SHOREBIRDS
OF NEW ZEALAND

SHOREBIRDS OF NEW ZEALAND

Sharing the margins

Keith Woodley

PENGUIN BOOKS

For Ray Pierce and John Dowding
— and for Mark Barter in memoriam

PENGUIN BOOKS
Published by the Penguin Group
Penguin Group (NZ), 67 Apollo Drive, Rosedale,
Auckland 0632, New Zealand (a division of Pearson New Zealand Ltd)
Penguin Group (USA) Inc., 375 Hudson Street,
New York, New York 10014, USA
Penguin Group (Canada), 90 Eglinton Avenue East, Suite 700, Toronto,
Ontario, M4P 2Y3, Canada (a division of Pearson Penguin Canada Inc.)
Penguin Books Ltd, 80 Strand, London, WC2R 0RL, England
Penguin Ireland, 25 St Stephen's Green,
Dublin 2, Ireland (a division of Penguin Books Ltd)
Penguin Group (Australia), 250 Camberwell Road, Camberwell,
Victoria 3124, Australia (a division of Pearson Australia Group Pty Ltd)
Penguin Books India Pvt Ltd, 11, Community Centre,
Panchsheel Park, New Delhi – 110 017, India
Penguin Books (South Africa) (Pty) Ltd, Block D, Rosebank Office Park,
181 Jan Smuts Avenue, Parktown North, Gauteng 2193, South Africa

Penguin Books Ltd, Registered Offices: 80 Strand, London, WC2R 0RL, England

First published by Penguin Group (NZ), 2012
10 9 8 7 6 5 4 3 2 1

Copyright © Keith Woodley, 2012

The right of Keith Woodley to be identified as the author of this work in terms of section 96 of the Copyright Act 1994 is hereby asserted.

Designed and typeset by Sarah Healey, © Penguin Group (NZ)
Photography as credited
Map on page 6 by Outline Draughting and Graphics Ltd
Prepress by Image Centre, Ltd
Printed in China by Leo Paper Products Ltd

All rights reserved. Without limiting the rights under copyright reserved above, no part of this publication may be reproduced, stored in or introduced into a retrieval system, or transmitted, in any form or by any means (electronic, mechanical, photocopying, recording or otherwise), without the prior written permission of both the copyright owner and the above publisher of this book.

ISBN 978-0-143-56750-9

A catalogue record for this book is available
from the National Library of New Zealand.

www.penguin.co.nz

IAN SOUTHEY

CONTENTS

Map of New Zealand and Offshore Islands   6
Author's Note   7
Acknowledgements   8

Prologue: Before the Fall   11
Introduction   15

PART I: BIRDS AND HABITATS

1 Divergent Fortunes: A Tale of Two Plovers   27
2 Only Game in Town: The Braided Rivers   37
3 Intertidal Food Factories: Coastal Wetlands   45
4 Life with a Twist: The Singular Wrybill   55
5 Shrinking Fortunes: Black-fronted Terns   67
6 High-Stepping in the Shallows: The Stilts   75
7 On Mussel-Pickers and Sea-Pies: The Oystercatchers   85
8 Transtasman Oddity: Banded Dotterel   95
9 A Game of Two Halves: New Zealand Dotterel   103
10 Piracy and Prejudice: The Gulls   111
11 Elegance Aloft: The Terns   123
12 Ancient Enigmas: The New Zealand Snipe   133
13 The Great OE: Migration   143
14 Tight Schedules, or Easy As? The Migration of Godwits   153
15 Specialisation Blues: The Troubled Future of Knots   165

PART II: TROUBLED FUTURES

16 Winners and Losers: How Are Our Shorebirds Doing?   175
17 Helping Hands: Recovery Groups and Plans   185
18 War without End: Dealing with Predators   201
19 Natural Flows: Essential Ingredient for a Shorebird Future   209
20 Aqua Blues: The Problems with Water   217
21 Coastal Pressures: Competing for the Margins   227
22 Shrinking Gas Stations: Flyway under Stress   237

Conclusion   247

Glossary   254
Abbreviations   254
Notes   254
Bibliography and Further Reading   264
Index   269

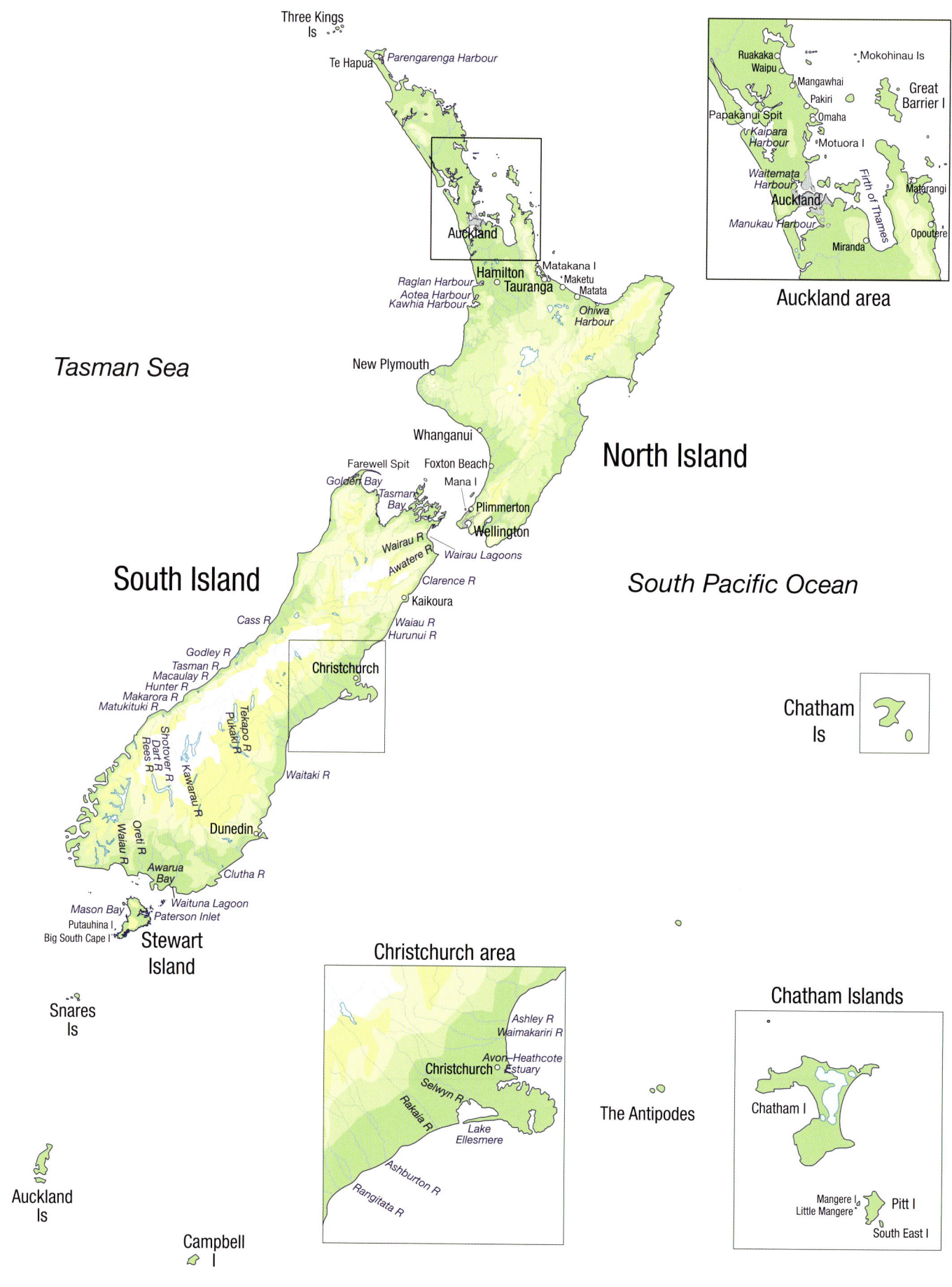

AUTHOR'S NOTE

The frigid wind descends the valley, pulling cloud down the weathered ramparts of Mt Earnslaw. To the west broad, tawny river flats extend away to the dark beech slopes of the Humboldt Mountains, where the Routeburn tumbles out of its valley. In early August 1994, in the lower Dart Valley at the head of Lake Wakatipu, my attention is diverted from the occasion – a small family gathering – in response to calls I have just heard. After several years living among the shellbanks of Miranda it is a familiar sound, but one I associate with the coast, with a tidal estuary and mudflats, not a high-country valley in the South Island. Years later there is a similar encounter, just before entering the first of the Poolburn tunnels on the Otago Central Rail Trail. In a place that is almost as far as one can get from the coast anywhere in New Zealand, I hear birds flying overhead. But from the deep cutting only a sliver of sky is visible, and there is only a quick flutter of shadow high on the cutting face before they are gone. Like the pair of oystercatchers in the Dart Valley, these ones prospecting over the Maniototo Plain belong in this environment as much as they do on a northern shoreline; for in the course of their annual cycles, our shorebirds inhabit many landscapes.

Decades earlier, on roadtrips north to Christchurch, crossing the Waitaki River marked the gateway to a singular landscape: sprawling over the plains, a succession of such rivers, broad gravel banks bisected by fast-flowing channels. The pinnacle was the immensely long bridge across the Rakaia, passing over channel after channel of churning milky green water separated by stony ridges – all viewed from a moving vehicle as if watching a jerky movie, each vertical crenellation in the sides of the concrete bridge a single frame. These journeys through the 1970s usually meant concerts and other good times in Christchurch; the rivers then were a vivid part of the landscape for me, but little more. Today, when I encounter such places, my thoughts are immediately on shorebirds.

A globally rare geographical feature, these braided river systems provide essential habitat for endemic species: black stilt, banded dotterel, black-fronted tern and black-billed gull are found here, all highly valued components of our avifauna. But among them there is one other that is *primus inter pares*: *Anarhynchus frontalis*, or wrybill. With nearly half the world population spending most of each year on the Firth of Thames, they are as much part of the landscape here as the shell ridges they roost on. But they are equally associated with the rivers. Aside from their singular bill – an instrument found on no other bird anywhere – wrybills are uniquely dependent on the braided rivers for their breeding habitat. So what are these river systems, and why are they so important?

Over the years at Miranda I have watched countless small flocks of oystercatchers departing southwards, in ragged and restless formations, usually against a clear blue backdrop and most often between early afternoon and nightfall, from late June through July. They are invariably noisy affairs, their calls tumbling from on high, urgent and constant. A few weeks later the wrybill are also on the move, but theirs are more discreet departures. Then a few weeks later the now sparsely occupied high-tide roosts begin filling again with newcomers, as the birds of the tundra arrive – the godwits and knots, turnstones and sandpipers. Where oystercatcher and wrybill combine North Island and South Island within their annual cycle, these newcomers combine hemispheres. They arrive with feathers that were grown here 10 months earlier, but with body tissue built of food found on the tundra and the coastal mudflats of Alaska.

At certain times, at certain places, these birds are prominent in our landscapes: the beaches and bays, harbours and estuaries, rivers and lakes around which many of us live, or where we gravitate for recreation. It may be where thousands of oystercatchers are pushed up onto a grass verge in suburban South Auckland; or a beach on the Coromandel where a single pair of dotterels are attempting to nest; or a mudflat on the coast of northern China where foraging options for knots and godwits are diminishing before a relentless tide of human constructions. This is the world where shorebirds find themselves living alongside us, sharing the margins. Yet from the tens of thousands of people I have encountered over the years at Miranda, it is clear that most people know little about these birds, let alone the problems they face. This book is one response.

ACKNOWLEDGEMENTS

Many people over the years have contributed in some way to our understanding and knowledge of New Zealand shorebirds, but as always there are a few whose contributions stand out, and without whose efforts this book would not be possible. Historically, it begins with the names that are threaded throughout the text: the early chroniclers of our avian fauna – such as Walter Buller, Thomas Potts, Frederick Hutton, Herbert Guthrie-Smith, Edgar Stead, Robert Falla, William Oliver, Charles Fleming, Graham Turbott and Dick Sibson – some of whom witnessed the beginnings of the problems that so beset conservation in this country today, particularly the impacts of introduced predators.

In New Zealand today there are a number of people who continue this work, contributing enormously to the knowledge base that is so essential if informed conservation decisions are to be made for shorebirds. This book is dedicated to two such people. It is a dedication that is not made lightly: without the work and advocacy of these two, knowledge of our shorebird species and what they require for their future wellbeing would be considerably lessened.

When Ray Pierce began research into some of our endemic shorebirds in the 1970s, he found much uncharted territory. Much of what we now know of the biology of species such as black stilt, wrybill, and banded dotterel emerged from his work. There also emerged a deep understanding of the complexities of the braided river systems: the interactions among species, both inter- and intra-specific; the differences in the habitat requirements of each; and the dynamics of predator–prey relationships. In subsequent work in Canterbury, Otago and Northland, Pierce has built a legacy of great respect among those who worked with him. In the course of researching this book I encountered several people who expressed great admiration and gratitude for his expertise and quiet mentoring. Currently based offshore, Pierce still has much to offer conservation management in this country.

The contribution of John Dowding to this book has been immense: his knowledge and experience, his guided tours of the riverbeds, his library and photolibrary, and his prompt response to queries. As the reader will discover, it seems that when it comes to New Zealand shorebirds, Dowding has been everywhere. What began as an encounter with New Zealand dotterel just north of Auckland in 1985, expanded to take in the dotterel population on Stewart Island, then out to the Chathams with its oystercatcher and shore plover. Subsequently there was considerable work with wrybill, both on their northern wintering grounds and on the riverbeds; and the likes of variable oystercatcher and fairy tern along the way. As with Pierce, the depth of Dowding's knowledge and expertise is impressive: for both men it is hard-won knowledge from field experience and observation, over which is laid the rigour of scientific method. It is unsurprising, therefore, that over the years both have featured regularly as expert witnesses at consent hearings and boards of inquiry.

During the final editing of this book I learned of the passing of Mark Barter. For over three decades, Mark was very involved in shorebird research and advocacy in Australia and throughout the East Asian–Australian Flyway, particularly in China. Readers of *Godwits: Long-haul Champions* will know of the huge contribution he made to our knowledge of shorebirds in the Yellow Sea. This book also draws on that knowledge – a small part of what is an enormous legacy.

This book also draws on the research of others: Rod Hay and Ken Hughey on wrybills and riverbeds; Colin Miskelly on snipe; Alan Baker on oystercatchers; Mary Bomford on banded dotterels; Rachel Keedwell on black-fronted terns; Alison Davis on shore plover; Rachel McLellan on black-billed gulls; Maida Barlow on spur-winged plovers; Gwenda Pulham on fairy terns; Rob Schuckard and David Melville on shorebirds at the top of the South Island; Adrian Riegen and Tony Habraken on everything; Jesse Conklin on godwits; Phil Battley, Bob Gill and Theunis Piersma on godwits and knots, and the biology and ecology of shorebirds in general. My thanks also to Dean Nelson, Kaki Recovery Programme; Chris Woolmore, Project River Recovery; and Sue Anderson, DOC Twizel and the Tasman River survey team.

The following gave of their time for interviews: Phil Battley, Colin Miskelly, Wendy Hare, Dean Nelson, Chris Woolmore, Paul Sagar, Andrew Crossland, Gwenda Pulham, Rachel Keedwell, David Melville, Frances Schmechel, Paul Scofield, Graeme Taylor, Ray Pierce, and John Dowding. Two further interviews occurred in Christchurch, on Tuesday 22 February 2011. I thank Andy Grant, DOC Canterbury, for an excellent overview of the situation in Canterbury and the problems and concerns about its rivers. I then found myself outside Lincoln University at 12.51 p.m. I am deeply grateful to Ken Hughey for an interview that could well not have happened; but despite the fact that the building was being evacuated, amidst the bustle of concerned people coming and going, and to the accompaniment of several aftershocks, Ken was adamant we should proceed. There followed a 45-minute conversation that proved immensely valuable, filling in many gaps and pointing out fruitful leads to follow up.

Various people assisted with support, useful comments and suggestions: Rob Schuckard, Adrian Riegen, Tony Habraken, Trevor Worthy, Jesse Conklin, Alan Tennyson, Gwenda Pulham, Dianne Brunton, Colin Miskelly, David Wilson, Sioux Plowman, Gillian Eller, Tony Beauchamp, Katrina Hansen, Richard Maloney, David Wilson, Tim Lovegrove and Theunis Piersma. And once again I am indebted to Ian Southey for many useful conversations and fruitful suggestions.

For comments and improvements to sections of the text I am grateful to David Melville, Ray Pierce, John Dowding, Colin Miskelly and Adrian Riegen. Any further errors or omissions are likely to occur in sections that they have not perused, and responsibility rests solely with me. The immaculately fine toothcomb of editor Gillian Tewsley resulted in a much improved manuscript. I must also gratefully acknowledge the support and encouragement of Jeremy Sherlock, Catherine O'Loughlin and the folks at Penguin.

This book is as much about images as it is text, and the following photographers are gratefully acknowledged: First and foremost Ian Southey for the generous access to his compendious image files; Cushla and the late Brian Chudleigh; John Dowding; Colin Miskelly; James Fraser; John Holmes; Janie Vaughan; Athena Drummond; Katherine Steeds; Steve Wood; Alex Scott; Brendon Doran; Adrian Boyle; Rohan Clarke; Bruce Shanks; David Boyle; Michelle Gutsell; Jan van de Kam; Chris Woolmore; Neil Fitzgerald; Rod Morris; and Dave Murray.

Research took me on the road, where a number of people were of great assistance. I am particularly grateful to Audrie McKenzie for a delightfully easy and flexible base camp for my comings and goings through Christchurch. In Christchurch, I am indebted to the extremely knowledgeable and generous Andrew Crossland, city council ranger and much else besides. The Christchurch City Council is to be commended for its continued enlightenment in employing Crossland; the council, the City of Christchurch and the birds of Canterbury are the better for it. I am also grateful to Betty and Alister Clay in Queenstown, David Seay in Wanaka, Chris Jones in Oamaru, David and Vicky Melville (and David's formidable library) in Nelson, and Brian and Sue Bell in Marlborough. And my thanks to Kate, for much support and encouragement: not the least the provision, from time to time, of a quiet and productive working space.

Once again this project required considerable absences from my duties at Miranda Shorebird Centre: my thanks for the continued support of Miranda Naturalists' Trust, particularly Gillian Vaughan, David Lawrie, Adrian Riegen and Ashley Reid. We are all indebted to Maria Stables-Page and Kristelle Wi for ably filling in for me, as well as to Alister Harlow. To other relievers, my grateful thanks: Terry Wyatt, Helen Cain, John and Stella Rowe, Stuart and Alison Chambers, Brian and Judith Tyler, Janie and Kevin Vaughan, Ann and Ray Buckmaster and Lynda Underhill.

Many people over the last few years have endured me banging on about shorebirds. But I have been gratified by the level of interest and support shown to me during the course of completing this book. I can only hope the finished product goes some way to satisfying that interest, as well as meeting the expectations generated for it.

Keith Woodley
Miranda, December 2011

Oystercatcher. KATHERINE STEEDS

A foraging wrybill on the Upper Rangitata River. KEITH WOODLEY

PROLOGUE
BEFORE THE FALL

Human impact on the New Zealand biota and landscape has eclipsed anything brought about by natural processes over the last 3 millennia. —Matt McGlone[1]

Among the stones at the water's edge there is slow, purposeful movement: a bird in the shallow riffle, predominantly grey on top and white underneath, coloured as if it were a stone, albeit one moving against the flow of the current. However, three features temper this illusion: a black necklace, a dark eye and a long black bill. And there is something rather odd about that bill: from the base it extends outwards in orthodox bird-bill fashion, until the last third when it shows a peculiar twist to the right. As it proceeds, the wrybill pecks on or below the surface of the water, taking small invertebrates. Now and again it tilts its head and probes around or under a stone as if seeking unseen prey.

Beyond the bank is one of the main channels of the river, its fast-flowing blue-green water laden with glacial silt. On a shallow shelf near the bank, the water breaks around the long pinkish legs of a dark bird, probing beneath the surface with its long tapered black bill. Further out over the channel three grey and white birds with bright yellow-orange bills hang elegantly on the breeze in flapping hover, before dipping towards the water surface and up again. In jerky zigzags the terns make their way up the river, past the shingle bars where a series of riffles and minor channels join the main one. There a strikingly black and white bird with vivid orange bill stands up from the shingle where it had been sitting and saunters away; its place is immediately taken by its identical-looking mate. Along one of the minor channels two more wrybill forage near their almost-fledged young. Some distance behind them

The full splendour of a male banded dotterel on the Dart River.
IAN SOUTHEY

there is further movement, as a bird of similar size but altogether different appearance slips down into the riffle and begins foraging. It is light brown above and white below, its bill short and dark, but around its neck and breast are two deeply contrasting bands; the upper one black, the lower one a deep chestnut crescent.

Beside the margins of the river where more stable shingle banks have been colonised by herbs, grasses and low shrubs, there are seepages and small ponds. From all around the riverbed and its margins there comes a series of low-pitched honks, from large stocky geese – about 70 cm tall, with short thick legs, very stubby bills, and no wings. Scattered among the geese but more numerous are small ducks: they too are short-legged and flightless. On the far side of the main channel a broad terrace several metres above the river is covered in swathes of cushion plant and scattered tussock. Here small plump brownish birds are busy fossicking for seeds and insects. Some of these quail have rufous faces and necks, and dark mottled breasts, but others are rather drab. Even further back, perhaps a kilometre away, a higher bank of tussock and low shrubs ends abruptly before a steep slope and its dark curtain of forest. The last of the morning mist is rising off the flanks of these mountains, as a bulky shape slowly browses amid scattered shrubs, matagouri and tussock. The body tapers to a long neck and small head ending in a stubby rounded bill. It is an eastern moa – one of several visible among the vegetation.

It is early summer and many of the wrybill that have nested on the riverbed are beginning to fly downstream. Several kilometres from the rivermouth they pass over a huge shingle island flanked by two major channels. A mass of white movement and loud noise is sprawled across it: thousands of black-billed gulls and white-fronted terns, some still on nests but many with chicks. Turning north the wrybill cross over lowland forest with patches of more open shrubland and vast swamps, to the edge of an enormous sheet of water. It is separated from the coast by a spit extending from the base of a range of hills towering over the otherwise flat land. Here the murmur of river water over shingle is replaced by the crash of surf on the outer beach, and the tang of salt-laden air. On the lake there is noisy bedlam: vast flocks of waterfowl, and around the margins hundreds of other birds, some long-legged with long bills, others short and dumpy, probing the exposed flats. Here the wrybills find others of their kind, and here a few will stay through the following winter. However, before long most are on the move again, heading north.

Passing over the strait separating the two great islands, the wrybill continue north up the west coast. Directly ahead of them land protrudes seaward in the form of a huge symmetrical peak. In late December there is only a scattering of thin snow patches still clinging to its upper slopes. Further north the birds strike the first of a series of shallow inlets. Some continue on the same course, landing only once they have reached the southern shores of an enormous harbour that sprawls on the western edge of a large bush-clad isthmus. Other birds have turned to the northeast and fly over tall forest, broken here and there by small lakes and wetlands. Further on there are more wetlands, these ones enormous. Ahead of the birds, on either side of their track, lie two ranges of hills. To the east, extending beside a wide flat valley, much of which is covered in swamps and tall kahikatea, is a jagged spine of forest-covered peaks and cones, bisected by deep valleys and ravines. The jagged ridges continue along the side of a broad, rectangular bay; on its opposite shore

River bed and tussock, Upper Rangitata. KEITH WOODLEY

the hills are lower and more rounded but also densely covered in thick forest, through which protrude thick stands of kauri.

The shore on this side of the bay is a broad white strip of shellbanks, clear and dazzling in the sun. From the shell edge and continuing in a wide band across the southern end of the bay, the ebb tide has uncovered vast sand- and mudflats, interspersed with countless gleaming strips and pools. As the wrybill descend towards the shellbanks, just 12 hours after starting out on their journey from Te Waihora, they pass over thousands of other birds foraging over the expanse. Many are of the same kinds they encountered further south. These godwits, knots and other sandpipers are, like the wrybill, mere visitors to this place, for they too breed elsewhere. In a few months' time they will begin their own northward travels, although unlike the wrybill theirs will be a journey of days and weeks – and tens of thousands of kilometres.

Foraging wrybill in the Upper Rangitata. KEITH WOODLEY

Manawatu Estuary, one of many harbours and estuaries around New Zealand that provide good habitat for shorebirds. KEITH WOODLEY

INTRODUCTION

Unfortunately for . . . shorebirds, our common definition of 'home' has engendered not only praise and affection but a growing threat of disenfranchisement. —Harry Thurston[1]

It has been a frustrating day trudging the sands of the Manawatu Estuary. The last few hours we have spent watching our bar-tailed godwit quarry flying everywhere but into the catching area. These are not just any godwits; seven of them are in possession of information about where they have been over the last two years. On an upper leg they carry a geolocator, a tiny device that records day length, and hence latitude and longitude, from which each bird's movements can be retrospectively plotted. As a research method it is brilliant – the information gathered is of incalculable interest and value – but there is one major drawback: to retrieve its data the bird needs to be recaptured. In its final stretch the Manawatu River sweeps north to form a hairpin bend before turning south, meeting the sea where the northern beach tapers to a sandy point. This spit is the point of a broad wedge of dunes extending around onto the northern edge of the inner estuary and ending in a smaller spit facing upstream to the east. This inner spit is where most birds roost at high tide, and where we try to catch them. While we are fixed on these uncooperative birds, there has been opportunity to absorb other avian flavours of this place.

Earlier, in dim morning light as we set up the nets, a flock of 30 or so Canada geese had wheeled off the estuary and over our heads, honking loudly as they passed. It was a sound of the northern tundra regions, yet it was unfolding on the west coast of the lower North Island. Out on the estuary there were shags and ducks, mainly mallards of course, along with a few black swans. Downstream beyond the dunes, the Tasman Sea thundered onto Foxton Beach, which was strewn with giant piles of sea-scoured timber and detritus. Amidst it all roosted small flocks of black-backed gulls and Caspian terns. Along the river edge, beyond a few roosting white-fronted terns, a scattering of godwits and red knots foraged.

As I walk up the broad sandy margins of the estuary, my eyes are drawn to movement just metres away. Ambling away, seemingly casually but with eyes steady upon me, are a dozen or so wrybills. Watching more warily from behind them are two similar-sized but

Manawatu Estuary: the curving sleeve contains a cannon net designed to fire over birds on a high-tide roost. KEITH WOODLEY

lankier birds: curlew sandpipers, summer visitors from the tundra of northeastern Russia. A shallow inlet divides the inner edge of the spit from the string of houses lining the riverbank. Along its muddy edge stand a dozen Pacific golden plovers, also from the tundra, accompanied by several banded dotterels, smaller and very distant New Zealand cousins. Roosting near the top of the spit among strands of driftwood are a pair of variable oystercatchers and about 40 pied oystercatchers. These we regard with some disfavour, as they are roosting in the very place we need the godwits to be in order to catch them.

But this is not just a place of birds. Foxton Beach is a surprisingly large, sprawling community. There is much human activity here on the estuary, especially off-road vehicles. About 500 m downstream of the spit a barrier of wooden bollards crosses the flats to the river edge; a sign advises this is a bird sanctuary, with no vehicles or dogs permitted north of the sign. Beyond, there are vehicles parked up and down the estuary margins. Up on the coastal dunes a 4WD sits immobilised, its bonnet up. A second vehicle is roaring down onto the flats, heading out to rescue the first. A van is also heading onto the flats; two large dogs emerge from it and sprint off towards the river edge and its roosting birds.

In many ways this place mirrors numerous others up and down the country. The long indented coastline of these islands, with their bays and harbours, estuaries and lagoons, marshes and beaches, is where many of us live, and where we go for recreation. Up to 90 percent of New Zealanders live within 40 km of the sea. It is an unusual statistic in world terms, although the world is catching up: by 2020, 75 percent of the world's population is expected to live within 60 km of the coast.[2] We have a tendency to take our coastline for granted – we overuse it, overdevelop it and pollute it. But how well do we know the creatures we share these places with?

Much shorebird habitat lies within the tidal reaches

Pied oystercatcher and Mt Earnslaw. KEITH WOODLEY

Within their annual cycle, shorebirds link habitats as diverse as alpine and coastal: this single pied oystercatcher near its nest in the shadow of Mt Earnslaw at the top of Lake Wakatipu could well be one of the birds in the mixed flock massed in this Napoleonic spectacle on the southern shores of the Manukau Harbour in March. IAN SOUTHEY

of our harbours and estuaries; but such places are only one part of the shorebird equation. With their catchments – draining high country, plateau, valley and plain – our rivers and streams are an obvious connection between land and sea. And there are birds that mirror this unity, combining, in their annual cycle, inland and coastal habitats at opposite ends of the country. Those wrybill on the banks of the Manawatu Estuary in early February are most likely transients, pausing on migration to a northern estuary such as the Manukau Harbour or the Firth of Thames. Exactly where they were migrating from we do not know, except that it was a braided river somewhere in the central eastern South Island. The strong probability is they were from the Rakaia or Rangitata rivers, or from the Mackenzie Basin. It is even possible that within this small flock there were birds from each of those places. Likewise, the pied oystercatchers on the estuary could be from the same locations, or from farmland in mid Canterbury, or a subalpine valley in western Otago.

If there is one group of organisms that best symbolises the connectedness of all life on our planet, it is surely the families of birds collectively known as shorebirds. Imagine a globe upon which has been drawn a line marking the annual track of every shorebird: there would be a mass of threads encompassing much of its surface. For they are among the most widely dispersed of any animals on earth, and there are few terrestrial areas that are either not inhabited or not visited by them. From the edge of alpine snowfields to the High Arctic tundra; from grasslands in central Asia to the sands of tropical deserts; from riverbeds in the shadow of the Himalayas to an old watercourse in central Australia; from braided riverbeds to coastal estuaries; or from pastoral farmland and ploughed fields to urban parks and even forest, various members of the shorebird clan may be found. Their travel is as diverse as the birds themselves. Some are strictly sedentary, occupying beach territory or a small subantarctic island throughout the year; others move a few kilometres along the coast to flock for winter; others migrate between inland breeding sites and the coast; and still others, such as the bar-tailed godwits, routinely traverse the hemispheres and the world's oceans in their migrations.

The expressions 'shorebird' and 'wader' are often used interchangeably, depending on where you happen to be. Geography may also determine which species are included in each term. In Britain and Europe 'shorebirds' can be understood to include gulls, herons and perhaps even some crows, whereas 'waders' in North America often incorporates herons, storks, ibises, flamingos and their various allies. 'Waders' was widely used historically in Australasia, but in recent times 'shorebirds' has become more frequently adopted. The editors of the magnificent series *Handbook of the Birds of the World* spend little time dwelling on the issue, dispatching it summarily: 'throughout the text the terms "shorebirds" and "waders" are used indifferently, as there appears to be no pressing need to establish a single term'.[3] They might be on to something, if one considers that some waders seldom, if ever, wade; and some shorebirds never visit a shoreline.

Eighty percent of shorebirds are maritime or coastal in their lifestyle.[4] Many are inland breeders but spend little time there, although there are always exceptions. The inland dotterel of Australia is, as its name suggests, not a coastal creature and indeed it rarely encounters running water.[5] At the opposite end of the spectrum are the phalaropes which, although shorebirds, seem closer to pelagics, or seabirds, in their lifestyle. While red phalaropes breed on the Arctic tundra, they spend more than 75 percent of their annual cycle at sea, which is more than some marine mammals.[6]

Most shorebirds, however, forage in and around water margins, or on substrate along the shores of lakes, rivers and the sea. A typical shorebird has relatively long legs in relation to body size, a long bill, and a streamlined body, powered by long pointed wings. Each of these physical characteristics has been furnished by evolution to suit an adaptable and highly energetic lifestyle.[7] Shorebirds nest mainly on the ground in open areas, where many of them rely on cryptic colouration or fast escape flight for safety.[8] Of course, herons, storks, rails and cranes share some of these features and are adapted to broadly similar ways of life, but they are structurally different and genetically quite distinct from the shorebirds: compare, for example, the lumbering, broad wing-flap of a heron taking flight with the rapid-burst flight of a sandpiper. The similarities that herons and others share with shorebirds are considered by some biologists to be excellent examples of convergent evolution.

All families and species covered in this book are found within the order Charadriiformes. Birds of six families occur here: Recurvirostridae, represented by two stilt species; three species of Haematopodidae or oystercatchers; three species of Laridae or gulls; and at least four Sternidae or terns. But the remaining two rather dominate the species list: Charadriidae, the plovers and dotterels; and Scolopacidae, the snipes, sandpipers, godwits and curlews. There are records of at least 60 species of shorebirds within the New Zealand region, including mainland and offshore islands, from the Kermadecs and Chathams to the subantarctic islands. Of these, 14 are classed as either endemic or native, which means they breed within New Zealand or on offshore islands. The other 46 breed elsewhere and have migrated or straggled to New Zealand.

New Zealand shorebirds reflect the great differences that exist between the earth's two hemispheres. The northern temperate regions are intensely seasonal, and the response of many birds in those regions is to be highly migratory. The southern regions do not have such marked climatic extremes, which means more birds can occupy a home range all year round; or they need migrate only short distances. Different social systems and breeding strategies are a further manifestation of this. Arctic breeding shorebirds are adapted to making the best of a very brief 'breeding window' during the few weeks of the year that the tundra is clear of snow, and food is available. They spend more of the year in the southern hemisphere than in the north, but have developed specialist adaptations for breeding in the higher latitudes of the northern hemisphere. The colours and patterns of their breeding plumage are

White-faced herons (top) share many of the characteristics of shorebirds – such as long legs and bills – and may be found in similar places; yet taxonomically they are quite different; similarly this royal spoonbill foraging alongside a bar-tailed godwit. IAN SOUTHEY

A massed flight. Such flock behaviour is typical of many shorebirds, including these godwits, knots and two oystercatchers. IAN SOUTHEY

superbly cryptic, so a bird sitting on a nest on the tundra is camouflaged. They lay big eggs, so that when chicks hatch they are fully developed and quickly commence growing. Their chicks depend on the brief burst of productivity that is the spring invertebrate emergence on the tundra. This means birds need to return to the tundra each year to complete their annual cycle. It also means, of course, that they have had to develop the means of doing so. Thus they have developed fuelling strategies that supply sufficient energy for long-distant migratory flights, as well as skills for the flight itself – navigation and weather pattern detection systems.

At least 15 species of tundra-breeding shorebirds reach New Zealand each year – some in small numbers, perhaps one or two, while others such as bar-tailed godwit and red knot occur in their thousands. On our harbours and estuaries they join many locals. Some of these are also migrants – such as the pied oystercatcher, which travels north after breeding in the South Island.

Others are very much residents, breeding locally and remaining throughout the year. Pairs of both northern New Zealand dotterel and variable oystercatchers – strictly coastal breeding species – may occupy a section of beach all year round. On the other hand, you would have to consider pied stilts to be generalists. Highly mobile within New Zealand, they are rarely found on ocean beaches or rocky shores, but could turn up almost anywhere else where there is any form of wetland. Some breed on the braided riverbeds and around high-country lakes in the South Island, where they may find themselves alongside banded dotterel or wrybill or pied oystercatchers. Or they may nest in a damp paddock or on the edge of saltmarsh in the Firth of Thames, with other birds such as New Zealand dotterel or spur-winged plover also breeding nearby. Later all of these locals may be joined by flocks of wrybill, pied oystercatchers and other pied stilts, returning after breeding elsewhere in the country; or even one of their

A tundra-breeding ruddy turnstone (foreground) side by side with a wrybill from a South Island braided river. IAN SOUTHEY

The long-bill club: sedentary and seemingly reluctant fliers, the annual cycle of these Chatham Island snipe (top) is rather different to that of the globe-trotting bar-tailed godwit, yet taxonomically they are in the same family. IAN SOUTHEY

distant relatives – kaki, the black stilt.

Intertidal areas support, for all or at least part of their annual cycle, a greater number of shorebird species and populations than any other ecosystem, apart perhaps from the world's tundra regions. But birds are on the tundra for two or three months at most, while the intertidal area – be it on the tundra edge, on the migration flyway, or on the wintering grounds – supports them for the rest of the year. For some species one estuary provides feeding, roosting and breeding habitat, and the birds are present there throughout the year. For others, the intertidal zone provides feeding and roosting habitat up to eight months of the year. For shorebirds, most food on the estuary is found in the intertidal zone, and can only be accessed during low tide. When feeding is impossible at high tide, birds need somewhere secure to roost. Large flocks congregate above the tideline to rest and preen, and at these times they are most vulnerable to disturbance.

The spectacle of large flocks of shorebirds lifting off a high-tide roost, or being gathered up in a wide sweep across the tidal flats – perhaps in response to a skua or harrier – is a characteristic of the clan. Loose formations wheeling overhead, or a tightly woven organism of several thousand birds twisting and turning as one – the aerial patterns can be as diverse as the birds themselves. Yet other shorebirds will never be found in these situations. Tiny snipe inhabiting the subantarctic islands are reluctant fliers; they take to the air only when flushed or, at certain times of the year, to perform an aerial display. In contrast with the 30,000 km annual migrations of bar-tailed godwits, these snipe are not only sedentary, but spend their entire annual cycle within just a few hectares of remote island, surrounded by the great empty expanse of the southern oceans. Unlike most other shorebirds, these are birds of the forest or other dense vegetation. Probing for invertebrates in the damp peaty soil, they seem to have more in common with kiwi than with a bird of the open mudflats.

The riverbeds and coastal lagoons of Canterbury play an essential role in the annual cycle of many New

Zealand shorebirds. Before human settlement, central Canterbury was a mosaic of vegetation types – forest, dense shrublands and riparian grasslands – all of it continually fluctuating at the whim of the braided rivers. These rivers were subjected to great floods that periodically uprooted and buried tracts of forest and shrublands, replacing them with gravel riverbed. Empty gravel areas were then gradually revegetated in stages, from cushion plants and grasses to successive covers of kanuka, kahikatea and totara forest, and marginal shrublands.[9] The result was a rich diversity of habitats available for many creatures, including shorebirds. Coastal wetland systems were no less diverse and important: a good example is Te Waihora/Lake Ellesmere, the remnant of a much larger lagoon and swamp system that is likely to have had far more wading-bird habitat than it does now. But 'as sea levels rose in the early Pleistocene, a changing pattern of coastal lagoons and wetlands preceded the advancing tide line and Canterbury could have supported large populations of wading birds and waterfowl'.[10] Mudflats and shellbanks in the estuaries of the Ashley, Waimakariri and Avon–Heathcote, as well as Ellesmere and other coastal lakes and lagoons such as Lake Wainono, would have attracted northern migrants.

There is much that we do not know about these places and how they were used by birds in pre-human times. Shorebirds are not well represented in fossil faunas, but the record for these areas is particularly poor. The most common shorebird was South Island snipe, found in at least 30 sites ranging from forest and shrubland to riparian grasslands, lake edges and the seashore.[11] There are no inland fossils of pied or variable oystercatcher, although it is suggested the latter would have been found along much of the coastline, and pied oystercatchers were breeding on the rivers. The modern palaeontologist, painstakingly piecing together a diminished or vanished avifauna, has a major collaborator – albeit one that has been extinct for over 100 years. Laughing owl deposits have proven a treasure trove of bird bones, including some shorebirds – snipe, banded dotterel, shore plover and black-fronted tern. The owls were less accommodating, though, when it came to birds of open riverbed habitat, such as wrybill and black-billed gull, because that was not where they hunted; so the fossil record for these species is much poorer than for, say, forest species. Fossils of other terns and gulls come almost exclusively from coastal deposits.[12]

Of the northern harbours and estuaries we know even less, except that the coastline has long been dynamic and constantly changing. Shifting river courses, sand dune formation and fluctuating sea levels – from either sea level rise or tectonic activity – all make for continual changes to coastal wetlands, but infertile conditions for the fossil hunter. Worldwide fluctuations in sea level occurred in the Quaternary glaciations, during the last of which the North and South islands were joined by a land bridge. Sea levels up to 120 m below today's level caused valley deepening in the lower courses of some rivers and the cutting of river terraces in earlier inland deposits. Post-glacial sea level rise drowned these deepened valleys, resulting in the northern harbours and the Marlborough Sounds.[13] While the glaciations dramatically altered vegetation patterns in the South Island and southern North Island, forests are known to have survived through the glacial periods in Northland and the Auckland region – which might suggest the intertidal areas supporting shorebirds in those regions remained largely unmodified once the sea reached its current level.

Most of our current coastal wetlands date from only around 7000 years ago, when the sea level reached its post-glacial high point; it has fluctuated only about 0.5 m since.[14] All current dune systems, many of which would have become forested, date from after this time.[15] Intertidal areas have followed a similar pattern. The total surface area of tidal flats on the planet has fluctuated over thousands of years, but there were probably larger intertidal areas when sea levels were higher. A higher sea level means more sediment is carried into the estuary; and if the sea level does not rise too quickly, tidal flats are built up. But once levels fall, less sediment inflow occurs and eventually tidal flats will dry out. New tidal flats may then form along the new coastline.[16]

A thousand years after people first arrived, very little of these landscapes remains unmodified. What has human presence in the landscape meant for shorebirds? The answer, for the most part, is not good. Much of their original habitat is now degraded or gone entirely. Some of the birds, too, are gone: North Island snipe to extinction; shore plover surviving only on the Chatham Islands and a few offshore sanctuaries. The northeast coast of the North Island still supports many birds, but it is also where our biggest concentrations of people occur. Coastal development and disturbance are two insidious, ongoing pressures on shorebird habitat in the region.

The quality of rivers is also under great pressure, again from development – be it water or gravel extraction, power generation or farm runoff – as well as from recreation. Altered flow regimes and the encroachment of exotic vegetation onto riverbeds have removed vast areas of breeding habitat for river specialists such as wrybill. And superimposed upon everything else, a pressure applying everywhere – coastal and inland – is the blanket of mammalian predators we have spread over these islands. No corner of the mainland is exempt: there are no safe boltholes for native species that evolved in a more benign environment, and are thus ill equipped in both their individual defence strategies and their population biology to withstand the onslaught of four-legged intruders. In a further perverse addition to the problem, human activities have created conditions for unnatural expansion of two native predators – harriers and black-backed gulls – and these have increased in numbers and in range.

Old-timer and newcomer: an endemic wrybill with a self-introduced native white-faced heron. ATHENA DRUMMOND

ORIGINS OF NEW ZEALAND SHOREBIRDS

How old are New Zealand shorebirds? Some are very old; and some of their ancestors are positively ancient. Worldwide, fossils believed to be shorebirds have been described from the Mesozoic in the late Cretaceous Period, 146 to 65 million years ago, and recent molecular evidence supports some diversification occurring over the same period. This recent consensus between fossil and molecular evidence suggests that while much of the diversification into modern orders took place in the early Tertiary, some orders diversified much earlier, as much as 139 million years.[17] The ancestors of shorebird lineages with us today – including terns and gulls, sandpipers and allies plus curlews, traditional plovers, and oystercatchers and allies – originated between 79 and 102 million years ago.[18]

Evidence from the early Miocene indicates that herons, rails, gulls and waders were present at least 16 million years ago.[19] Many terns originated in the Oligocene or Miocene, with our two endemic species, black-fronted and white-fronted terns, emerging during the Miocene.[20] But some of our endemics are even older. Shore plover, wrybill and the Coenocorypha species of snipes 'appear to have a long history extending back into the Eocene or Oligocene so may be long-standing members of Zealandia's avifauna'.[21] For other shorebirds, it all began considerably more recently. DNA studies suggest that although gull and skua genera may extend back into the Miocene or even the Oligocene, some modern gulls and skua emerged mainly during the last million years. By comparison, pied and variable oystercatchers are new kids on the block, and may have separated only 15–13,000 years ago.[22]

Those shorebirds still around at the beginning of the Pleistocene proved to be rather adaptable. They needed to be, for there began a succession of severe glaciations that shook up the playing field for everyone. Warm climate species were weeded out early, but these losses were balanced by endemic speciation, as new habitats such as braided riverbeds and alpine areas appeared, and birds adapted to exploit them. This appears to be particularly true of the shorebirds: 'Wrybill, shore plover, black stilt, black-billed gull and black-fronted tern can all be regarded as having nesting requirements adapted to conditions prevailing on periglacial tundra and braided river beds.'[23] While recurring glacial and interglacial periods further tested the mettle of most species, 'the composition of late-Pleistocene fauna was stable for the past 100,000 years, with few or no extinctions and as few colonisations during the last glacial-interglacial cycle'.[24]

High water at the coastal village of Kaiaua on the Firth of Thames: at such times birds like these pied oystercatchers may be pushed into close proximity to humans. BRUCE SHANKS

Birding is a growing interest in New Zealand, and our endemic shorebirds also attract many overseas visitors. BRUCE SHANKS

Spur-winged plovers. IAN SOUTHEY

PART I: BIRDS AND HABITATS

A newcomer now well established: spur-winged plovers are a seasonal feature on some of our shorelines, as seen here with red knots (foreground) and wrybills (rear) on the southern Manukau Harbour.
IAN SOUTHEY

CHAPTER ONE
DIVERGENT FORTUNES: A TALE OF TWO PLOVERS

Outside the perimeter fence of the Invercargill Borstal, one day in 1932, there lurked some strangers. Although they were shy, their persistent raucous cry attracted attention.[1] They were birds, but they were unusual. First, consider their appearance: stocky white body with brown back and long reddish-brown legs, and below their black cap a pendulous bright yellow mask across the face. Then look at their location: they should have been somewhere in eastern Australia, rather than outside a correctional facility in southern New Zealand.

It turned out to be the beachhead for a successful invasion: these spur-winged plovers or 'alarm birds' are now a noisy, obtrusive presence in paddocks and urban fringes, on beaches and riverbeds, up and down the country. Their success undoubtedly owes much to their nature – for they are by no means demure or backward creatures. They have been recorded nesting in the middle of a busy tractor track outside a farm shed; or on the roof of an office building in central Auckland; or hatching eggs from a nest on the grass verge of the Invercargill Airport runway.[2] They are given to spectacular aerial manoeuvres, noisily turning tables to harry a passing harrier or anything else that intrudes into their nesting territory.

Decades earlier, there was another bird: the shore plover – a strictly New Zealand species once common around our shores, particularly in the South Island, until its world was upturned by the arrival of dangers for which evolution had not prepared it. By the time spur-winged plovers began to establish, New Zealand shore plovers were gone from the mainland, pushed to one last refuge – a tiny island more than 700 km off the coast.

If we were to think of modern New Zealand as a laboratory, then spur-winged plovers (*Vanellus miles*) would be a good study species. The contemporary New Zealand birdscape is a highly modified one,

Spur-wings can forage in a range of habitats whether along the tideline or in an inland paddock.
IAN SOUTHEY

populated by numerous exotic and self-introduced species that exist alongside those native and endemic species that remain, in some cases precariously. The newcomers, usually birds of open country, have for the most part thrived in the environment formed by several hundred years of human activity. Self-introduced species – invariably from Australia – are part of a long tradition of birds drifting across the Tasman. Perhaps we could think of the process as COR: Closer Ornithological Relations with Australia. Millions of years ago, once New Zealand had separated from Australia, followed by both Australia and South America separating from Antarctica, the Antarctic Circumpolar Current (ACC) was established. There was no longer any land mass to impede the great southern oceans; now the 'roaring forties, fifties and sixties' were initiated, 'creating a powerful agent of wind- and current-driven dispersal between eastern Australia and New Zealand that continues today, bringing birds, insects and plants across the Tasman'.[3]

Before human settlement of these islands, such wanderers may have found the heavily forested land unsuited to their purposes, and never became established. Or perhaps they never arrived at any one time in sufficient numbers to establish a viable population. One researcher points out that 'all the birds present and breeding in the fauna when people first reached New Zealand were present 30,000 years ago. It is probable that potential colonizers arrived constantly but that most were unsuccessful.'[4] But once that land was modified, some may have found it easier to find a foothold. It may surprise many New Zealanders to learn that three of our most common birds are comparatively recent Australian immigrants. The silvereye (or waxeye), for example, became established here only after the mid nineteenth century. The white-faced heron and welcome swallow are more recent arrivals, only becoming established from the 1940s and 1960s respectively, and yet both are now ubiquitous. The establishment of spur-winged plovers offers a very good case study of how a bird colonises a new land; and as it happens, their dispersal throughout the country is reasonably well documented.

If habitat requirements are the key to understanding the success of spur-wings in New Zealand, you could not consider them overspecialised in this regard. Even a brief summary of dietary items would include molluscs, worms, millipedes, centipedes, spiders, insects, crustaceans and occasionally seeds, wheat, barley, leaves and frogs.[5] A description of suitable places – a wide range of open habitats – includes:

> low vegetation, moist grasslands, pasture and playing fields to the margins of wetlands . . . on almost any grassy habitat in urban areas, even . . . areas close to busy traffic, lawns, golf courses, roadside nature strips and median strips, parks, airfields, and sewage ponds . . . sheltered coastal areas, including intertidal flats, estuaries, and lagoons; muddy, sandy or rocky beaches; glacial lakes, bogs, and short tussock grassland at 600–1100 m above sea level.

They are also common in braided riverbeds. Spur-winged plovers 'generally avoid areas of uncleared timber and scrub';[6] a fact of particular relevance given today's much-altered New Zealand landscape.

The original distribution of spur-winged plovers, also known as masked lapwings, encompasses much of eastern Australia, Papua New Guinea and the Maluku Islands (the Moluccas), with two subspecies recognised. The nominate race *Vanellus miles miles* occurs in the northern section of this range, including North Queensland; and the second race, *V. m. novaehollandiae*, extends to the south as far as Tasmania. However, there is a broad zone where the two overlap around Townsville: at Cairns, 280 km further north, only *V. m. miles* occur; and at Mackay, 330 km south of Townsville, only *V. m novaehollandiae* are found.[7] The two subspecies are quite different in appearance, and plumage characteristics, particularly the black strip down the back of the neck, suggest the New Zealand birds originated in southeast Queensland or northern New South Wales.[8] *Vanellus* is a diminutive of the Latin *vannus*, winnowing fan, and *miles*, soldier, refers to the wing spurs that suggest armaments – although their function is more for display.[9]

Small numbers of spur-winged plovers were most likely drifting across the Tasman – although sporadically – long before they became established here. Oliver lists two records from the nineteenth century: one bird shot at Kai Iwi Lakes in 1886, and another seen at Hokitika in 1892.[10] The next record appears to be the Invercargill Borstal birds, of which there were five in 1932. In 1946, by which time there were around 50 birds within a 10-km radius of the city, they became fully protected. Five years later the population was in excess of 100, and numbers then increased slowly but steadily until, during the 1971 breeding season, 1240 birds were estimated to be within a 16-km radius of the Invercargill Post Office.[11]

Meanwhile, having consolidated and expanded their original beachhead, the spur-winged invasion proceeded inland to northern Southland, and on from there. In 1966 they were still rare outside Southland, but a decade later flocks of over 100 were being reported from Canterbury, Marlborough, Nelson and Westland, with the North Island clearly in their sights. In 1967 two or three birds were seen at Lake Horowhenua and at Hokio Beach; but the first confirmed record of breeding in the North Island was near Gisborne in 1970. By 1980 they were considered common in Manawatu and spreading inland. In the decade after 1984, numbers at Lake Wairarapa increased from 211 to 852. Eleven surveys of Wellington Harbour between the 1970s and 2011 recorded an increase, from 1 to 81 birds.[12] By 1991 they were widespread throughout the North Island, with rapid increases in South Auckland, Waikato, Bay of Plenty, Taranaki and Hawkes Bay.[13] They are now well established in Northland.

But this rapid expansion has not been an isolated phenomenon: since the late nineteenth century, a similar process has unfolded within Australia. Before European settlement, spur-winged plovers were confined to southeastern Australia and Tasmania, occupying grassland and shingle areas near lakes and rivers. With conversion of forest and brush to pasture, swamp drainage, and irrigation, available habitat increased and they expanded as far north as Townsville. They were not particularly common in Tasmania until the 1880s, but gradually increased after a major drought on the mainland in 1888. Considered a scarce visitor to the Alice Springs area before 1970, by 1977–81 they were being recorded throughout the district.[14] It seems likely the periodic arrival of birds in New Zealand may be part of this overall range expansion and dispersal back in Australia. It also seems likely that the expansion of the population within New Zealand has been augmented from time to time by further arrivals from across the Tasman.

Certainly this was the view of Maida Barlow, then living in Invercargill, who closely studied these birds and their establishment here. Indeed she can be regarded as the spur-winged plovers' very own chronicler. She considered the '1932 arrivals in Southland were a pair that by chance found themselves in a vacant niche where breeding conditions were ideal. These birds formed the nucleus of the present population.' However, she was sure some wind-assisted birds had probably continued to reach Southland since 1932. This seemed likely given that vagrants of other Australian species, then as now, regularly landed in New Zealand. This may be the explanation behind the record of two adults and three chicks at Makarora Station at the head of Lake Wanaka in November 1952, at a time when the Southland population was still largely confined within a broad radius of Invercargill. If these birds had originated from Southland 'they would have bypassed many suitable breeding areas en route, and it seems reasonable to suppose they were wind blown vagrants'.[15]

The spur-winged immigrants expanded in two ways. One, known as the 'inkblot', is where the established breeding area is gradually expanded outwards as new territories are established on the perimeter. The other is where birds, most often juveniles, arrive in a previously unpopulated area, commence breeding and so begin a new 'inkblot' pattern. Population increase is likely to be more rapid in the earliest stages of colonisation, where opportunities are at their maximum: low breeding densities mean larger territories in the most optimal habitat, such as pasture with low stock numbers; and reduced probability of predators finding nests or chicks. But once the population expands, habitat limitations begin to take effect.[16] From 1965 to 1970, numbers around Invercargill remained quite stable, suggesting that an optimum breeding population had been achieved. A map of the dispersal of birds out of the original perimeter around the city resembles a large stain creeping through central and northern Southland

Despite their name in New Zealand, spur-winged plovers actually belong to a group of species known as lapwings. More rounded wings and shallower wingbeats distinguish this group from most other shorebirds. Note the spurs each wing. IAN SOUTHEY

The first spur-winged plover nests were on Southland farmland; but other habitat is also suitable, such as this riverbed location. JOHN DOWDING

and then up the South Island. The longest distance a banded bird moved was 19.3 km.[17]

In consolidating and expanding their Southland beachhead, spur-winged plovers found unwitting allies in local farmers. Most of their nests were in pasture or on cultivated land, and from mid May to mid August sheep and cattle were concentrated in small areas, leaving paddocks largely unoccupied and available to early breeders.[18] But from mid August birds needed to contend with stock being moved back into paddocks, and with spring ploughing. Birds clearly preferred sites with few or no stock; otherwise they did what they could to cope. Flocks of sheep tended to congregate around an incubating bird, eventually trampling the nest, though not without, on occasion, spirited actions by the aggrieved victims. One such pair was observed confronting a mob of sheep, with the on-duty bird straddling the eggs 'in half-sitting posture, calling loudly and striking with its wings', while its mate stood by, 'making a great demonstration'.[19] Birds will often fly in the face of sheep and cows to prevent them treading on eggs, and will even stand and peck the nose of a sheep. Cattle are an entirely different proposition, and few if any nests remain safe in their presence – which means conditions in Southland for spur-winged plovers are rather different today, with extensive dairy conversions and fewer sheep operations.

Both spur-winged plover adults incubate, tend the young, and defend against intruders, yet despite their vigilance and long periods of brooding chicks, mortality among chicks is high, with over half dying in the first two weeks. Beyond this period, however, mortality drops sharply so that around 25 percent of chicks fledge. As Barlow pointed out, 'you don't have to be a maths expert to realize that this is a high survival rate for a bird which can breed at the end of its first year, lives to at least 11 or 12 years, and whose annual clutch size is 3.7 eggs'.[20] Young are led away from the nest to feeding areas soon after hatching. Birds that have nested on urban rooftops have been observed descending to the ground, carrying a chick by grasping a leg, while the chick hangs on to the adult's facial wattle.

Young are feeding independently within 24 hours, although they remain dependent on their parents for many months. In response to danger, young have been seen crouched in shallow water with only their bills above the surface. One chick, just two–four days old, was seen swimming 12 m across the strongly flowing Taieri River and struggling up a sloping rock retaining wall 1.8 m high on the other side.[21] Family groups remain together for up to 10 months, during which time parental behaviour remains protective. Juveniles may still be around for the beginning of the next breeding season when the parents are copulating. In Australia there is a record of a juvenile helping to defend the territory until the first egg was laid. Generally, after about 10 months adults become 'increasingly hostile' to any junior overstayers.[22] For a successful pair this makes for an exceedingly long breeding season.

Spur-winged plovers have received a somewhat chequered response from New Zealanders over the years, particularly given their activeness at night – usually accompanied by a very loud and shrill cackle

A male shore plover on South East Island/Rangatira. JOHN DOWDING

– but there is no doubting they do possess character. In the early days they were hugely exotic, a colourful (if noisy) addition to the rural landscape. For some they were a tonic: 'Early nesters, presaging new life, raise the spirits of some people, especially in the long dark winters of southern New Zealand.'[23] Clearly they have been successful here – in fact they have been too successful. After receiving legal protection in 1946, in June 2010 (for reasons we shall return to) they were removed from the list of absolutely protected species. Their fortunes are a telling indicator of what has happened to the New Zealand landscape, the transformation of forest to farmland creating opportunities for open-country Australians like white-faced herons, welcome swallows, and spur-winged plovers. In marked contrast are the fortunes of another shorebird, a once common New Zealand endemic that was quickly reduced to a remnant population clinging to a tiny wind- and wave-lashed island over 700 km from the mainland.

It is a very rare assemblage of birds – perhaps the first time it has occurred on mainland New Zealand for over 100 years. There is nothing unusual about the New Zealand dotterel pair on this shellbank at the mouth of the Taramaire Stream in the Firth of Thames, for they are resident. Banded dotterels are regularly seen here as well, although at this time of year most are away breeding, so this individual – perhaps a young bird or a failed breeder – is slightly uncommon. But there is nothing at all commonplace about the third bird in view. Its dark head and throat, the orange-red and black bill and orange-red eye ring mark it as quite distinct from the other two more drably coloured species. So too does the manner in which it is being harassed by the New Zealand dotterels; clearly to them it is a stranger. As indeed it is; although over a century ago it may not have been. Though they were more common in the South Island, there are a number of nineteenth-century records of *Thinornis novaeseelandiae*, or shore plover, in the North Island. But by the 1880s they had vanished from the mainland, surviving only in the Chatham Islands. The trajectory of the shore plover population negatively mirrors that of the spur-winged plover in New Zealand.

The altered landscape, while it created opportunities for the latter, spelt near extinction for the former, mainly because of the other new inhabitants.

Johann Forster, naturalist on the *Discovery* during Cook's second voyage, collected specimens of shore plover in Dusky Sound in April 1773, and at Queen Charlotte Sound in May, which suggests they were widely dispersed in the South Island. Yet by the mid nineteenth century most records came from the southern regions. Canterbury's Thomas Potts, indefatigable naturalist and observer, wrote: 'this pretty plover is sometimes frequently seen in the southern parts of this island fossicking about the sandy shores at the mouth of rivers. It is very hardy, with a strong inclination for the neighbourhood of the sea.'[24] According to another account, 'the sand plover was once common in sandy bays from the Great Barrier Island southward to Otago, but it is now very rare. It never went inland'.[25] It was widely reported in the North Island until the late nineteenth century, with records from around the Hauraki Gulf, Great Barrier Island and Coromandel Peninsula, as well as Wellington Harbour. Walter Buller reported it to be 'comparatively plentiful at the mouth of the Piako, the broad flats of the Manukau Harbour and the sandbanks of Tauranga Harbour associating freely with the flocks of godwits'.[26] However, these reports are now considered doubtful as they made no mention of red knots or turnstones, species that are more likely to have been present at those sites.[27] As Charles Fleming noted, there is scope for confusion among observers: 'on the wing the shore plover is reminiscent of the turnstone, the wing pattern, glistening white breast, dark collar, orange legs and general manner in flight being remarkably similar'.[28] Fossils from the Waikari Valley in North Canterbury suggest that, despite the name it has been given, it may also have been distributed inland as well.[29] If so, the riverbed populations were the first to go, disappearing before 1850. Its subsequent decline is not well documented, though Otago specimen collector Percy Earl considered it to be rare by 1845, with the last mainland records in the 1870s.[30] A more recent researcher observed: 'Their decline has been plotted from lack of records rather than from records of actual disappearance from parts of their former range. Unlike many threatened species in New Zealand, most areas of former shore plover habitat remain intact, so other factors need to be investigated.'[31] What, then, did happen to it?

Shore plovers. ALEX SCOTT

Ruddy turnstones in nonbreeding plumage. It is thought that early witnesses who reported shore plovers in large numbers on the Firth of Thames are more likely to have seen turnstones. IAN SOUTHEY

As with the narrative of so many of our native species, there is a four-legged thread running through this book. In this case it was kiore (Pacific rats), Norway rats and cats, all of which were well established by the early nineteenth century. Ship rats, mustelids and hedgehogs are, for once, not in the dock; as by the time the first two spread throughout the country, and just as hedgehogs were being introduced, the shore plover were largely gone. Subfossil and midden evidence indicate birds occurred on all islands in the Chathams group, although by 1871 they were found only on Pitt and Mangere, and not on Chatham. Sometime in the 1880s, following the introduction of cats, they disappeared from Pitt, and were last recorded on Mangere in 1898.[32] By the end of the nineteenth century they were confined to a single island – South East or Rangatira. But even there the numbers continued to plummet, in part, it is believed, because of their growing rarity. After they were found in the Chathams in 1872, 'the eyes of collectors both scientific and commercial were turned in that direction; and the incredible number of specimens in museums both local and overseas proves how eagerly these beautiful little plovers were sought after and what a good price they would fetch'.[33] In a further twist, if the introduction of exotic animals was the main reason shore plovers disappeared from most of their original range, a further decline in the population occurred after 1960 due to the *removal* of exotic animals. Once grazing by domestic stock ceased on Rangatira in 1961, the island's open spaces began reverting to forest, which meant reduced habitat for shore plover.[34]

A common theme among New Zealand birds is evolution in the absence of mammalian predators, and shore plover seem to have been particularly vulnerable. Most plover species nest in the open, such as on beaches, gravel or shellbanks, tundra or low turf. But shore plover are unusual in that they nest under cover, be it dense vegetation such as muehlenbeckia, tussocks or sedges, or in the crevices under boulders, or in a deserted seabird burrow; in one study only two of 141 nests were completely open to the sky.[35] This may be a factor of their breeding biology, in which there is a long laying period before a clutch is completed; from laying the first egg to the start of incubation can be up to 15 days, meaning eggs may be unprotected for long periods, thus increasing exposure to climatic conditions.[36] Perhaps that is why nests are under cover; or it may also be a defence against aerial marauders such as harriers, skua or gulls. But whatever the reason, nesting in such a manner made them particularly vulnerable once mammals arrived: with reduced visibility a bird may not even see a predator approach, let alone escape quickly.

Yet what we do not know is whether all shore plover nested under cover or whether this behaviour is a feature of the Rangatira population. Eggs from Rangatira were used to establish a captive breeding population at Pukaha Mount Bruce Wildlife Centre, and all birds descended from them that have nested, did so under cover. The behaviour of other species on Rangatira may also be significant. White-fronted terns nest on the mainland on riverbeds, beaches and spits, while red-billed gulls nest on offshore rock stacks. Yet on Rangatira both species nest under cover. This

Tidal rock platforms along the aptly named Thinornis Bay on South East Island/Rangatira, last bastion of shore plovers, and also habitat for Chatham Island oystercatchers. JOHN DOWDING

Not as strongly coloured as males, a female shore plover on Mangere Island. IAN SOUTHEY

is suggested to be a response to brown skua, which regularly prey on nests in the open.[37] Whether or not they nested in similar fashion on the mainland, shore plover were clearly ill equipped to cope with the inexorable advance of mammals.

Most of the 218-ha island – its highest point 207 m – slopes gently to the north and is covered in forest and shrubland. The south-facing slopes are mainly cliffs, except for the southeastern shore, which has raised salt meadow and tussockland sloping down to the coast. There are no sandy beaches on the island. In the prevailing southwesterly conditions southern areas are cooler and windier than the northern coast, and spray and wash from large swells are more common.[38] Shore plover on the island are most commonly found foraging on wet, bare or algae-covered intertidal rock platforms, and 'brackish seeps'.[39] In 1999 a second population of 21 birds was discovered on Western Reef, a tiny islet off Chatham Island where, it is thought, they had been undetected and separate from the Rangatira population for over 100 years. The Western Reef habitat was primarily rocky shore platform with little terrestrial vegetation present.[40]

From this one could surmise that intertidal rock platforms are critical habitat for shore plover. But this may only be so on those tiny wave-lashed islands, the last bastions of the species, where the remnant population survived. On the mainland they were found in a wide range of coastal habitats: from exposed and sheltered rocky coast and sandy beaches to rivermouths and sand- and mudflats of estuaries. So could this be a situation where, like the remnant population of takahe in the Murchison Mountains of Fiordland, a species that was once widely distributed now clings to existence in an otherwise marginal habitat? Noting the absence of sandy beaches from its present range, Fleming dispensed with 'sand plover', the common name used since Buller, in favour of 'shore plover'.[41] He also argued that so closely was the species associated with the rock platform habitat that it was 'fundamental in the make-up of the species and not a secondary adaptation to South East Island conditions'. He pointed out that mainland references to other types of habitat were scanty and undocumented.[42] However it has since been found that rock platforms may not be so essential after all. Birds introduced to Motuora Island in the Hauraki Gulf in the late 1990s had a choice between rock platforms and sandy beach, and spent 90 percent of their time on the beach.[43]

A study of the breeding biology of shore plovers on Rangatira revealed evidence of a remnant population coping with extremely limited habitat. Shore plover live around the island, but the best habitat tends to be on the more sheltered northern and eastern coasts: the more exposed southern coast seems to be poorer habitat for plovers.[44] For instance birds on the southern shore had longer laying intervals than northern birds, which suggests southern females may find it more difficult to gather sufficient nutrients for making eggs. The southern birds also needed to disperse more widely in search of food, meaning less time was spent caring for chicks. This possibly explains the higher predation rate on chicks on the southern coast.[45]

Between 1937 and 1994 the population remained nearly constant at around 120 birds, but with a large pool of nonbreeding birds. Perhaps unsurprisingly, if suitable habitat is in limited supply, birds show an extremely high degree of mate and site fidelity. Habitat quality may also explain wide variation in fledging periods, from 31 to 61 days; chicks on the southern shore take on average twice as long to fledge as chicks on the northern side. Habitat limitations would also explain why birds do not double-brood or renest, as many other plovers do, and as shore plovers in captivity on the mainland do. In the overall population mortality is relatively low, a factor perhaps of the sedentary nature of the species, a relatively stable environment and the absence of mammalian predators. Population models predict the population should expand, but the constant number of breeding pairs and the pool of nonbreeding birds within the population – presumably those that cannot find a territory – suggest habitat limitations are the key obstacle to growth.

So there is an extraordinary divergence in the relative fortunes of spur-winged plovers and shore plovers in New Zealand. One has been so successful that, in just 80 years, it has gone from being newly established and absolutely protected wildlife, to having that protection removed. The other has been driven from the mainland to its last refuges on just a few offshore islands, and then pushed further until only on one tiny island did it cling precariously to existence. Human transformation of the New Zealand landscape in modern times has driven both trajectories. The replacement of indigenous forest with farmland greatly benefited spur-wings, but it should not necessarily have impacted on shore plover, because much suitable coastal habitat remains for them to this day. They just could not cope with the other main change – the introduction of exotic predators.

But if much of the country was originally covered in forest and shrublands, what habitats were there for shorebirds other than snipe? In the contemporary landscape there are several key regions – areas where scale and diversity of habitat support the biggest numbers of birds and widest range of species. These are North Island east coast beaches and estuaries; the large northern harbours – particularly the Manukau and Kaipara and the Firth of Thames; the northern South Island coast – Tasman Bay, Golden Bay and Farewell Spit; the coastal lakes and lagoons of the central east coast of the South Island; and the braided river systems. In the following chapters we shall focus primarily on two of these: northern North Island beaches and harbours, and the South Island rivers.

Foraging male shore plover on Mangere Island. IAN SOUTHEY

A feature of the northern approaches to Christchurch: despite its proximity to the city, the Lower Waimakariri River still supports considerable numbers of shorebirds. JOHN DOWDING

CHAPTER TWO
ONLY GAME IN TOWN: THE BRAIDED RIVERS

Usually it is that dramatic spine of the island, backdrop to any traverse of the Canterbury Plains – the Southern Alps – that catches the traveller's eye. Or it could be the complex patchwork of human endeavours that marks the plains themselves. But cutting a broad swathe across the chequerboard land is a feature found in few other places on earth: the gravel bars and twisted channels of the braided rivers. From the air their scale and grandeur are always impressive: twisted tangles of shiny ribbon, tying together mountain and sea.

These rivers are playgrounds to many people. They feature in films and tourism publicity: river and gravel and a backdrop of snowy peaks; a rider on horseback, perhaps accompanied by dogs, in a high-country sheep operation. Just as often there will be 4WD vehicles in the landscape, or a jetboat: here also is good habitat for anglers. But for some of our endemic birds the braided rivers are essential habitat; and for one in particular, the only game in town. Without these river systems in their natural state, wrybill would quickly follow so many of New Zealand's fauna into oblivion.

The eastern South Island's braided rivers are often described as dynamic. 'They are', noted one study, 'the product of high-energy environments where . . . variable discharge regimes and heavy sediment loads interact to produce dynamic riverscapes.'[1] Immense quantities of eroded material are carried away and deposited by the very rivers that flow across and through the landscape. Twisting streams of water separate and rejoin around islands and channels and are further divided by gravel bars – a system in continual flux. It is a land of water and wind: the river does its work, sorting and resorting, removing and depositing its load; and strong gusts of wind work on the fine sediment, carrying and distributing it as dust.

Braided rivers would not exist without two key ingredients supplied by the Southern Alps: a source of highly erodible material – the product of active mountain building and glaciation; and a physical barrier high enough to create its own weather.[2] The material forming the uplifted Alps is mainly greywacke and argillite, sedimentary rocks that are highly prone to erosion. Great glaciers carved and shaped the mountains into the form we know today, and rock continues to be chipped away by smaller glaciers and frost action. But erosion is also continuous at lower altitudes below the permanent snowfields, where water is busily at work. Prevailing westerly weather systems lifted by the great barrier of the Alps can produce rain or snow at any time of year, though it may be unevenly distributed. Average rainfall along the divide in the Waimakariri catchment, for instance, is 8000 mm, but drops to less than 700 mm at the coast. Eleven percent of this annual precipitation is stored as snow and ice from April to September, and released from October to February. Meltwater or seepage-fed streams carry scree from the higher slopes and deposit it in giant fans against the lower walls of the larger valleys. The rivers occupying the valleys carry this debris further downstream, depositing it along the valley floors and over the floodplains beyond: 'Interactions between rainfall, sediment size and slope of the floodplain may create conditions that cause a river to form multiple sinuous channels across its floodplain'.[3] Such floodplains may develop where the river is not constrained by some geographical feature, such as where it emerges from a gorge.

The three great rivers of Canterbury – the Waimakariri, Rakaia and Rangitata – share broadly similar features. They all rise in the Southern Alps and discharge into the Pacific; upper reaches of the rivers occupy old glacial valleys with broad braided floodplains above narrow gorges; both above and below the gorges

Tasman Valley: Vast stretches of riverbed remain exposed during times of low flow, but periodic floods prevent the establishment of vegetation. KEITH WOODLEY

the floodplains can be kilometres wide; and they are strongholds for much of what remains of our native and endemic shorebird fauna. The great fans of alluvial and glacial outwash deposits on the beds of these and other rivers have built up the Canterbury Plains over thousands of years. Layers of this alluvium – gravel, sands and silt – extend to great depths; at Chertsey, between Christchurch and Ashburton, borings to 610 m did not reach bedrock.[4] Despite being glacial in origin, the rivers descend quickly into country with a temperate climate that enables growth of invertebrate fauna populations sufficient to support birds such as the wrybill.[5]

Southwest of the Upper Rangitata valley, beyond the Two Thumb Range, lies another region of critical significance to shorebirds – the Mackenzie Country. Eroded material – glacial outwash gravel and moraine deposits from the Main Divide that forms its northwestern edge – formed this intermontane basin. Moraine deposited by retreating glaciers around 17,000 years ago dammed three river systems, creating a trio of lakes: Tekapo, Pukaki and Ohau. The Ahuriri River to the southwest joins the overflow from these lakes to form another of the great braided rivers: the Waitaki.

What we see on the surface – the alluvial floodplain and the braided gravel beds of these rivers – is only part of an extremely complex hydrological system. The bed over which a river flows is quite porous and may be many metres deep. Water flows both horizontally and vertically through the gravels, becoming groundwater that may emerge as a wetland or a spring some distance away from the riverbed itself. This means 'the lateral and vertical limits of the "river" include the entire width of the floodplain and the saturated depths of the alluvial aquifer, within and across which the river moves as a single body of water'.[6] It is a diverse and complicated three-dimensional ecosystem, a mosaic of connected aquatic habitats linking surface and subterranean areas – turbulent main braids, quiet side braids, groundwater, springs and spring-fed streams.[7]

The flow regime itself is also rather complex. A river may have one or more major channels flowing fast and deep all year, along with many side channels, riffles and pools, each with its own microhabitat and each subject to fluctuations at any time. Some are ephemeral channels, flowing only immediately after rainfall or snowmelt; or intermittent streams fed by seepage or underflow but which dry up during drought. Large floods, on the other hand, may cause large-scale

(top) A typical view of the Upper Rakaia during a period of low flow: a series of channels and riffles, with plenty of raised gravel areas exposed, create perfect conditions for nesting wrybills. KEITH WOODLEY
(above) Its historical breeding range is believed to have been more widespread, but now the endemic black-fronted tern is largely confined to breeding on braided riverbeds. JOHN DOWDING

modification to the entire riverbed, so even 'perennial' channels may be abandoned and the flow contained within a channel previously considered to be ephemeral or intermittent.[8] Mean annual flow on the Rakaia between 1958 and 1981 was 200 cumecs, with peak flows in late spring and early summer, and lowest flow occurring in winter. But floods in excess of 600 cumecs could occur in any month; one massive flood of 4320 cumecs occurred in December 1979. In addition there was the material carried within the water: the mean average suspended sediment yield of the river, much of it glacial silt, was 1640 tonnes/km^2 per year. Such flood events may occur on any of the rivers at any time of the year, posing considerable challenges to any life forms existing there.

If these rivers are subject to such frequent and dramatic changes, how can any invertebrate life exist? Indeed, because of this extreme disturbance, early accounts of the natural history of the rivers referred to them as 'relative [biological] deserts'. But more recent studies have revealed a great complexity of braided river floodplain habitats with extremely rich biodiversity.[9] Waterflow over and through the riverbed creates a diversity of lentic (standing or slow-moving water), lotic (flowing water) and semi-aquatic habitat types, each at various successional stages. This variety in habitat conditions explains not only the high biodiversity found within river floodplains, but also how biological communities survive in highly unstable conditions: the key lies in 'the relative proportion of each habitat in any particular floodplain [remaining] roughly constant over time'. That is, a particular habitat may be destroyed in one place but will remain intact or be forming in other places, so there will always be habitat at different stages of development. This means 'mobile taxa will persist within the floodplain, and form part of a meta-population within the river system'.[10]

The food chain in the rivers begins with biofilm – an accumulation primarily of algae or periphyton, with fungi, bacteria, and organic and inorganic particles. A major food source for invertebrates, biofilm determines the structure of communities. The all-important periphyton is influenced by local physical and biological factors such as flow regime, wave action, nutrients, light, temperature, and invertebrate grazers.[11] It is a challenging environment, even for biofilm, as fluctuations in river flow may cause physical abrasion during time of flood, or desiccation during prolonged dry periods. But it is habitat for shorebird food – mayflies, chironomids and elmid beetles, typical creatures of fast-flowing, clean, gravel-bed rivers. Sandflies, stoneflies and caddisflies are also common.[12] The composition of these communities varies widely across habitats. In one study, the main river and side braids of the Waimakariri had similar faunas, dominated by mayflies, worms and midge larvae; but the greatest diversity was found elsewhere on the riverbed, particularly in springs and spring-fed streams. Some invertebrates, including the mayfly *Deleatidium* and some chironomids, were ubiquitous throughout the study area, while others had restricted habitats.[13]

Downstream, the physical character of the rivers changes, as does the composition of biological communities. A wider floodplain and smaller and better-sorted stones create more heterogeneous habitats. Here the effects of flooding are mitigated, as high flows are less confined and there is less substrate movement. The result is increased species diversity and abundance in the lower reaches. Higher nutrient levels in central and downstream sections of the river, along with greater bed stability, allow green filamentous algae to succeed and dominate. Relatively stable habitats, such as spring-fed creeks that are rarely washed out during floods, allow colonisation by invertebrates that do not tolerate the unstable, flood-prone environment of the active river channel. They also seem to act as repositories, collecting other life forms that migrate downstream from the wetlands, pools and creeks that feed the headwaters of the river.[14]

At any time of the year a river may be subject to bank-to-bank flooding, affecting every habitat within the riverbed and its margins. This complex, ever-changing

Foundation stone of the braided river food chain: filamentous green algae provide habitat for the aquatic invertebrates that are staple food sources for birds on the riverbed. KEITH WOODLEY

Key food for shorebirds: a swimming mayfly, favourite foraging item for wrybill, among others. ROD MORRIS

Milky glacial silt-laden water is a typical feature of braided rivers like the Tasman. KEITH WOODLEY

environment has implications for the fauna and flora of the riverbed, especially for aquatic invertebrates trying to make a living in a world that could be upturned at any time. The churn of water and the material travelling within it have a direct effect on both invertebrate abundance and community composition. Increased water velocity and movement of material carried by the river mean that some animals are just swept away. A big spring flood will strip periphyton and filamentous green algae from river stones, thus carrying off a major food source. Movement of the riverbed itself may cause catastrophic drift or physical damage to aquatic life forms. Some animals may be smothered by increased levels of suspended sediment carried in floodwaters.[15]

Many invertebrates demonstrate a range of adaptations to cope with these potentially disastrous conditions. For one thing, such events seldom last very long, and the river level may fall just as quickly as it rose. Invertebrate communities then bounce back with remarkable resilience. Quickly making up for losses – replenishing the population – is the key, and the diversity of habitats on offer facilitates this. As one writer notes, this is where these rivers differ from single-channel rivers:

> Braided river floodplains moderate the physical and biological effects of floods by dispersing the flood water's energy over a greater area, and the presence of an extensive mosaic of habitats provides refugia and sources of recolonists. In contrast, a confined river channel provides fewer refugia for invertebrates or internal sources of colonisers, and the full scouring force of a flood is concentrated within the single channel.[16]

Invertebrates have different responses to increased river discharge. Cased caddisflies move down into the substrate, protected by their respective case or shell; while others, such as mayflies, use their low, flattened profile to cling to stones and are rarely dislodged from a stable substrate. But when substrate does move, the animals may move into the stream voluntarily: drifting downstream into areas of lower current velocity is a very effective strategy for many. Once they find refuge – in stable substrate patches, spring creeks or tributaries – they not only avoid the flood, but rapidly recolonise once it recedes; and as river levels drop, invertebrate communities can rapidly recover to pre-flood levels:[17] during a two-week period of stable flow in the Rakaia in winter, invertebrate abundance doubled, with mayfly densities of 200–775 per square metre recorded.[18]

Along with good dispersal ability, increased reproductive output – producing multiple annual broods – is another adaptation to a highly unstable environment. For some species an asynchronous (non-seasonal) lifecycle is one such strategy. Pupae attached to the underside of stones may be adversely affected by floods, but their annual cycle means the timing of a flood is not as important for them as for more seasonal fauna, because if mobile larvae are available through most of the year, there are always individuals at various stages of the lifecycle. This means there are always some individuals that not only survive a major disturbance, they can be present in the water at any time of year, and are thus ready to re-establish themselves.[19]

The iconic scene appears on countless calendars, postcards and tourism promotions: Aoraki Mt Cook, usually depicted against a cloudless sky, presides over an empty expanse of river gravel. In essence it is an image of both the source and the rubble: billions of pieces of rock sheared off the Alps and ground up, planed and rounded by thousands of years of ice and water action. In the postcard image the smooth, rounded stones extend away in a flat plain toward the mountain flanks. But if you stand out on the riverbed itself, the reality is quickly apparent: far from an even, featureless plain there is an astonishing variety of contour, substrate, and vegetation patterns. The landscape is pitted with ridges and hollows, shallow ravines and plateaux, bisected by pools and channels. There is similar diversity in the size and shapes of the stones, and where they lie. The flow of the river sorts shingle into different sizes: banks of big stones adjoin flat areas of sand; a stretch of rounded stones gives way to flat ones. Such areas may change repeatedly over time; while others, away from the main channels, can remain unaltered for years. In some of these areas, stones and boulders are embedded in firm substrate that resembles concrete, and here and there tiny patches of moss and lichen have established. Adjacent to a section of cushion plant and tiny tussocks is a plateau of small rounded stones, recently shuffled by the river and thus empty of any debris or vegetation.

From beside the airfield at Mt Cook we cross a kilometre or so of short dry grass, tussock and matagouri and descend several metres down a steep bank to the riverbed. From there we spread out across the width of the valley as far as the main channel, running fast and deep along the east side of the valley. The high U-shaped slopes are all rock, scree and tussock. Behind us the enormous valley bends away towards its namesake glacier. Today, at 27 km long, it is less than a fifth of the length it was during the last ice age. Lying across the bottom of the valley is our destination, the turquoise sheet of Lake Pukaki: our elevation and the clear alpine air make it seem very close, but it is nearly 20 km away. I have joined eight Department of Conservation personnel tasked with a bird survey of the river, which means covering the length of the riverbed.

Line abreast, we set off walking to the lake, recording any birds encountered along the way. Birds are only counted once they are upstream of us. Within minutes the first wrybill is flushed from its nest. In this environment a sitting bird is perfectly adapted to avoid visual detection, and will not be found unless it moves; but birds flush when the intruder is within a few metres of the nest. The survey procedure is to retreat a few paces and allow the bird to return to the nest. This is essential, for both the nest scrape and the eggs are even less conspicuous than the adult, and hence susceptible to trampling. A short time later the first banded dotterels are recorded, along with one or two black-fronted terns working the edge of a channel. Soon a dozen or so agitated terns are circling close overhead, some swooping to within a metre of me, their vivid yellow-orange open bills screaming angrily. I am standing near a shallow depression in which they appear to have begun nest-building. Just ahead, another startlingly loud commotion erupts in the form of a Canada goose lumbering into flight, leaving a clutch of eggs tightly packed in a nest lined with down. Paradise shelducks, black-billed gulls, black-backed gulls, pied oystercatchers, pipits and redpolls are also encountered on the riverbed. The redpoll is a reminder of another place, another remote, hard landscape 12,000 km north of here: the snowbound tundra of the Yukon–Kuskokwim Delta in Alaska. There it was within its natural range, spread across Eurasia and northern North America; here it is an exotic introduction, but seemingly at home. And so the survey progresses, each person walking as straight a line as this braided river will permit; major channels are skirted where necessary, and crossed where possible.

By afternoon we are two thirds of the way down the river. Here, on older, more stable sections of the riverbed, there is extensive vegetation – *Raoulia* cushion plants, small clumps of tussock and scattered matagouri; a yellow-green mosaic extending into the distance. Banded dotterel are notably more numerous in these sections. Here also, two more people join the western end of the survey line; but as the riverbed is now 4 km wide they remain distant, and invisible for much of the

(top left) *Black-fronted tern in flight.* JOHN DOWDING
(top right) *The dry bed of the Tasman above Lake Pukaki.* KEITH WOODLEY
(bottom left) *Like a stone rolling upstream: a wrybill chick on the move.* KEITH WOODLEY
(bottom right) *Tasman delta: the turquoise expanse of Lake Pukaki at the mouth of the Tasman.* KEITH WOODLEY

time. Eventually we reach the river delta, an area of mud, sand and small stones leading to the lake edge, where a few wrybill forage. For hours under the hot sun we have traversed a rough desert-like bed of stones, with Aoraki looking over our shoulders the entire way. Now – as T.E. Lawrence found on the shore at Aqaba – desert is replaced with dazzling blue-green water.

Today we have counted 99 wrybill, compared with 143 in the 2008–09 breeding season.[20] We have also recorded 402 banded dotterel, 65 pied oystercatchers, 165 black-fronted terns, 3 stilts (1 black and 2 pied), 12 black-billed gulls and 239 black-backed gulls. Of course we will have missed some birds, such as any wrybill that managed to sit tight as we passed by, or birds on the far side of the main channel. But this count is a repeat of previous years, and has followed exactly the same methodology. So it represents a snapshot only, an index of the birdlife on the river. The data will be analysed and used to chart trends in bird numbers and distribution, an essential tool for conservation managers. The task facing those managers is complex and challenging, as we shall see.

Typical high tide scene: the tide approaching the outer shell bank at Miranda has pushed these godwits into shallows along the shoreline, where many of them will roost until the ebb. KEITH WOODLEY

CHAPTER THREE
INTERTIDAL FOOD FACTORIES: COASTAL WETLANDS

The long New Zealand coastline is blessed with a wealth of estuaries. Like Cleopatra they have infinite variety which custom cannot stale. Perhaps the time of their scientific neglect is coming to an end. —R.B. Sibson[1]

Detritus. There is often a negative flavour to the way we use this word, which derives from the Latin for 'rubbing away', by way of French, and means 'an accumulation of disintegrated material or debris'.[2] But in the world of shorebirds, detritus is a beginning, a foundation for life itself. Fine particles of organic matter – collectively known as detritus – accumulating in the margins where land and sea meet are the basis for a complex life-sustaining web in some of the richest ecosystems on earth. Derived from the decomposition of plant material and animal remains, it is the beginning of an organic food chain that, if we follow it upwards, culminates, for example, in the massive journey of godwits and other migratory shorebirds to the other end of the planet.[3] Repositories for detritus are our harbours and estuaries, beaches, inlets and lagoons, where it is raw material in these 'food production lines' for shorebirds.

The other building block for these coastal food factories is sediment. The minute beginnings of life on an estuary can begin close by, or hundreds of miles away in either direction. Sediment and nutrients from the open sea, carried in by tide and current, join eroded material carried from high up in the catchment by rivers and streams; or,

Mixed flock of waders at Miranda.
BRIAN CHUDLEIGH

closer to the shores, rainfall runoff. Tidal action then moves these fine particles in a continuous process of deposition, erosion and removal.

Two key characteristics of estuaries help to explain what happens to this sediment. First, their enclosed or partially enclosed nature make most estuaries relatively sheltered places, where calm conditions allow fine inorganic particles carried in suspension to settle out. Second, by definition they are places where fresh water meets salt water. In a process known as electrolysis, positively charged ions – or cations – that have more protons than electrons, migrate towards a negatively charged cathode. Salt water contains high concentrations of cations, so that when fine river-borne particles encounter saline water, the particles clump together and become heavier, and so sink more easily. Where they settle they form the estuary floor. Though there is little about an estuary that remains settled for long: like a braided river, it is a highly dynamic environment, with sand and silt, channels and even whole islands endlessly moving. Those areas of the sea floor that are left exposed by the receding tide are the tidal flats, and they can be found in all climate zones from the equator to the Arctic and subantarctic.

The composition and origins of these sediments determine the nature of an estuary. Dominant sediment may be sand particles brought in by seawater; or it may be mud – a mixture of silt and clay particles – originating inland and deposited by rivers; or it may be a mixture of both. There is a broad spectrum of sediment types and particle size, ranging from coarse sand to the finest silts, known as lutum. The type of sediment and where it occurs determine which organisms can live in a given area. Coarse sediments are more difficult to get into suspension than fine silt, and so they settle out more quickly. This is why sand flats are more likely to be found in exposed parts of the tidal zone, whereas silt flats generally occur in more sheltered areas. Oxygen-carrying capacity is also determined by sediment size: in sandy flats, coarser material allows oxygen to penetrate several centimetres deep; but in fine silty areas it may barely get 2 mm below the surface. Finer sediments also have higher water-holding capacity; in some areas a sample may be 70 percent water and 30 percent sediment – which is why we find sand flats easier to walk on than soft mudflats.[4] Finally, biological processes, such as burrowing and feeding by invertebrates, further sort and modify sediments. So between a combination of sediment types, their distribution, and biological activity, each estuary is unique.

Biofilm on the mud surface supports communities of tiny invertebrates – the foundation of a complex food web. KEITH WOODLEY

On the Firth of Thames the abundant mud crab is an important food item for many shorebird species. KEITH WOODLEY

TIDES

Dominating all life forms on any estuary or other coastal area is the tidal cycle, the gravitational pull of the sun and moon on the earth's surface, which causes the sea to rise and fall. As the positions of the sun and moon change in relation to the earth, so this pull varies; at any given time only one half of the earth faces the moon. The pull of the moon draws towards it all the water on that side of the earth, thus producing a high tide. At the same time, because the pull of the moon on the other side of the earth is less, water also flows in that direction, creating a simultaneous high tide. These surges of water on either side of the planet cause corresponding decreases in water level elsewhere, resulting in low tides. This tidal movement is kept in constant motion by the movement of the moon around the earth, and the earth's rotation on its axis as it moves around the sun. As the earth rotates every 24 hours, the moon also is moving, and it takes 24 hours 50 minutes for the two bodies to take up the same position relative to each other. This determines the occurrence of high and low tides every 12 hours and 25 minutes, and the advance of the tide time by approximately 50 minutes each day.[5] Meanwhile, every 24 hours the earth rotates relative to the sun, and every 29½ days, at the time of the new moon, the sun and the moon lie roughly in line with each other on the same side of the earth. At the time of the full moon 15 days later, this alignment occurs again but on opposite sides of the earth. At such times, the sun's gravitational pull reinforces that of the moon, resulting in much bigger ranges in tide height, called spring tides. At the other end of the cycle are much smaller tidal ranges called neap tides. These occur during the first and last quarters of the moon when the sun and moon are at right angles to the earth, at which time their gravitational pulls work against each other.

The two most common tundra-breeding species found in New Zealand: bar-tailed godwit (right) and red knot (left foreground) feeding side by side, although with quite different bills. IAN SOUTHEY

Above all else, it is tidal movement and the meeting of salt and fresh water that make estuaries such dynamic environments – presenting both challenge and opportunity to the organisms living there. At the very least, animals and plants in the intertidal zone need to contend with salty or brackish water. But their environment is transformed every few hours – from exposure to air and sun, to complete inundation. The mixing of fresh and seawater is not constant: the shape or topography of the estuarine basin, the level of river flow at a given time, changes in the height of tide each day, strength and direction of wind action – all these serve to alter the composition of the water column in any part of the estuary. At different times, fresh and saltwater may be completely or only partially mixed; or there may be vertical stratification, with lighter river water flowing over denser saline water. Estuaries are like no other marine ecosystems – and if you are an animal trying to live there, you must be highly adaptable to survive.

Broadly speaking there are three basic groups of benthic animals: free-swimming species such as fish or shrimps; surface-dwelling animals such as crabs, snails and some shellfish; and those that live buried in the sediment such as worms and most shellfish. Which takes us back to where we began. From nutrients, water and exposure to sunlight, life is synthesised. Detritus becomes mixed with fine inorganic particles and is soon colonised by large numbers of bacteria, protozoa and other microorganisms. Breakdown of detritus particles releases nutrients, which are then used by estuarine plants such as benthic algae. This interaction of detritus and microorganisms makes estuaries richly productive in plant matter, 'typically four times that of good New Zealand grassland'.[6]

Two major forms of animals dominate the lower levels of the estuarine food chain: benthic species (living in or on the substrate); and free-swimming or pelagic species. There are some animals, though, that are both, at different stages in their lives. Most benthic invertebrates reside permanently on the shore, but some may spend part of their early lifecycle as floating plankton. During this phase they, along with bacteria and other microorganisms, may end up as food for microinvertebrates: tiny animals – nematodes, crustaceans or polychaetes – less than 1 mm in size.

Further up the chain we find the macroinvertebrates: other forms of crustaceans and polychaete worms; but also molluscs, various sea anemones, other types of 'worms' and even some insects. Most are detritivores, and are either suspension feeders filtering food from the water, or deposit feeders scraping food off the sediment. Some benthic animals actually eat the substrate; others are predators feeding on other animals. In this second group are secondary consumers such as predatory polychaetes, whelks and crabs. Gastropods, bivalves and crustaceans dominate the macrofauna of many New Zealand estuaries, and one of the most important groups among them is the crab – which also features in the diet of many birds.

Distribution and densities of benthic fauna are strongly linked to the distribution of sediment types on an estuary. Oxygen-dependent filter feeders such as mussels avoid living in silt, while others such as lugworms prefer a mixture of silt and sand. Animals living in areas of coarser or sandy sediments, which are often near the mouth or on less sheltered areas of the estuary, must contend with waves and current continually rearranging the landscape. In the more sheltered silty areas more often associated with the upper tidal zone, there is less danger of being swept away, but the anaerobic nature of the substrate limits what can live there. So the highest densities of animals tend to be in the mid-tidal zone. The time an area is submerged or exposed during the tidal cycle also determines what lives where. Areas uncovered for the longest time at low tide are not ideal places for animals that are intolerant of such lengthy exposure. True filter feeders like cockles or mussels can only feed when the tidal flat is submerged, so they do less well in areas that are submerged for less time. Deposit feeders, on the other hand, can continue feeding at low tide and can occur throughout the tidal zone.

Some animals live deeper in the substrate than others. Some species burrow more deeply in winter months, becoming less accessible to probing bird bills. The presence or absence of competitors or predators is also a factor. But a good estuary has much to offer: areas of suitable substrate and little wave action, good amounts of phytoplankton and zooplankton for the filter feeders, patches of algae for the grazers, and plenty of detritus for the scavengers.[7] So for a number of reasons – a rigorous physical environment with fluctuating salinity, distribution of particular sediment types, variable exposure to air and extremes of temperature as well as pressures from competitors and predators – benthic fauna, or shorebird food, is rather unevenly distributed both in time and space.

Getting down to it: foraging in soft mud for their favourite polychaete prey can be a dirty business for bar-tailed godwits like this one at Miranda.
IAN SOUTHEY

A high tide flock of godwits at Miranda. KEITH WOODLEY

It could be a coastal settlement anywhere in New Zealand: lining the coast road, a string of houses facing several hundred metres of tidal flats at low tide. On broad strands of dark pebbles interspersed with wet sand and shallow pools, a few pied oystercatchers are thinly scattered, with others sub-roosting or loafing, concentrated in loose huddles near the waterline. A pair of sleeping variable oystercatchers – entirely black lumps – are only just visible among the black stones. Two white-faced herons scrutinise the contents of a long shallow pool, while a couple of second-year black-backed gulls – looking particularly scruffy, neither black nor white, nor the spangled brown plumage of their first year of life, but off-white and dull, patchy grey – stand motionless but intensely curious, watching. Movement gives away the presence of two small brown-backed birds – banded dotterel foraging in the mid-tide zone. Just ahead a small hunched shape breaks the flatness, then disintegrates into movement, a flash of iridescent blue as the kingfisher moves to another perching spot. It could be anywhere; but there is one clue, one presence here that reveals a more confined geography. The northern New Zealand dotterel standing preening near the waterline means this place – the tiny community of Kaiaua on the Firth of Thames – could only be somewhere in the upper North Island.

Diversity of bills: (clockwise from top left) New Zealand dotterel JOHN DOWDING; *Chatham Island oystercatcher* BRIAN CHUDLEIGH; *bar-tailed godwit; and red knot* IAN SOUTHEY.

Seven kilometres south along the coast, the strip of exposed flats off Kaiaua start to seem rather narrow in comparison. For here, extending along the entire southern coast of the Firth, is where the major mudflats begin – all 8500 ha of them. These flats explain why the Firth of Thames supports up to 35,000 wading birds each year.[8] On the ebb tide the flats are a bird pantry – and not just for shorebirds. The surface is a mass of footprints and probe holes; godwits and gulls, knots and other sandpipers, stilts and oystercatchers, herons and dotterels and even ducks all forage here. The incoming tide diminishes foraging opportunities, gradually concentrating birds towards the shore. Reaching unseen parts of the bay, the tide forces more birds off distant flats, and shortly afterwards they appear on this side – strung across the sky in loose echelons, heading for the growing ranks on the flats immediately off the shellbanks. These massed flocks will remain here; or, if it is a tide higher in the cycle, they will be pushed off the flats completely. Only when the ebb begins and the first mud is exposed will they return. And so the cycle of the estuary and its life forms continues.

As we have seen, the estuary is a complex place and shorebird food may be distributed very unevenly within the intertidal zone. How do birds find and harvest this food? From the air, the texture of a given area of

A variety of bills suited to foraging in the intertidal zone: from left, knot, oystercatcher and godwit. ILLUSTRATION KEITH WOODLEY

mud, its proximity to a channel, its location within the tidal zone, or the presence of other feeding birds, may offer clues as to food availability. At ground level there are other visual clues – perhaps a burrow or a trail of excreta – to indicate the presence of prey. When it comes to harvesting this food, shorebirds come equipped with a dazzling diversity of tools for the job.

In most birds the bill has two basic functions: feeding and preening. Among the Charadriiformes there is almost every size and shape of bill imaginable, reflecting the great diversity of food resources exploited by its members over a wide range of habitats. All are different in some way – long or short, curved or straight, sturdy or extremely slender – each adapted to a particular niche. Differences are almost impossible to detect among some species; but for others, the extremes are dramatic. At the small end of the scale are the sparrow-sized stints, whose bills are shorter than the length of their heads; likewise the smaller plovers. The straight bill of a red knot is about the same length as its head. The bill of a terek sandpiper or a curlew sandpiper is longer; upturned in the former, and decurved in the latter. Aptly named turnstones have short, relatively strong, wedge-shaped bills, used to push aside objects or tip them over in search of prey. Stilts have long, thinly tapered bills used for picking prey items from the surface of mud or shallows; while those of oystercatchers are thick and robust, a necessity for levering open or drilling holes in the shells of their mollusc prey. Then there is the godwit, where the long and slender bill, slightly upturned towards the end, is noticeably longer in females than males. At the top end of the scale are the somewhat improbable curlew family: in the largest – the eastern curlew – the long and decurved bill seems to go on forever.

Regardless of this diversity of bill length, shape and function, all birds share the same basic bill structure: each has an upper and lower mandible. The upper mandible is anchored to facial bones; the lower is based on the jawbones. In many shorebirds the tip of the upper mandible is flexible, allowing it to be opened and closed while probing, to grasp prey. The upturn in a godwit bill is an extension of this function. Studies of curlews show their curved bills are more manoeuvrable within cavities and around corners in burrows than are straight bills, and are better suited for grasping prey within a confined space. This applies to godwits as well, because the same advantage appears to exist whether the bill curves upwards or downwards. Bills are covered in 'a horny layer that resists wear by growing continuously, rather like our fingernails'.[9] In many species the bill tip is slightly swollen, and internally honeycombed with hexagonal cells. Located here are tiny mechano-receptor organs – including Herbst corpuscles, which measure pressure – to which sensory fibres are attached.[10] Birds are able to interpret and react to vibrations made by quickly moving or buried prey. This is known to be particularly the case in red knots, where these adaptations may be more highly developed than in some other species.[11]

The 9654 km-long coastline of New Zealand has an estimated 301 places that can be broadly defined as estuaries or lagoons – an average of one every 32 km. Of course there is great variation in size, ranging from less than 100 ha to over 15,000 ha, and complexity. Over half New Zealand estuaries are known as 'bar-built' – shallow areas with a bar across the mouth and an outlet that may shift position – and over 50 of them are drowned rivers resulting from changed sea levels.[12] In the Firth of Thames seven rivers or streams contribute to the wider system, forming what is called a 'compound estuary'.[13]

These larger estuaries contain a greater diversity of habitats and invertebrate fauna, and so accommodate larger and more diverse bird populations. Collectively our estuaries support over 160,000 birds of New Zealand breeding species, and similar numbers of northern hemisphere migrants.[14] For most New Zealand birds, estuaries are where they spend the nonbreeding season, moving elsewhere to breed. The vast majority of them tend to use relatively few sites – mainly the northern harbours, Farewell Spit and Nelson bays, and the southern South Island. However a number of smaller estuaries – such as Ohiwa Harbour, Kawhia Harbour and the Avon–Heathcote – support large and diverse wader populations.

Other areas are more properly defined as coastal lagoons – semi-enclosed bodies of predominantly fresh water with a connection to the sea, but which may not always be fully tidal. Yet such places share some features with estuaries and can be important sites. A good example is Te Waihora/Lake Ellesmere, a shallow lagoon of mostly open water fringed with areas of raupo, rush and willow and 6000 ha of saltmarsh and mudflats. It is not tidal like a true estuary, yet it may be subject to daily water fluctuations – a phenomenon that partly mimics the tide. Here it is not the lunar cycle but wind that is responsible. In strong winds, water from one side of the lake is pushed 2 km out, leaving exposed mudflats on one side and flooding low-lying areas on the other. One consequence of this is that the mudflat habitat is continually changing and renewing itself. Lake Ellesmere is one of the most important shorebird sites in New Zealand. It regularly supports over 90,000 wetland birds, including 14,000 shorebirds; on occasions up to 10,000 pied stilt have been recorded there.[15] Other important sites include Vernon Lagoons near the mouth of the Wairau, Lake Wainono in South Canterbury and Waituna Lagoon in Southland. Of course birds are found in other coastal environments as well, such as ocean beaches and rocky shores, but it is the estuary and its tidal flats that are our primary focus, for that is where most shorebirds occur most of the time.

Ohiwa Harbour. BRIAN CHUDLEIGH

The aerobatics of a wrybill flock never fail to enthral. This characteristic behaviour increases in intensity and duration as winter progresses, before the birds migrate southwards from late July. KEITH WOODLEY

CHAPTER FOUR
LIFE WITH A TWIST: THE SINGULAR WRYBILL

After many preparatory stoops, they alight with an inexpressibly graceful, butterfly gesture, common to many small waders before and after flight: arching slender, tapering wings vertically above their backs, revealing the soft white silk of their under surface: a lovely moment suggestive of infinite luxury of physical contentment. —Richard Perry[1]

The evening tide is almost full and the shellbank roosts a festival of chattering, preening, jostling birds when the eruption occurs: a sudden deafening rustle of wings and vocal clamour. No obvious reason for the disturbance is apparent – no harrier hanging in the mauve and peach sky, no skua marauding over the bay. But then this is the nature of shorebirds outside the breeding season – drawn together in large sociable roosts, restlessly lifting off into wheeling manoeuvres, before settling once more. Perhaps it is merely a real-estate reshuffle – adjustment to roosting space dwindled by the tide. Gradually the skies empty as birds resettle. First down are the thousands of oystercatchers, claiming the end of the spit as their own; sprinkled among them are a few Caspian terns and black-billed gulls. The wintering flock of godwits and the few dozen remaining knots alight on the middle reaches of the bank, some spilling down into the edge of the tide. Only the wrybill remain airborne, over 2000 individuals meshed into a kinetic spiral directly above.

As I leave at dusk, 20 minutes later, they are still up there. It has been a fantastic display – frenetic twists and turns followed by languid loops as the flock teases apart then coalesces, flashing white underparts twisting to dark as they turn away. A string of birds peels off and spirals down, like unravelled wool hung across the sky, before twisting and spooling upwards. Soon the sky is almost dark, but still the wrybill are aloft, the murmur of wings and soft voices drifting down.

What is this all about? Why are these birds expending energy in this way? I idly muse that it *is*, after all, Saturday night at Miranda, and maybe that is what wrybills do at this time. Such a notion of course would never pass muster with biologists, most of whom seem highly suspicious of any notion that animals 'do' recreation. For them, every behaviour has a function. It is late June, so is this a social mechanism prior to migration and dispersal over the breeding grounds?

Wary and watchful: a female wrybill with her two eggs at a nest on the Ashley River.
JOHN DOWDING

Whatever its purpose, it is a display I have witnessed countless times, yet it never stales; each time is fresh, new, fascinating. It has also enthralled countless visitors to Miranda. It is one of the endearing features of this singularly charismatic little bird.

From late December, as their breeding season winds down, nearly half the entire population of wrybill flock to Miranda on the Firth of Thames, where their quicksilver aerial ballets enchant the visitor. They are a magnet for birders, and a flagship species for the Miranda Naturalists' Trust (MNT).

A species by definition is unique. But could it be that some are more unique than others? Take the wrybill, for example: Germans call it *Schiefschnabel* or 'bent-nose', though the species does not occur there. In fact it does not occur anywhere outside New Zealand. *Anarhynchus frontalis*, the wrybill or ngutu pare – known also as sand-lark, crook-billed plover or scissor-bill – with its twisted bill is alone among nearly 10,000 bird species.[2] *Anarhynchus* combines the Greek *ana* 'upwards and backward' with *rynchus* 'bill'; and *frontalis* is from the Latin 'fronted' or 'browed'.

As the Age of Discovery unfolded and ships from Europe spread across the globe, specimens of exotic flora and fauna flowed back into museums and private collections. Some plants, birds, animals and insects bore similarities with specimens already familiar to natural scientists. Others, though, were downright weird; and among the strange new birds exposed to Old World scrutiny an inordinate number seem to come from New Zealand. The kiwi, for instance – at first thought to be a mischievous collector's composite; or the giant moa – too big to be a bird, surely? The first European record of wrybill comes from Quoy and Gaimard, naturalists on the 1827–29 voyage of the *Astrolabe*, who recorded small flocks 'on mud-flats and saltwater estuaries around the Hauraki Gulf'.[3] On 25 February 1827 the ship entered the Waitemata Harbour, where several were collected on the North Shore.

Of particular note to the discoverers was the lateral curvature of the bill, and their hunters shot a number of other specimens to confirm its occurrence as a normal species characteristic. All birds had their beak bent to the right, although only one could be preserved because the others were badly shot-damaged.

Despite this information, in 1862 G.R. Gray of the British Museum dismissed the bill on the intact specimen before him, named *Charadrius frontalis*, as a mere deformity. 'The bird is represented in the *Voyage of the Astrolabe*, with a deformed bill; the bill is perfectly straight in most specimens.'[4] This 'very remarkable note' clearly surprised T.H. Potts: 'Where could the author have met with those specimens with perfectly straight bills? Or perhaps he was confused with other species such as banded dotterels.'

In his reading before the New Zealand Institute in 1870, Potts described the bill as:

black, longer than the head, pointed, curved to the right or off side, [and] curled slightly in itself in a leaf-like manner . . . From the base of the bill the upper mandible is flattened on the top for a distance . . . it then assumes a raised and slightly rounded form, till it gradually sweeps down into the point.[5]

But the bill is not just curved laterally. Another account describes what is quite a complex structure.

In the zone of curvature the mandibles are not simply horizontally bent but are also twisted and curled in the vertical plane. At the base, the bill is symmetrical in section, with the mandibles being of similar width. In the region of the curve, however, the concave edge of

Unique structure: complexities of the 'wry' bill.
KEITH WOODLEY

JOHN DOWDING

each half of the bill curls inward while, on the convex side, the upper mandible closes over and overlaps the lower. This asymmetry becomes less pronounced towards the tip of the bill where the edges of the mandibles meet normally and the section is once more symmetrical.[6]

The result is a structure which, when closed, leaves an opening on the concave side in the region of the curve which, for Potts, resembled 'a curved pipe, with a very slight twist'. The effect is that 'with the left side laid lowermost, it has the potential to be used like a spoon'.[7] Even within the bird kingdom, with its diversity of bill shapes and sizes, this is an odd instrument. What is its purpose?

Observing the birds on their riverbed breeding grounds, Potts concluded the bill was specifically adapted for that stony environment: 'The horny point of the bill . . . is sufficiently strong to be used for thrusting between and under stones and pebbles.' The very structure of the bill – the long grooves and flattened form of the upper mandible – 'tends materially to assist the bird in fitting its curved bill close to a stone, and thus aids it in searching . . . beneath the shingle for its food, while at the same time the closed mandibles would form a tube through which water and insects could be drawn up, as water is sucked up by a syringe'. This enables the bird to follow its prey 'by making the circuit of a water worn stone with far greater ease than if it had been furnished with the straight beak of the plover, or the long flexible scoop of the avocet'. For Potts this was conclusive:

It must clear away any little cloud of doubt . . . that this singular form of bill, so far from being an accidental deformity, is a beautiful provision of Nature, which confers on a plover-like bird the advantage of being able to secure a share of its food from sources whence it would be otherwise unattainable.[8]

Walter Buller certainly supported this interpretation; but others, including one of his regular sparring partners, were not so sure. Frederick Hutton, then assistant geologist to the Geological Survey Department, questioned whether, in making the circuit of the stone in pursuit of prey, the wrybill would need to see around a corner. He also correctly pointed out:

the bird is just as common . . . on the mud-flats of the Manukau Harbour, where there are no stones, as it is in the shingle-beds of the rivers of the South Island; and . . . I have often watched the bird feeding and never yet saw it run round a stone more than any other bird might do.[9]

Hutton pointed out that a favourite food of wrybill was minute but numerous organisms hidden among fine algae.

By slightly inclining its head it could lay a considerable part of its bill flat on the ground, and thus, in the first case, take up a much larger quantity of those minute organisms at a time, or, in the latter, could search over a greater extent of Algae for creatures that it could not see, than if it used only the point of the bill. The broad bill of the duck performs the same office in a different manner.

However, he was also careful to point out that he had not directly observed this for himself.

I by no means assert . . . that this is the use of the peculiar shape of the bill; for I have had no opportunity of observing one through a telescope when feeding, neither have I examined the contents of the stomach to ascertain on what they feed; but it must be remembered that the curve in the bill would not prevent the bird from eating insects and other animals also.[10]

Canterbury ornithologist, hunter and collector Edgar Stead was also sceptical. He thought there 'can be very few occasions when the peculiarity is of any decided benefit to its possessor, for over nearly all the river-beds on which the bird feeds, the stones are so much buried in sand as to make the bent bill quite unnecessary'. Stead joined Hutton in pointing out that wrybill spend only a few months on the riverbeds, and the rest of the year living 'on mud-flats, and sea beaches, where its abnormality can be of no benefit'.[11] Hutton's point was well made: if a bird spends more of its year on soft mudflats than among river gravel, should it not be adapted more for that habitat?

In one of his classic works on New Zealand fauna, *Birdlife of Island and Shore*, Herbert Guthrie-Smith pondered the same question. Watching wrybill foraging over sand flats on a receding tide, he speculated 'whether the sweeping scythe-like action in feeding, a skimming of the surface of the wet sand, had helped to modify the remarkable crooked bill of the species, or had been adopted in consequence of it'.[12]

The debate continued into the 1970s. Graham Turbott, then director of Auckland Museum, and familiar with wrybill from the harbours around Auckland, was intrigued not only by the bill shape, but also by the feeding actions employed.

The birds as they feed over the soft mud predominantly sweep the head sideways, the action being from right to left, that is, against the 'right handed' curve of the bill; such an action means the whole side of the front . . . portion of the bill from angle to tip becomes functional as a grasping and gathering mechanism, and it seems justifiable to suppose that the bill possesses a relatively high efficiency for mudflat feeding when used this way.[13]

Turbott observed that the bill tip was also used in more conventional fashion, to merely pick up an item, but when doing so 'the stroke is also down and to the left'. He considered that '[there] can be no doubt concerning the adaptive significance of the shape of the bill'. Other waders, such as pied stilt, on mud will turn the bill 'along the flat' to pick up food items – but with a straight bill this is done with some effort, and 'the bird's face may in extreme cases go down until almost touching the mud; in comparison the wrybill's action against the side of the bill is both deft and effective'. Turbott was also of the view that food taken on shingle beds during the breeding season is derived mainly from 'soft muddy drifts in the river beds and softer interstices between the shingle', and is comparatively rarely sought under the stones themselves.[14]

In 1979, ecologist Ray Pierce published a seminal paper addressing the wrybill debate. He considered the 'gaps and contradictions in the knowledge of wrybill feeding on riverbeds, [were] largely because authors have formed impressions rather than made quantitative measurements'. Pierce grew up in South Canterbury and, through family camping and fishing trips, came to know the lakes and riverbeds of the central South Island very well. 'I would get on the end of a fishing line and would not do very well food wise but would see a lot of things passing by – terns, grebes, coots and . . . I saw my first wrybill on a fishing trip on the Rangitata, and black stilts at the mouth of the Cass.'[15] In considering a subject

For the experienced observer, the characteristic twist of the head as it forages on the mudflats can always identify a wrybill, even at a great distance. IAN SOUTHEY

Despite its peculiarity, a 'wry' bill can be used most effectively as a more conventional tool as well: plucking a polychaete from its burrow for instance. IAN SOUTHEY

Much of what we know about the ecology of wrybill was learned at this study area on the Upper Rakaia in the 1970s. KEITH WOODLEY

for his postgraduate diploma, he found in the wrybill a prime candidate. Surprisingly, apart from some Wildlife Service riverbed counts in the 1960s, no one had actually focused on them. His paper reported findings from an extensive study of birds on the Rakaia, and on the Cass River, which flows into Lake Tekapo.

In the study area on the Rakaia, patches of sand were sometimes extensive at the edge of streams; and silt commonly settled on streambeds in areas of quieter water, but was generally absent from riffles or rapids. Stones were typically smoothly rounded. Main food items for wrybill were caddisfly and mayfly larvae, and their location was quite significant.

> In both study areas mayfly larvae were found to be negatively phototactic, clinging to the undersurface of stones during the day. Stones that were free of silt and partly covered in algae normally supported mayflies. These conditions were characteristic of the riffles and it was here that mayflies were most abundant and wrybills most frequent.[16]

The highest mayfly densities on both rivers were found in riffles, and not in the 'soft muddy drifts on the riverbeds and softer interstices between shingle' mentioned by Turbott and others. Pierce found such areas, as well as backwashes and transitional areas, had low mayfly densities and were not favoured by wrybills.[17]

Pierce noted three feeding actions: a *direct peck* consisting of a rapid movement after which the bill is quickly withdrawn; a *clockwise movement* where the head is tilted to the left followed by a left to right bill movement; and *probing* where the bill is pushed at a steep angle into the streambed. Nearly 60 percent of bill movements in both study areas were direct pecks, most of them 'in-water' and 'probably directed mainly at benthic prey, because bottom-dwelling mayfly and caddisfly larvae were frequently seen captured'. Moving targets were often suggested: 'It is likely direct pecks to the base of stone may have been directed at mayfly larvae which, having detected the approaching bird, were seeking shelter of stones.' About 25 percent of bill movements were clockwise movements; in most such cases the bill was pushed under a stone where prey seemed to be felt for rather than seen. In some cases, clockwise movements were used exclusively throughout the period of observation, though usually

Adapted to cooler conditions, some black stilts are able to remain on the inland riverbeds during winter, when most other birds have departed. Their more robust bills are better adapted to riverbed foraging techniques than their slender-billed pied stilt cousins. IAN SOUTHEY

Two oystercatchers foraging around stones on the Upper Rangitata. KEITH WOODLEY

this method was interchanged with direct pecks. Pierce found probing was used less often than other feeding techniques, usually occurring only in areas of small stones.[18]

Of course wrybill habitat on the northern harbours and estuaries is quite different. On the Firth of Thames they are seen feeding on worms such as *Nicon* and *Orbinia*, commonly found in the upper stratum of the mudflats. But much of their foraging is closely associated with wet sediment, where they appear to be feeding on biofilm. In Auckland, they sometimes shift from the Manukau Harbour to the Tamaki Estuary, to feed in the soft mud exposed by the outgoing tide.[19] Having noted the spoon-like structure formed between the upper and lower mandibles, Rod Hay, during a PhD study in the late 1970s, looked for an apparent use of it on the riverbeds, and found no indication that 'spooning' or 'sweep feeding' was common. On the northern mudflats, however, it was characteristic – being used 31 percent of the time.

In each feeding action the bill was thrust sideways, as it was being closed, to the right and into water overlaying the surface of the mud or into the mud itself. Only a step or two was taken before the next bill movement took place.

Using a probe in the mud to simulate this action, Hay found the disturbance caused large numbers of small crustaceans resting on the mud surface to enter the water column. Once the disturbance stopped the animals took less than a second to settle, so a bird had to be quick to take advantage – explaining the high feeding rates recorded in the study.[20]

In cooler conditions on the riverbeds – such as early in the morning, or during late winter and early spring when water temperatures are cooler – much aquatic fauna is inactive, so wrybill food is less available. At such time most feeding actions were tactile, particularly with clockwise movements, where the 'curvature of the bill assisted prey capture. The bill appears to be pre-adapted for obtaining mayfly and caddisfly larvae from their inactive diurnal positions on the underside of submerged stones.' The bent bill was also useful for gleaning visible larvae from the curved surfaces of stones; it can be opened parallel to the surface of a stone, giving freedom of movement for catching prey. Birds with more orthodox bills, such as banded dotterels, or even the upturned bill of a terek sandpiper, lack these advantages. The terek's bill in particular is quite unsuitable, as the mandibles cannot be opened effectively under a stone. During poor feeding conditions, Pierce noted that other species also employed tactile methods: black stilts and pied oystercatchers were observed probing under stones; and black-billed gulls used foot-paddling to try and stir up benthic insects. But with mayfly and stonefly emergence in early afternoon, river birds were then able to forage by sight alone.[21] It is these observations during times when food was scarcer that led Pierce to speculate on possible origins of that peculiar bill.

Pierce looked at wrybill in comparison with other species in similar habitat, such as the two stilts. The lateral asymmetry of a wrybill is advantageous during really difficult feeding conditions when prey is less accessible. He suggests pied stilts are at a disadvantage at such times, using a lot of energy walking around seeking prey, or moving from the channels to better feeding areas. Black stilts are better able to cope with cold conditions: their larger, stronger bills, and greater insulation from their darker plumage, mean they can get in the river and rake. Pied stilts seem reluctant to do this, probably because their finer bills are more sensitive and prone to abrasion.[22] The wrybill adaptation for foraging in soft sediments also applies in the Mackenzie Basin. On exposed mudflats around lake and lagoon edges, when water levels drop, chironomid larvae and tubificid worms can be really abundant for a time. It 'is great tucker, especially the chironomids, and wrybills really go beserk on them'. During extreme floods when breeding conditions are particularly poor, birds leave the rivers as soon as they can, but 'even in those hard times we would sometimes see them go to muddy edge lagoons'. However such habitats occur in only about 10 percent of wrybill breeding range; for example, there are few associated damp areas on the Rakaia.[23]

Pierce suggests that 'Any behavioural or morphological modification that increases the ability of these birds to capture prey during this potentially difficult time, clearly has survival value', and that such adaptations were probably more important to wrybill than other species. Their shorter legs prevent foraging with stilts in deeper water where prey density is often high, and small birds are probably susceptible to heat loss in very cold conditions; so a combination of subzero temperatures (which frequently occur in late winter and spring), and a low intake of food could be fatal. 'One can speculate', wrote Pierce, 'that a bent bill had even more survival value during the glacial epochs of the Pleistocene Period, when many New Zealand bird species probably became extinct'.[24] The shorebird fossil record for New Zealand is rather sparse, and there may be important absences from it. For instance, suggests Canterbury Museum vertebrate curator Paul Schofield, a species such as the wrybill may have had more than one relative or competitor at a given time, all of which became extinct, it being the only one to survive because of its adaptation.[25]

Confined to Central Asia, the ibisbill is also a gravel riverbed specialist, using its decurved bill to forage over and around stones. However its food is usually more accessible than wrybill prey that clings beneath stones. JOHN HOLMES

Because of high mortality rates, evolutionary forces are strongest during bad years, [and] in the case of wrybill, such forces may have been particularly strong during prolonged cool periods. A scarcity of riparian insects and comparatively stable river beds (both results of a cold climate) coupled with heat-loss problems, would have selected for improved feeding techniques in the aquatic habitat. The bent bill may have permitted efficient food intake, allowing the species to persist through adverse climatic conditions, such as occurred during the glacial epochs.[26]

But if that is the case, why has such an adaptation not occurred elsewhere in the bird kingdom where, presumably, similar habitat factors occur? Hay presented three hypotheses: a feature could arise rapidly in a small and isolated population; conditions in New Zealand are unique; or the occurrence of mutation giving rise to the curvature is so rare it has simply not occurred elsewhere.[27] Certainly the braided river systems are rare globally, and only one other shorebird – the ibisbill in the Himalayas – appears to be restricted to such areas. Investigating this, Pierce found that while habitat conditions in the Himalayan rivers were broadly similar to those in New Zealand, the nature of ibisbill invertebrate prey was different, 'because they were on the river beds with large prey actually sheltering under stones so they could go around or over stones and still open their beak and grasp them. They didn't have an issue where larvae would cling to the undersurface of stones.'[28] For Hay, the small wrybill population, the insularity of its range, and the 'relatively unusual nature of its braided river habitat' suggested the origin of the curved bill was 'most likely the result of selection of natural variability in the breeding grounds'. As a result of competition on mudflat habitat, further 'selection acted on this structure . . . to produce feeding behaviour and secondary asymmetry that characterise this species'.[29]

Another question arises: is the oddly shaped bill reflected elsewhere in wrybill anatomy? There is no asymmetry in skull structure, nor are there any other unusual features in the rest of the skull, which is closely similar to plovers in the genus *Charadrius*. Interestingly, some asymmetry of the skull at the base of the bill is found in oystercatchers, 'which also lay the head to the left when feeding, but in this case the bill is used to make forceful attacks on molluscs while in this position'.[30] In the wrybill, no asymmetry is found in the jaw and tongue muscles, or in neck muscles. Typical of most shorebirds is rhyncokinesis – where the upper mandible is flexible and can bend upwards. In most plovers the bending zone starts relatively close to the skull, while in other birds, such as snipe and curlews, it is narrower and is situated farther forward in the bill. The wrybill is a typical plover with a wide bending zone centred near the midpoint of its bill.[31]

Yet it is not only bill shape that make wrybills so superbly adapted to their riverbed breeding environment. Stead considered the uniform steel grey of its upper plumage was of greater benefit to a bird than its bill. 'It is sincerely to be hoped that this most interesting bird does survive, for, on its nesting ground, it exhibits in all its stages – adults, eggs, young – the most amazingly perfect protective colouration that there is among New Zealand birds.'[32] Likewise for Guthrie-Smith, watching a bird on the lower Rakaia: 'the grey-blue boulders, the splashed water edges, the stones half dry, half wet, darker or grey, the dusts and sands and gravels of the river. Everyone of them is blended into his plumage.'[33] Shingle riverbeds are high-contrast environments with strong light and deep shadow, but they are nevertheless very open, 'with few hiding places even for a small bird'.[34] In such terrain a colourful bird is rather obvious: oystercatchers and paradise shelducks are two examples of this.

Tactile feeding requires a bird to move more or less continuously, which makes it more visible to predators. Foraging along the stream edge may reduce its ability to detect predators so developing a more cryptic pattern and colour would increase its chances of survival.[35] Hay suggests avian predators are a key factor behind wrybill colouration. At least two raptors – the New Zealand falcon and the now-extinct Forbes' harrier – occurred on or around the riverbeds. Since human settlement, both the black-backed gull and the Australasian harrier have occurred in increased densities. During Hay's study, there was little predation of wrybill eggs, but he did note the response of adults guarding chicks to the presence of black-backed gulls. This, together with indications that wrybill avoid nesting in the vicinity of black-backed

The cryptic colouration of the wrybill shows perfect adaptation to its riverbed nesting environment. KEITH WOODLEY

Spot the bird: a wrybill chick in 'frozen' posture in the righthand third of this photo. JOHN DOWDING

Beyond camouflage: wrybill, along with many other shorebirds, use distraction displays to try and divert the intruder. JOHN DOWDING

colonies, 'provide strong evidence for the influence of avian predation on wrybill evolution'.[36]

The Hi-Lux bounces across paddocks of matagouri and tussock, following a path that is part track and part creekbed. Across the valley, tussock and scree slopes ascend to remnant snow patches on the tops. On a wooded knoll behind us are the buildings of our base at Mesopotamia Station; in front flow the many strands of the Upper Rangitata. The tyranny of the gorge downstream will shortly confine them to a single channel, but for now they are spread over several kilometres of flood plain. We park on the river edge. Over the channel nearest the bank a black-fronted tern is flying upstream, proceeding jerkily in its hovering, dipping fashion. The sun is touching the tops but has not yet reached into the valley as we cross this first channel. The current is stiff and the ice-cold water knee-deep; instantly my feet are like iceblocks. Our purpose is to catch and band wrybill.

The near side of the first gravel bar is steep-edged, over a metre high, but then slopes gently towards the next channel 50 m away. Here, within a few minutes, we flush the first bird of the day. It sidles around us, displaying at a distance. Stead described a bird in a similar situation, displaying 'with the wing near the intruder trailing on the ground, the other lifted in the air; the tail spread fanwise, and depressed so that the tip is almost on the ground; and the bird all the time makes a continuous purring noise'.[37] But it appears the resources of cunning in wrybills are of shorter duration than those of some other shorebirds. Once we back away a few metres, the bird quickly returns to the nest and sits. As we approach once more, the bird again flushes, revealing the nest location. A rock tied with pink ribbon is immediately placed a metre or so away. Such is the cryptic nature of both nest and eggs that this is an essential measure. The nest is barely a scrape among stones, lined with smaller stones, and the two eggs are stone-grey with minute black specks. Even standing close by, it is astonishing how quickly one can lose sight of it, and the wisdom of marking it is revealed. Inadvertently trampling these eggs would be ridiculously easy.

Several metres from the nest, ecologist John Dowding places a noose mat – a firm lattice about a metre long, with a grid of nylon loops. He walks slowly back and forth in an arc around the end of the mat, as the adult bird approaches and displays. Eventually the bird walks across the mat and is caught. It looks simple, but Dowding cautions that it has taken him 20 years to perfect this technique. The bird is banded with a metal band around its left tibia, followed by a colour combination on the tarsi, or lower legs. Placing the metal band around the upper leg is a comparatively recent measure. With most bird-banding the lower leg is used, however, such is the nature of this environment – with wrybill spending much time wading in water laden with glacial silt, and exposed to wind-blown dust abrasion – that the metal bands were being sanded smooth of any information within just a few years. The colour combination enables individual birds to be subsequently recognised in the field. Once it is processed the bird is carefully released, although not before the beribboned rock is removed from the nest area.

Finding some nests is easier, as colleagues have spent the last few days locating and recording them with GPS. Others are more problematic, especially where the eggs have hatched and the chicks are now mobile. Almost all the nests are on high shingle banks devoid of any growth or drift debris, with close access to a stream edge. Of five nest pairs in part of Hay's study area, four had access to a stream edge where they could forage, but a later arriving pair were forced to nest further back from the channel. This pair attempted trespass to gain stream access but were apparently not successful enough; of the five, only this pair failed to raise young. While this could have been a result of their lateness in breeding, it was also 'evidence that access to stream margins is an important aspect of territory quality'.[38]

Ecologist John Dowding places a noose mat before a displaying wrybill. Within minutes the bird is caught, banded and released back to its parental duties.
KEITH WOODLEY

Early twist: curvature of the bill is already evident at hatching.
KEITH WOODLEY

Banded dotterel tend to nest on lightly vegetated areas away from the channels, but clearly for them stream access is also important. At one site a tongue of lightly vegetated dotterel habitat reached to within a few metres of a stream margin that was frequented by a territorial pair of wrybills. A wrybill was observed moving along the water edge while, on top of a bank 1 m above the stream level, five banded dotterel stood and watched. Once the wrybill was 50 m downstream the dotterels ran to the water edge and foraged in the riffle until the wrybill turned and started heading back. The dotterels quickly returned up the bank and remained there until the wrybill had passed. This happened three times during an hour of observation, during which there were no 'agonistic encounters'.[39]

There is movement on the edge of a riffle ahead of me – what appears to be a small stone rolling upstream. But then it stops – and disappears. A short distance away an adult wrybill stands on a shallow ridge, calling softly. Its chick has responded to the alarm by freezing; adopting the perfect posture and appearance of one of the small stones among which it crouches. A few metres downstream a second chick also freezes. Like most shorebird chicks, newly hatched wrybill can hit the ground running; fully developed legs and feet make them immediately mobile. Within a day or two they can swim well. Stead believes a wrybill chick hatched at a nest on an island in the Rakaia, and later found with adults on a shingle bank further downstream following a major flood, had swum there when the island was covered by the flood, 'having been carried half a mile by the swift current'.[40] But while mobility is important to a young bird needing to forage for itself as well as deal with suddenly rising river levels, the ability to cope with aerial intruders is no less important. The fluffy bundle crouched at the water edge in front of me is doing just that. Nevertheless, despite such cryptic skills, by the end of the day we have caught both chicks and their mother, along with a further five chicks and nine adults.

Most shorebird chicks are cryptically coloured in the form of streaks, spots and speckles, designed to blend in with their various surroundings, often including vegetation. Young wrybill are quite different, although the outcome is the same. The eye, bill, legs and feet of the young bird in my hand are all dark, but the rest of it is a uniform light grey without other markings. Already, at just the length of my thumbnail, the bill shows that particular sideways twist. The two chicks are quickly banded and released, following a well considered procedure. Release occurs at the riffle edge in full view of the female being held several metres back, so she can immediately see and follow the chicks. Otherwise there is danger of the family being dispersed, with chicks heading upstream and the adult heading downstream, especially if that is where the chicks were first caught and where they were last seen by the adult. On the other hand, a calling chick appears to be detectable by an adult at a considerable distance. But as there is a

Wrybill banding mission: crossing the Upper Rangitata River. KEITH WOODLEY

small black-backed gull colony just downstream, as well as patrolling harriers, all steps are taken to maintain a cohesive family unit. Once the adult is released we all back off quickly. Shortly afterwards the adult is seen brooding both chicks.

By mid afternoon the sun is scorching the riverbed. A few tiny fluffs of cumulus hang above the ridge across the river, but everywhere else the sky is clear. A faint whisper of a breeze begins, and ends almost immediately. This is very different from the testing conditions that other people working in this environment routinely encounter – gale-force winds hurling down the valley; and eddying winds whipping up spinning clouds of rock flour and silt, reducing visibility to zero. Ray Pierce recalls a time when he was camped out on the Upper Rakaia and spent the night wrapped up in his gale-demolished tent, anchored by small round boulders rolled against him by the wind.[41] Today the only sounds are the rustle of water over the riffle and the clamour of other riverbed residents – the tedious honk of a pair of Canada geese, and the shrill female shriek and the male grunt of paradise shelducks.

In the middle of the riverbed we traverse an enormous area, perhaps several hectares, completely bare of anything except shingle. Dowding says it is rare to find such places now, as most other rivers have been degraded in some way. Even on the generally less modified Upper Rangitata, exotic species have established. Sure enough, we pass several clumps of dead broom that have been sprayed. But birds are also absent from some of these large stretches of seemingly pristine wrybill habitat. This is the case on other good 'wrybill rivers', too. Clearly, then, it is not always limited habitat that constrains the wrybill population. The most likely explanation for there being fewer birds here than the area can support – and something we will return to repeatedly when looking at New Zealand's shorebirds – is predators.

Adult black-fronted tern and chick: Bealey River. IAN SOUTHEY

CHAPTER FIVE
SHRINKING FORTUNES: BLACK-FRONTED TERNS

Upstream, the river looped around a huge shingle bar before a backdrop of the Eyre Mountains, the tops still snowbound in early November. Against a green wall of willow were three white flecks of movement, as if snowflakes had peeled off the peaks and drifted towards the river. They hovered, dived and climbed, their trajectories forming a corkscrew pattern. Steadily they came nearer, and I could see each had a large dark spot; from even closer, they showed more grey than white. As they passed, the black spot revealed itself as a black cap, leading to a short yellow-orange bill. These black-fronted terns, working down the channel of the Upper Oreti in northern Southland, were hawking insects above the river; although they swooped low towards the water, they never actually broke the surface. A few minutes later they were gone, swept out of view around the next bend in the river. I had been watching a particularly elegant component of this country's endemic birdlife, but one that is facing a precarious future.

The first scientific record of black-fronted terns came from Johann Forster, in Queen Charlotte Sound in 1773. Percy Earl collected it at Waikouaiti in North Otago in 1840, from which G.R. Gray named it *Chlidonias albostriatus*.[1] The bulk of the tern family are considered to be 'sea terns', grouped together in the genus *Sterna*. The smaller genus *Chlidonias* contains three species of 'marsh terns', which is where, based on its dark plumage and inland nesting habits, *albostriatus* was assigned. Some taxonomists, however, were not comfortable with this; and in 1980, based partly on its non-marsh nesting habitat, a case was made for black-fronted terns to be reclassified as *Sterna*. Subsequently,

A tern apart: while they all share a black cap, the predominantly grey black-fronted tern (left) differs markedly from our other tern species, which are primarily grey and white. It is named for the black cap extending to the base of the bill, distinguishing it further from the white-fronted tern. IAN SOUTHEY

in a not uncommon development in modern biological science, DNA analysis published in 2005 proved the original status was correct: 'Our results confirm that this taxon belongs in *Chlidonias* and that its plumage reflects its systematic affinities more strongly than does the absence of marsh nesting.'[2] And so *Chlidonias* it became once more. For Maori, it is tarapiroe.

The original range of black-fronted terns within New Zealand is not entirely clear, although they did occur in parts of the North Island. Buller received an account from his brother-in-law Gilbert Mair who, in December 1879, watched 'hundreds flying around clumps of black birch trees' just after sunset, near the southeastern slopes of Ruapehu. The curious Mair climbed one of the trees and watched them 'darting hither and thither, very much in the zigzag manner in which bats pursue their prey'. He found they were 'chasing small moths, beetles, etc., and now and then when a large green beetle came booming along in its flight from the plain seeking a resting-place in the trees, a score of these pretty little birds would dart after it, uttering soft plaintive cries.'[3] Stead recorded them breeding near Waiouru.[4] But it would appear their stronghold lay in the South Island, primarily east of the divide. Potts described them as being 'exceedingly abundant' in Canterbury: 'numerous flocks made up of vast numbers, scattered themselves over the wide plains, with restless, untiring activity searching for grubs, caterpillars, locusts, lizards etc.'[5] There were many nesting colonies scattered over the riverbeds and adjacent alluvial plains, but while it still 'occurs in flocks of considerable size', wrote Stead in 1932, 'all those nesting sites are gone owing, I think, to the presence of sheep'.[6] Sheep and many other things too, it turns out, for having declined markedly since human settlement, these birds are now classified as Nationally Endangered.

All indications are that, unlike wrybill, this species is not strictly a braided river specialist. Some black-fronted terns once nested in habitat not associated with the riverbeds, and their current range is really a case of occupying 'remnant habitat'. Yet today that breeding range is confined almost exclusively to the braided riverbeds of the eastern South Island, from Marlborough to Southland, and may be continuing to contract. It is suggested that the Upper Waitaki Basin holds up to 50 percent of remaining suitable braided river habitat in New Zealand;[7] and it is also where around 30 percent of the black-fronted tern population breed.[8]

Considering the status of this endangered endemic, it is surprising that they are so little studied. While there are mentions in early writings by the likes of Potts, Buller and Stead, and in more recent papers on other braided riverbed species, there are very few accounts specifically related to them. A master's thesis by Chris Lalas, focusing on food and feeding behaviour, appeared in 1977, and was followed by a long hiatus. The next major contribution was not until 2002 when Rachel Keedwell, in her PhD thesis, addressed some of the substantial gaps. During a logistically challenging four-year study on the Ohau River, Keedwell investigated breeding biology and survival.

These terns are not the easiest of birds to study. There is the dispersed nature of their breeding and foraging ranges, for one thing; and their physiology for

Adept and graceful: black-fronted terns hawk for their insect prey. IAN SOUTHEY

Their short legs make black-fronted terns a difficult species to study, as there is room for only one colour band; and the band combination can be read only when a bird is standing in an exposed position, or sometimes when it is in flight. IAN SOUTHEY

another. One of the most potent tools for studying a wild bird population is marking individuals with unique colour band combinations. The normal method is to use at least three or four bands, thus expanding the number of potential combinations. However, the lower legs of black-fronted terns are so incredibly short that only one band will fit on each. Furthermore, they are usually seen either in flight or on a nest, where their legs are concealed. Bands are more easily seen on birds roosting in flocks at the start or end of the breeding season, or in the air when the observer is under attack. They are, wrote Guthrie-Smith, 'an emotional fowl, excited to pugnacity, easily roused, soon soothed'.[9] Another observer found them

> *fearless in defence of their nests, unmercifully and effectively harrying invading gulls, dogs, human beings and hawks with a concerted dive-bombing attack pressed home with angry, grating cries. Where human beings are concerned the attack is accompanied by a devastatingly accurate discharge of regurgitated matter or faeces – Inspecting a tern colony is a job that demands old clothes.*'[10]

Since such moments were often the only opportunity for reading band combinations, Keedwell took to wearing a motorcycle helmet visor as she looked up at an angry bird with its legs stretched out in frontal attack. Focusing on survival rates and causes of mortality, she found a species in sharp decline: 'Low survival rates and low productivity suggest that concerns about the species' survival are well founded.'[11]

Black-fronted terns begin nesting from the last week in September, and the season may extend to late January. Loose colonies of varying sizes are formed, usually in areas of bare or sparsely vegetated shingle, though clearly there is no firm rule about this. Stead found nests 'up near gorges and in back country where hard nor'west winds are prevalent during spring and summer, [and] birds almost always choose nooks deep down among big stones, behind tussocks, or little bushes, or on banks, where they are sheltered from wind'.[12] This was also the case with a small breeding colony found at over 1700 m in the Pisa Range in Central Otago. In an area of 'low hummocky tundra' all nests were located 'in the dead hearts of clumps of the low-growing alpine daisy *Celmisia viscosa*, where they would gain considerable protection from the winds and storms of this mostly inhospitable environment'.[13] Stead was admiring of what he considered to be a hardy little bird.

> *When a howling gale is driving clouds of sand and grit down the river-beds, so that it stings like a needle when it strikes bare skin – even with the shelter of a neighbouring stone, sitting on a nest on the ground must be an uncomfortable business. Yet the terns do not seem to mind, and I have never known them to desert even the most exposed nests on account of the weather.*[14]

Over three breeding seasons from 1998 to 2001, 1022 nests were monitored at 11 colonies on the Ohau River. Of these 50 percent successfully hatched, but only 28 percent of chicks survived to fledge. Predators were directly responsible for nearly 26 percent of nest failures, with desertion accounting for another 21 percent. Hatching success varied widely among colonies, depending on densities of predators.[15] So who were the offenders?

Fifty nests monitored by video camera revealed cats, ferrets and hedgehogs as the major predators on the Ohau. Cats were filmed killing adults and chicks at the nest, as well as being the likely cause of nest desertion. A cat visited a nest, sniffed at it but did not take the eggs, yet the adult birds abandoned. This was just one of a considerable suite of hazards that nesting terns need to cope with.

> Video footage also showed non-fatal nocturnal desertion after terns were disturbed at night by hares, rabbits, hedgehogs, mice, possums and deer. At two videoed nests, nocturnal desertion resulted in the death from exposure of one chick at each nest. A further 19 chicks were found dead at the nest with no sign of predation and 17 of these were found within the same week that the chicks at the videoed nests died.[16]

Perilous margin: unlike wrybill, nesting black-fronted terns are not confined exclusively to the riverbeds, as revealed by this nest immediately beside a road near Twizel. BRIAN CHUDLEIGH

A study of black-fronted tern breeding success on the Wairau River in Marlborough in 2010 used observations, video footage and DNA analysis and found a similar suite of predators, but added two further species: black-backed gull and harrier.[17]

Yet while the actual number of predators may vary in different sections of a riverbed, it takes only one animal to discover a 'tern supermarket' and wreak enormous damage.

Colonies may provide an easily accessible and concentrated food source for individual predators. The sudden declines in numbers of active nests at colonies coinciding with videoed predation events and the appearance of chick carcasses suggest that predators such as hedgehogs and Norway rats use tern colonies as a constant food supply.[18]

Stead watched a stoat on the Rakaia as it discovered a tern colony on the opposite side of a major channel. The colony was no longer in use but the accumulation of droppings and moulted feathers gave rise to 'a fishy smell that is apparent at some distance'. The stoat walked up the riverbank 'pausing at intervals and raising his head to get the wind', and then swam across the channel. Despite the big volume of water and a stiff current, it had no difficulty landing on the other side about 100 m from the colony. It then worked methodically across an area of about a quarter-acre before returning across the river. Had it been a nocturnal visit to an active colony, the stoat would 'easily have caught as many sleeping birds as he wanted'.[19] The Ohau study confirmed that other animals such as Norway rats and hedgehogs can have similar effects on a colony.

But what happens on one river may be quite different to conditions occurring elsewhere. Suites of predators certainly vary in different areas: Norway rats and hedgehogs were important predators on the Ohau, but on the Tasman a lot more damage may be attributed to stoats. Unfortunately for riverbed birds, cats appear to be a common factor throughout. Then there are other factors affecting productivity. As part of a hydroelectric power scheme, the Ohau is subject to controlled flow. So while predation was a major cause of nesting failure, only minimal losses occurred from flooding; whereas elsewhere, indications are that flooding may be a major cause of losses. Stead reported that to be the case on the Rakaia; and in 1982, 11 out of 21 colonies on the Ahuriri River were entirely or partially flooded.[20] Severe flooding in December 2010 destroyed all tern nests still active on the Wairau.[21]

So do these terns have any defensive strategy against predators? Well yes, though they would be more effective if we could turn the clock back 1200 years or so. Nesting strategies and behavioural responses correlate with a species that evolved in the presence of mainly diurnal and avian predators. Nesting in colonies

Black-fronted tern egg and newly hatched chick. JOHN DOWDING

is a useful strategy, allowing combined forces for nest defence. That they do actively try to defend their nests will be borne out by anyone straying near breeding terns, as birds mob intruders loudly, vigorously and at extremely close quarters. Yet at night, tern colonies are silent places where adults not only make no attempt to confront nocturnal intruders, they are also likely to temporarily or permanently desert eggs or chicks. Given that virtually all introduced mammalian predators operate more by night than by day, Stead's surmise that the stoat on the Rakaia could have caused the utmost carnage during its visit to the tern colony is all too correct. While it was once a good adaptation for a low predation environment, colonial nesting in today's transformed landscape is 'probably detrimental to black-fronted tern survival'.[22]

Incubation times and slow growth rates of chicks may be further adaptations to a world long gone: 'The incubation period of black-fronted terns may be longer than expected because the species evolved in the absence of high predation, which would lessen selective pressures towards shorter incubation periods.'[23] In addition, birds begin incubation once the first egg is laid, so later eggs hatch later, leaving first-hatched chicks with a survival advantage. This is thought to be an egg protection measure, where incubation may lessen the chances of avian predation of the newly laid egg, while also reducing the overall time the egg and chick remain vulnerable. There appears to be a trade-off, however, in that it dispenses with an insurance policy for loss of the first chick. While first-laid eggs tend to be larger, chicks from second-laid eggs are generally smaller and have slower growth rates. Keedwell found a greater proportion of second-hatched chicks died within the first five days than did first-hatched chicks. Today, however, with introduced, mainly nocturnal mammals known to prey on eggs, early incubation provides no additional protection at all. Moreover, not only is hatching asynchrony no longer an advantage, the difficulty in producing more than one chick now becomes a factor in lowering overall reproductive output in black-fronted terns. This may be further compounded by an overall slower growth rate for chicks than in most other tern species. The net result is low productivity for these birds.

This was further highlighted in a comparative study of survival rates of black-fronted terns and banded

They may not have been strictly confined to the riverbeds historically, but black-fronted terns have remarkable adaptations to that environment, such as the cryptic plumage of this chick hiding among stones. JOHN DOWDING

dotterel. Both species nest in similar habitat, often in close proximity to each other. The terns actually have shorter incubation periods and chick-rearing periods than banded dotterels, which decreases the time breeding birds are vulnerable to predation. The dotterels, however, have higher productivity: their offspring are fully independent at fledging; they produce more young at each nesting attempt; they have a longer breeding season; and they can successfully raise a second clutch in one season. Banded dotterel attempt to surreptitiously leave the nest to avoid detection, and have better nest camouflage; while terns stay on the nest longer and then rely on colony-based mobbing of intruders once they are disturbed. Yet 'predation rates at nests of banded dotterels and black-fronted terns in the Ohau River were almost identical and chick survival was very similar for both species'. So if the two species are subjected to the same level of predation pressure, in the same habitat, why do banded dotterels survive better? Higher rate of renesting for the dotterels is thought to be the key. 'The ability to re-nest, produce more young and a shorter generation time are critical factors in allowing banded dotterels to survive well in the same environment where black-fronted terns are doing

Black-fronted tern in flight: Bealey River. IAN SOUTHEY

poorly.'[24] As we have seen, colonial breeding may also be a contributing factor; the solitary nesting dotterels are not affected by what happens at neighbouring nests.

Keedwell concluded her thesis with an attempt to estimate the current population of black-fronted terns. Published estimates ranged from 2000 to 20,000 – clearly problematic for developing conservation strategies. Using all available data the best population estimate she could establish was somewhere between 6000 and 10,000 individuals. Undertaking an accurate census is rather difficult for such a widely dispersed population. Unlike wrybill, which concentrate mainly in two or three flocks on their northern wintering grounds, black-fronted terns are not quite so accommodating. In winter they scatter over coastlines north and south, as well as inland. During the breeding season they are no less difficult to find, as colony locations may change both within and between years. Furthermore their colonies are not easy to find from the air, so aerial surveys, such as occur for tightly packed colonies of white-fronted terns or black-billed gulls, are also not an option. To get around these problems Keedwell advocated nationwide surveys during the breeding season, where all rivers with black-fronted tern populations are surveyed within a two-month period.[25] With the breeding population now confined to the riverbeds, the ecological integrity of those river systems becomes an essential part of the equation if the species is to have a future. Which is something we shall return to in a later chapter.

Loud teenager: immature black-fronted terns lack the fully black cap of adults. IAN SOUTHEY

Hybridisation between black stilts and pied stilts is a complication for conservation managers. Recent evidence shows that black stilts show a strong preference for selecting black stilt mates, which helps reduce the prospects of interbreeding – although given the very low numbers of black stilts remaining, it is still a potential problem. BRIAN CHUDLEIGH

CHAPTER SIX
HIGH-STEPPING IN THE SHALLOWS: THE STILTS

It is as if the soundtrack is shaped like a graph: the vertical axis a skylark, directly above at full throttle, its bubbly trill pouring down a warm mantle; and on the horizontal plane to my right, the relentless, high-pitched 'yap-yap-yap' from what sounds like a mob of irrepressible puppies. The creatures responsible are visible through a screen of 2-metre-high fennel. Lanky elegance, high-stepping in the shallows, they are poaka or pied stilts. Teetering on improbably long pink legs, they forage with their long, finely pointed black bills for tiny prey from the pool surface. Their scientific name, *Himantopus himantopus*, is from the Greek for 'strap' and 'foot', derived, it is suggested, from Pliny via an 'awkward metaphor implying the legs are slender and pliant as if cut out of leather'.[1] They have also, over the years, acquired a host of common names: black-winged, white-headed, white-necked or black-throated stilt, stilt bird or stilt plover, long-legged plover, longshanks, or dog-bird.

The Recurvirostridae family – the stilts and avocets – are wading birds *par excellence,* with the longest legs, relative to the body, of all birds.[2] 'It would be gratifying certainly to know just how this bird disposes of its legs when nesting,' wrote Charles Abbott in 1899. Abbott was referring to flamingos; but Gilbert White, 120 years earlier, *was* referring to stilts when he pointed out that 'their legs are marvellously long for the bulk of their bodies. To be in proportion of weight for inches the legs of the flamingo should be more than ten feet in length.'[3] Many an observer of these birds has pondered such matters, particularly in regard to nesting. Michael Soper, for many years a rural GP in the South Island, was also an astute observer and photographer of New Zealand birds.

> Settling down on the nest to incubate is for the long-legged stilt a matter requiring much care and nicety of judgment. Approaching the nest the bird steps up on to the nest mound and vigorously shakes the water from each foot in turn. Then by a series of little shuffling steps it centres its feet accurately on each side of the eggs. The bill is lightly touched on the far side of the nest for balance, and the bird gradually lowers itself down. The action is very graceful – until suddenly the knuckle joints give way and the bird performs the rest of the manoeuvre with a rather undignified bump.[4]

Such scenes may be witnessed in many parts of the country any time from early July to December, for these birds are relatively common and widespread. But this only became the case comparatively recently: until the mid nineteenth century, pied stilts were rather rare in New Zealand.

Indeed, at the time of first European contact, pied stilts appear to have been quite unknown here. The naturalists accompanying Cook did not report seeing any; nor did those sailing with D'Urville. Early observers and collectors such as William Yate, Ernst Dieffenbach and Percy Earl did not record them. As late as 1865 Buller was of the view the country was inhabited by only one stilt, the range of which 'does not extend north of the Waikato'. In 1868, however, he did add a species known then as *Himantopus leucocephalus*, based on several records, the earliest being a specimen shot in 1854 in the Waikato.[5] 'Although Buller was not always reliable,' wrote Charles Fleming,

> it would be inconceivable today for him to have grown up in the North Island without encountering Pied Stilts until he was thirty years old, so they were certainly much less abundant than they later became, and they may well have colonised New Zealand for the first time in the early nineteenth century.[6]

But they did not stay rare for long. While seldom recorded north of the Waikato River, from the 1870s they spread east, west and south through the rest of the North Island. Only in the early twentieth century did they become more common in the north, and by the 1940s large post-breeding flocks were regular sights on the northern harbours. The species was already widespread in the South Island by the 1870s, and subsequently expanded its range into Nelson and Marlborough and either side of the Southern Alps.[7]

In comparison, and in marked contrast to their current status as one of the most endangered shorebirds in the world, black stilts were, for early ornithologists, commonplace. In fact it was probably, as Buller suggested, the only stilt in New Zealand. During the mid nineteenth century they were relatively common around

In flight the long trailing legs of a pied stilt give it a profile unlike any other New Zealand-breeding shorebird. IAN SOUTHEY

All legs I: pied stilts at Miranda. IAN SOUTHEY

All legs II: getting those long legs settled over a nest seems an awkward enterprise for a pied stilt. BRIAN CHUDLEIGH

the Rotorua lakes and Hawkes Bay, and were 'generally found in all river courses of the Wellington district and further south'.[8] Like pied stilts, they were rare north of the Waikato, though small numbers were recorded as far north as Parengarenga until the late nineteenth century. There then followed a dramatic decline, with no breeding recorded in the North Island after 1900; although given the scarcity of observers throughout the region, some breeding may have continued unnoticed into the twentieth century. Yet, as Ray Pierce noted, it is no doubt significant that none of a trio of such acutely aware observers as Buller, Hutton and Guthrie-Smith reported black stilts from anywhere in the eastern or southern North Island.[9]

In the South Island, however, it was quite a different picture, for at the turn of the century black stilts were still both widespread and relatively common. But through meticulous research of early records and diaries, Pierce has charted in some detail their subsequent decline – even as their pied cousins inexorably increased in both range and numbers. During the late nineteenth and early twentieth centuries, large numbers of black stilts could be found on the riverbeds of Canterbury and Otago, but their range then contracted in a distinct pattern – from north to south and from lowland to inland basins. Stead noted reduced numbers between 1900 and 1910, and in 1924 Guthrie-Smith reported pied stilts but no black stilts from the rivers of North Canterbury. On the plains of South Canterbury they persisted longer, and between 1920 and 1940 were nesting in the lower reaches of most rivers between the Rangitata and the Waitaki. The diary of one resident indicates that in 1928 'one pair of black stilts may have occurred for every two km of lowland riverbed in South Canterbury. [But] by the 1930s or early 1940s, all observers recorded a decline in numbers – although some nesting persisted until the 1950s.' The last record of lowland nesting in New Zealand by a black stilt pair was on the Orari River, South Canterbury, in 1957.[10]

In inland Otago from 1930 to about 1964 they nested at Naseby and Cromwell and on the Shotover, Nevis, Arrow, Timaru, Dingleburn and Hunter rivers, but there has been no nesting record since. Likewise they disappeared from elsewhere in the South Island, albeit places where they may never have been in big numbers. For instance there are records from Westland and also Fiordland, with pairs of both black and pied stilts reported from Amelia Arm of Charles Sound.

Internationally important proportion of the population: three black stilts foraging on the Tasman River delta. IAN SOUTHEY

Three mustelids: one of the main factors in the precipitous decline of black stilt. L to R: weasel, stoat and ferret. JOHN DOWDING

'It has always been a rare bird in Westland at least,' wrote South Westland explorer Charles Douglas. 'A pair trotting about now and again in certain localities, represent the black snipe [black stilt] both now and thirty years ago.'[11] In the late nineteenth century both species were 'widely but sparingly distributed' in Marlborough, and black stilt specimens were collected on the Wairau River and at Collingwood. But since 1900 there has been no nesting record anywhere in Westland, Nelson or Marlborough.[12]

Which leaves us with the central South Island. During the 1930s and 1940s black stilts were common in the Upper Waitaki Basin, but a marked decline in the inland population occurred during the 1950s, about 20 years after similar declines in coastal areas. In 1947–49 an area of wetland near the Tekapo River had 40–50 birds, with a further 20 pairs on the Tekapo Flats. Both areas now lie beneath Lake Benmore, but the birds had disappeared by the early 1950s – before the lake was formed. During the 1960s the black stilt's breeding range was largely confined to the Upper Waitaki Basin, with a population of just 50–60 birds. Looking at the extent of suitable habitat in its former range, Pierce estimated the region's population in the 1940s may have been 500–1000 birds, but within 20 years numbers had crashed to less than 100. The number of valleys used for nesting dropped

Smudgie: a hybrid stilt at Miranda.
IAN SOUTHEY

from at least 24 to 12. The rate of decline slowed after 1960, but contraction of range continued, with nesting birds disappearing from the Waitaki and Hakataramea valleys. By 1982, while the pied stilt population stood at about 30,000 birds, there were just 32 black stilts left.[13] What had happened?

An explanation for this divergence in the fortunes of the two stilts lies in their history and ecology. We have seen how pied stilts escaped the attention of the first naturalists in New Zealand. Indeed, the belief that only one species occurred here is reflected in John Gould's name for black stilts – *Himantopus novaezelandiae*, described in 1841 from two specimens shot in Wellington Harbour. But as the century progressed, considerable confusion accumulated. Part of the problem was the different plumage phases of immature black stilts. Only when a bird is over 16 months old does it attain its full black plumage, before which it goes through several phases where it is overall more white than black. Adding further difficulty for the early naturalist, there is considerable variation among individuals. The net result was much muddle in the literature, with black stilts variously seen as a 'seasonally dimorphic species', a 'mutant form of white-headed (pied) stilt', a 'subspecies' and a 'full species'.[14] "They are,' complained Buller, 'probably the most puzzling group of birds we have in New Zealand.'[15] Once the presence of pied stilts had been established, the situation was compounded by the possibility of hybridisation between the two. Since 1841, 10 species names have been applied to the two New Zealand stilts in an attempt to account for these different plumage forms.

Confusion continued well into the twentieth century. For Oliver, in 1930, black birds were 'merely a mutant of the white-headed species'.[16] Stead, on the other hand, suggested variations in plumage pattern of pied stilts in New Zealand resulted from a long history of interbreeding with black stilts.[17] This proved to be a rather prescient observation. In 1949 bones of a stilt were excavated at Pyramid Valley in North Canterbury. Initially described as being from a pied stilt, they were actually from a black stilt, according to a reassessment published in 1995. The fossils were dated to between 4280 and 2620 years before the present.

> *The differences in length and proportions of the limb bones between the fossil and recent black stilts support the contention that the black stilt was the only stilt in New Zealand 3000–4000 years ago. The intermediate position of recent black stilts, between the fossil and pieds, may indicate that the black stilt has converged in proportions to the pied because of long-term introgression between the populations.*[18]

The accepted view today is that our stilts are the outcome of a double invasion from Australia. Black stilts *evolved in New Zealand from pied stilt ancestors, but they were not isolated from the ancestral species sufficiently long to evolve differences great enough to prevent the two forms from interbreeding when the ancestral form colonized New Zealand for a second time.*[19]

Nevertheless they did evolve a number of morphological and behavioural differences from their transtasman cousins, such as darker plumage. For Fleming this was an example of a common trait among New Zealand birds, the 'tendency for melanism [darker colour] that became "fixed", presumably because the natural selection that normally maintains countershading or disruptive patterns is relaxed in a land with few predators'. He pointed out such melanism occurs, in varying patterns, among a number of species, such as shags, weka, oystercatchers, fantails, tits and robins.[20] For palaeontologist Richard Holdaway, the larger body size, longer wings and colour of black stilts suggested:

divergence from a pied ancestor in response to the colder, windier environments of successive Pleistocene glaciations. Increased body size, dark plumage, shorter legs, and better flying ability would have enhanced survival through better heat retention, quicker warming, and greater power of movement in a windier environment, respectively. Shorter legs made for 'lower geared' gait suited to wading in swift streams.[21]

Another adaptation is the greater flexibility of black stilts in habitat use. Though primarily thought to be birds of braided shingle riverbeds, they do occur in a wide variety of wetland areas such as swamps, tarns and ponds. As we have seen, at times of low food availability on the rivers, during winter or early in the day when low water temperatures mean aquatic larvae may be inactive and sheltering beneath stones, the black stilt has advantages over the pied stilt. Its more robust bill allows it to probe and 'rake' in search of prey, unlike the more slender-billed pied stilt.[22] This wider feeding repertoire enables it to achieve its energy requirements 'under extremes of weather and climate in a relatively small area. It is therefore able to remain relatively sedentary within smaller geographical areas', while pied stilts need to leave the riverbeds for other areas such as ponds or springs.[23]

Pied stilts occur through most of the country, although they are rare on Stewart Island and the Chathams, and largely absent from Fiordland. Their extension of range in New Zealand coincided with an expansion of nesting habitat through the clearing of forests and the creation of seasonal wetlands – and the decline of black stilts. The wide variety of nesting habitat includes flooded paddocks and pasture, ephemeral lakes, swamps, pond edges, estuaries, riverbeds, bare sandy or muddy ground, small islands, sandbars, shingle, grassy banks, sedge or tussock hummocks, floating vegetation, lignum, cane grass, rushes, sarcocornia and other bushes in water.[24]

The breeding season is a rather protracted affair, with birds in lowland areas commencing as early as June, while birds in the central high country may not finish until February. Post-breeding movement patterns are complex, depending on where the nesting area is. Birds breeding in northern New Zealand are primarily sedentary, apart from some local movements of up to 20 km. Birds in central regions exhibit a combination – some sedentary, some moving locally and others migrating long distances. Birds from riverbeds or inland wetlands mostly move to coastal sites, while some birds in coastal Canterbury, Otago and Southland stay at

All-dark plumage and shorter legs are thought to be adaptations to colder conditions, which may explain why some black stilts remain in the Mackenzie Basin during winter, while all pied stilts move elsewhere. IAN SOUTHEY

Kaki on ice: black stilt foraging during winter in the Mackenzie Basin. DAVE MURRAY coastal lagoons and estuaries all year round. However, most birds from mid Canterbury, the Mackenzie Basin, Central Otago and Southland migrate to northern harbours from Kawhia to Parengarenga.[25] Clearly the north is appealing, for more than half of all birds counted nationally are in the Auckland and South Auckland regions, with the Firth of Thames being now the most important site nationally.[26]

While black stilts have some advantages over pied stilts, in other areas of comparison they fall short, and nowhere is this more evident than in their responses to predators. One study showed black stilts clearly cope with natural threats such as flooding and cold weather; except in severe conditions their nests were not susceptible to flooding because birds tended to nest in stable situations with high food availability. Moreover, there were no known nest desertions after light snowfalls of up to 10 cm. However 64 percent of nest failures were the result of predation by mammals or birds, compared with 49 percent of pied stilt nests. A comparison of trapped and untrapped areas produced stark results: 41 percent of unprotected black stilt nests were destroyed, compared with only 19 percent of pied stilt nests. The offenders were ferrets, cats, Norway rats and harriers, all of which ate eggs.[27]

Pierce identified a number of factors that make black stilts more vulnerable. For a start their colouration may be a disadvantage: adults lack the disruptive pattern of other riverbed birds, including pied stilts, which helps camouflage them. Black stilts begin nesting as early as August, a time when rabbit numbers may be low and predators hungrier. The banks of small streams or side braids of rivers that are often favoured as nesting sites are also areas where predators tend to be more active. Sites in swamps or on river islands – where there are likely to be fewer predators – are also used, although the downside is the risk of flooding. Whereas pied stilts tend to nest in loose groups or colonies, black stilts may nest more than 100 m from each other, depriving them of the group vigilance and joint response to predators that give pied stilts an advantage. Black stilt chicks at night foraged up to 150 m from their parents, while pied chicks were seldom more than 40–50 m away. They also remain vulnerable longer, taking 39–55 days to fledge, compared with 30–37 days for pied stilts. If a nest is lost, black stilts show strong site fidelity and will renest at the same site, leaving them vulnerable to repeat predation. Broods may be present as late as February, when predator young are dispersing and predator density is

Awkward-looking procedure for a highly successful species: the copulation of pied stilts.
IAN SOUTHEY

greatest.[28] Anti-predator responses in the two species are also revealing. Black stilts frequently used dive-bombing, which can be very effective against avian predators, but quite ineffectual against a terrestrial mammal. Pied stilts used this method less often, although Stead recorded one occasion when they did employ it.

> I once saw a Harrier flying against a heavy wind over a colony of Stilts, numbers of which were attacking it. They flew at it from a height, and, having passed screaming close over it, spread their wings to the wind and soared up, to turn back, and over, and swoop again. The effect was very curious, for it seemed as though the Hawk was proceeding with a Catherine-wheel of Stilts above its tail.[29]

Breeding success for pied stilts in this study was similar to that of many other shorebirds, including other members of the stilt/avocet family. 'Low annual production of black stilts,' concluded Pierce, 'plus existence of much unoccupied habitat suggests predation has contributed considerably to the population decline.' Together with low recruitment, this 'facilitates mixed pair bonds and hybridisation'.[30] The breeding biology of pied stilts, on the other hand, indicates a different evolutionary path in which they have been exposed to many ground predators, meaning their defensive capability in New Zealand is higher.

As black stilt numbers plummeted, interbreeding with pied stilts emerged as a serious conservation issue. Yet interbreeding has been occurring since at least the late nineteenth century and perhaps even longer. Measurements of the Pyramid Valley fossils 'support the contention pied stilt has hybridized extensively with black stilts in New Zealand, and that both pied and black have now sufficient admixtures of the other's genes that both differ noticeably from their respective parent populations'.[31] Molecular evidence showed the genetic distance between black stilts and Australian pied stilts was similar to that between hybridising species, and the differences between black stilts and New Zealand pied stilts were within the range commonly reported between bird species. How serious an issue is it? For conservation managers there is cause for optimism: 'After over 100 years of hybridisation, the finding of any difference suggests that black stilts have maintained their genetic identity and that gene flow has largely been one-way from black to pied stilts.'[32] For instance, the lower legs of pied stilts in New Zealand appear to have become shorter than Australian birds, which may, it is suggested, 'indicate a transitional stage in speciation process'.[33]

There is now clear evidence that when given the option a black stilt will almost always choose a black stilt partner: 'Black stilts predictably mate according to the sex and plumage node of stilts in the winter area.'[34] In the absence of another black stilt, a black will also choose a dark hybrid over a pied, while hybrids prefer hybrid or black stilt mates. In the 1979–80 season, 70 percent of black stilts mated with other black stilts; in the 1986–87 season 60 percent did; and 87 percent in the 1987–88 season. Of black stilts in mixed pair bonds, most chose a hybrid rather than a pied stilt mate. 'This behaviour confirms they are separate species.'[35]

This evidence of selective mating led Pierce to conclude that, while interbreeding has been a contributing factor to the decline of black stilts, it is by no means the primary cause. If reproductive isolation had broken down in the nineteenth century, the then rare pied stilts would most likely have been absorbed into the black population. Furthermore, the much smaller contemporary black stilt population has been maintained without being absorbed into the, by now, larger pied stilt population. Separate wintering grounds and different habits of the two species have helped

A pied stilt nest – more elaborate than many – on the bare stones of a riverbed.
JOHN DOWDING

Pied stilt chick. JOHN DOWDING

A juvenile pied stilt forages near a flock of roosting godwits. KEITH WOODLEY

maintain this. For instance, black stilts form pair bonds before pied stilts return inland; and the rarity of pied stilts in the Upper Waitaki Basin study area in winter and early spring, when unpaired resident black stilts are usually forming pair bonds, meant there was less likelihood of mixed pairs forming. Pierce suggests that 'if all black stilts wintered alongside pied stilts in scattered coastal localities, mixed pairings would have been more likely than they are'. Black stilts declined because they 'could not adapt to man-induced changes in the environment, particularly increased predation pressure and habitat alteration'.[36] But while habitat degradation and loss is important, the number one factor outweighing all others is predation.

Yet given the precarious status of black stilts today, the issue of hybridisation remains a potent one. 'The chances of a black stilt finding a suitable black stilt mate,' writes Pierce, 'become less as the population decreases, and the potential for reproductive isolation between the two species also decreases.' If a small number of black stilts are scattered over the one million hectares of the Mackenzie Basin, the chances of finding a black mate takes on the appearance of a lottery, especially as most black stilts are not known to range far from their natal area. Pierce concludes: 'because black stilts select other black stilts for breeding if they can, and because of their morphological and ecological differences from pied stilts . . . [they should] retain their full specific status'.[37]

Living up to its name: a variable oystercatcher with a Pacific oyster.
ATHENA DRUMMOND

CHAPTER SEVEN
ON MUSSEL-PICKERS AND SEA-PIES: THE OYSTERCATCHERS

Beneath a leaden sky on a morning in late May, the mudflats are leached of colour. The incoming tidal edge a few hundred metres away occasionally whispers, otherwise the world is silent. Oystercatchers are strewn across the flats, many already sub-roosting – heads turned, bills tucked away – while others forage languidly. Even in the flat light they remain prominent. As the flood edges softly across the flats, it begins shepherding birds – individuals, twos and threes – all quietly drawn together. Roosting birds unsheath their bills and begin walking. Numbers accumulate, all stepping shorewards. Often at this time of the tide birds will lift off and fly to roost, but today they remain earthbound. The congregation grows; tens become hundreds. The shoreline is all shell – metre-high piles ending here as a spit, encased on three sides by soft mud. The boundary between the two is pencil thin. Their footfalls smothered by soft mud, the advancing oystercatchers make no sound. Reaching the shell, they amble up its flanks, more and more crossing over from the mud. Now audible is the only sound in the universe – the clatter of shell beneath a thousand oystercatcher feet.

From late January these South Island pied oystercatchers (SIPO) begin to dominate the landscape of the Firth of Thames and other northern estuaries; and even more so from early April once the thousands of tundra breeders – godwits and knots – have departed. For the oystercatchers, too, long-distance movement is an integral feature of their annual cycle, if not on quite the same spectacular scale. During autumn and early winter the Firth of Thames and Manukau, Kaipara and Kawhia harbours are where the biggest concentrations are found, but many smaller sites such as Whangarei, Tauranga, Ohiwa and Raglan also receive big flocks. The largest wintering South Island flocks

From January to July, large flocks of pied oystercatchers are a common sight on the northern harbours and estuaries, such as here at Miranda on the Firth of Thames. The other birds are black-billed gulls. BRUCE SHANKS

are found at Farewell Spit, Waimea Estuary, Motueka and the Avon–Heathcote Estuary. Banding records show that females generally migrate earlier than males, and that members of a pair may winter at separate sites. Samples of birds caught on the northern harbours show increasing proportions of juveniles over time, suggesting their migration is slower and that some may be stopping off on the way north.

Among the shorebird clans, oystercatchers tend to stand out. Unlike many of their cousins of the mudflats and other coastal margins, where plumages of greys and browns predominate, they are either black and white or entirely black. The reddish or pink legs also draw attention – although here the distinction is less marked, when one considers the stilt family as well as an assortment of others, such as ruddy turnstone and the two redshank species. But when it comes to bills, oystercatchers truly distinguish themselves. There are of course shorebirds in possession of bills either fully of partly coloured; the red scimitar-like appendage of the ibisbill of Central Asia, for instance; or the bicoloured bills of black-fronted dotterel and New Zealand's own shore plover; or even the peculiar wattle and bill arrangement of the spur-winged plover, all of it bright yellow. Nothing, though, quite matches the long, thick stabs of bright red or orange of the oystercatchers.

Why the name 'oystercatcher' when, as is often pointed out, many birds may have never even seen an oyster let alone caught one? According to one account the name first appeared in 1731 when American naturalist Mark Catesby used it for a bird that was commonly seen on oyster banks along the coast of the Carolinas. Gradually the name was applied generically, eventually displacing 'sea-pie', the name commonly used

Once all birds have returned after breeding, roosting space on the shell bank may become a scarce resource for oystercatchers. KEITH WOODLEY

Variable oystercatchers in flight: note one bird has a short white wing bar. A more extensive wing bar in pied oystercatchers, along with white rump and back, are distinguishing features. ATHENA DRUMMOND

A pied oystercatcher in flight. IAN SOUTHEY

in Britain for the European species of oystercatcher.[1] There were, of course, other common names in use throughout Europe: the German *Austernfischer*, literally 'oyster fisher', for example, or the Spanish *ostrero*, or the Dutch *scholekster*. If we were to think of 'oyster' as a generic term for mollusc, then New Zealand oystercatchers would be aptly named, as they seek out cockles, tuatua, pipi and other shellfish. The scientific name of the genus, *Haematopus*, comes from the Greek words for 'blood' and 'foot';[2] not only are they red, oystercatcher feet are also 'much more fleshy than are generally seen in the Plover family'.[3]

Oystercatchers are absent from the polar regions and remote oceanic islands, except the Galapagos and the Chathams; otherwise, they occur from northern Russia to Cape Horn.[4] The northwest coast of North America and the southwest coast of Africa have one species of black oystercatcher each, while western South America and Australia have both a black and a pied species. As a general rule, the black forms are typically specialists of the rocky shore, while the pied forms tend to favour softer substrates such as tidal flats. A similar pattern applies to the three species found in southern South America, where the rocky shore habitat is occupied by the blackish oystercatcher; soft substrate niches by the pied American oystercatcher; and marshy and inland habitats by the Magellanic oystercatcher.[5] As is so often the case in the avian affairs of these islands, though, New Zealand's oystercatchers do not necessarily toe the line.

At Mercury Bay on 5 November 1769, Joseph Banks recorded the shooting of several birds that 'looked like sea pies' but were 'black with red bills and feet'.[6]

So began a long tradition of looking at New Zealand shorebirds through gunsights. So also began a good deal of confusion for the natural scientist. These were clearly oystercatchers, but over the next 200 years the nature and status of our oystercatcher species, not unlike Buller's 'puzzling' stilts, continued to intrigue and perplex ornithologists. The pattern elsewhere of either pied or black species did not seem to apply to these islands where, along with birds that always fitted those two descriptions, were others that could be anywhere in between. In addition there was yet another bird in the Chatham Islands which, though always black and white, not only seemed quite different to the pied version on the mainland, but shared many features with the variable form. Who would not be confused?

In 1773 Forster collected a specimen of what we now know to be variable oystercatcher in Dusky Sound, and this was formally described in 1844 as *Haematopus unicolor*. Oystercatchers were subsequently reported during the early years of European settlement, but just which form was not clearly identified. A pied specimen collected at Saltwater Creek near Timaru, and which had made its way to Hamburg, was described and named after Otto Finsch, a German naturalist and one-time imperial commissioner for the German colony in New Guinea. But this was subsequently dismissed by Buller as a variant partly albino.[7] By the late 1930s Robert Falla, later director of the Dominion Museum in Wellington, had recognised that the pied oystercatchers breeding on the riverbeds and tussock uplands of the South Island were different from the variable pied-form birds found on northern beaches. Moreover these southern birds formed large coastal flocks after breeding, before some migrated to harbours and estuaries in the north; whereas the birds breeding in northern coastal regions were clearly sedentary.

Yet as late as 1939 Falla still thought of the larger non-migratory birds as belonging to two species, calling the black form *H. reischeki* and the birds with varying degrees of white plumage *H. unicolor*.[8] Oliver, in 1955, further muddied the water by thinking the black form of *H. unicolor* was a separate species while the Australian pied oystercatcher, the Chatham Islands form, and the pied form of the variable, were all one species.[9] In the 1970 Ornithological Society of New Zealand (OSNZ) Checklist, both *reischeki* and *unicolor* were combined into one species, which seemed to make sense as interbreeding had been known to occur between these forms, whereas no interbreeding between the forms and the all-pied *finschi* had been recorded, and the latter clearly occupied different breeding habitat. Nevertheless, the idea of two subspecies persisted for a few years longer.[10] Finally, in 1974, Alan Baker published a paper demonstrating that both *reischeki* and *unicolor* belonged to a single breeding population with no subspecies. 'This confirms,' wrote Baker, 'the "informed guess" of the 1970 Checklist and allows the taxon *reischeki* of other publications to sink into oblivion.'[11]

As a general rule, though with exceptions, the two New Zealand mainland species occupy different habitats, especially during the breeding season. Most SIPO may be found throughout inland eastern South Island, anywhere from farmland to braided rivers to alpine bogs. After breeding they generally move to the coast, with large numbers migrating to northern New Zealand. The variable oystercatcher (VOC), on the other hand, is only found breeding on or near the coast – with one breeding record up to 30 km inland being exceptional. Many VOC specialise in foraging on rocky shores, a trait they share with other black species elsewhere. But while these rocky-shore birds do not breed inland, they may change their habitat during the year, moving to soft shores particularly during the nonbreeding season.

Researchers in the early 1970s hypothesised that VOC and SIPO are the outcome of a double invasion by the Australian pied species *H. longirostris*. In the intervening period between the two invasions, the original colonists evolved towards melanistic or darker forms. The presence of other species here, such as black stilt, black robin, and Snares Island tomtit – all of which have pied

Chatham Island oystercatchers are always fully pied, but in most other respects seem closer to variable oystercatchers, particularly with their shorter legs and stout bills. IAN SOUTHEY

Farmland in northern Southland in August is a long way removed from a crowded high-tide roost in the North Island, where, several weeks earlier, this solitary pied oystercatcher may have been part of a flock of thousands. KEITH WOODLEY

counterparts across the Tasman – is used to support this view.[12] Enough time had lapsed before the second wave arrived that pied birds were now sufficiently different to preclude interbreeding with the earlier (now dark) birds. However there were still similarities that allowed for competitive factors to arise, which, it is argued, forced the pied birds inland to breed.[13]

More recent molecular work found that Chatham Island oystercatchers are genetically distinct from the mainland birds. However there was surprisingly little genetic variation between VOC and SIPO, despite their morphological differences. 'It seems likely that the oystercatcher group currently includes taxa recognised as species with fewer genetic differences than in many other bird species.' The authors of the molecular study observe that, while their sample size was very small, they believe the two species radiated within New Zealand comparatively recently, and that they 'began to separate once the braided river beds of the Canterbury Plains started to form about 30,000 to 15,000 years ago'. Alternatively, the two may have parted even more recently, which is supported by the recent discovery of a population of hybridised birds in coastal Canterbury.[14]

Tidal platforms around the Chatham Islands are the places to look for our third oystercatcher. Despite being slightly smaller than the VOC, it has much in common with the mainland birds: it is similar in shape although its short stout legs perhaps make it look heavier than it is; its stout bill is similar in structure, although generally shorter; and it forages in broadly similar fashion, although almost exclusively on tidal platforms, mainly at low tide. This predominantly rocky habitat may explain why it has markedly hypertrophied (abnormally large) feet, a feature it shares with only one other oystercatcher – the similarly remote Galapagos form.[15] Apart from being endemic to the Chathams, it has one further distinction: it is the most highly endangered oystercatcher in the world – a dubious distinction that we shall return to.

As befits their name, oystercatchers specialise in capturing and eating shellfish; and they are equipped with a perfect tool for that purpose. The long straight bill is well adapted for opening shells and prising

Pied oystercatchers foraging on an ebbing tide. KEITH WOODLEY

reluctant molluscs off rocks. This blade-like instrument consists of a bony core that contains nerves and blood vessels covered with a protective outer layer of keratin. The outer layer, thickest towards the tip, contains numerous Herbst corpuscles.[16] Bills come in a range of shapes and sizes: a blunt and square-tipped bill may be useful for a bird chiselling barnacles off rock; whereas one specialising in foraging in soft sediments will find a more pointed and presumably more sensitive bill better value. It may also be a clue concerning the origins of these birds.

The highly sensory nature of the bill tip suggests that oystercatchers evolved from a tactile foraging ancestor. This, in turn, suggests that the use of rocky shores, and its link to black plumage, are derived rather than primitive features of oystercatchers, providing further support for a pied ancestor.[17]

The observer of foraging oystercatchers is left with one clear impression – these birds are workers! 'Admiration for the birds' industry and their skill in opening shellfish, found expression in the saying – *Haere. Mahi kai mau! Ka whati te tai, ka pao te torea* – Go and work to get yourself food! When the tide goes out, torea cracks open the cockles.'[18] Considerable strength and skill are required to breach the defences of molluscs, barnacles, chitons or limpets, and feeding techniques vary with the type of prey. It may take individual birds a long time to become proficient at tackling different prey items.[19] But along with a stout bill, there come strongly developed jaw and neck muscles. This is readily seen when watching a bird extracting a mollusc from the mudflats. Its short thick legs are braced as the bill makes contact with the prey, which is then levered out of the ground, the bird swivelling if necessary, the required effort revealed as rippling neck muscles catch the light.

To eat a shellfish such as a cockle, an oystercatcher first needs to find it. Sometimes the prey item itself may offer a visual clue: when water covers the substrate in which it lives, a cockle feeds by extending siphons from its gaping shell; but when the tide ebbs, these siphons are retracted inside the shell. Unfortunately for the cockle, the siphons advertise its presence to a passing bird. A study on the Avon–Heathcote Estuary found that birds foraging in shallow water were clearly able to detect prey using such clues. Birds foraging during one hour either side of low water – the optimum time for finding feeding cockles – were successful in locating one at approximately every second attempt. This represents, for the biologist, a 'much higher rate of success than would be expected if probing were random and no

Hard at it: despite the seeming proliferation of some of their prey, oystercatchers may need to work hard for their food. BRIAN CHUDLEIGH

Like those of all our beach-nesting shorebirds, VOC nests are vulnerable to human activities: wheel tracks on Matakana Island. BRIAN CHUDLEIGH

visual location was involved'.[20]

When the substrate is completely exposed and all mollusc siphons are retracted, a bird must resort to more tactile means of finding prey, using a series of short vertical probes with its bill slightly open beneath the surface.[21] Areas where the surface is littered with dense concentrations of old opened shells make prey detection more difficult, particularly for the inexperienced. Younger birds 'painstakingly investigated each shell', while older birds seem to quickly differentiate between occupied and empty shells, by tapping each one sharply two or three times: in an uninhabited shell the valves flex with this applied pressure; but they remain rigid and immovable if an animal is at home. Both variable and pied oystercatchers use these methods of prey detection. At other times, however, such as at night or when a breeze ruffles the water surface, such visual clues are not available.

Detecting and catching a mollusc is one thing; extracting its flesh is quite another – and here the value of the particular dimensions of an oystercatcher bill is revealed. If a shellfish is found with its valves gaping, the bill – often less than 1 mm wide at the tip – is inserted and the valves parted. Further pressure against the substrate immobilises the animal, before the bird and its bill rotate through 90 degrees so that the 9–12 mm height of the bill forces the valves apart. This snaps or seriously weakens the adductor muscles that hold the shell closed. But if the bivalve – by holding its shell firmly closed with no gape showing – does not cooperate, the persistent bird has two possible measures: hammering and thrusting. The shell is hammered, usually at its thinnest point, until an initial hole is made, which is then enlarged so the animal can be removed. Sometimes an oystercatcher receives assistance in its task from the marine boring worm *Polydora ciliata*, which, as its name suggests, bores into shells. Of a sample of 100 unopened shells weakened by borers, 92 were hammered by birds at the site of borer activity.[22] Bivalves on oceanic beaches tend to have noticeably thicker shells than those in estuarine environments, which makes hammering less useful. In this case, oystercatchers resort to persistently thrusting at the closed gape of the shells until they are opened.

On a rocky shoreline, the main problem for an oystercatcher is not *finding* favoured prey items such as barnacles and chitons – for they are clearly in view, albeit firmly attached to the rocks – but *removing* them. Here VOCs are the specialists, and only they consistently take large limpets, 'probably because this species alone possesses a robust bill and correspondingly massive musculature'. When first uncovered by the tide the exposed foot of the limpet may create a gap between its shell and the substrate. On such occasions the bird lowers its head and delivers a sharp horizontal blow to the side of the shell with its bill. Small limpets can be knocked over by this, but larger ones sometimes require several blows before they can be separated from the rock. The shell contents are removed by placing the

(From top) Newly hatched pied oystercatcher chick JOHN DOWDING; Variable oystercatchers: note the indistinct 'shoulder tab' of the pied-phase bird on the right JOHN DOWDING; Comparison of the two species: the variable oystercatcher is notably larger and has a heavier bill than the pied oystercatcher IAN SOUTHEY.

upturned limpet in a suitable crevice, then 'paring the flesh from the shell with scissor-like movements of the bill'.[23] Similar ability is required to deal with chitons, where the bill is pushed underneath, 'flat' side against the rock, and the animal cut from the rock by scissor-like movements of the bill. The flesh is then removed in one piece and swallowed whole. All New Zealand oystercatchers have been recorded taking chitons.

While there is considerable overlap in behaviour and even habitat use by our two mainland oystercatchers, there is also evidence that each may be superior to the other in particular environments. A study in the early 1970s compared rates of foraging success between the two species feeding on tuatua at Jackson Bay, Westland. The long slender bill of the SIPO appeared to give it a distinct advantage in the soft substrate, and it was able to gain an average daily quota of tuatua equivalent to about 52 percent of its body weight, while VOCs at the same time could gain only 32 percent. On the rocky coast at Kaikoura, on the other hand, the short robust bill of the VOC allowed it to consume limpets equivalent to 44 percent of its body weight, suggesting it was more efficient foraging in rocky areas than in soft substrate. This niche utilisation would be a distinct advantage for VOCs, particularly in districts with large flocks of SIPO, and may have been 'an important factor in the speciation of New Zealand oystercatchers'.[24]

The different plumage phases of VOCs are not equally distributed. While all forms occur throughout the country, all-black birds predominate in the south, and the incidence of intermediate and pied-form birds increases further north. Yet even in the Far North, the black form is still the most abundant. One hypothesis links darker plumage to colder climates. Black plumage in birds generally has three physiological effects: increased absorption of radiant energy; reduced oxygen absorption when exposed to solar radiation at low temperatures; and increased 'metabolic economy'.[25] Bills and legs get shorter from north to south. Longer bills and legs are in accord with Allen's rule that states 'extensions of the body tend to be larger in warmer parts of a species range and shorter in cooler parts'. It is suggested oystercatcher bills and legs could be subject to considerable heat exchange. For instance, shorter legs should be better in colder areas than longer ones. But despite such differences in relative size and distribution, the three forms of VOC seem to interbreed freely and randomly. 'Pairs of extreme black or pied birds tend to breed true, producing mainly black or pied offspring respectively.'[26]

Unlike most shorebirds, oystercatcher parents feed their chicks for several weeks – even, in some cases, until fledging. BRIAN CHUDLEIGH

A noisy feature of the northern harbours from late June: formations of pied oystercatchers migrating south. IAN SOUTHEY

They may be rocky shore specialists, but variable oystercatchers still like a good sandy beach, and that is where 78 percent of nests are found.[27] SIPO, on the other hand, are rather more catholic in their tastes. Some may nest on shingle riverbeds just a few kilometres from the coast; others will be found in pasture or cultivated farmland; while still others will be far inland, on top of a dry, well-drained frost hummock in the subalpine tundra zone, somewhere between 1200 and 1800 m.[28] Soper found nesting pairs on the riverbeds tended to be widely spaced, usually over 180 m between them, on more stable sections less disturbed by the river. Some nests are quite close to the river but strategically placed so that 'it takes a freak flood to catch them'.[29] Since the 1950s increasing numbers of SIPO have nested on farmland in the eastern South Island. The first birds begin leaving the Firth of Thames from mid June, but most arrivals in Canterbury occur from early July. Many birds linger near the coast before heading inland, with arrivals in the Upper Waitaki Basin from late July through August.[30] Further south, things are even later getting underway; it is not until November, as snows retreat from the Old Man, Dunstan and Pisa ranges of Central Otago, that oystercatchers arrive.[31]

Within the oystercatchers there is a high degree of both mate and site fidelity, and long-term monogamy appears to be the norm with all New Zealand species. Two pairs of Chatham Island oystercatchers are known to have remained together in the same area for 10 years, and similar patterns are known for both SIPO and VOC. Charles and Peg Fleming watched the same pair of VOCs at Waikanae Estuary for 18 years.[32] There is one major way, however, in which oystercatchers depart from behaviour evident among almost all other shorebirds. In most species of Charadriidae, chicks are precocial and, from within hours of hatching, will begin finding their own food; but within the oystercatchers there is an extended period of parental care. Both SIPO parents incubate, brood and – until they fledge at around six weeks – feed chicks. Chatham Island birds are similar, although fledging may take up to seven weeks. VOC chicks are totally dependent on their parents until around three weeks, after which they do some foraging for themselves – the amount increasing closer to fledging. VOC chicks fledge at six to seven weeks and are usually evicted about a month later. However some may stay with their parents over the next winter, still begging for food some months after fledging.[33]

Most VOC pairs are sedentary and will remain on or close to a territory all year round. Others move and congregate in winter flocks at certain favoured sites, such as Ruakaka, Waipu, and Mangawhai in Northland, and in the South Island at Golden Bay, Tasman Bay and South Westland, where flocks of up to nearly 200 birds have been recorded. Immatures in particular are known to set out to see the world; in one study the mean dispersal of 27 youngsters was 36 km, but one bird banded at Waipu was found 15 months later 570 km away, near Wellington.[34]

Flock of banded dotterels, including juveniles, in flight in March. IAN SOUTHEY

CHAPTER EIGHT
TRANSTASMAN ODDITY: BANDED DOTTEREL

When it comes to standing out in a crowd, none of our endemic shorebirds can match a banded dotterel male in full breeding plumage. Around the upper chest a dark band, beneath it a white strip followed by a broad rufous crescent and white belly. The effect is stunning: even from a distance it dazzles the eye. He exhibits the classic plover structure – rounded body, large head, large eye and short bill, as well as behaviour common to his tribe. A few metres away another bird, approximately the same size as the dotterel, is foraging along the channel edge. It is more elongated in appearance, with a long narrow bill with which it is probing just below the mud surface. In contrast with the uniform brown upperparts of the dotterel, this bird has a strikingly scalloped appearance, dark streaked centres to its feathers, fringed with chestnut and broad pale edges. The reddish-brown of its crown confirms it to be a sharp-tailed sandpiper, a long way from its breeding grounds in northern Siberia.

So markedly different in appearance, structure and behaviour, these two birds, side by side on an estuary in New Zealand, represent the rich diversity found among shorebirds. As much of their food lies buried in the substrate, sandpipers usually need to probe to find it. Of course such tactile foraging requires suitable implements, and we find among the various species an astonishing diversity of bills – in both shape and length – used for that purpose. Among the plovers, however, the 'eyes' have it, for they are primarily visual foragers, picking much

Plovers and sandpipers: the two largest shorebird families are represented here. This banded dotterel shows the rounded head and body shape and the large eyes common to the plovers. The sharp-tailed sandpiper has a more elongated body, smaller head and eyes, and long narrow bill. IAN SOUTHEY

of their prey, mainly small invertebrates, from the surfaces of substrates or from low vegetation cover. Large eyes set in a rounded head are characteristic of the plover family, as is their manner of feeding. For them foraging is a stop–start affair – a short run before stopping with head held high, then either pecking at something or running some more. Biologists believe these pauses allow plovers to detect prey at quite large distances, using a particularly acute form of monocular vision; and brain structure has been found to reflect this visual hunting style: the relative size of the optic lobe of plovers is almost twice that of probe-feeding sandpipers.[1] However, it is thought an auditory detection system may also be used in foraging.

This acute eyesight also allows plovers to forage in dim light conditions or at night. Compared with the sandpiper family, plovers have higher retinal density of rods, useful under poor light conditions, and a greater ratio of rods and cones for diurnal vision and colour discrimination.[2] Even so, it may be that birds will do better on a moonlit night: a study of banded dotterels in

A male banded dotterel in full breeding plumage, showing his bands to full effect. JOHN DOWDING

A foraging banded dotterel: while much of its food may be surface-dwelling creatures, it is not averse to extracting a worm from the mud if it happens upon one. IAN SOUTHEY

Australia found that when they continued feeding after dark they switched to a more continual pecking strategy, suggesting a more tactile method of prey detection. During days following a moonlit night they also roosted longer, suggesting energy intakes are greater on nights when some light is available.[3]

A further contrast with the probing sandpipers is bill structure: the characteristic shape for plovers is a short bill that narrows in the middle and then bulges at the tip. This is not the elongated, highly flexible bill of a typical sandpiper; yet like those of sandpipers, plover bills contain high densities of Herbst corpuscles, though they are arranged in less complicated ways than in probe-feeding sandpipers, and perhaps are used more for 'inspection of captured prey items rather than prey detection'.[4] The foraging manner of plovers is highly adapted for finding prey in flat, compacted substrates that may be hard to penetrate with a long and sensitive bill. Such feeding areas are more likely to be found higher in the tidal zone, where surface-living prey, such as amphipods, provide good plover food. Foraging plovers tend to be thinly dispersed over the flats – and there is an antisocial element to this. Their food may occur in low densities, and because they are relying on visual clues for prey detection, it would be useful not to have other birds in close proximity disturbing prey before they get to it. Using the higher tide zone also helps avoid busy groups of probing sandpipers, which more often forage lower in the tide zone. But plovers like to keep to themselves at other times as well, often keeping their distance from big flocks of other waders, or standing dispersed along the fringes of a roost.

The terms 'plover' and 'dotterel' are often used interchangeably to describe some members of the genus *Charadrius*, and both seem to originate in the realms of myth and misconception. Plover is derived from the Old French *plovier* which, in turn, is probably from the Latin *pluvia* meaning rain. It is thought to refer to the grey plover and the golden plovers – members of the genus *pluvius* – in the belief they flocked together and called before rain.[5] Another suggestion is that it denotes the distinctively spotted upperparts of those species, reminiscent of raindrops.[6] 'Dotterel' has less benign origins, being a diminutive of 'dolt' in one account, for a person who is foolish or easily duped. One suggestion is that it may come from the energetic courting and distraction displays of the Eurasian dotterel *Charadrius morinellus*, named by Linnaeus, but first used by third-century Roman writer Caius 'with a double meaning – being a diminutive of *morus* a fool, and having reference to *Morini*, the ancient name of the people of Flanders, where he had found the bird common'.[7] For Maori, banded dotterel are pohowhera, meaning 'burnt breast', referring to a myth concerning an ancestor in Hawaiki called Tuturiwhatu 'who burnt her breast while cooking kumara in a hangi. This woman became the bird.'[8]

The subspecies Charadrius bicinctus exilis is confined to the Auckland Islands. It is a slightly larger, more robust-looking bird than the mainland population, with heavier legs and toes. Male breeding plumage is considered closer to that of a mainland female, with the breast bands often more mottled and not as sharply defined as a mainland male. IAN SOUTHEY

The scientific name *Charadrius bicinctus* stems from the Latin *bi* 'two' and *cinctus* 'banded' or *cingere* 'girdled or encircled', referring to the chestnut and black bands.

Why the double band? Mary Bomford, who studied banded dotterels on the Cass River delta, suggested a functional value for this striking plumage. In one example, a territorial bird runs rapidly towards an intruding bird with its body held in a horizontal posture, its throat puffed out, but clearly displaying the upper black chest band, while the lower chestnut band is largely hidden. This presents a striking pattern of dark bands across the forehead, face and chest, each alternating with white. White feathers along the flank of the bird are raised over the closed wings, in effect making the bird appear wider. Then, facing the intruder, the bird stops and stands in an upright posture, with its chest lifted and thrust forward, so that the broad chestnut band is now prominently displayed while the black upper band is largely hidden: 'This sudden flashing of the chestnut band must be very striking to an observer at ground level.'[9]

According to another account, when an intruder enters a pair's territory, all three birds may stand around in erect posture displaying their breasts at each other. In this display the bands are shown 'to best advantage, particularly the black upper one, because of the upward stretching. They must surely look intimidating to each other . . . at close quarters.'[10] But while these accounts indicate conspicuous display, the bands may help with the opposite as well – reducing the bird's visibility. When sitting among shingle, the drab back plumage helps with camouflage, while the dark chest bands resemble the shadows of stones thus 'visually [disrupting] the bird's image'. When an intruder is still 50–100 m away a sitting bird may leave the nest in a crouch run, keeping its 'drably coloured back and sides to the intruder so its conspicuous chest bands can't be seen'.[11]

The sharp-tailed sandpiper is clearly a long-distance migrant, but what about the dotterel? Well, it depends on where in the country it comes from. If wrybills are extremely specialised in their breeding habitat, banded dotterels are quite the opposite. Nesting records occur throughout the country, from coastal beaches to inland areas such as the Central Plateau of the North Island. They are widely dispersed through the central South Island, sometimes at high altitudes, and also overlap with wrybill on the braided rivers. Yet their pattern of post-breeding migrations reveals a curious thing; after breeding a bird may, depending on the location of its nest site, stay put, move to the coast, move north, or head across the Tasman. Dotterels breeding inland or at high altitudes are almost all migratory, while most birds breeding on beaches, coastal lagoons or estuaries anywhere in the country tend to remain sedentary. A further sedentary population is the subspecies occurring on the Auckland Islands.

Birds breeding in inland North Canterbury tend to migrate elsewhere in the country; Westland birds move north to Farewell Spit; while most North Island birds winter around Auckland and the Bay of Plenty. However, birds breeding inland in the southern South Island follow a longstanding Kiwi tradition by migrating to Australia. Of banded birds recovered in Australia, the

Banded dotterel nest and clutch on the Ashley River. JOHN DOWDING

A banded dotterel nest on the sand at Ohope Beach. BRIAN CHUDLEIGH

An interesting feature of some banded dotterel nests is that eggs can be virtually burried. Once a clutch is complete only a small part of the eggs, barely a dimple, may show above the surface. BRIAN CHUDLEIGH

proportion from each breeding region presents a clear picture of this: inland Southland 74%, Central Otago 95%, Mackenzie Basin 65%, Canterbury 27%, Westland 15%, Marlborough–Nelson 3% and the North Island 1%. On the other hand, the proportion of South Island birds moving to the North Island is 62% from Marlborough, 15% from Westland, 5% from the Mackenzie Basin, with no records from Otago or Southland.[12] Like most things in biology this pattern of movement is food related; inland areas above 600 m may be snow-covered in winter, and rivers are more unreliable at this time as well; but in coastal areas avian food emporiums remain open all year round. Birds nesting inland, especially those at higher altitudes, are also later breeders, which means by the time they are finished, limited coastal wintering habitats in New Zealand are largely occupied by lowland birds.

Yet not all birds leave the high country in winter. Ray Pierce found 100–200 dotterels, including juveniles, wintered in the Tekapo area; and if a juvenile had wintered once in the area it would do so again in successive years. There is perhaps an element of 'missed-the-bus' in this. Such birds were normally late-fledging chicks, whereas all winter sightings of chicks from the area that had fledged earlier – in November or December – were in Australia. 'Migratory and sedentary behaviour among partial migrants is thought to be under genetic control. It seems, however, that this genetic base can be modified by other factors, including timing of fledging.' Pierce suggests such late fledgers may not have enough time to deposit pre-migratory fat.[13] There are at least three interesting things about this movement of banded dotterels to Australia: apart from some white-fronted terns, it is the only instance of east–west migration known among shorebirds; birds undergo a name change when they arrive there – Australians know them as double-banded plovers; and while it may be a species endemic to New Zealand, the first scientific description of it came from a specimen collected in Australia in 1827 by a Scottish naturalist, Sir William Jardine. Only afterwards was it found to be a New Zealand-breeding species.[14]

On the riverbeds where wrybills breed, it is common to see banded dotterel also nesting nearby. Typical nesting habitat may be dry, open and stable areas of shingle, sand or stones, sometimes with patches of low vegetation cover. Herb fields adjoining the riverbed, ploughed or stony paddocks and pasture areas are also used. In coastal areas nests occur on 'sandy, shelly

Dotterel on ice: while most banded dotterel migrate away from the central South Island for the winter, some do linger – where they may find rather cold conditions, such as this bird in the Mackenzie Basin. DAVE MURRAY

or shingle beaches, spits and backing dunes'.[15] But these birds are not particularly picky, so modified environments are also acceptable; hence gravel pits, quarries, gravel tracks and roads with wide gravel edges have all been used. They can also be found at higher elevations, with nests in Central Otago found at between 900 and 3000 m on bare rock, among tussock, mixed subalpine herb fields, and on the fell fields on top of ranges.[16]

When it comes to homeland defence, banded dotterels seem adept at taking care of business. Like many shorebirds, they have a toolkit of dissimulation displays to try and divert attention from nest, eggs or chicks. Jules Tapper, farming in the Waiau Valley in western Southland in 1909, reported two encounters with them which compelled him 'to unseat the owl from his pedestal as that of the wisest of birds and instead to place the dotterel thereon'. While heading to a fishing spot he encountered a dotterel that began displaying to him using 'its usual box of tricks', before it crouched alongside a stunted tussock, remaining there until approached. It was stationed immediately beside the nest of a 'ground-lark' or pipit. On returning the next day Tapper watched the bird repeat the performance. 'I then understood her motive. I think it was the cutest and the most cunning act I have heard of any one of the feathered tribe.' The inference was that the dotterel was deliberately trying to lead the intruder to the pipit's eggs rather than its own. The second example came while driving a flock of 300–400 sheep across a level stony paddock: Tapper watched the mob separate into two columns and then rejoin again. Curious, he rode up to the spot and found 'a dotterel standing alongside its nest of two eggs with its wings revolving like an electric fan. The sheep in consequence had divided with the result the nest and eggs were untouched.'[17]

Compared with other similar-sized shorebirds, dotterels have quite long incubation times. This is believed to be an evolutionary adaptation to ensure chicks hatch 'fully mature with respect to neural function, so they are capable of detecting and capturing highly mobile insects from the start'. Even so, chicks require a lot of parental care. In their first two to three weeks they may struggle to keep up their normal body temperature of about 40 °C when foraging in very cold conditions. At such times they need to be brooded at regular intervals, which 'may lead to "bizarre scenes" – where three or four chicks, three weeks old and close to fledging, want to be brooded by one of the parents'. There are benefits and costs to this strategy:

> The lower metabolic rate of young birds has the benefit of considerably reducing the energy costs of growth, giving chicks an increased capacity to survive temporary food shortages or inclement weather. But the downside is they remain dependent on parental care for such a long time.[18]

Black-fronted dotterel, Hokio Beach. IAN SOUTHEY

When camouflaging of nest and eggs is not sufficient, banded dotterels have a full repertoire of dissembling and distraction tricks for luring away intruders. JOHN DOWDING

Dotterel chicks have particular defensive postures, scattering, running and then squatting, head and neck stretched out in front, and pressed tight to the ground, making them hard to see. JOHN DOWDING

RECENT IMMIGRANT

Another recent Australian immigrant, the tiny black-fronted dotterel is considered to be so distinct it has its own genus, *Elseyornis melanops*. Widespread throughout much of Australia, it established in New Zealand relatively recently, with the first nest record near Napier in 1954. Since then it has expanded into much of the lower North Island, Marlborough, South Canterbury and Southland. Its preferred habitat appears to be the muddy margins of riverbeds, 'keeping to freshly exposed slippery mud'.[19] During floods it can be found in muddy areas elsewhere such as on adjacent farmland. Unlike the run–stop–peck action of other plovers such as banded dotterels, the black-fronted dotterel tends to walk 'carefully and quietly, picking as it goes'. Where it occurs in New Zealand it sometimes overlaps with banded dotterel, but the latter tend to be the predominant species, and it has been suggested that differences in habits make 'competition between them unlikely'.[20]

Newcomer: established as a New Zealand breeding species only in the 1950s, black-fronted dotterel are still sparsely distributed in the lower North Island and parts of the eastern South Island. IAN SOUTHEY

Watchful: New Zealand dotterel alert for prey. KEITH WOODLEY

CHAPTER NINE
A GAME OF TWO HALVES: NEW ZEALAND DOTTEREL

The bird pauses a few metres in front of me, its right leg held slightly in front, its foot shaking the surface of the sand. Darting forward a couple of paces, it pecks at the sand, taking what is most likely a sandhopper. It seems quite proficient at this foraging technique, known as foot trembling, for it takes prey at about every third attempt. It is a handsome bulky sort of a bird, mainly brown above and pale below, although on its belly is a broad swathe of reddish-orange. It has a large round head with a brown cap, a pale band above the eye from its forehead to neck, prominently large eyes, and a stout dark bill. On its right leg this New Zealand dotterel carries three colour bands: from top to bottom, blue, orange and white – 'We call her BOW,' says David Wilson from the Warkworth office of DOC. She was banded as a breeding adult in November 1994, so is now at least 19 years old, and has nested at this site every year since. Thirty minutes later a second bird is in front of us, and both birds are doing it in perfect tandem, trembling in unison.

We are sitting on a sand dune looking south beyond the spit at Pakiri, to the cliffs and headlands leading to Cape Rodney. Behind us, the jagged profiles of the Hen and Chickens islands straddle the horizon. To the east the steep form of Hauturu or Little Barrier lives up to its name of 'resting place of the winds' – the sky and horizon are clear except for a slab of grey cloud lying across its summit. To our right, the Pakiri River emerges into a broad lagoon filling with the flood tide. The stream used to flow directly out, but a few years ago it changed course and now loops south past the cottages of the holiday park, and around the end of the spit. The park is largely deserted at this time of year but that will change dramatically come summer at this very popular beach. Then, the dotterels before us – one of 13 pairs known to be breeding on this spit – will be sharing space with hordes of New Zealanders at play.

The endemic New Zealand dotterel is the largest member of the

On a mission: a New Zealand dotterel on the southern Manukau Harbour. IAN SOUTHEY

Part of the sand spit at Pakiri Beach. KEITH WOODLEY

Hapless crustacean: New Zealand dotterel on the Manukau Harbour dealing with a mud crab. IAN SOUTHEY

cosmopolitan plover genus *Charadrius*, and in northern New Zealand they are, with one or two exceptions, very much coastal birds. They will usually be found foraging in the typical stop–start fashion of the plover family, on firm mudflats, and sand or stony beaches. Prey include molluscs, amphipods, insects, crabs, or even small fish – in short, whatever opportunity presents that is of suitable size. Apart from the foot trembling observed at Pakiri, a number of techniques are employed, such as turning over an object to search for prey beneath, not unlike the turnstone. They have also been seen raking small mounds of seaweed covered in wind-drift sand, then pausing with head cocked, before pecking or probing the sand. They will dismember small crabs by shaking them until limbs fall off, eat the legs then the body whole; smaller crabs will be consumed whole. One dotterel was seen feeding on a small fish dropped by a white-fronted tern returning to a nearby colony.[1]

New Zealand dotterels nest primarily on the coast – on beaches, sand dunes, sandbanks, shellbanks, or even short pasture adjacent to the beachfront. As always however, there are exceptions. 'They are opportunists,' wrote Dick Sibson, 'with a quick eye for spotting new breeding grounds, such as the untidy fringes of a great airport or the stony waste around pits and pools where gravel is excavated.'[2] Road construction engineers working on Auckland's Northern Busway discovered this; as have workers at other motorway extension sites around Auckland. In recent years dotterels have nested at numerous sites around the city: next to the runway at Auckland airport, on Wynyard Wharf on the edge of the CBD, in a quarry in Mt Wellington, on an industrial construction site in Avondale, in a residential area near Devonport, beside the Albany Mega Centre, at MOTAT, and near the runway and helipad at Ardmore airfield.[3] In a move that subsequently proved beneficial to conservation, dotterels nested on the edges of a goldmine tailings dam at Waihi (see Chapter 17). But seemingly aberrant behaviour aside, it is on the beach that one is more likely to find a nesting dotterel – which is where its troubles begin. Before looking at this more closely, we need to get a historical perspective.

Human settlement of these islands impacted wildlife in a variety of ways, but perhaps the most curious outcome for shorebirds was what became of these dotterels. We could begin with the very name assigned to it when first described by Gmelin in 1789. *Charadrius obscurus* it became, for it was certainly of the plover family, but *obscurus* is from the Latin – dark or dusky. Once again Johann Forster and Dusky Sound enter the story, for it was collected there in April 1773 and painted by Forster's son Georg. But as no specimen survived, Gmelin described the species from Forster's unfinished image. So we know it occurred in that part of

Opportunists? Or perhaps merely resisting eviction from a traditional nest site: dotterel nest on the edge of a development area at the Port of Tauranga. BRIAN CHUDLEIGH

A more conventional dotterel nest site: the footprints show much activity, but they may also the attract attention of a passing predator. BRIAN CHUDLEIGH

Fiordland, and according to Johann Forster it 'was found on gravelly shores in the South Island'. It may also have been the plover recorded by Gaimard at Tolaga Bay in February 1827.[4]

In 1882 Buller described dotterels as 'nowhere very plentiful, [but] dispersed along the whole of our shores, frequenting the ocean beaches and sand flats at the mouths of all our tidal rivers. It moreover inhabits the interior, and appears to affect very high altitudes.' During an ascent of Mt Egmont one of his informants 'discovered a pair of these birds on the slope of the cone at an elevation of at least 1800 m' (although it is more likely that these were banded dotterels). Another assured him 'that he met with it in small flocks on the Spencer Ranges, in the province of Nelson, at an elevation above the sea of fully 2440 m.'[5] Charles Douglas, singular bushman and explorer of South Westland, said

> it frequents the sea beaches and river flats during the winter, but in summer I have often found them in the mountains, almost to the snow line, where they lay their eggs and rear their young. But what they feed on in such high latitudes, I don't know. Perhaps they fly down to the low country every day. With their extraordinary speed of flight, they could fly from the top of Mt Cook to the sea in a few minutes.[6]

Yet, although there are plenty of such records from inland South Island, there are no records of coastal breeding in either the South Island or in the southern part of the North Island. More than a century after Forster, T.H. Potts wrote: 'This excellent game bird formerly bred on Canterbury Plains whence I have taken the nest in the month of October; since then farms and settlements have occupied the waste lands of the plains, for the most part it has retired to the mountains of the back country.'[7] According to T.N. Brodrick, a surveyor from Makarora at the head of Lake Wanaka, writing in 1881: 'Above the bush are to be found the . . . mountain plover or dotterel. It is about twice the size of the common [banded] dotterel and has more colour on the breast. It makes its nest in coarse grass and its eggs are a great delicacy.' Commenting on this observation in 1993, Maida Barlow wrote: 'I have found no published record of South Island breeding later than Brodrick's 1881 nest and egg description.'[8]

There are a few records of inland breeding from the lower North Island, including one from the Rangitikei River near Bulls, but none from the coast. It was suggested the dividing line between the two populations lay in the southern half of the North Island. If that was the case, breeding birds have disappeared completely from both there and the entire South Island, leaving us with the situation today: two completely separated populations – the northern birds and a tiny population breeding on southern Stewart Island.[9]

Dotterels today are scattered unevenly around their northern range. Beginning on the central east coast of the North Island, prior to 1988 they were rare south of Te Araroa but have since been recorded at Napier and Porangahau. There are a few pairs all around East Cape and into the Bay of Plenty, with good numbers from Ohope to Matakana Island. The eastern Coromandel, especially Matarangi, is a stronghold, with a few around the Firth of Thames and the coast of Auckland. There is then a string of sites further north – Tawharanui, Pakiri,

The well developed legs and feet of a dotterel chick. JOHN DOWDING

Mangawhai, Waipu – all of which support significant breeding populations. They also occur around Northland but become noticeably scarcer along the west coast. They are entirely absent from the southern North Island and most of the South Island, the exceptions being Awarua Bay in Southland, where some of the Stewart Island population move after breeding; and Farewell Spit, where occasional wanderers turn up.

So what happened to the southern birds? Much of what we currently know about both dotterel populations stems from an encounter with a banded bird at the Weiti River mouth north of Auckland in 1985. The observer was John Dowding, who became curious about who had banded it and why. He found the person responsible was Sylvia Reed, an active member of the OSNZ, who had died several years earlier. Discovering that no one appeared to be carrying on her work, and realising there were large gaps in what was known about these dotterels, Dowding put together a study plan.[10]

After spending 15 years in overseas laboratories as a biochemist working with bacteria and viruses, Dowding had recently returned to New Zealand, seeking something different. There began an attachment to dotterels and other New Zealand shorebirds that continues to this day. Shortly after starting the dotterel work, he met his future wife, Elaine Murphy, and moved to Dunedin to work for the Natural History Film Unit. During subsequent holidays, having worked with the northern birds, Dowding and Murphy started visiting Stewart Island, curious about the southern population. This was to be an important development.

> *After just a few years there we realised they were plummeting in numbers, they really were in dire straits, and suddenly the academic focus went out the window and it became conservation – how do you conserve these threatened species that are going down the tubes, and from then on just about everything I did, even on northern dotterels, was with a view to how you manage them.*[11]

In marked contrast to the northern population, which nests almost entirely on or near the coast, southern birds nest on the high country of southern Stewart Island. Before the mammalian onslaught, many birds in the South Island most likely nested in similar situations.

Southern Stewart Island is rough country, and remote, with weather that is often challenging. Between December 1988 and April 1992 Dowding and Murphy made 10 trips, each of two to four weeks, to survey the island for dotterels. What they found was a population in deep trouble. It is not known how many dotterels were once on Stewart Island. The first record appears to be specimens of two breeding birds collected on Table Hill in the centre of the island, south of Paterson Inlet, and described by Buller in 1896. Subsequent reports over the next few decades referred to them 'being plentiful on beaches and also on the mountain-tops' and 'it occurs [on Stewart Island] in fair numbers'. In May 1955 a flock of 218 birds was recorded at the mouth of Paterson Inlet, and in 1969, 40 birds were roosting on Cook Arm of Port Pegasus, with a further 51 birds at Awarua Bay on the mainland. The Paterson Inlet birds have been found to be regular commuters: foraging mainly on tidal flats at the mouth of the Freshwater River on the western side of the inlet, they fly to roost at Mason Bay on the west coast of the island during daytime high tides, but during night-time high tides, they flock at The Neck on the east coast, a round trip of about 60 km every 24 hours.[12]

Southern New Zealand dotterels are slightly larger and much darker than northern birds. JOHN DOWDING

Southern dotterel and nest on Mt Anglem, Stewart Island. JOHN DOWDING

Blaikies Hill, Stewart Island: unlike northern birds, southern dotterels breed inland, often at high elevations. JOHN DOWDING

These places – Cook Arm, Mason Bay and The Neck, along with Awarua Bay – are now known to be the only flocking sites for the southern population.

By April 1992, 49 birds had been colour-banded, which allowed monitoring of movements between breeding and flocking sites. There was no obvious link between where a bird nested and where it flocked, with instances of breeding pairs dispersing to different sites. For example the mate of one bird seen at Awarua Bay on the mainland was at Mason Bay. However all adults were faithful to their flocking site over the period of the study, which is helpful if one wants to rely on flock counts to assess the population. There had earlier been some speculation as to the origins of the birds regularly seen at Awarua Bay, but A.T. Edgar in 1969 suggested that 'in the absence of proof that dotterel breed on the Southland coast it must for the present be assumed that these birds came across Foveaux Strait'.[13] By 1993, bird-banding had confirmed that Edgar was right.

Analysing these results along with earlier count data, Dowding and Murphy concluded the population in the 1950s was probably around 350, but that it had fallen, probably to a minimum of 230, by the 1970s. At the end of their survey period in 1992, the estimated population stood at a maximum of just 25 breeding pairs in three flocks, all of which showed steep decline. The largest flock, at Paterson Inlet, was just one fifth of the size it had been 37 years earlier, yet this flock averaged 66 percent of the Stewart Island population. At the current rate of decline, they added, 'the southern population will be extinct in five to ten years'.[14]

Unlike the northern dotterels, southern birds do not need to contend with much in the way of human disturbance. There also appears to be abundant habitat available for them. The population was found to contain a high proportion of juveniles, which suggested a lack of productivity was not the problem. The major finding was that annual mortality of adult birds was about three times that seen in the northern population.[15] All of which pointed in one direction: as in so many other facets of New Zealand biodiversity under stress, predation was the problem. There are no mustelids on Stewart Island, but there are rats. There is also an abundance of *Felis catus*, which is where the accusing finger ends up. Birds, especially ground-nesting species, turn up in 44 percent of cat scats on the island.[16]

However, if, as seems the case, cats have been on the island since the mid nineteenth century, and if they had been killing dotterel at the rate indicated in these surveys, the dotterel population should have been long extinct. It is suggested, therefore, that the 'density, distribution, behaviour or diet of cats on the island may have changed in the last 40 years'.[17] In the early 1980s a similar incidence of high mortality was noted for kakapo, and there was some evidence that a few cats had learned to target kakapo and were having a disproportionate effect. Other species have also suffered: in the 1950s weka were described as abundant on the island, but by 1992 they were virtually extinct; and brown teal had also disappeared by 1972. It is likely a similar pattern was affecting dotterels. Cats take birds on the nest at night, and because males mostly do the incubation night shift, there is a shortage of males in the population. One result is female pairs, infertile eggs and extensive but futile incubation.[18]

The colour-banding of birds in the Stewart Island population answered several puzzling questions. Apart from confirming the origins of the flock at Awarua Bay, it also showed that the few dotterels seen at Farewell Spit were not ones that had drifted down from the north, but rather wandering juveniles from the south. A recently fledged juvenile banded in January 1991 was seen in early February at Farewell Spit – 835 km and 13 days after banding. A bird banded as a recently fledged juvenile in January 1991 was seen two months later 770 km away at Motueka Sandspit, but by December 1991 it was back on Stewart Island. Of 265 juveniles colour-banded in the northern North Island over 41 years to 1992, none had been recorded at Farewell Spit or anywhere in the South Island. Yet of only 21 birds banded on Stewart Island in three and a half years, two birds had already been seen twice in the northern South Island.[19] Then a southern bird set a new record when it was photographed alongside a northern bird at Shoal Bay, Auckland.

A world apart: rather than a windswept plateau on Stewart Island, a sandy beach on the Coromandel is a good nest site for this female northern New Zealand dotterel. JOHN DOWDING

Early observers of the southern dotterels noticed they seemed to be darker and slightly larger than the northern birds. Plumage on the upperparts of southern birds is a darker brown compared with the more mid grey-brown tones of northern birds. In breeding plumage the flanks and bellies of southern birds tend to be a darker brick-red than the more orange-red of northern birds. Southern downy chicks are also noticeably darker. Dowding suggests selection may be favouring more paler plumage in northern birds because of their nesting habitat on pale substrates such as sand or shell, compared with the southern birds which nest on darker cushion plants or among rocks.[20]

But for all the differences between northern and southern birds, there is one that stands out rather dramatically – one in which the two populations could not be more different: breeding locations. The northern birds are coastal – for them a piece of sandy beach or shellbank is prime real estate; whereas southern birds breed inland above 300 m. One observer noted the southern nests were lined with much more material than was found in northern nests, perhaps a strategy to raise it above damp ground.[21] Dotterel eggs on Stewart Island are also larger and darker on average than those of northern birds.

It is interesting that these birds nest in such places, even though 'there is clearly much suitable coastal habitat in the South Island and southern North Island similar to that now used in the northern North Island'.[22] One possibility is that the ancestral New Zealand dotterel population was a typical mountain plover, and the northern birds are atypical ones, having taken to breeding on beaches as the range expanded northwards and they found no unforested tops inland.[23] Today, not only are habits of the southern birds quite different, their breeding range is separated from the northern birds by 1100 km, with no overlap in nonbreeding range. Citing all these differences in measurements, plumage, habitat and behaviour, along with separated breeding ranges, Dowding concluded there are two subspecies of New Zealand dotterel. Given that the first scientific record came from Dusky Sound, according to taxonomic procedure that makes the southern birds the nominate species, with the northern population a subspecies, given the name *aquilonius* from the Latin for 'northern'.[24] The southern birds are now *Charadrius obscurus obscurus* or southern New Zealand dotterel.

From a study of northern dotterels breeding at

Rare meeting of populations: juvenile birds from Stewart Island are known to wander as far as Farewell Spit, but seldom further north – which makes this meeting at Shoal Bay, Auckland rather remarkable: a southern New Zealand dotterel (foreground) with a northern bird. JOHN DOWDING

Northern New Zealand dotterel eggs (top) and southern dotterel eggs (bottom). JOHN DOWDING

Omaha, 60 km north of Auckland, much has been learned about their breeding ecology. For one thing, compared with many other plovers – some closely related – they show remarkable site fidelity. Habitat conditions, including climate, may account for this. For southern dotterels, climatic conditions are harsh and food is scarce on their breeding grounds during winter, so they disperse and do not return until late July or August. Wrybill remain in nonbreeding flocks in the north until late July or August, while most banded dotterel breeding inland in the South Island spend the winter elsewhere in New Zealand or in Australia, not returning until August or September. In comparison, northern dotterels face rather benign conditions – a milder climate and food available all year round. Consequently they can occupy breeding sites at any time of the year, and birds may be back on a territory by the second week in May; they may even become quite sedentary.

It is not, however, entirely plain sailing for them. For example, a good breeding territory is in demand, and it is necessary, especially if it is a good one, to defend it. Both site fidelity and pair bonds that endure much longer than in other plovers are thought to be a result of this. They can also be long-lived: the species is believed to hold the longevity record among Charadriiformes. A bird seen on the Manukau in 1991 had been banded at Mataitai as a chick 41 years and 1 month earlier.[25] In February 2011 a bird seen at Big Sand Island on the Kaipara had been banded in 1980, giving it a minimum age of 32 but more likely 33 – the oldest known living dotterel.[26]

In other species, breeding site fidelity is strongly correlated with successful breeding the previous season. Although breeding success was very low during the study period at Omaha, site fidelity remained high: 'This suggests high quality breeding sites are rare and holding one is more important than moving to try and improve breeding success.'[27] While dotterels are usually fairly solitary when choosing nest sites, in some places they do nest in close proximity to others. At particularly favourable sites, such as near stream mouths like Pakiri or at estuaries like Omaha, there may be anywhere from two to ten pairs in such an arrangement, each in smaller territories. On longer beaches away from streams, densities are lower, so that further up the beach at Pakiri there may be one pair in 5 km.

A further outcome of relatively benign conditions is what can be an extraordinarily protracted breeding season. The earliest known nest initiation is 25–29 July and the latest 22–25 January at Omaha, where chicks were present on 10 March but were not seen again after a major storm. Assuming a fledging period of 36–46 days, if those chicks had survived they would have fledged in early April, so 'in exceptional circumstances therefore, the entire breeding season may extend for a little more than eight months'.[28] Early nesting is most likely climate-related, and research in the northern hemisphere indicates it may occur in years when temperatures are higher than average.[29]

But while benign climatic conditions may apply for breeding birds from the northern population, they also face circumstances that are anything but favourable. While the overall season may seem protracted, most breeding activity takes place in the spring and early summer, at just the time when human activity on our beaches increases. In addition, the various predators occupying our coastal environment are ever-present, day and night. All of which, as we shall see, leaves us with a species requiring considerable help.

Black-backed gull, over the Avon–Heathcote, Christchurch.
IAN SOUTHEY

CHAPTER TEN
PIRACY AND PREJUDICE: THE GULLS

The commotion downstream grew steadily louder. Tall grasses obscured all but the narrow view directly in front – three little black shags preening on a stranded log in the middle of the river. For the last 30 minutes I had sketched them, oblivious to my surroundings, focusing only on these sleekly elegant birds with their emerald-green eyes and glossy black plumage shining silver where it caught the sun. All the while there was unseen activity down the river to my left. There had been gulls drifting past in ones and twos but I paid little attention: they were only gulls. But the noise and clatter increased, until eventually I stood and looked. Strung across the river was a bathing party of black-backed gulls, nearly 100 of them – dipping, splashing, shaking, preening, chattering. The hubbub extended the width of the channel. Bright yellow bills clapped, heads and bodies gleamed white and black, revolving wings churned the water. *They were only gulls*. As a pageant of colour, form and movement, this scene near the mouth of the Waikanae River was quite beautiful – and a reminder to temper what for many of us seems an almost innate prejudice towards these birds.

If we were to award a prize to the New Zealand bird attracting the highest levels of disfavour, this gull must be a prime contender. We call it the southern black-backed gull, *Larus dominicanus dominicanus*. It is found from South America to New Zealand and Australia, and is one of five subspecies of kelp gull; the others are spread from southern Africa and Madagascar to the southern Indian Ocean and Antarctica.[1] The Latin *larus* refers to a 'rapacious seabird' from the Greek *laros* 'gull or some other seabird'.[2] To Martin Lichtenstein, physician, traveller, ornithologist and founder of the Berlin Zoo, who in 1827 named it from a specimen collected in Brazil, its distinctive black and white plumage suggested the monastic habits of Dominican friars or Jacobins, prominent among the missionaries to Latin America.[3] The monastic tradition of Christianity suggests virtue, goodness and piety, but of course history is strewn with instances of clerical behaviour that is anything but.

Scavengers, bullies, marauders, thugs or predators – these are some of the words that spring to mind when we think of gulls. We associate

Big, strong and aggressive: fighting black-backed gulls. BRUCE SHANKS

'Its lovely purity of plumage imparts such an air of virtue that one is loath to believe it a cowardly assassin.' — Thomas Potts. IAN SOUTHEY

A more familiar impression of black-backed gulls. BRIAN CHUDLEIGH

them with refuse tips and other places where we deposit our waste. Yet they are impressive creatures, striking in appearance, strong and robust, and highly successful. Oliver called them a 'most useful scavenger'. However, he continued: 'against these good qualities must be placed the fact that whenever the opportunity presents itself, it kills birds and preys on their eggs and young, not sparing chickens around the homestead'.[4] Nor are they averse to theft from their neighbours. During nest-building, observed Stead, 'one of the birds is always in attendance at the nest, this being necessary to stop neighbouring birds from pilfering the material or the eggs, which they would not hesitate to do if chance offered'.[5] Potts was similarly torn between appreciation and disapproval: 'Of the large black-backed gull . . . we shall be obliged to give a character somewhat mixed for good and evil, it is not possible to approve of all that it does; yet on the other hand it is so useful that its absence would leave a blank in our bird system not to be readily supplied.' Nevertheless in his description of a gull attacking a cast sheep, he writes, 'its lovely purity of plumage imparts such an air of virtue that one is loath to believe it a cowardly assassin'. In Dusky Sound he observed gulls taking teal chicks that were 'tossed up and swallowed whole'.[6]

Maori, too, appear to have mixed feelings towards the karoro. Ngati Porou, when confronted by northern tribes armed with muskets, had cause to lament, 'The people will be driven away, unhappy as the karoro flying around the beach, homeless as driftwood and seaweed cast up on the shore.'[7] In Maori tradition, according to Margaret Orbell, the zone between land and sea was seen as 'a kind of no-man's land', a place that was 'neither one thing or the other, a place for the broken and homeless', so it was 'appropriate that the karoro – so closely identified with the beach – should . . . be regarded as unhappy'.[8]

Gulls fall somewhere between shorebirds and seabirds: taxonomically they are included with the shorebirds under Charadriiformes, yet they bear superficial similarities with the true seabirds – the albatrosses, petrels and shearwaters. However, the major factor distinguishing them from seabirds is that they are generalists. Despite their wide-ranging nature, most seabirds tend to be highly specialised in foraging techniques, food types and habitats, whereas gulls are quite the opposite. Worldwide, they occupy a

In its first year the black-backed gull (above) has a strikingly spotted or spangled appearance, but by the second year (bottom right) it seems to be stuck in between, neither smartly patterned nor the vivid black and white of an adult. ATHENA DRUMMOND

Vociferous parenting: gull family. BRUCE SHANKS

tremendous diversity of habitats – from the Arctic to the Antarctic, from coastal regions to inland deserts, from sea level to mountain ranges.[9] They are better adapted for operating on land than seabirds are. Of course some seabirds also nest far inland – before human settlement of New Zealand extensive colonies of seabirds could be found throughout the country – but a petrel or shearwater on land is awkward and clumsy. Their body shape makes gulls more agile on land, while also allowing them to be good fliers and swimmers. Over the sea, gulls may forage in a manner similar to many seabirds – feeding on underwater prey from above the surface.

These 'seagulls' are indeed also birds of the high country. They are 'ubiquitous in the mountains of the South Island', and are more often encountered, and at greater altitudinal range, than birds usually thought of as high-country species, such as kea or rock wren.[10] Standing above Arthurs Pass at over 1800 m, Oliver observed several gulls 'sailing overhead and calling in the manner they do when their nests are approached'.[11] In a colony at over 900 m in the Paparoa Range, pipi and gastropod shells were found, the nearest source of which was the coast over 9 km away.[12] But gull nests are also found at sites well beyond coastal commuting distances – on rock outcrops 900 m up in the Rock and Pillar Range;[13] or at 1500 m overlooking Lake Wakatipu.[14] Takahe chicks in the remote Murchison Mountains have been seen to cower when a gull flies overhead. Downtown Auckland is a long way from the Remarkables or the Paparoas, yet it has something in common with both in providing sites for gull nests with a view: in the 1968–69 breeding season, birds fledged from four of six nests around the central city.[15] Most gull colonies, however, will be found in more likely places – along the coast or in the nearby hinterland.

Black-backed gulls appear to be assiduous parents, with both sharing incubation and brooding duties. Parents stop feeding the chicks at about 12 weeks, although food begging may occur for up to six months, usually unsuccessfully.[16] Chicks may stay with parents for at least several months after they are flying and able to feed themselves, during which time, according to some observers, an adult's patience must be sorely tested. 'The cry of the immature bird', wrote Stead,

> is a peevish whistle. So far as I know, Buller was the first to apply this adjective to the young black-back's call, and it fits exactly – it was coined for the job; and it always amazes me that the parents should show no sign of irritation when, hour after hour, they are persistently pestered by their young, and that exasperating cry.[17]

The fortunes of black-backed gulls on these islands have expanded immeasurably since European settlement – for they were not at all common prior to that. Fossils are 'comparatively rare for such a large bird and almost confined to dune deposits, but they have been found twice in swamp deposits associated with moa and other birds, indicating that the scavenging habit is of long standing'.[18] It is thought the role of prime scavenger around our coastal areas before human settlement was that of the now long-extinct New Zealand crow. In a pattern reflected in many species worldwide, black-backs have directly benefited from human settlement; the development of refuse tips is one obvious example. In some situations, such as the critical time immediately after fledging, in 'less than one hour at a dump a gull can usually obtain its daily food needs',[19] thus reversing a previous pattern of high chick mortality. Greater survival of birds beyond their first year can mean measurable population increases – or the reverse, if controls are implemented. In 1972 there were an estimated 27,000 gulls in the Auckland city area, but they declined dramatically once the dumping of rubbish in the sea off Rangitoto was halted, and compulsory rubbish bags for domestic collection were introduced. Within a year, successful hatching at the colony on Rangitoto fell from over 65 percent to 15 percent.[20] The current national population of black-backed gulls is estimated to be around one million.[21]

The wrybill, just 3 m in front of me, is working hard. It holds one end of a polychaete in its bill and is tugging firmly, its back tilted downwards and its legs locked in unison. It makes a quick stab as if to get a better grip, and eventually levers the worm out of the mud, a large curling mass drooping from its bill as it trots to a puddle to wash its prey. It is a quick wash, followed by hurried consumption, for the wrybill is clearly as aware as I am of the presence of potential muggers nearby. For three red-billed gulls are vigilantly at work. The wrybill has appeared unconcerned at my close proximity, but the nearest gull is less comfortable and remains several metres beyond. Further out it is another matter, as another successful wrybill discovers. As a gull approaches, the wrybill runs while trying to swallow its meal, but drops it and the gull is instantly upon it. As I watch, wrybills continue to forage, and the gulls continue hanging around expectantly – an age-old tussle on the mudflats.

This second type of gull with which New Zealanders are most familiar is 'an unmitigated robber'.[22] Stead watched as a young shag that had just been fed by a parent was forced to disgorge the food, which was immediately eaten by other gulls. Fleming observed a gull 'pounce open-mouthed upon a piteously-squeaking plover chick and swallow it whole, still cheeping, in mid-air'.[23] Another observer reported, 'I have seen a Caspian tern distracted by one gull, have its egg snatched by another, which in turn was lost to a third. The gulls were not hunting together, but the effect was the same.'[24] Fleming studied a gull colony on the Mokohinau Islands in the 1940s: 'About a third of the birds, at a rough guess, remained on the nesting sites during the day, mainly building nests, *robbing their neighbours' nests*, indulging in courtship activity.'[25] The offenders in all cases were tarapunga or red-billed gulls, the ones most commonly seen at the local shopping centre or takeaway place, clustering and squabbling for scraps and handouts, or following ferries and other vessels on harbours and estuaries.

It is not all about theft and scavenging, though: one could admire these gulls as omnivorous, opportunistic and enterprising. Their methods of foraging are many and varied, and include behaviours that, in other birds, are specialised techniques. They are proficient at

For Buller this was 'a pretty little gull'. IAN SOUTHEY

Watchful pirate: the long bill of an oystercatcher is an efficient foraging tool. Well aware of this, red-billed gulls may lurk nearby ready to indulge in acts of piracy. 'The Oystercatcher may succeed in flying off with his prey; but the plunderer, being swifter on the wing, pursues, overtakes, and compels a surrender.' —Walter Buller, 1888. IAN SOUTHEY

hawking, or catching insects such as beetles in flight, operating from near ground level to over 60 m.[26] Hovering over water or mud, they dip to take prey from the surface, like a tern or a kestrel. At Gisborne in 1962 they were observed behaving like skimmers; three gulls flew just above the surface with their trailing legs causing a slight ruffling, and their open bills held just above the water. 'During each flight a sprat, and on one occasion a flounder, leapt from the water under the tip of a bill and was caught.'[27] A variation on this was recorded at Miranda, with birds flying over a thin film of water on exposed mudflats, from which were emerging hundreds of squirts of water: 'Birds hung on the wind with wings slightly arched and legs dangling just above the surface. After each quick peck the feet would lightly pat the surface . . . the arch in the wings would increase and the bird would move forward to peck again.' The observer was reminded of storm petrels.[28]

These gulls in their pearl-grey and white plumage, with their stridently red bills and feet, hold considerable appeal for some people. Certainly Buller was all in favour of them. The presence of this 'pretty little gull' helped relieve the monotony of travel 'over such dreary stretches of sand as the Ninety-mile Beach and the coast-line between Wanganui and Wellington'.[29] They presented pleasing images 'as they rest on the wharves and jetties, or hover lightly among the shipping at its anchorage'. But they were useful as well as ornamental, doing 'good service to mankind as scavengers – by devouring the garbage which will inevitably find its way into the water in the vicinity of human habitations'.[30]

New Zealand red-billed gulls, or *Larus novaehollandiae scopulinus*, are currently recognised as one of three subspecies; the others occur in Australia (*L. n. novaehollandiae*), and in New Caledonia and the southwest Pacific (*L. n. forsteri*). It was first named in 1843 from yet another Forster specimen from Dusky Sound. Of course Maori had already named them – tarapunga; and Buller listed two other Maori names – makora and akiaki. The population at the time of European settlement is unknown, but they seem to have been widely distributed in all coastal areas. Numbers clearly increased in association with human activities, such as around whaling stations, urban areas, freezing works, farms and ports.[31] In the mid 1960s the population was estimated to be about 40,000 pairs and increasing.[32] In Australia, where the subspecies is known as silver gull, dramatic increases were also recorded in association with expanding urban centres. A colony

Red-billed gull family at Kaikoura. KEITH WOODLEY

near Wollongong in 1940 had only a few breeding pairs, but by 1962 had 17,800, and nearly 50,000 by 1992. At another colony 82 percent of gull food came from human sources.[33] Yet while they may be closely associated with human activities, and have benefited from our presence in these islands, some of their major nesting sites could not be further from human society.

Unlike black-backed gulls, red-bills are mainly coastal, with most colonies on the coast, or on offshore islands and rock stacks. They are densely settled, busy places. Oliver described a closely packed colony, where sharply demarcated territories made trespass impossible to avoid, as a 'place of continual uproar – an unceasing din of squabbling, raucous, bad-tempered gulls screaming abuse over boundary disputes'.[34] Colonies are often situated in association with other species such as shags, terns or other gulls.[35] The reason for proximity to other species is a ready supply of alternative food – be it eggs, chicks, or dropped food.

However, the location of the larger red-billed colonies is determined by another food-related factor, and may also be an indication that these birds, seemingly common and known to all of us, may be more specialised – and less common – than we think. They are found in areas where the sea is rich in euphausiids or krill, a form of planktonic crustacean on which chicks are fed. The most common of these is *Nyctiphanes australis*, a species restricted to the coastal continental shelf regions of New Zealand and southeast

Australia, optimally in 12–18 °C water.[36] Usually living 22–100 m below the surface, they swarm at the surface during breeding – and when they swarm, they do so in spectacular numbers. One study estimated *N. australis* schools off the coast of Tasmania as ranging from 3000 to over 450,000 individuals per square metre, with the biomass of an individual school being in excess of 100 kg wet weight.[37] The outcome of such a phenomenon can also be spectacular; swarms may occur erratically over a wide area, 'usually attended by sprats, kahawai

Copulating red-billed gulls, Kaikoura. KEITH WOODLEY

and thousands of gulls along many miles of coast'.[38] When schools of predatory fish such as kahawai are also in attendance, birds need to be mindful of peril from below. 'Gulls are forced to feed in restricted areas away from the frenzied feeding of the fish to avoid their legs and feet being bitten.'[39]

Most gull colonies are along the east coast of New Zealand; the largest concentrations are on the Three Kings and Mokohinau islands, followed by others off the Coromandel and Bay of Plenty, around Cook Strait and at Kaikoura, with further smaller colonies scattered elsewhere. Long sections of the west coast are uninhabited, except for colonies at Muriwai, New Plymouth, Kapiti, Mana, Okarito and Fiordland. Investigating the location of gull colonies in relation to plankton distribution and marine hydrology, biologist Jim Mills found some clear correlations. Plankton abundance on the surface depends on the availability of nutrient salts and sunlight, and nutrient salts tend to be abundant in areas where there is extensive, free and vertical circulation of water from lower levels. This mixing of surface water with deeper layers is promoted by turbulence and ocean currents along irregular coastlines and around islands; wind movement of surface water; and upwellings caused by diverging currents. These areas of convergence and sinking create 'fronts' where plankton capable of resisting the downward currents tend to concentrate. Plankton densities may be unevenly distributed: upwelling and vertical mixing of nutrient-rich water may create enrichment zones up to 100 km wide but the concentration of organisms at a convergent front may only be a few metres wide.[40]

Mills found that submarine canyons at Kaikoura, Cook Strait and off Cape Reinga produced suitable conditions for plankton concentrations within 45–65 km of the coast, well within red-billed flying range. Tidal currents in Cook Strait produced turbulence and water movements promoting production of 'fronts' and nutrient renewals for the 13 gull colonies in the area. Fronts and eddies formed around islands in the Hauraki Gulf and off the Bay of Plenty, while the irregular coastlines of Banks and Otago peninsulas created suitable turbulence. On the west coast, wind action on surface water was the major factor, inducing upwellings of colder water close to the coast.[41]

Recent research has established strong correlations between La Niña and El Niño climate cycles, plankton supply, and gull breeding success. As a relatively stable environment is necessary for the survival and growth of plankton populations, fluctuations in water temperature, and the time of year in which they occur, can be critical factors. For instance, major incursions of warm subtropical oceanic water from the north severely limit plankton availability. As well as reducing euphausiid productivity, warm water affects the availability of gull food by overlaying colder water, preventing the upward migration of plankton. Conversely when inflows of colder water from southern regions are higher, *N. australis* begin to reappear, meaning there is more food for gulls. In the Kaikoura region upwellings are also associated with northeasterly winds, so it is predicted higher food availability occurs on average in La Niña conditions when such winds are more frequent.[42]

This research also demonstrated the scientific 'gold dust' that may derive from a large data set gathered over a long period. Studies of the red-billed colonies at Kaikoura began in the late 1950s and have continued

The long stretch: a red-billed gull drinking. ATHENA DRUMMOND

Investigation: an inquisitive juvenile red-billed gull. ATHENA DRUMMOND

ever since. Over 71,600 chicks have been marked, resulting in a large proportion of the population being of known age.⁴³ For an adult gull there are alternative food sources – small fish, garbage and kelp flies – to keep it going, even during the breeding season. But to breed successfully, an abundance of food is required; they are, in fact, quite dependent on plankton swarms. The feeding ranges of gulls from breeding colonies near Kaikoura are known to extend approximately 40 km north and south of the colonies, although most of the plankton shoals are located north of the peninsula. During times of plankton abundance, numbers of breeding birds increased; young birds entered the breeding population at 2–4 years old rather than the usual 5–6 years; laying dates were earlier; clutch size increased; and females produced larger eggs. And benefits for gulls expanded exponentially: earlier laying and larger eggs have been shown to improve overall breeding success.⁴⁴

But the advent of global climate change may be a cloud on the horizon for the gulls of Kaikoura and elsewhere:

> . . . *westerly winds over New Zealand are expected to increase gradually with time, especially in the winter months and, to a lesser extent, in the spring. The potential consequence could be a decrease in the frequency of the NE wind type and a corresponding decrease in plankton availability, leading to the continued decline of the red-billed gull population in Kaikoura.*⁴⁵

This decline is also mirrored at the two largest colonies – the Mokohinau and Three Kings islands – which means our ubiquitous common 'seagull' needs to be considered a species of conservation concern.

The third New Zealand gull probably suffers from being 'tarred with the same brush' as the others. It is certainly a gull and it looks very similar to red-billed gulls – pearl-grey and white but with a longer, more slender black bill. That it is a more elegant, streamlined bird than the similar-sized red-bill is perhaps underlined by one aspect of its behaviour: while it may be opportunist, unlike the two other gulls it is less likely to be seen scavenging refuse.⁴⁶ That alone, in the popular conception of gulls, should mark it out as somewhat odd. But there are at least three other features about it that, for our purposes, are of the utmost significance: it is endemic to New Zealand, so found nowhere else; it is classified as endangered; and that alarming status is a comparatively recent development. In 1988, and again in 1994, the black-billed gull *Larus bulleri* was listed by the International Union for Conservation of Nature (IUCN) as a species of 'Least Concern'. Just six years later it was upgraded to 'Vulnerable' and then, in 2005, to 'Endangered'. The reason for this change in status was an observed 'very rapid decline throughout its breeding range, equivalent to an overall decline of more than 50 percent in 32 years (or three generations)'.⁴⁷ It is, in fact, one of the world's most endangered gull species.

We do not really know how many black-billed gulls there were prior to the 1970s, but indications are that they too increased markedly following European settlement. From the mid nineteenth century virtually all of lowland

The bulk of the black-billed gull population nest in riverbed colonies, such as this one on the Ashley River. JOHN DOWDING

Southland – now their major stronghold – was cleared of forest and tussocklands and converted to pastoral agriculture. Gull diet prior to this is largely unknown, although there are early reports of birds hawking for moths and beetles over forest, tussock grassland and wetlands. One of Buller's correspondents reported gulls taking large moths, 'pursuing them very much as other insectivorous birds would do'.[48] They also hawk for emerging mayflies and other insects, taking them from the surface of the water.[49] Beetles, crustaceans and fish also feature in the known diet, all of which would have been available prior to human settlement, but it is thought farmland created a more consistent and predictable food supply. This is backed up by contemporary evidence: chicks in Southland breeding colonies are fed almost exclusively on agricultural invertebrates such as earthworms, taken from nearby sheep, dairy, beef and deer farms. Pastoral invertebrates also dominated the diet of black-billed gulls studied in Canterbury.[50] Indeed one Southland farmer advanced the case, based on his own observations, that gulls were beneficial to his operation. During sowing of a swede crop he watched a constantly changing flock of 40–60 birds behind his tractor taking, among other things, grass grubs and porina grubs. 'With over 200,000 black-billed gulls [then] in Southland, it is interesting to contemplate the volume of agricultural pests they take annually.'[51]

Black-billed gulls are predominantly concentrated in the southern South Island, though their breeding range gradually expanded northwards in the twentieth century. Initially mere visitors to the North Island, they were recorded breeding at Rotorua in 1932 and in southern Hawkes Bay in 1948. A nesting record from Miranda in 1968 remained the northernmost colony until the 1990s, when further colonies were established on the Manukau and Kaipara harbours. The best estimate of the black-billed population is around 90,000 birds, most of which breed in Southland. OSNZ surveys in the mid 1990s found between 69 and 77 percent of the total population breeding on riverbeds in the region, particularly the Waiau, Aparima, Mataura and Oreti, with the biggest numbers occurring on the Oreti. Which makes the following figure very disturbing indeed: there has been an 83 percent decline in gulls on the four rivers since 1977 – the equivalent of a 6 percent decline each year. The extent of population decline elsewhere in the country is unclear, but there is some data indicating a worrying trend. Monitoring of gulls breeding on the Ashburton River over a 25-year period shows a decline of over 58 percent. Sparse data from the Waitaki suggests a decline of 76 percent over 32 years, while densities in inland Canterbury and Otago decreased on six of nine rivers surveyed. All of which suggests a population in considerable trouble. One study concluded: 'There is clearly some indication that current survival and recruitment of black-billed gulls may be too low to sustain a stable population.'[52]

Black-billed gulls nest in large dense colonies on gravel-bedded rivers, which tend to be highly unstable habitats, subject to flooding at any time. Gravel patch size and the absence of vegetation appear to be important factors in both colony location and size. But our rivers today are far from what they once were: original vegetation on riverbeds such as those in Southland would have been highly specialised groundcover species with nothing particularly tall; but since European settlement over 2500 species of exotic flora have become naturalised. This, together with land clearance and river modification works such as planting willows to stabilise banks, have brought huge changes to the riverbeds: 'These rivers now support one of the most invaded riparian plant communities in the world.'[53] The spread of vegetation modifies riverbed habitat on a number of fronts: it stabilises banks and gravel islands; increases river incision; increases predation risks for nesting birds; and may force nesting closer to water levels, leading to a higher exposure to flooding.[54]

Gravel extraction from the lower Oreti since the 1970s has impacted habitat on a large scale: in 1974, over 190,000 cubic m of gravel per annum was being taken out of a 12-km section. Regional council data shows historical extraction rates on this and other Southland rivers far exceed what the rivers can supply, and one study found the Oreti had been lowered by over 1 m as a result. In addition, stopbanks and groynes were employed to further modify the river, leading to a narrower and straighter channel. The largest and third-largest black-billed gull colonies in New Zealand were on the lower Oreti in 1977 and 1986; by 2002 all gravel areas at these sites were largely vegetated. So does this mean loss of habitat through human activities and vegetation encroachment is responsible for the decline in the gull population? Yes, but it is not the entire picture.

Rachel McClellan completed a major study of the gull colonies in Southland in 2009. She points out that while vegetation encroachment has reduced suitable areas, there are still large areas of what appears to be suitable gull habitat remaining on all four rivers. However evidence did suggest that productivity at some colonies had reduced as birds were being forced to establish nests nearer the waterline, with increased exposure to flooding. But reduction of habitat per se

Flock of black-billed gulls, Ashley River.
JOHN DOWDING

was not the complete answer. For that we must return, yet again, to our four-legged theme. During McClellan's study, 80 percent of all observed chick mortality was the result of predation.[55]

Black-bills are distinct among gulls in that, not only do they nest exclusively in colonies, they do so in greater densities than any other species. They also exhibit a marked degree of breeding synchrony, with most birds in a colony laying within a week of each other. Breeding synchrony in other species may be related to limited habitat availability, but this does not seem to be the case with black-bills. One researcher suggested black-bills' synchrony was the result of intense selection, because nesting habitat can be rapidly and unpredictably flooded. 'Breeding synchrony could develop as a mechanism to avoid wasted parental investments by early nesters that would desert their own eggs if later-arriving colony mates decided to abandon that colony breeding attempt – a frequent occurrence.'[56]

McClellan suggests extreme coloniality could be, at least in part, a response to predator pressure. Black-bills co-evolved with a variety of potential avian predators, many of which – like Forbes' harrier, the adzebill and the laughing owl – are now extinct or, like weka, are absent from contemporary breeding locations. While harriers and falcons are both present today, their impact appears minimal.[57] Black-backed gulls, on the other hand, are the main avian offender. Stead clearly recognised this, recording that two pairs of black-backed gulls nesting near the mouth of the Rakaia 'fed their young almost entirely on the young white-fronted terns and black-billed gulls from a colony nearby'.[58] But if fossils indicate they were largely confined to dune deposits and were relatively uncommon at the time of European settlement, these impacts are a recent development. The evolutionary significance of coloniality in these gulls, then, is unclear, but 'it is plausible that avian predation was at least a partial reason for [its] development'.[59] If so, how effective might it be in enabling the gulls to withstand modern predators?

A black-billed gull colony is a highly obvious feature in the landscape, busy, noisy, and smelly, so finding such a place is hardly a challenge to a cat or mustelid. In a densely packed colony a single predator can have an enormous impact, not just through the actual killing of a chick or adult, but through the disturbance such a visit causes. McClellan found half of egg mortality was indirectly caused by cats or ferrets disturbing incubating gulls, with eggs being knocked accidentally out of nests, desertion of nests, or predation by other black-billed gulls.[60] Location of the colony was significant: birds on islands had much higher nest success than those on banks, most likely because they were not as easily accessible to predators, and they were also less exposed to disturbance from human activities. Adults on islands were also heavier, and so presumably in better condition than birds at bank colonies. Of the 48 colonies studied in 2004–06, 71 percent were located on banks, and so subject to greater predation and disturbance during breeding.

The size of a colony is also important. A densely populated colony may assist in containing the damage, in that the presence of one cat or ferret may exclude others of the same species. But this would very much depend on the size and density of the colony, together with its exact location – factors which McClellan demonstrated to be of the utmost significance for gull breeding success.[61] In what is known in ecology as the Allee effect, below a certain size a gull colony tends to be less successful. The density of a population has an effect on population growth: greater population density may improve reproduction and survival rates, while there is a fall in reproductive rate at very low population densities.[62] Where a predator encounters low densities of prey with inefficient anti-predator strategies, the low survival rates that ensue could generate the Allee effect. Another factor may relate to habitat quality: a small colony, perhaps comprised of lower quality individuals, may be restricted to poorer quality habitat, whereas larger colonies tend to occur in habitat of higher quality.

McClellan's finding that smaller colonies tend to be less productive has major implications for management of black-billed gulls throughout the country. The three smallest colonies in her study, containing 120–550 gulls,

A sorry end for these gulls is even more alarming, given that this endemic New Zealand species is one of the world's most endangered gulls. JOHN DOWDING

failed to produce fledglings. The colonies most affected by black-backed gulls had approximately 120–1200 birds. These colony sizes happen to be typical in all other regions except Southland, where the mean colony size from 2004–06 was about 2400 gulls. The net outcome is a vicious circle of decreasing prospects: 'The relationship between productivity and colony size as well as the Allee effect has major implications for this rapidly declining species as the size of colonies will gradually decrease leading to overall productivity decline.'[63]

The situation in South Canterbury is a further case in point. Between the outlying suburb of Tinwald and the southern edge of Ashburton, State Highway 1 crosses the Ashburton River. On the immediate downstream side of the bridge the river flows in two channels separated by a broad reach of gravel. In October 2010 this entire section of gravel was covered in a dense, seething mass of gulls – over 3000 of them. The Ashburton is one of the most important Canterbury rivers for birdlife – one of five outside the Mackenzie Basin that are rated 'outstanding'. It has held nationally important populations of black-billed gulls, black-fronted terns, banded dotterels and black-fronted dotterels, along with regionally important populations of wrybill, pied oystercatchers and pied stilts. Between 1982 and 1990 there was a decline in all species; and the black-billed gulls here in late October 2010 were only a fraction of the number that were once on the river. From 11,000 on the south branch of the river in 1986, numbers plummeted to 1500 in 2005, although by 2007 numbers had increased to 3200.[64] The most likely causes include habitat loss from weed encroachment, low river flows and predation. But there may also be a human factor. At the Ashburton colony there is easy access to the riverbed from both sides of the river for walkers and dogs, and there are numerous vehicle tracks up and down river. A vehicle driven through a colony is known to have killed at least 110 adults and an unknown number of young.[65] In January 2008, several hundred adults and chicks were shot in a large Canterbury colony, a loss of more than half the birds present.[66]

Changing farming practices may also be limiting breeding success. The early development of farming in places like Southland clearly benefited this species. Indeed, so good and reliable was the food supply offered by farmers – such as winter fields left fallow – it is believed to have altered the migration patterns of some gulls, in that they had no need to move out to the coast. It is not known whether this also allowed them to double-brood and so increase productivity, but some researchers have suggested this could have been the case. Higher productivity and increased survival from the cessation of migration may be behind the population increase that is believed to have occurred through the mid twentieth century.[67] However, farming operations in recent years have become more intensive. Conversions to dairying, for instance, lead to more compacted soils and longer grass length, both of which could reduce gull prey availability. Higher use of herbicides and pesticides, year-round maintenance of grassed pastures, direct drilling of seed crops, and less ploughing are also likely to have affected invertebrate populations, meaning less food for gulls. Whatever the causes, the net result of all these factors is one of the most endangered gull species in the world. Indeed, strange as it may seem, the current trajectory within the population, and the lack of management targeting this species, mean it is in greater danger of extinction than the kakapo.

The black-billed gull colony beside State Highway 1 at Ashburton, October 2010.
KEITH WOODLEY

The patterns of a juvenile white-fronted tern gave the species its scientific name – *striata*.
IAN SOUTHEY

CHAPTER ELEVEN
ELEGANCE ALOFT: THE TERNS

Few sights are more elegant than such a colony in repose, the beautiful birds in hundreds facing one direction, settled into the sand as if floating on water, each with the same pure greys below, the same black cap above, the same dark bill, the same long pinions crossed above the back like the forked tails of a great Brazilian butterfly, each bird sheltering the same long tapering delta of bright, clean, shining sand.
—Herbert Guthrie-Smith[1]

The constant procession up and down the coast is visible from the Shorebird Centre, several hundred metres away to the west. But in the stillness of a cloudless evening at the end of December, it is also audible. A raspy *krrrr* or *kgrra* comes from dazzling white flecks radiating the low sunlight. The seaward paddock ends in a line of mangroves, beyond which is the mouth of a small stream called Taramaire, which drains part of the narrow coastal plain and its farmland. Here there is much activity, the white forms dipping and climbing, wheeling and dipping. On the incoming tide are schools of tiny sprats – the purpose for the continual flights of these birds. Two kilometres to the south, where the beach ridge ends in a broad shell spit, there is family business to attend to: a loud congregation of adults and chicks sprawled across the shell. The birds swoop and prick the water surface and, once successful, proceed back to the colony, a single fish drooping from each bill.

These tara, or white-fronted terns, are among the most elegant and graceful of birds. A flock of terns, 'a host of restless spirits housed in perpetually volatile silver bodies',[2] is exquisitely beautiful to watch, working a stretch of coast – passing over or in front of breaking waves, or roosting on a beach. The soft grey of their upperparts may not always be detectable at a distance; they are essentially delicate scraps of white, a jet-black cap and a long black bill. The white forehead

Elegance aloft: white-fronted tern. BRUCE SHANKS

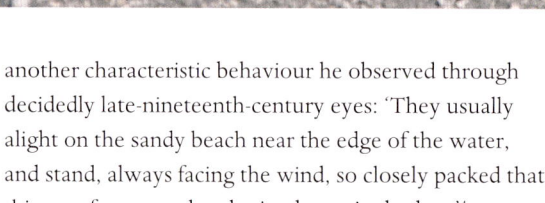

Tern takeaways: fish and chick. BRIAN CHUDLEIGH

separating cap and bill gives them their name.

The terns and gulls are thought to share a common ancestor, but in many ways they are quite different. Where the gulls tend to have a round, robust shape to them, the body shape of terns is more slender and elongated, with relatively shorter legs, longer and narrower wings and longer bills.[3] Perhaps most distinctive of all, particularly with white-fronted terns, is the long, deeply forked tail. In adult birds the two extremely elongated outer tail feathers form long streamers that project well beyond the tip of wing of a bird at rest. In a sitting bird the tail tends to be cocked at an acute angle, accentuating this feature even more. No less elegant is the slender bill, longer than the length of the head, and slightly decurved towards the tip.

A tern flock is seldom still. 'They shuffle about,' wrote Buller, 'with a constant low twittering, and occasionally stretch their wings upwards to their full extent, presenting a very pretty appearance.' But another characteristic behaviour he observed through decidedly late-nineteenth-century eyes: 'They usually alight on the sandy beach near the edge of the water, and stand, always facing the wind, so closely packed that thirty or forty may be obtained at a single shot.'[4]

It was a white-fronted tern that brought to a close the first period of European ornithology in New Zealand. One evening off the southeast coast of the North Island, as the *Discovery* sailed north from Queen Charlotte Sound at the end of February 1777, a bird flew on board. The 'Eggbird or Tern,' wrote ship's surgeon William Anderson, 'differ'd from all any of us had seen before. It was about the size of the common tern or sea swallow with the head, back and coverts of the wings finely variegated with black and white, the rest of the body nearly white and the bill and feet black.'[5] Captured and painted by William Ellis, it was 'the last animal collected in New Zealand waters for some years, the last new species for decades'.[6] The variegated plumage indicates it was an immature bird, but it became, by way of Ellis's painting, the type specimen. Anderson described the bird, but the official taxonomy begins in 1789 with Gmelin, who named it *Sterna striata*, based on the painting. 'Sterna' comes from the Old English *stern*, *stearn*, or *starn* – referring to black tern; but there is also a likely Scandinavian link with the Swedish *tärna* or Norwegian *terne*. 'Striata' or 'striated' comes from the Latin *striare* 'to striate or straight furrow'.[7]

The white-fronted tern is our most common tern, with one population estimate in the 1980s of over 100,000 pairs. Their current status is unclear, although a partly completed survey in the 1997–98 season counted 11,500 nests. Virtually anywhere around the

White-fronted tern colony, Stewart Island. IAN SOUTHEY

The stretched neck and strut of displaying terns – an elaborate courtship ritual as if to compensate for short legs. IAN SOUTHEY

A white-fronted tern family on the southern Manukau Harbour. IAN SOUTHEY

White-fronted tern. IAN SOUTHEY

New Zealand coast you may encounter them – either a single bird, a pair or a flock of hundreds, or anything in between. Breeding colonies vary similarly in size: in 1903 Stead recorded a colony of around 35,000 birds on the south branch of the Rakaia River, about 5 km from the sea.[8] Birds disperse widely after breeding, although banding data suggests movements within the country may be somewhat limited; banded birds from the South Island have only ever been recovered there, and a similar pattern occurs with North Island birds. Yet there are some that don't appear to recognise this 'rule', dispersing as far as Australia. Thought to be mainly subadults, such birds thus join banded dotterels and gannets in bucking the otherwise almost universal pattern of west to east bird movements across the Tasman. In another 'breach', some birds have taken things a step further and now breed over there. However this is a small population confined to the Furneaux Islands in Bass Strait, where birds were first recorded nesting in 1924.

Down at the shellbank colony there is much hubbub, many comings and goings as birds take care of family business. A few weeks earlier, courtship proceedings were just getting underway. The display posture of a courting male tern suggests an attempt to compensate for what he lacks in stature. On his short legs he struts, his wings held stiff and drooped; but the observer's eye is drawn to the extended neck and head held high, a fish drooped in his bill. One or more females will approach, their necks also extended, until the male takes off with admirers in pursuit. Flight will continue until only one female is left following, at which point the male may land and present her with the fish. But, as Stead writes, not always: 'for I have often seen a bird, perhaps disapproving of the looks of his pursuers, or disappointed with their powers of flight, settle on the ground again, and eat the fish himself'. If he is successful, however, and has passed the fish to a female, he will then resume his erect posture and walk slowly around her.[9] They are monogamous and are thought to pair for several years, or possibly for life.[10]

Just as the size of breeding colonies may vary, so do both location and nest structure. Nest sites can be anywhere from an offshore rock stack or on top of a rock precipice, to a sand or shell spit or even an old harbour groyne. Rock stack or cliff nests may be elaborately built with vegetation stalks, while a nest on a shell spit may be a shallow scrape and nothing more. One or two eggs, elaborately patterned with blotches and fine lines, are incubated for about 25–27 days. For two to three weeks after hatching the young are helpless, and continue to be fed by parents for some time after leaving the nest. They are fully fledged at around 35 days.

The huge dagger-shaped bill makes the Caspian tern look fierce and formidable. ATHENA DRUMMOND

Caspian terns roosting with pied oystercatchers: a common sight on the Miranda shell banks. IAN SOUTHEY

Its 'actions and attitudes lack the grace of other terns" says one of the bird bibles.[11] But that is not the only way the Caspian tern differs from the others. For one thing, it is the biggest of the terns, being closer to black-backed gulls in body size. It is basically shaped like a tern and has the black crown common to most of them, but its rounded body shape also reminds one of the gulls. Overall it is a stocky, heavy-looking bird. Apart from size, its most prominent feature is the thick bill, shaped like a dagger. The 'huge red bill and flat head with short crest and angular nape give [it a] fierce expression,' says another bible.[12] In flight its slow, heavy wingbeats are also like those of a large gull; and its forked tail is relatively short compared with many other terns. Many of the tern species land on water to bathe, and 'a few actually feed from the surface, but for a family with webbed-feet, so closely tied to water, swimming is remarkably unusual and uncommon'. The Caspian however, settles 'freely on the water, riding high and buoyantly and feeding like a gull'.[13] Finally it is the most cosmopolitan of all the terns: its range extends – if somewhat erratically – throughout much of the world, with the notable exception of most of South America, as well as the polar regions and the central Pacific.

Today Caspians are recorded from much of the northern North Island coast, with scattered sightings elsewhere from the east and south coasts and around Taranaki. It is also not uncommon to find some around the lakes of the Central Plateau. They can be seen around much of the South Island – though rare in Fiordland – and also extend throughout most of the braided river systems including the headwaters. There is no evidence of Australian or New Zealand banded birds crossing the Tasman – so the New Zealand population, which one estimate in 1985 put at about 3500 birds, may be isolated.[14] That they are so comparatively widespread and familiar through most of the country was a puzzle for Sibson, because they seemed to have escaped the attention of all the early naturalists who followed in the wake of Cook. That many of these early observers came from western Europe, where it occurs but is not common, only deepened the mystery. 'Surely,' he wrote, 'such a striking species would have called for comment, and if possible taxidermy, if it had crossed the path of those early collectors.'[15]

Sibson found the earliest mention of Caspians was in an account published in the *Zoologist* in 1861. J.B. Ellman, an 'itinerant Englishman', referred to a 'very noisy bird confined to the coast', and called it Great Tern or *Sterna major*, unaware 'that he was adding a new bird to the New Zealand list'. Sibson also found a painting from around 1865 by Richard Laishley, a church minister who settled at Onehunga, showing a Caspian alongside a white-fronted tern. Laishley named it *Sterna strenua*.[16] In 1870 Potts published an account of Caspians nesting at Lake Ellesmere, but in Buller's writings as late as 1888 the inference seemed to be that they were 'rather scarce or else that they seldom came to the attention of the few naturalists who might be interested'.[17] This continued into the twentieth century, with writers referring to them as 'solitary' or 'occurring in pairs' or, as Oliver put it in 1930, 'never seen in large numbers'. Weighing all this led Sibson to suggest they may have colonised New Zealand comparatively recently. Few bone fragments have been found in middens, and yet 'midden deposits yield widespread evidence that white-fronted terns and our three native gulls . . . frequently formed part of the Polynesian diet'.[18] Another view is that it did occur much earlier but was largely confined to the northern harbours and long beaches, because 'its large bones have been found only in Northland and not in extensive collections from dunes further south'.[19]

In the sometime arcane world of the taxonomist there occur, from time to time, minor eruptions over correct nomenclature and order of priority. Thus the Caspian tern was named *Sterna caspia* by one of the greatest naturalists of the eighteenth century, Peter Simon Pallas, in 1770. However, in the same work in which Pallas's description appeared there also occurred reference to the same bird as *Sterna tschegrava* by Russian naturalist Ivan Lepekhin. In the late nineteenth century an attempt was made to change the name from 'caspia', because 'tschegrava' had 'priority by several pages'. Buller, for one, was having none of this, summarily dispatching the idea: 'the word is not only barbarous, but exceedingly cacophonous, and especially as *caspia* has become so well established by common consent, I do not think it would be expedient to supersede Pallas's name in view of the very slight priority of that of Lepechin'.[20] It is now included in its own genus – *Hydroprogne*, derived from the Greek for 'water' and 'swallow'. There is, however, a further name change that might be usefully employed today. The common Maori name for Caspians is taranui, an extension of tara, but Ellman referred to the Maori name as tara kakao which, as Sibson wrote, has 'onomatopoeic merit'.[21] It is a name that certainly conjures very well the croaky rasp of a Caspian flying over a New Zealand estuary.

A large proportion of New Zealand birds breed at

Tradition long past: for early settlers the Caspian tern colony at Mangawhai was a source of eggs for Christmas cakes. KEITH WOODLEY

Newly hatched Caspian tern chicks at Bowentown, Bay of Plenty. BRIAN CHUDLEIGH

long established colonies such as Whangarei Harbour and Mangawhai in the northern North Island, but there are also regular colonies in Nelson and Marlborough, and at Invercargill, the world's southernmost, where it is thought birds have attempted to breed every year since the 1890s.[22] According to one account, the colony of about 200 nests at Mangawhai 'has been permanently established in the area since the days of the early settlers'. It was also something of a larder for the locals. 'Each year it was the local custom to raid the colony when laying commenced in early November, to obtain a supply of eggs for baking the Christmas cakes.'[23] Preferred nesting habitats include shell- or sandbanks immediately above the high-tide level, provided they have ready access to the tideline and flats for unfledged chicks. 'Low scrub and maritime grasses provided some shelter and possibly protection from aerial predators for chicks not being brooded.'[24]

Nesting where they do, Caspian terns join the long list of species confronted by human modifications to the landscape. Of the factors reducing breeding success – predation and disturbance by humans, cats, dogs, sheep, cattle, mustelids, red-billed gulls, skuas and black-backed gulls – the latter are considered to be the most serious problem. Their effects on nine colonies studied were considered to be major. An increase in gulls adjacent to the Invercargill colony after 1987 had a severe impact on tern success, and only active management by DOC staff over the next few years – by puncturing gull eggs – alleviated the situation.[25]

Similar in size to fairy terns, and considerably smaller than white-fronted terns, small numbers of the little tern regularly visit New Zealand, but do not breed here. BRIAN CHUDLEIGH

Croaky calls draw attention to the arrival of three tiny birds from behind the dunes. They fly up the beach a short distance and land on the inner edge of the spit. If, in contrast to the bulky Caspian tern, the ethereal grace and elegance of white-fronted terns instil pleasure in the observer, one would think a bird with the name 'fairy tern' might elevate such feelings a notch or two. Yet there is a surprisingly stocky look to the newly arrived trio. The black cap and dark patch in front of the eye, and the robust yellow bill, suggest top-heaviness. Their wings in flight are noticeably darker than the white-fronted tern, with a darker leading edge. Yet there is still a delicacy to them, perhaps because of their diminutive size. 'When resting on the sands,' wrote Buller, 'it appears, owing to the shortness of its tarsi, to be actually lying on its breast.'[26] Furthermore they are certainly graceful in the air, turning, hovering and dipping in classic tern-like fashion. But there is one distinction that sets New Zealand fairy terns apart from all the other terns; indeed from every other species featured in this book. It even separates out from this particular equation three of the iconic species of New Zealand conservation – black stilt, kakapo and black robin. For the birds in front of me on the sandspit at Pakiri are the most rare, and by definition the most critically endangered bird currently breeding in this country: the three individuals here represent about 8 percent of the population.

Of course, as with so many other New Zealand species, the situation used to be quite different. Fairy terns were once widespread around the North Island coast, and on the east coast and inland rivers of the South Island. Buller considered them in 1888 to be 'tolerably common'.[27] However, some confusion then enters the picture in the form of another species that is very similar in size and shape to fairy terns. Populations of the little tern *Sterna albifrons*, some of which are migratory, occur in Europe, Asia and northern Australia. In the 1950s, as the birdlife of the Firth of Thames was coming under increasing scrutiny by eminent ornithologists of the day, diminutive terns were found to be present most years in small numbers. It was only once these had been closely studied that the nonbreeding range of the little tern was confirmed to include New Zealand.[28] Because of its similarities to the fairy tern – and in some plumages it takes considerable skill to separate them – historical records of what were thought to be fairy terns had to be reconsidered. Nevertheless, one key distinction between the two meant a degree of certainty could sometimes be achieved: fairy terns breed here; little terns do not.

A foraging fairy tern hovers over the channel at Mangawhai. IAN SOUTHEY

A significant proportion of the world population of New Zealand fairy terns – most endangered bird species in the country – in flight at Papakanui Spit on the Kaipara Harbour. IAN SOUTHEY

Plunge diving fairy tern at Mangawhai. IAN SOUTHEY

Described by John Gould in 1843, the type specimen of *Sterna nereis* (now *Sternula nereis*) – in Greek mythology one of the 50 daughters of the sea god Nereus was a nymph called Nereis – came from Bass Strait. The range of the species consists of three widely separated regions: the western and southern coasts of Australia, New Zealand and New Caledonia. One source describes them as 'gregarious . . . usually seen in small groups, sometimes in large flocks of up to 150'.[29] Buller, however, reported them as 'less sociable than the other Terns, never assembling in flocks, but always associating in pairs'.[30] Of course it rather depends on the location of the observer, for the first description is from Australia where fairy terns are more numerous – although even there they may never have been particularly abundant; one recent estimate of the population is just 2000 pairs.[31] There is no evidence upon which to base an estimate of the New Zealand population before human settlement. Most terns are very rare in the fossil record, although that may be more to do with the vagaries of fossil deposits than the rarity or otherwise of the birds themselves. Nevertheless, in the nineteenth century they were widely distributed.

During the 1930s and 1940s fairy terns were known to be breeding at Tauranga, Horowhenua, Manawatu, Hawkes Bay and near Blenheim. In the 1950s the population stood at just 18 pairs, but by 1983 it had plummeted to the brink of extinction with just three known pairs – at Mangawhai and Waipu, south of Whangarei, and at Papakanui Spit on the Kaipara Harbour. 'These three remained the only breeding sites since that time, until the recent establishment of a breeding pair at Pakiri in 2003–04.'[32] This last pair was a return to a breeding site last used over 40 years ago.[33] Protection of known breeding sites began in 1984, and an intensive management plan has been carried out over the years since. Yet the population today is still just 35–40 birds, meaning its current threat ranking is Nationally Critical: a species with a very high risk of extinction.[34] Why are they doing so poorly?

To understand what has happened to fairy terns we need to look at their ecology. They are restless creatures – 'active, noisy and excitable'. Their diet is almost entirely fish, which they catch by plunge-diving in shallow water. Foraging habitat is strictly coastal – sheltered coasts, harbours and estuaries or along ocean beaches – and they are 'rarely out of sight of land'.[35] Breeding sites are generally on low-lying sandspits, near sheltered estuaries; and the birds tend to be most particular about the actual nest site – an open area of beach with a scattering of shell seems to be ideal. Eggs are laid in November to mid January, with an incubation period of 21–23 days. Once hatched, it takes chicks about the same amount of time to fledge,

Fairy tern family at Mangawhai.
BRIAN CHUDLEIGH

and then about three weeks to learn how to forage for themselves. This protracted process from nesting to full independence equates to a long period of vulnerability. At the end of the breeding season, birds move to flock sites on both the east and west coasts, particularly the Kaipara Harbour.

The location of their remaining habitat – on beachfronts and estuaries immediately north of our biggest city – is one of the great obstacles to fairy tern breeding success. Growing recreational pressures and coastal subdivision, together with industrial activities such as sand extraction, pose continual threats of disturbance and degradation of habitat. These areas are particularly under pressure during the spring and summer, which is exactly when birds are attempting to breed. Here the nesting ecology and cryptic plumage of these birds, especially the chicks, may work against them. Unlike other New Zealand terns, fairy terns do not nest in noisy, conspicuous colonies. When confronted with such a colony, people have the option of moving around it to avoid disturbance. (That only

some, and not all people, take that option rather than heading straight through the colony is part of the ongoing problem for our shorebirds!) But fairy terns nest as solitary pairs; some may nest within 8–10 m of each other, while other pairs can be separated by several kilometres. Camouflage is so stunningly effective they can elude even seasoned observers. The colouration of adults – grey back, black cap, yellow bill – mimics their beach surroundings. There is, for example, a particular conical shell that, when freshly washed up, exactly replicates a fairy tern bill. When alarmed a chick will freeze, huddling close to the ground so it casts no shadow. Its plumage – grey feathers with black subterminal bands and golden fringes, and even, for a time, a golden crown – all provides disruptive camouflage while replicating nearby shell fragments.[36] What chance, then, that members of the public walking or driving on a beach will see them?

Yet again, predation poses a problem – and that regular litany of villains: mustelids, hedgehogs, rats, cats and black-backed gulls. Against the latter, fairy tern cryptic skills give them a chance; against all the rest, there is no contest. Since management of fairy terns began there has been considerable success at reducing this particular threat: loss caused by predation has decreased from 32 percent to 12 percent. But when we are considering only a handful of breeding pairs each year: any loss to predators remains a disaster.

Finally there is a natural threat: the weather. Extreme weather events, which may be coupled with high tides, are clearly a natural phenomenon, but cause problems simply because of where birds nest, on sandspits and beaches that are subject to spring tides and storms at any time. It is suggested fairy terns may be particularly sensitive to climatic conditions accompanying the El Niño–La Niña oscillations. Between 1951 and 1975, La Niña-dominated conditions – increased rainfall, higher frequency of onshore easterly winds, more storm events and storm surges – may 'correspond with the noticeable decrease in sightings of fairy terns' on the east coast in the 1950s. From 1976 to the late 1990s, El Niño-dominated weather patterns produced more benign conditions which, coinciding with the beginning of management of terns, may 'have made breeding conditions easier'.[37] Bird populations, of course, are usually adapted to cope with natural events such as these; it is only when you add all other unnatural threats, together with the tiny number of birds remaining, that it then becomes hugely significant.

Minimalist nest: a patch of sand with a scattering of shell seems to constitute ideal real estate for fairy terns. BRIAN CHUDLEIGH

Particularly productive male: this bird has produced 15 chicks in eight consecutive seasons. Photographed at the end of the breeding season, he is just beginning to moult into eclipse plumage; note the worn feathers, an indication of a busy summer providing for his offspring. IAN SOUTHEY

Rare calm day: Eboule Peninsula and Jacquemart Island, last bastion for Campbell Island snipe. COLIN MISKELLY

CHAPTER TWELVE
ANCIENT ENIGMAS: THE NEW ZEALAND SNIPE

One kilometre off the southern tip of Campbell Island is a steep-sided remnant of basalt lava known as Jacquemart Island. Named during the French Transit of Venus Expedition in 1874, the 200-m summit of the 19-ha island is crowned by windswept tussock grasses, and cushion plants along the clifftops. The great sweep of the Southern Ocean, driven by fierce westerly gales, crashes relentlessly on its sheer rock walls. It is there, one morning in November 1997, that science – in the form of three blokes and their dogs – reconnected with a fragment of our long-lost bird fauna. The group had landed by helicopter on the summit to search for a second population of the flightless Campbell Island teal. While they found no sign of any ducks, within minutes Fiddich, one of the bird-locator dogs, was on to something else. He followed a tiny bird for about 20 m around the base of a bluff before it flushed – and landed 15–20 m away. 'After a brief discussion,' says the official science record, 'and realising the significance of the find, the team determined to catch a specimen to confirm identification.'[1] About 50 m down the slope Fiddich pointed to a bird in a clump of low tussock; it was surrounded, caught, photographed and released. Over the next two hours one or more birds were encountered at 10 locations, and evidence of probing was found at two further sites. What the teal team had discovered was a previously unknown subspecies of snipe – descendants of a family that was once widespread throughout all the islands of New Zealand, the Chathams and the subantarctic. While populations still exist on the latter islands, snipe are long gone from the mainland.

Long-lost relic: the first Campbell Island snipe caught in November 1997. JEREMY CARROLL (DOC)

The interesting thing about the location of this discovery is that it is next door to the most studied of our subantarctic islands. During the Second World War, coastwatchers were permanently stationed on Campbell Island, and a weather observation station was fully staffed until 1995. Among those stationed there over that time were trained naturalists, as well as others who assisted with various ornithological projects. The presence of a permanent weather station provided good infrastructure for researchers in an otherwise remote place, making Campbell an 'accessible and appealing research site'.[2] But while the main island was well covered, the offshore islets – about a dozen of them – remained remote and not well known. Given that Jacquemart is just off the coast, and snipe, while they seem to be reluctant fliers, are known to cross narrow water gaps, presumably some birds must have been crossing to the main island during that time, especially if the population reached saturation. So why were snipe not encountered before this?

In 1840 Robert McCormick, surgeon and naturalist on the *Erebus* and *Terror* expedition, noticed that unlike the Auckland Islands, Campbell appeared to have no land birds. 'His failure to record pipits, snipe, teal, parakeets, falcons, bellbirds or banded dotterels – all now known originally to have been present, or assumed to have been,' is a clear indication of an event that had preceded McCormick by some years: the arrival of Norway rats on the island.[3] In the historical record there are some accounts that refer to snipe being there, although almost all turned out to be incorrect. For instance, Carsten Egeberg Borchgrevink, a Norwegian naturalist, visited Campbell in 1894 and secured three 'snipe specimens', which now reside in the Museum of Victoria. They are in fact bar-tailed godwits, a few of which regularly straggle to Campbell. Lord Plunket described a snipe-catching expedition in 1907, although it appears he confused his islands, for the event actually happened on Adams Island in the Auckland Islands group. The most tangible record is from 1952 when Brian Norton, a weather observer, had a close view of a snipe in an area immediately across from Jacquemart, but did not recognise the significance of what he had seen. It was only in January 2007 'on the way back from a nostalgic visit to his old haunts on Campbell Island' that he saw snipe on the Auckland Islands and the penny dropped.[4] A further likely sighting by another observer was made in the same area later in 1952.[5]

Despite its remoteness, Campbell Island has seen much in the way of human activity, with rodents just part of the legacy. In 1828 the brig *Perseverance* was wrecked on the island, and it is believed to be the source of the rats that subsequently ran amok. Cats are thought to have been present from about 1916; and there were also attempts at sheep and cattle farming. Then with the 1975 rediscovery of Campbell Island teal on Dent, another of the offshore islands, new conservation priorities began to emerge. Feral cattle were shot out in 1984 and the last sheep were gone by 1990. Interestingly, cats seem to have died out naturally by the 1990s, although this was not realised for some years.[6] It is thought vegetation changes once grazing stock went may have helped push out the cats. With sheep gone, the tussock and megaherbs grew taller and thicker, making hunting more difficult for cats. The very wet climate meant cats pushing through wet vegetation would be continually cold and wet, inhibiting their survival.[7] There still remained *Rattus norvegicus* – and with cats gone, their population is estimated to have fluctuated seasonally between 50,000 and 200,000. Now the discovery of the Jacquemart snipes delivered added impetus to an 'audacious proposal to eradicate rats from Campbell Island'.[8] But not only was it remote, the 11,300 ha island was much larger than any island where pest eradication had been achieved. Yet in July 2001, with the assistance of three helicopters and much hard work, that seemingly insurmountable goal was achieved, with breathtaking results.

In May 2003 snipe footprints were found near Monument Harbour opposite Jacquemart. In March 2005 further birds were seen and one chick, estimated to be about seven weeks old, was caught. Birds were already back breeding on the main island. During a survey in January 2006, 12 adults were caught, along with five chicks from three different broods; a nest was

Colin Miskelly (right), James Fraser and Percy searching for snipe on Campbell Island. MICHELLE GUTSELL

Campbell Island snipe, showing the strongly striped head pattern common to all the snipes, and the eyes set further back in the head than in most other birds. JAMES FRASER

found; and aerial displays were observed.[9] 'Given the expected small size of the Jacquemart population and the absence of acceptable records from Campbell, it was not expected that snipe would colonise Campbell at a sufficiently rapid rate to locate, mate and breed within four years of rat eradication.' Presumably, researchers concluded, 'many dozens of snipe must have attempted to colonise Campbell from Jacquemart over the preceding 170 years, and been killed by rats or cats before being detected by humans'.[10]

Woodcocks and snipe form one of the most distinctive branches of the Scolopacidae shorebirds, with species occurring in most parts of the world. If their long bills give them something in common with cousins such as the godwits and dowitchers, their overall shape sets them apart from other shorebirds. Their large eyes are set high and further back on the head than other waders. The earholes are located beneath the eyes, rather than behind the eyes as with other birds, 'so they can function when the flexible and sensitive beak is plunged into soil grasping for prey as if with forceps'.[11]

Snipe habitat is, on the whole, more terrestrial than most other shorebirds; they forage within the cover of vegetation such as marshy grasslands and even forested areas, rather than on estuaries and beaches. Within the group are several well known species such as Eurasian woodcock, breeding in a broad area across Eurasia; and common snipe, widely distributed across most of the northern hemisphere. Also within the group are some of the least known and most enigmatic of shorebirds, and these include the New Zealand snipes – an ancient element of our fauna.

If New Zealand was once a land of birds, it was also a land of snipe. More snipe species were breeding in the New Zealand region than any other wading bird; but of the 11 forms in an area encompassing Fiji and New Caledonia to mainland New Zealand, the Chathams and subantarctic islands, six are now extinct.[12] Kiore are thought to have exterminated them from the North, South and Stewart islands as well as some offshore islands, through predation of eggs and chicks, and possibly through competition for food. Snipe still remain on some islands in the Chatham and Auckland groups, as well as populations on Campbell, the Antipodes and the Snares; however even in those remote places they have been under siege from predators. Only on the Snares and Antipodes do they still occupy their full former range. Those populations that survive share a particular distinction within the Scolopacidae family: while numerous species occur here as nonbreeding migrants or stragglers, the New Zealand snipe are the only ones breeding within Australasia.[13]

Two leading researchers into our fossil past point to something of a tradition in ground birds evolving long probing bills. New Zealand 'is unusual in having high populations of terrestrial amphipods (*Talitridae*) which may process much of the plant detritus in forest soils'. In the absence of competitors such as rodents or hedgehogs, invertebrate faunas were abundant. 'Potential food for insectivores (or more accurately micro-carnivores) included one of the largest faunas of terrestrial snails, large earthworms and insects and no specialist mammalian insectivores – although short-tailed bats did their best to fill that niche.' To exploit this rich litter fauna, kiwi and rails evolved long probing bills, although 'the snipes presumably already had them'.[14] Those litter- and soil-probing species that survive tend to be nocturnal or crepuscular. In the presence of only avian predators it is suggested that species now extinct most likely fed within thick cover 'or emerged only at night or on overcast days'.[15]

Probing in the damp soils of the subantarctic islands can be a dirty business, which presumably is the origins of *Coenocorypha,* the rather unprepossessing name borne by this genus. From the Latin comes *coenum* 'mud or slime', and from *coryphaeus*, Latin derivation from the Greek *koryphe*, 'head or summit'.[16] These snipe are largely absent from the earliest ornithological investigations of New Zealand, and the reason is quite simple: by the time Europeans came they were essentially gone from the mainland; the first definite record was McCormick's Auckland Island specimens. One of those, collected on Enderby Island, is the type specimen for both the Auckland Island snipe, and also for the genus *Coenocorypha*. Although formerly occurring on all major vegetated islands except the Kermadecs and Macquarie, even now they struggle to make our radar screens. 'Paradoxically,' writes Colin Miskelly, curator of vertebrates at Te Papa and leading authority on New Zealand snipes, they 'are among the least known New Zealand birds; they are unknown to the general public and few details of their life histories are available to ornithologists and conservation managers'.[17] Then again, these birds are hardly show-offs. 'Displays are rarely seen as [colouration] and behaviour [are] cryptic, habitat is dense, and displays [occur] only occasionally, with some displays performed only at night.'[18]

Of North Island snipe *Coenocorypha barrierensis* there are few records – all of them from the Hauraki Gulf. Nearly as small as the 80-g Chatham Island snipe, the only known specimen – now in the Auckland Museum – was collected on Hauturu/Little Barrier in 1870. Yet Maori middens and the fossil record indicate it was once widespread throughout the North Island. While nothing is known about its biology, its body proportions indicate it could fly very well, and 'we can infer from other snipe that the species was active both day and night and fed on invertebrates'.[19] That the only modern records come from northern islands in the nineteenth century suggests they were virtually gone from the mainland before Europeans arrived. That places responsibility for their demise firmly with kiore.

The snipe bill is an excellent instrument for probing damp soils and forest litter in search of invertebrates. IAN SOUTHEY

Unique specimen: the only known specimen of North Island snipe resides in the Auckland Museum. KEITH WOODLEY

Fossils show South Island snipe – tutukiwi (*Coenocorypha iredalei*) – were once on Stewart Island and throughout the South Island. That there is virtually no live record indicates that it, too, was probably eliminated soon after kiore arrived. There is, however, one possible glimpse of it still existing on the mainland when Cook arrived on his second voyage. In Dusky Sound in 1773 Forster referred to a 'woodcock' brought back to the ship by a hunting party. It obviously reminded him of at least two familiar birds in the northern hemisphere as – having a bob each way – he called it *Scolopax gallinago* – the first being the name for woodcock; the second the common snipe. In northern Japan, Sakhalin Island and the west coast of the Sea of Japan there breeds a bird that migrates to eastern Australia and, periodically, turns up in New Zealand as a vagrant. Known as Latham's or Japanese snipe *Gallinago hardwickii*, this could have been the bird collected in Fiordland. As no specimen, adequate description or drawing exists we shall never know for sure, although there is also the possibility it was the once common *C. iredalei*. There is further circumstantial evidence: Dusky Sound is not normally known as the haunt of migratory waders; and while the *Discovery* was there two other species – New Zealand dotterel and shore plover – were also collected and described. Both are ground-nesting species that may have bred there at that time, and 'they obviously survived into the historic period in that locality, but were never recorded there again'.[20]

Whatever the identity of Forster's 'woodcock', there can be no doubt that South Island snipe did survive into the 1960s, and then featured in one of the great tragedies of New Zealand biodiversity. Once gone from the mainland it survived for a time on Stewart Island before disappearing. Small populations continued to exist on islands around Stewart Island, then one by one each of them became subject to the depredations of ship rats, weka and cats. That left only Taukihepa or Big South Cape Island, a rugged 939-ha island off the south coast of Stewart Island. Unlike the mainland populations of both North and South Island snipe, for which there is largely a vacuum of information, we have here at least the benefit of observations made by two noted naturalists: Guthrie-Smith visited the island in 1913 and 1923; and Stead spent time there with Major Robert Wilson in 1931. The bird is described as short-legged even for a New Zealand snipe, with more rufous and cinnamon colouring in the upperparts than other species. Guthrie-Smith watched birds foraging:

'The long bill is held well forward after the manner of the kiwi . . . a Lilliputian stride or two, five or six rapid spearings into the ground, a brief hesitation, a prolonged sniff, a deeper more assured perforation of the spongy soil, a quick mouse-like run, a pause, an advance, a downward thrust of the beak, so they moved ahead.'[21] As a later researcher noted: 'That Guthrie-Smith was able to stroke a bird sitting on its nest is a vivid demonstration of the species' utter vulnerability to mammalian predators.'[22]

Taukihepa is one of the 'Muttonbird Islands' – ancestral food-gathering sites for the Rakiura hapu of Ngai Tahu. Muttonbirders tell of how good the island

SUCCESS AND FAILURE – THE CHATHAM ISLAND SNIPES

In his 1869 description of Chatham Island snipe, Buller named it *pusilla* – meaning small, which seems appropriate for the smallest of all the New Zealand snipe with the shortest bill. A comparison of *pusilla* and the extinct *chathamica* in 1915 led one observer to conclude they are 'generalised or primitive scolopacines and as such are living fossils'.[23] Sometime after 1500, following the introduction of kiore, *C. pusilla* became extinct on Chatham and Pitt islands – accompanying, in the process, another bird which has been described as 'one of the most mysterious of many extinct birds known from the Chathams'.[24] Although there are no live records of Forbes' snipe *Coenocorypha chathamica*, there are plenty of fossils. It may have continued to survive on outlying islands within the Chathams group but, if so, it vanished once cats reached the islands during the 1800s. Meanwhile about 1900, after the introduction of rabbits, sheep, goats and cats, *pusilla* disappeared from Mangere Island. For the next 70 years it was believed to be confined to 218-ha Rangatira Island, although it may have persisted on the nearby, rarely visited, Star Keys.[25] That one snipe survived and one did not suggests there may have been important differences in the ecology of the two. 'Perhaps Forbes' snipe was flightless, or less inclined to fly, or had a slower breeding rate than the surviving species.'[26] Or maybe it was just bad luck; perhaps there was only room for one on the Rangatira liferaft.

Since the 1970s *pusilla* has been reintroduced to Mangere, and birds have subsequently been reported from nearby Little Mangere island.

was for birdlife: 'it was like going back to New Zealand as it used to be . . . a little paradise on its own,' said one. Another said, 'the air always smelt sweeter when he got back on the island'.[27] Among the island's birdlife were the last populations of South Island saddleback, Stead's bush wren and South Island snipe, together with another relict of our ancient fauna – greater short-tailed bats. Sometime before 1964, probably by way of a moored fishing boat, rats arrived on the island, and that year discovery of a major irruption caused Wildlife Service staff to launch a hasty rescue mission – not an easy task for a remote island subject to extreme weather. That the saddleback was saved became one of the great early milestones in New Zealand species conservation, rightly lauded around the world. A tiny population of wren was established on nearby islands but did not breed, and the last reliable sighting of the species was in 1972.[28] Attempts to capture and transfer snipe failed, and so it too joined the long list of birds – and the bat – consigned to oblivion.

New Zealand snipe have a finely tuned probing instrument for a beak. The tip of the upper mandible overlaps the lower, and is thought to contain sensitive Herbst corpuscles that help sense the presence of prey. Birds can manipulate prey within soil using these pliable mandibles, and most prey is swallowed without taking the bill from the soil. All vegetated areas with moist soil and dense groundcover offer snipe habitat on the islands where they still survive. In the three weeks prior to egg-laying, males courtship-feed females – a behaviour that appears to occur nowhere else within the Scolopacidae.[29] Nests are concealed in dense ground vegetation. One factor behind having overhead cover is thought to be protection against 'crash-landing petrels'.[30]

The nature of parental care is another common trait among snipe. The standard clutch size is two eggs, and if both hatch, each parent cares for only one chick. Two adults have never been seen caring for the same chick, nor is there any interaction between a chick and its sibling, or with the other parent. A chick is fed entirely by its attendant parent for the first two weeks, and does not become independent until 41 days old on the Chathams, or up to 65 days on the Snares.[31] On virtually all occasions when feeding of a chick has been observed the process was the same. Once the parent had extracted prey from the soil it stood motionless with its bill held over the spot. The chick then moved forward and took the prey; the adult 'never carried prey to the chick, nor even orientated its bill to the chick'. It is thought the sudden cessation of the adult's otherwise constant motion while foraging is a cue for the chick that food is on offer.[32]

When comparing the New Zealand snipe with their northern hemisphere relatives, Hutton thought they more closely resembled the South American snipe of the genus *Chubbia*, and suggested they may be related. Fleming thought a northern Palaearctic ancestor was more plausible rather than a dispersal across the South Pacific, 'even if such a dispersal took place while Antarctica was still vegetated, in the early Tertiary'. The specialised feeding behaviour of snipe, probing soft substrate for invertebrates, made them poorly adapted for coping with frozen ground. He pointed out most northern hemisphere species cope with this during the northern winter by migrating elsewhere. 'Thus,' he concluded, 'snipe probably did not colonise the subantarctic islands until post-glacial times, in the past 10,000 years.'[33] Investigation of the newly discovered Campbell Island population revealed that

Chatham Island snipe. JOHN DOWDING

Chatham Island snipe clutch. JOHN DOWDING

morphologically and genetically they were more closely related to the Auckland and Antipodes birds than to the other *Coenocorypha* snipes. The three locations share a similar geological history and vegetation patterns.

The Auckland Is. and Campbell Is. were glaciated during the Pleistocene ice ages up to 15,000 years ago, but snipe appear to have persisted on the Auckland Islands through this time, as C. aucklandica *was estimated to have been isolated from the other Coenocorypha snipe for c.96,000 years . . . The radiation of* C. aucklandica *to Antipodes and Campbell Is was estimated to have occurred within the last 10,000 years following the end of the Pleistocene glaciation.*[34]

To disperse in such a manner to outlying islands requires good flying ability, yet this seems to be much reduced in the remaining species of New Zealand snipe where 'no form is considered capable now of prolonged flight'.[35] It is suggested that once they were established on their remote new homes, selective pressures against flying began to operate. If food was available all year round there was no need to migrate. If there were no ground predators then escape flights became less important, especially if there was plenty of cover from aerial predators. Those aerial predators – skua, gull, harrier or falcon – could also make flying between islands hazardous.[36] However, in one particular respect flight remains essential for these birds, and for many people it is *the* most characteristic feature of the snipe clan: their aerial displays. It is also a feature in which there may be a clue suggesting Hutton may have been right about the origins of New Zealand snipe.

Most snipe in the world have a mixture of vocal and non-vocal displays in their repertoire, and these are believed to have arisen before the split of the *Gallinago*, *Chubbia* and *Coenocorphya* lineages. Structurally very similar, the *Chubbia* snipes of South America are considerably bigger than the New Zealand ones. They mainly exhibit non-vocal aerial displays immediately followed by non-vocal acoustic displays. It has been noted that Cordilleran, Andean and Imperial snipe display only at night or at twilight, and that their displays are not unlike those of the *Coenocorypha* snipe. The similarities in their displays, it is argued, 'supports a common ancestry for these two groups of Southern Hemisphere snipes'.[37]

In the folklore of the muttonbirders around Stewart Island there are stories of Hakawai – a legendary bird that remains unseen; its loud eerie call is heard only at

Colin Miskelly catching Snares Island snipe for translocation.
JAMES FRASER

night. In a competition with Kahu the harrier to see who could fly the highest, Hakawai flew so high that he did not return to earth – though sometimes in the night he derisively calls out his own name.[38] 'A series of 3–6 dysyllabic whistles variously described as *"queeyoo, queeyoo, queeyoo"* or *"hakawai, hakawai, hakawai"* was given by birds tens of metres above the ground, followed immediately by a "roar" or undulating whistle of air rushing through feathers, that we likened to a jet aircraft passing close overhead.'[39] The last time any of the muttonbirders recall hearing Hakawai was on Big South Cape in the early 1960s, just as rats began to establish. This seemed to be strong evidence that the hakawai was most likely the *iredalei* snipe, and so would be heard no more. This view was strengthened by the fact that the aerial display had never been observed on the Snares, about 100 km to the south – the nearest snipe population to Stewart Island, and also the most studied. It was hypothesised that because Snares birds had higher wing loadings and reduced flying ability compared with Chatham Island birds, 'they had progressed further towards flightlessness, apparently losing the hakawai display as part of their repertoire'.[40] The vibrational

Return of the hakawai: snipe release on Putauhinu Island, April 2005. ROS COLE

stress on a displaying snipe's tail feathers causes distinctive damage; the shafts near the tip snap, leaving a V-shaped gap. This tail feather wear had not been found in the Snares birds, although it was noticed on the Auckland Islands where, subsequently, aerial displays were also heard. Could it be the hakawai had not gone completely?

Their significance for muttonbirders was such that, once islands were cleared of rats, they were keen to get 'hakawai' snipe reintroduced. However instead of birds known to give 'hakawai' displays, conservation imperatives dictated that any translocations should be from the Snares population. A combination of proximity, habitat use, similarities in morphology with the Stewart Island birds and the conservation needs of the Snares population determined this decision. In April 2005, 30 birds from the Snares were translocated to Putauhinu Island off southwest Stewart Island, where they successfully established. Following a return visit to the island in March 2011, Miskelly estimated the population to be over 500 birds, which was an astonishing outcome. 'The rapid growth of the population . . . indicates that both productivity and survival rates greatly increased in the colonising population compared to the source population.'[41] Which creates a rather intriguing situation: 'this is a rare, if not unique, example of conservation management resulting in a species becoming more abundant than at any time in its evolutionary history'.[42] In a further irony, it was during this translocation that characteristic tail damage was found in two of the Snares males. Did this mean they performed the displays after all? It is now known that all the *Coenocorypha* snipe, including the Snares, Campbell and Chathams birds, perform the aerial displays. So, in the best traditions of folklore, the hakawai had returned to the Muttonbird Islands.[43]

So the story of the New Zealand snipe is one of very mixed fortunes, with a number of populations clinging – if somewhat precariously in some cases – to remote islands. This brings with it considerable problems for conservation managers. Recent genetic studies show the Snares and Chathams populations are clearly isolated from each other, and from populations of *C. aucklandica* on the more southern islands. There seems to be very little genetic diversity within each population – a problem familiar to us from the black robin and kakapo stories, where populations recovering from an extreme bottleneck show little if any variation in DNA. On a world scale, the Chatham, Snares and Campbell Island snipes rank second, third and fourth after kakapo (*Strigops habroptilus*) in genetic impoverishment. The Antipodes Island snipe is sixth after the Mariana crow; the Port Ross population of the Auckland Islands snipe is eighth after the great bustard.⁴⁴ At least they are still here.

The discovery of the Jacquemart snipe revealed a previously unknown population – an unprecedented event in recent New Zealand ornithology. Not since the discovery of Westland black petrel in 1945 had anything like this occurred. However the situation was critical: a tiny population in an extremely confined place stood the risk of being wiped out by one catastrophic event. The recovery plan for New Zealand snipes published in 2003 stated it was essential that a second population of the Jacquemart Island birds be established. There was, however, a big hurdle: before the translocations of Snares Island birds, not a lot was known about catching and transferring snipe. The one attempt in 1964 to rescue birds off Big South Cape Island had failed completely; of three birds captured, one escaped and two died. So great care was needed. 'Managers must have complete confidence in the techniques chosen to recover this taxon. A failed translocation attempt could result in total extinction through the loss of both the source and transfer populations.'⁴⁵

But as we have seen, once rats were removed from Campbell Island, nature did the rest. In 2006, Miskelly and a colleague published a paper documenting that within five years of rat eradication snipe had successfully re-established on Campbell Island. They cautioned, however, that given that the total area occupied by birds seen in 2006 was probably less than 40 ha, and with probably fewer than 100 individuals in the population, its official threat ranking should remain Nationally Critical. Nevertheless the paper concluded with a phrase that must have been welcomed by hard-pressed conservation managers coping with ever-diminishing budgets: 'we . . . recommend that their natural recolonisation be left to continue unaided'.⁴⁶

There was still one issue outstanding. These birds were previously unknown, and still required a name; and in describing the subspecies for science, it fell to Miskelly to come up with one. The brig that wrecked on its shores unleashing its complement of rats in 1828 was no stranger to Campbell Island; it was in the *Perseverance* that Captain Frederick Hasselborough had first discovered the island 18 years earlier. Its major geographical feature he named Perseverance Harbour, on the shores of which, in 2006, two snipe were seen from the population that had persevered on Jacquemart. Hence the official taxonomic title for these birds: *Coenocorypha aucklandica perseverance*.⁴⁷

Antipodes Island snipe: all populations of subantarctic snipe are on large islands without mammals, except the Antipodes birds, which share their island with mice; and this food competition could explain the lower bird densities on the island. DAVID BOYLE

The vastness of the tundra: the Yukon–Kuskokwim Delta in western Alaska forms a small part of the circumpolar tundra zone where millions of shorebirds breed. KEITH WOODLEY

CHAPTER THIRTEEN
THE GREAT OE: MIGRATION

Thinning patches of snow and ice along the edges of marsh and slough are all that remain of the winter coverall at Old Chevak. Tundra – undulating ochre, black and browns and, here and there, the faint wash of new green – extends in all directions. The surface of the vegetation is dry and brittle, desiccated by the constant wind, yet just a few millimetres deeper it is sodden. As days lengthen, water and land are heaving with life. There are burgeoning insect populations, and everywhere birds: tundra swans and sandhill cranes, ducks and geese, sparrows and longspurs . . . and shorebirds – a constant soundtrack with every pitch and note imaginable. There are nesting godwits and plovers, turnstones and sandpipers and, monotonously circling above, the curious *w-w-w-w-w-w* sound of a displaying snipe. Scenes like this, on the coastal fringe of western Alaska, are mirrored across the tundra regions – a giant circumpolar factory of biodiversity. But it is one of comparatively short duration: within two months all this activity will be ending, and most birds will be dispersing to make preparations for their great journeys south. For one writer the region resembled enormous lungs: 'I came to think of the migrations as breath, as the land breathing. In spring, a great inhalation of light and animals. The long-bated breath of summer. An exhalation that propelled them all south in the fall.'[1] South – for godwits, the greatest of these travellers, down the Pacific to the harbours and estuaries of New Zealand. Hundreds of kilometres to the northwest, across the Bering Strait in Chukotka, other birds – red knots and sandpipers – will be preparing for similar journeys, and similar destinations.

These great migrations are for us an extraordinary phenomenon. For the birds they are normal life; an essential component of an annual cycle, tuned not so much to seasonal changes as to the vast fluctuations in conditions and resources they entail. Returning each year to the tundra, shorebirds capitalise on a wealth of invertebrates produced during the long productive northern spring and summer – an abundance of food to sustain the demands of breeding, and raising young. Long before the next snow, they have already returned to their southern latitude 'wintering' sites, exploiting the productivity of the southern spring and summer. These are, though, the extremes of migratory shorebird journeys. They are broadly similar to the movements of oystercatchers and wrybills between South Island pastures and riverbeds and the northern estuaries; or to the annual movement of some banded dotterel across the Tasman. The New Zealand shorebirds between them encompass the entire spectrum – the sedentary overlapping with the transequatorial. Old Chevak is over 13,000 km from the Auckland Islands and their stay-at-home snipe; yet a few bar-tailed godwits are regularly recorded there, so it is theoretically possible that one of the godwits on the tundra now has been there.

Diminutive travellers: breeding in eastern Siberia, the sparrow-sized red-necked stint (top foreground), seen here with a wrybill, is the smallest shorebird to visit New Zealand. It is named for the bright breeding plumage it assumes before returning to the tundra each year.
IAN SOUTHEY

THE LONG AND THE SHORT AND THE TALL

If, within the shorebird families, there is exhibited a wide diversity of size, shape and ecology, nowhere is this more starkly revealed than in the chasm between smallest and largest. If the scale of transequatorial migration impresses us, then the annual journeys of the sparrow-sized stints astound. While red-necked stints are not the smallest wader in the world – in that, they are pipped by the least sandpiper *Calidris minutilla* –they are certainly the smallest of those found regularly in New Zealand. After breeding in northeastern Siberia, the bulk of the population heads for Australia, where they are the most common tundra-breeding shorebird. Up to 200 have been recorded in New Zealand – a few in the northern harbours, and at Porangahau, Farewell Spit and Lake Grassmere; up to 70 percent occur at two particular strongholds: Te Waihora/Lake Ellesmere and Awarua Bay.[2] In nonbreeding plumage they are a nondescript brown-backed bird with a white belly; it is their deep brick-red breeding plumage that gives them their name.

At the other extreme we find the eastern curlew *Numenius madagascariensis* – the world's largest wader. Not only does it tower above all others; its most distinctive feature is an improbably long decurved bill. As with all the curlew family, plumage is strikingly patterned, with an overall smart spangled look. Its breeding range extends around the Sea of Okhotsk and Kamchatka and into northeast China. Most birds migrate to Australia after breeding, with just a few crossing the Tasman. One place it does not occur, despite its scientific name, is Madagascar. French naturalist Buffon bestowed the name in 1760, apparently confusing the large Indian Ocean island with Macassar, in Sulawesi; and Linnaeus maintained it six years later. 'Linnaeus no doubt meant to write *macassarensis*,' says one charitable account.[3] The population, which is thought to be under 10,000 and most likely considerably less, has been declining for some time. This is reflected at the extreme edge of their range in New Zealand, where numbers have fallen from an estimated 100 birds in the 1960s to an annual average of just 18 in recent counts.

At the other extreme is the somewhat improbable eastern curlew, seen here with oystercatchers and godwits. Largest of the shorebirds, it too breeds in the Russian Far East and migrates mainly to Australia. The species is in sharp decline. IAN SOUTHEY

The need to migrate away from the breeding grounds before the northern winter is quite understandable; but why do some birds migrate as far as they do? Are there not suitable 'wintering' sites located anywhere from northern temperate regions to the tropics? Would not such sites have the additional advantage of a shorter journey back to the breeding grounds? The answer is yes – and birds of many species do occupy such places. In the theory of competitive displacement, birds try to settle as close to breeding grounds as they can, but are forced further away by competition from other individuals in the population. This is believed to be why some banded dotterels find it necessary to migrate to Australia.[4] It may also be why some bar-tailed godwits from northern European and Russian populations winter in Holland and the United Kingdom, while others go to West Africa. Yet hundreds of thousands of birds go even further, crossing the equator to arrive in the southern temperate zone.

It is not known precisely why more birds do not stay in the tropics, though there are several possible reasons. Living in open exposed areas – as most shorebirds do – they may be subject to heat stress. Or it could be to do with their immune systems; there is probably a higher risk of disease in the tropics than in the 'relatively clean habitat' of southern tidal flats; energy otherwise invested in an elaborate immune system can be utilised on journeying further south. Or maybe it is those very same southern tidal flats that are the main attraction. It is thought mudflats in the temperate zones support more abundant shorebird prey than those of the tropical regions. Some birds have been found to achieve higher rates of pre-migratory mass gain in temperate regions than in tropical regions.[5]

If there is so much food available in the southern temperate zone, though, why don't those birds stay put? Why do they then return all the way to the northern tundra to breed? Nature, it is said, abhors a vacuum. If no birds migrated to the higher northern latitudes in spring, a large seasonal surplus of food would go largely unexploited. Conversely, those birds that do move north would find lengthening days and an increasing food supply, giving them a higher chance of breeding success than if they stayed in the south competing with residents.[6]

There is more to it than that. Unlike many other birds, in most shorebird species, parents do not feed their young. Precocial chicks are mobile and seeking their own food soon after hatching. It makes sense therefore for birds to nest where the food is – and on the tundra, or on coastal margins or riverbeds of the southern temperate zone, such food is readily available. However the vast bulk of tundra species that winter in the southern hemisphere – godwits, knots and other sandpipers – are adapted to foraging on intertidal flats; but while the food is there the nesting habitat is not – unless they were to evolve some way of coping with daily inundation by the sea. Ultimately, the origins of these birds lie in those high northern latitudes: the Arctic region is their ancestral home and migration is in their genes.

There are of course costs attached to this strategy – not least the hazards of the journey itself. Storms or unseasonal weather, exposure to pathogens, or encountering predators are all factors that make migration a risky business. Then there are the flight costs: the need to store sufficient fuel to make the journey possible, and then navigate successfully to the correct destination. So for the system to persist, these costs must be outweighed by the benefits of migration. These, for the tundra breeders, are the abundance of food, and long daylight hours in spring and summer that maximise their prospects of breeding success. For non-migratory species it is the reverse: the benefits of staying at home outweigh the costs of seasonal movement.[7]

For a shorebird the need to migrate is one thing; the ability to do so is quite another. To perform their massive seasonal journeys, birds have had to develop a toolkit – a set of strategies that enable them to migrate successfully. The main requirements are timing mechanisms, seasonal fat reserves, and orientation skills.[8] The annual cycle of shorebirds is governed by an endogenous timekeeping system that responds to changes in day length. These circannual cues stimulate the phenomenon known as *Zugunruhe* – 'migratory restlessness' – which is the prompt for birds to make preparations for the next phase of the cycle. Prenuptial moult is one such preparation; hyperphagia – the stimulus to begin the loading of extra fat reserves – is another. The navigation system includes a set of celestial and magnetic compasses, each of which is more useful at different stages of the migration. Clearly these are remarkable birds.

We turn off the Tiwai Road onto a gravel track – one of the white stone trails snaking through vegetation that I remember from growing up in this area, decades ago. It is one of those calm big-sky Southland days; multiple layers of high cloud and patches of bright light, a medley of blues, greys and pearl, and many tones besides. Under this arch the flatlands give a broad sweep to all horizons. There are hills in most directions – Bluff Hill and Greenhills opposite the entrance to the bay, and the distant Takitimu Range to the northwest – but all sit low on the horizon. The giant stack of the Tiwai aluminium smelter sits prominently at the tip of the spit guarding the entrance to Awarua Bay; yet somehow even it struggles to dominate these quiet flatlands, this broad expanse of estuary with its sandflats and *Samolus*-covered hummocks. Eastwards lie most of the 16,000-ha Awarua Wetlands and the Waituna Lagoon. Along the edge of the incoming tide there is noise and activity. Scattered flocks of birds are steadily being drawn together, and pushed towards the hummocks around the top of the bay.

Around the margins of the growing ranks, standing widely spaced and watchful, are what appear to be sentinels. They are stocky, upright creatures on long legs. Their plumage is a striking three-part affair: the crown, hindneck and back strongly spotted black, white and golden; while the face, foreneck and belly are jet black. Separating the two, like a snaking border fence, is a pure white strip from forehead to rump. Other birds – small, compact, and very busy – are foraging on the edges, and sometimes in the very midst of the flocks. Their plumage pattern, likewise, is strikingly visible: black and white head and face; broad strips of black, mahogany and chestnut on the back; and pure white belly. As if that were not vivid enough, their short legs and feet are bright orange. Though they may be utterly different in appearance, these two species have a number of things in common, other than the startling dark/light contrasts of their breeding plumage. Both visitors from the northern tundra have enormous breeding and nonbreeding ranges; both are conferred with scientific names derived from vagaries of the Swedish language; and even though they are the third and fourth most numerous of the tundra birds that come to New Zealand each year, we know surprisingly little about them.

The orange legs belong to ruddy turnstones *Arenaria interpres*, a species that may turn up on almost any coastline on earth – except Antarctica. Their circumpolar breeding range, generally north of 60°N, encompasses Scandinavia and across northern Russia to the Bering

Third most numerous tundra-breeding species occurring in New Zealand, the strikingly patterned ruddy turnstones are among the most easily identifiable shorebirds. IAN SOUTHEY

Like turnstones, a Pacific golden plover in breeding plumage is also easy to identify; it stands out clearly among these knots and godwits on the southern Manukau Harbour. IAN SOUTHEY

Strait; and from Alaska and northern Canada to Greenland and Iceland. The nonbreeding range is even broader, and birds may be found along most continental coastlines, as well as throughout Oceania. Each year approximately 2500 spend the southern summer in New Zealand, mainly around the northern North Island and at Farewell Spit, Tasman Bay and the coastal wetlands of Southland – with scattered records from many points in between. They are regular visitors to the Chathams, as well as Snares and Auckland islands; as for Campbell Island . . . perhaps that is an island too far, for there is just the one record.[9]

Compared with turnstones, Pacific golden plovers *Pluvialis fulva* have rather a narrow breeding range, although it still stretches over 135° of longitude from the Yamal Peninsula in northern Russia to western Alaska. Moreover if you were to combine with it the ranges of the Eurasian and American golden plovers, they almost rival the turnstone in extent; they are absent only from Greenland. When it comes to nonbreeding range, however, Pacific golden plovers too, are veritable globetrotters, wintering in coastal areas from East Africa to China; and from Australia, New Zealand and Oceania to coastal California.[10] They occur throughout New Zealand, although – like the turnstones – the sites particularly favoured are the northern harbours and estuaries, Farewell Spit, Lake Ellesmere and the Southland coast.

Arenaria comes from the Latin for sand, or sand-coloured, and presumably refers to the seashore habitat of turnstones. One explanation advanced for *interpres* is that it means going in between the tides. Reverend Morris, in his classic seven-volume *British Birds*, expressed another view: 'I conjecture [it comes] from the bird's habit of careful investigation, and turning over, as a translator does in the case of the words of a book.'[11] However it seems he was unwittingly led astray by Linnaeus himself. During a visit to Gotland in 1741, the great taxonomist received the mistaken impression that the local word 'tolk' referred to turnstones. In standard Swedish the word refers to an interpreter or translator, but in the local dialect it means 'stalk' and was actually used to describe another wader, the common redshank.[12]

Turnstones have attitude, and it is difficult not to be impressed: they have been variously described as 'alert and bustling';[13] 'pugnacious and quarrelsome';[14] and 'an opportunistic forager, with a wide diversity of techniques to locate, capture and consume prey and

Linguistic confusion – and the turnstone's habit of careful investigation and turning over of objects – saw it bestowed with the science name interpres, meaning interpreter or translator. IAN SOUTHEY

food wastes'.[15] And when it comes to food, you would not call them fussy. In a standard biological reference, their diet is described as 'carnivorous' and lists 'insects, worms, molluscs, crustaceans, spiders, occasionally eggs and carrion'.[16] Investigate further and one turns up an astonishingly catholic array of fare: fish eyes and gills, tern eggs, raw and cooked meat, raw fat, raw and fried fish, chipped potatoes, banana, uncooked rice, bread, biscuits and chocolate. Many of the items associated with humans come from a 1971 account of a bird that landed on a ship south of Fiji. Over the three days it remained on board it came to take food from the hand, and was clearly keen to try anything on offer.[17] At a campsite in Queensland turnstones were recorded foraging around the feet of people sitting at picnic tables, or entering closed sleeping areas and kitchen areas.[18] Another account of its diet refers to 'unhealthy morsels' – perhaps a reference to the record from Britain of a turnstone seen feeding on a human corpse that had washed up on a beach.[19] But this cornucopia applies more to the turnstone nonbreeding season. Back on the tundra their diet is more prosaic: for a short period after arrival they eat mainly plant material, before switching to invertebrates once they become available.[20]

Evolution has produced, among the shorebirds, a wide variation in feeding apparatus and methods; and the structure and behaviour of turnstones is a prime example of this. The sturdy wedge-shaped bill, deep at the base and tapering sharply with the lower mandible upturned towards the tip, is a versatile tool operated by powerful jaw and neck muscles. Short, stout legs and strong toes accentuate this image of a tough little bird.[21]

Versatile tool: the sturdy, wedge-shaped bill of a turnstone is slightly upturned at the tip, a useful adaptation for tipping over any objects that may conceal prey. IAN SOUTHEY

Oceans are no barrier: widely dispersed throughout Oceania, Pacific golden plovers are among the greatest of migratory birds. The dark speckled bellies of these two, photographed in March, indicate they are moulting into breeding plumage. IAN SOUTHEY

Its predominant method of foraging gives it its common name, although 'turnthing' may be more accurate.

The bird bends its legs, inserts its bill under the stone, clod, shell, or other object and with a vigorous jerk throws it over, or if this has been only partially successful sometimes completes the operation by pushing against the upturned edge with its breast.[22]

Pacific golden plover also have a wide, seasonally variable diet, which includes molluscs, worms, adult and larval insects such as grasshoppers, beetles, and grubs, spiders, cranefly larvae, small molluscs and crustaceans, earthworms and annelids. They are occasionally known to eat seeds, leaves, lizards, bird eggs and small fish; and on arrival and prior to departing the breeding grounds, berries are also taken.[23] Golden plovers appear, in varying degrees, to have adapted to human habitation throughout the Pacific and are recorded in a variety of inland and coastal habitats, both natural and man-made, including pastures, tilled land, burned fields, golf courses, cemeteries, parks, playing fields, residential lawns, roadsides, airports, mudflats, shorelines, estuaries and beaches.[24] Yet in New Zealand and eastern Australia they follow only some of this pattern. For instance, far from being seen on pavements and lawns, they are among the most shy and wary of the shorebirds found here. They are more likely to be seen – and often only from a distance – foraging on mudflats, saltmarsh, amid tidewrack on beaches, and sometimes in pasture. This strongly suggests the Pacific Island birds and those found in New Zealand are most likely from separate populations.

In the Latin *pluvia* lie not only the possible origins of 'plover' but also the genus *Pluvialis* – and once more Linnaeus is on the job. His notes from a lecture he attended around 1728–29 refer to Eurasian golden plovers *P. apricaria* as being called 'regnpipare', from their perceived habit of flocking together and calling before rain. 'Regnpipare' is from an obsolete Swedish word which means literally 'rain caller'.[25] *Fulva* is 'tawny' or 'yellowish brown' and aptly describes the general appearance of golden plovers.

In the Bering Sea during his last voyage in late August 1778, Cook observed golden plovers flying south and pondered what it meant: 'Does not this indicate that there must be land to the North where these birds retired in the proper season to breed and were now returning to a warmer climate?' This insight is 'perhaps the first recorded statement concerning migration in the North Pacific region'.[26] Its migrations are also thought to have been of assistance to early Polynesian navigators, leading them north to the Hawaiian Islands and beyond to the fringes of Alaska. The wide distribution of both golden plovers and turnstones throughout the Pacific region has long been an indication they must be good fliers; for how else could they bridge the enormous expanses of ocean to reach remote islands, let alone New Zealand or Australia? Nineteenth-century ornithologists certainly thought so; and the seasonal appearance of golden plovers on oceanic islands 4000 km from the nearest landmass clearly suggested long-distance migrations were involved. Research into both species in the North and Central Pacific in the 1960s was the first step towards answering some questions about them, and throwing light on shorebird migration in general.

Golden plovers usually begin arriving in New Zealand in September, with the main influx occurring in October. Northward departures may extend from late March to May, although it is believed most birds have left by mid April. Birds are known to be back on the breeding grounds by early June, although just where those areas are is not known. However a record from southeast Australia of a bird banded on the Pribilof Islands is possibly a clue our birds may be from Alaska. Wherever they come from, these birds are clearly capable travellers. In 1910 it was confirmed they could perform overwater flights of 3860 km between Alaska and Hawaii, the earliest observational study of long-distance shorebird migration. In 1967 researchers on Wake Island measured the weight of birds arriving in August during southward migration, and in April just before northward departure.[27] From flight speeds, fat deposits and metabolic rates, estimates were made of potential flight distances to and from Wake. The fattest April birds had an estimated flight range of 9975 km; while for those in August it was 8040 km. This suggested that nonstop flights between Wake and the Aleutians or Kamchatka, or further north, were well within range. In 1972 two New Zealand researchers investigated arrival weights of birds on Niue, 5000 km further south of Wake, and calculated they could have reached there in one nonstop flight from the Pribilofs.[28] Since then, of course, it has been discovered that bar-tailed godwits are capable of making nonstop flights of at least 12,000 km, so it seems quite possible some birds could even be reaching New Zealand in one flight.

So what are the turnstones doing? Between 1964 and 1967 over 16,000 birds were banded on the Pribilofs, and subsequent recoveries gave some idea of likely migration routes, albeit with sizeable knowledge gaps remaining.[29] Most birds seemed to fly directly to Hawaii, or the Marshall Islands, which appeared to serve as a 'centre of distribution for further southward migration'. One bird, last recorded at the banding site on 27 August, was found four days later in northwest Hawaii, 3656 km away – representing 1044 km a day at an average speed of 43 kph. From there, birds moved to wintering grounds throughout the southwest Pacific – Kiribati, Phoenix Islands, Fiji, the Solomons and Australia and New Zealand. One Pribilof bird was found in the North Island, and another was recorded at Sydney: at 10,723 km this represented the longest distance from the banding site.[30] Northward migration patterns were less clear, although Japan and Taiwan appeared to be major stopover destinations.

Alert and wary sentinels: golden plovers in New Zealand are easily alarmed and difficult to approach, unlike the situation on Pacific islands where they may be found foraging around picnic tables. Bar-tailed godwits in the background, red knots and ruddy turnstones in the foreground. IAN SOUTHEY

It was not until 2009 that researchers in Australia produced an important breakthrough that filled in some gaps in our knowledge of turnstone migration, and also confirmed a pattern which earlier data had suggested. Geolocators are used to measure and record day length, from which latitude and longitude and hence a bird's movements can be retrospectively plotted. The technology has long been used on seabirds such as albatrosses – producing research that revolutionised our knowledge of albatross movements in relation to deep-sea fisheries, with, in some cases, dramatic outcomes for conservation – but only recently have the devices become miniaturised enough to make them suitable for use on smaller birds such as turnstones. In April 2009, six turnstones in South Australia were fitted with leg

Easiest of shorebirds to identify, the striking black and white contrasts of turnstone plumage is particularly evident in flight, as seen here in this flock landing on a Bay of Plenty beach. BRIAN CHUDLEIGH

flags to which geolocators were attached. The accuracy of data recorded could place a bird within 300 km of a given location – which seems a large margin of error until you remember the tens of thousands of kilometres these birds travel on their migrations.

The first stop for four birds leaving Flinders between 27 April and 4 May was Taiwan, 7400 km from the point of departure. They then left in staggered intervals, after a stopover ranging from eight days to 17 days. All then followed similar though not identical routes to northeast Siberia, over 5000 km away. However their return journeys revealed something rather extraordinary: in 2009 and 2010 no two birds followed the same route each year. For example, in 2009 one flew 7800 km from the Aleutians to Kiribati, where it stopped for six weeks before flying 5000 km back to Australia. In 2010 the same bird stopped in the Marshall Islands and Vanuatu before returning to Australia. Why these different routes were followed is not known. What we do know is that, given that turnstones can live for up to 20 years, a bird making this 27,000 trans-Pacific migration could conceivably fly over 500,000 km in its lifetime.[31]

Annual metamorphosis: as with many shorebirds, a curlew sandpiper is transformed once it moults from its winter, or nonbreeding plumage (left), into breeding plumage (right). IAN SOUTHEY

FIRST MIGRATIONS – THE CHALLENGES OF YOUNG SHOREBIRDS

Nowhere is the story of shorebird migration more remarkable than in the way young birds make their first migration journey. In some species, this first outing is in the company of adults – easily explaining how it happens; in many others the youngsters are embarking without adults. One example is the curlew sandpiper *Calidris ferruginea*. It was once a relatively common migrant to New Zealand, albeit in small numbers, but is now increasingly rare – a trend mirrored in Australia, where the once considerably larger population has also crashed. This is unfortunate, because they are remarkable birds, even if their model of parental care may leave something to be desired. Breeding in the high Arctic of northern Siberia, their nonbreeding range encompasses central and east Africa to Australia and New Zealand. Once incubation begins the male is out of there, heading south on migration. Within three weeks of hatching the female too is gone – leaving any surviving chicks to their own devices. Which makes the following record rather remarkable indeed: a chick banded on the Yana Delta at four weeks old on 5 August 1994 was recovered two months and 25 days later on Perkins Island, Tasmania, some 12,579 km from the banding site.[32]

How do young birds make such long migrations on their first time out? One hypothesis is that the onset of *Zugunruhe* or migratory restlessness holds the key. This restlessness, triggered by photoperiod cues, has been shown to last for a certain period before it fades and birds become more settled. It has also been confirmed that this trait is heritable, so young birds are already wired for migration.[33] The hypothesis is that birds are born with a time programme which, together with inherited migration directions, sets them on a course to cover the distance between breeding and wintering areas. The young bird travels for as long as the period of restlessness continues, and once it comes to an end, the bird should have arrived at its destination. This helps 'explain why young birds, with no previous knowledge of a wintering area, can find their own way to an appropriate locality without help from experienced adults, although other behavioural responses may also be involved'.[34] Of course adult birds were once in this situation too, but since their first journey they have made repeated migrations to and from the breeding area, during which they have also developed 'maps' so they can then use 'bi-coordinate navigation' as well as a compass.

Classic features of a bar-tailed godwit include the upturned bill, the long pointed wings common to most shorebirds, and the barred tail for which this species is named. IAN SOUTHEY

CHAPTER FOURTEEN
TIGHT SCHEDULES, OR EASY AS'? THE MIGRATION OF GODWITS

The flat deck of the oyster barge carries us down the channel towards the harbour entrance. Across the still water to the north the tiny settlement of Te Hapua straggles over its ridge to the harbour edge. On the shore sits the Ratana church with its twin towers; and further along horses graze among derelict vehicles. Immediately to the south is the long flat peninsula at Paua, dominated by one of *the* landmarks of Parengarenga Harbour – the high gabled roof of an old fish-processing shed. The landmark in front of us, however, is in a different league entirely: the enormous white dunes of the Kokota Spit glisten like a snowbank beneath the low grey sky. A fringe of small dunes lines the edge of the spit, dotted with vegetation patches – toetoe, and both marram and pingao. Passing around the northern end of the spit we move from the lee of the harbour to where the Pacific registers its presence. Silky green swells push the barge beam-on towards the metre or so of flat sand along the beach, where we clamber ashore.

Immediately beyond the coastal dunes an astonishing new world is revealed: a broad vista of undulating sand and shallow pools extends southward around two massive dune systems. Scattered clumps of vegetation are mirrored in the grey-blue panels of water, and everything is bathed in a soft white light. Immediately we disturb two pairs of variable oystercatchers and the first of numerous banded dotterels. Further along a ragged line of perhaps 3000 waders is spotted – still over half a kilometre away. They are bar-tailed godwits – birds that, along with this location, are fused in the popular imagination of many New Zealanders. The myth engrained in generations of schoolchildren is that godwits from all over New Zealand gather here in the Far North, before setting off on their massive migrations.

There is a kernel of truth to this, for in March each year birds do leave from this very harbour. But they also leave from locations south of here – everywhere from Houhora Harbour 20 km away, to Awarua Bay near Invercargill . . . and all points in between.

The surprising thing about these godwits is that, although they have long been in the popular consciousness of New Zealanders, and are the most numerous of our annual Arctic visitors, until comparatively recently we knew very little about them. There was a second hard-wired myth that 'our' godwits breed in Siberia – and again there is a degree of factual basis to this. Two major populations, and one recently recognised smaller one, occur in the East Asian–Australasian Flyway (EAAF) – the network of migratory routes used by hundreds of thousands of waterbirds between Australasia and breeding grounds on the tundra. The western population *Limosa lapponica menzbieri* from north-central Siberia winters primarily in northern Australia, while the eastern population, *L. l. baueri*, breeds in western Alaska. Almost all of the godwits occurring in New Zealand are thought to be from the latter. Intermediate between the two is a small population in eastern Siberia called *L. l. anadyrensis* – and it is likely some birds from this population also reach New Zealand – but to all intents and purposes, most New Zealand godwits are from Alaska.

For the Maori, godwits, or kuaka, were birds of mystery: they arrived in New Zealand in early spring and remained throughout the time when most resident birds were breeding; then many of them changed colour, fattened up and disappeared again. From the 1860s onwards, godwits are regularly mentioned in the work of early New Zealand ornithologists such as Hutton and Buller, and their presumed migration routes became the accepted wisdom in both popular imagination and the scientific literature.[1] They were said to breed 'in north-eastern Siberia and Alaska and, during the northern winter migrate through Japan, China, the Philippines, and the Malay Archipelago to . . . winter quarters in New Guinea, Australia, Tasmania and New Zealand'. This 1950s account then offers a tantalising glimpse of a quite different possibility, referring to 'evidence indicating that the main migration route . . . to and from New Zealand is further to the east than has hitherto been believed . . . that the route lies over the south-west Pacific well to the eastward of the Solomon Islands'.[2] The assumption was that a stop or stops would be needed along the way, as it would be quite impossible for a bird to make it in one flight.

The reference to Alaska is intriguing, but it was some years later before this was confirmed. A dead godwit found on Tauranga Harbour in October 1967 had been banded the previous year on St George in the Pribilof Islands, 9800 km to the north. Not only was this the first overseas recovery of a bar-tailed godwit banded in North America, it was also the first direct link between New Zealand and Alaska. It was another 23 years before the next link was established: a bird banded as an adult in 1990 on the Seward Peninsula, which returned to nest at the same location over at least two successive seasons. The same bird was seen at Miranda on the Firth of Thames in four out of five years between 1994 and 1998.[3]

By the 1990s there were still substantial gaps in our knowledge of these godwits. We knew they departed New Zealand each March and arrived in Alaska from early May, yet we knew little of the enormous gap between. While there were nuggets like the Pribilof record, evidence from banding data was still somewhat thin, perhaps not surprisingly given some of the odds involved. It was calculated, after six years of shorebird-banding in New Zealand, that 350 birds would need to be banded to get one band recovery from overseas. Even then it took two years for the news to reach banders in New Zealand that one of their red knots had been recovered in Russia. So relying on banding data alone

Who has seen the nest of kuaka? Birds of myth and mystery for Maori, godwits were in New Zealand during the season when all resident birds were breeding. However at the end of summer most of them assumed their bright breeding plumage, fattened up, and departed again without nesting. A male godwit nesting in western Alaska. KEITH WOODLEY

This male godwit was banded at Miranda as an adult in 2004. Sighting records since then show he usually does not depart New Zealand until late March, which indicates he is most likely breeding in northern Alaska. IAN SOUTHEY

Muddy business: a foraging godwit getting right down to it. ATHENA DRUMMOND

suggested that unfolding the story of what the godwits were doing was going to be a long haul indeed.

There were, however, other avenues of research underway. Much early investigation of bird migration focused on songbirds, birds of prey and waterfowl. Then, in the late 1980s and 1990s, came a period of intensive research into the physiology and biochemistry of shorebirds – much of it taking place in western Europe, especially the Netherlands. This work literally got down to the guts of what makes birds tick: their metabolism and energy needs; the biochemical and physical changes within them before and during migration; and the aerodynamics of endurance flight. This work heightened our awareness of what some of these long-distance migrants may be capable of. As we have seen with golden plovers, if we examine a bird's physiology and mass, its use of energy, and the aerodynamics of its flight, we can calculate its possible flight range. Researchers in Australia calculated great knots (*Calidris tenuirostris*) and godwits were capable of reaching the coast of China in one flight. Subsequent research on departure mass for godwits in both New Zealand and Alaska indicated their potential flight range was much longer than just Australia to China, and that a single trans-Pacific flight may indeed be within the capacity of bar-tailed godwits.

In 2003 Phil Battley began postdoctoral research on godwits and knots. A strategy of individually marking birds with colour bands had a number of purposes. Tracking individual birds over time can provide demographic information such as age structure of a population, survival rates and breeding success. A further component of his research, in association with OSNZ, was to track movements of birds within New Zealand: knowing something about which birds use which sites, and when, can be essential information for conservation management. One thing that emerged early from the project was evidence of remarkable site fidelity: one bird was seen and photographed at the same stopover site in South Korea during northward migration in four consecutive years – each time between 13 and 15 April.[4] Then there is the astounding story of a bird colour-banded on the Firth of Thames in March 2004 and recorded in northern China, Alaska, and back in New Zealand eight months later, after a migration of at least 29,000 km. Not only was this further evidence for the predicted migration pattern of the *baueri* godwits, it strengthened the case that Alaskan biologist Bob Gill had been compiling. That birds were becoming immensely fat before departing Alaska triggered Gill to investigate further. Could it be these birds were preparing for a single flight to New Zealand? Looking at a range of evidence, including predicted flight ranges, weather data in relation to flight departures, and the historical pattern of godwit sightings throughout the Pacific, Gill concluded a nonstop migration route was indeed possible.[5] However, compelling though his case was, it remained largely circumstantial . . . until satellite technology entered the story.

In 2007 and 2008, 12 godwits fitted with implanted satellite tags departed New Zealand between 15 March and 2 April, and were tracked to the Yellow Sea – an average distance of 10,000 km nonstop. After a refuelling stopover of five to six weeks, the birds moved on to Alaska, most departing during the first three weeks of May. They were tracked across the Korean peninsula and Japan and out into the North Pacific before turning north to the breeding grounds – an average distance of 6770 km, completed in around four and half days. However one bird added substantially to this when it struck a low-pressure zone and associated headwinds in the northwest Pacific. About 450 km from the Alaskan coast it turned and flew 1300 km west to Russia, where it remained for eight days before resuming its migration to Alaska. By the time it arrived, it had flown 8910 km since leaving the Yellow Sea in just over seven days' flying time.[6]

Between 11 June and 17 July all birds with functioning transmitters were recorded moving to the Kuskokwim Shoals on the southern coast of the Yukon–Kuskokwim Delta (YKD) – a traditional pre-migration staging site for godwits. Power levels in the transmitter battery of one female, E7, were extremely low by 30 August 2007, and reporting was expected to cease at any time. Somehow the device kept going as she took off from Cape Avinof that day; and it continued to do so during her flight into the record books – and not a little media attention. For when she landed at the mouth of the Piako River in the Firth of Thames on 7 September, she had completed the 11,680-km nonstop flight in just over eight days. It was a feat of stamina and endurance unknown in any other non-seabirds. Indeed it was a world record, eclipsing the previous record set by the same bird during her 10,215 km flight to the Yellow Sea in March. And this record flight 'is by no means the longest flight expected', say researchers. About 25–30,000 godwits winter up to 1000 km further south than E7, and a godwit tagged in Alaska and recorded in

One of the godwits fitted with satellite transmitters, showing the trailing antenna and part of the flag attached to the upper leg of the bird. ATHENA DRUMMOND

Confounding bird: the black leg-flag coded D0 indicates this godwit was fitted with a satellite transmitter in February 2008 at Miranda. Its size and measurements suggested it was a male, but it subsequently turned out to be a small female – one of the smallest birds to have a transmitter surgically implanted. Not only did she survive, she was tracked to breeding grounds on the north slope of Alaska, 1000 km north of where E7 landed in 2007. In October 2008 she was retrapped at Miranda and had her antenna removed. IAN SOUTHEY

Departure terminal: godwits at Cape Avinof, Alaska, the major staging site for godwits bound for New Zealand. JAN VAN DE KAM

Australia after transmitter failure is likely to have flown over 12,200 km.[7]

For many biologists these results were astounding: 'When coupled with the extraordinarily high metabolic rates of prolonged exercise of these long distance movements, some migrants are truly performing at the upper limits of what is known for vertebrates.'[8] Migration is clearly a rigorous task, and not all those that set out will survive – though countless birds do, either by way of a direct flight or by stopping at some refuge short of the final destination. Satellite tracking confirmed this: towards the last section of their migrations, some birds drop out. One bird tracked via a geolocator appears to have made a short stop, probably in New Caledonia, before continuing to New Zealand. Another bird, E5, stopped in New Caledonia at the end of September 2007 for an unknown period before being recorded on the coast of New South Wales in mid December. She did not return to the Firth of Thames – her original destination – until February 2008. Other New Zealand banded birds have been recorded in eastern Australia during southward migration.

Such diversions are believed to be adaptive responses to adverse weather conditions encountered en route. Weather data from the track of E5 showed she encountered unavoidable headwinds for several days north of Hawaii – presumably at the cost of time and energy – before experiencing favourable conditions until just north of Fiji, when a major southeasterly system across her path meant headwinds for the final 1800 km to New Zealand. For southbound birds, Fiji is the last resort; around 1000–1250 km to the west are New Caledonia and Vanuatu, with Australia only 1200–1500 km beyond that; 'so islands such as these may provide an alternative route when conditions do not favour a non-stop flight to New Zealand'. This also correlates with historical godwit records from the Pacific that showed a marked increase in sightings further south in the migration track, particularly in September and October. Of course this is a persuasive interpretation of the tracking data; what is not known is whether 'visiting Australia is part of the regular migration strategy for some individuals'.[9]

SAME SPECIES – DIFFERENT SCHEDULES

Satellite telemetry was also used to track birds from the *menzbieri* population that winters mainly in northwestern Australia, and when the data was compared with the *baueri* population some intriguing results emerged.

Birds generally departed from Roebuck Bay three weeks later than *baueri* birds leaving New Zealand, but they too stopped in the Yellow Sea region after an average four-day flight of around 5860 km. After five to six weeks they then flew an average of 4170 km in two and a half days to breeding sites across 800 km of eastern Siberia, from northern Yakutia to northwest Chukotka.

On southbound migration these godwits then did something different: they stopped in the Yellow Sea for around 40 days before completing southward migration. Some birds then flew nonstop back to Roebuck Bay – 6100 km in just over four and a half days. *Baueri* depart earlier than *menzbieri* on northward migration and return later; indeed, some birds have arrived back in Australia by late August, before *baueri* birds begin leaving Alaska. Not only do the Alaskan birds travel further, 'the total distance to the breeding grounds for *menzbieri* is about the same as the length of just the first flight of *baueri*, from New Zealand to Asia'.[11]

Why, then, does one population stop during southward migration and the other not? Given similarities in morphology and flight speeds, and the fact that the flight distances on southward migration are similar, the answer is not clear. One suggestion is that the obviously extremely rich staging habitat available to birds on the southern YKD – sufficient to allow them to store fuel for a journey in excess of 11,000 km – is not available to the Russian birds. It is thought that, as fuelling rates on the tundra are likely to be lower than on tidal flats, a stopover further south may be required.

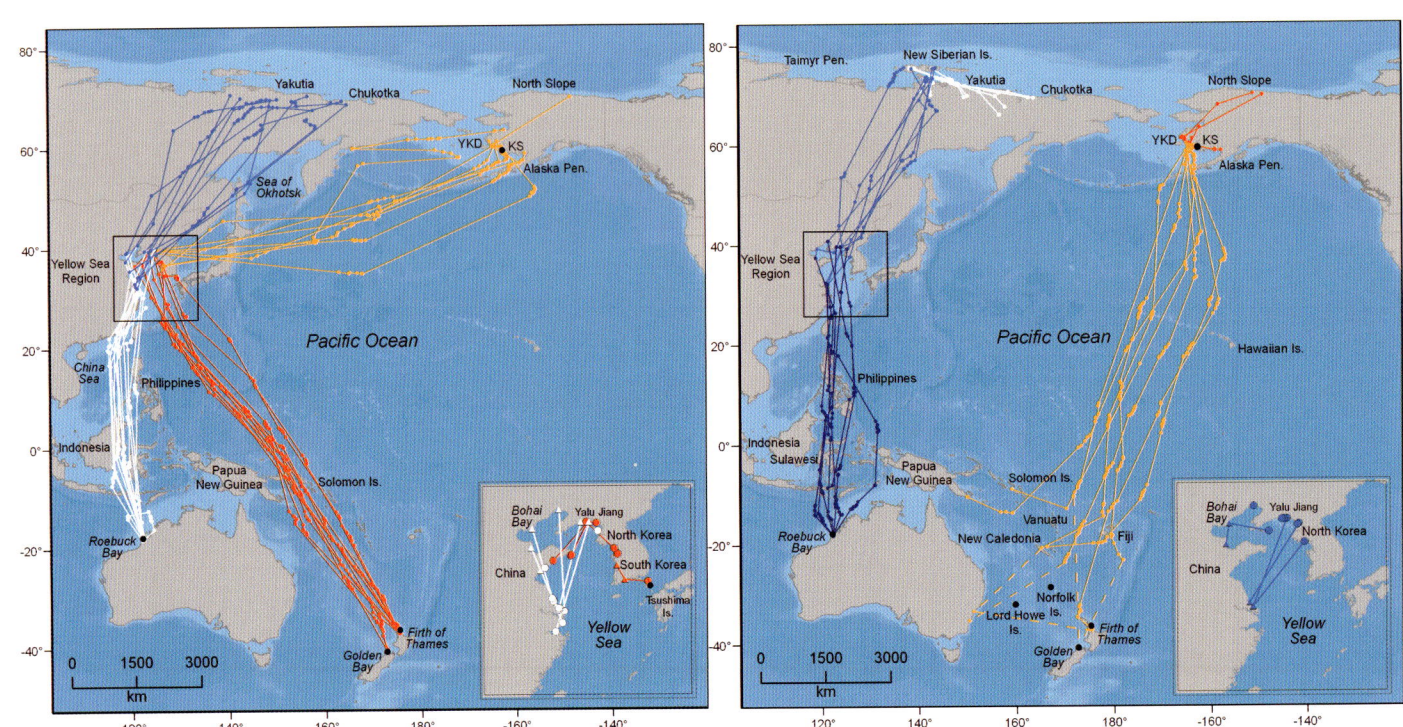

Tracks of godwits during northbound migration. Blue and white represent the menzbieri population, and orange and yellow the baueri population. US GEOLOGICAL SURVEY

Tracks of godwits during southbound migration, showing the marked divergence in migration strategy of the two populations. Dotted lines represent birds for which signals were lost, but for which there were subsequent sightings. US GEOLOGICAL SURVEY

GREAT UNKNOWNS – ORIGINS OF MIGRATION ROUTES

Wind is a critical factor in bird migration strategies: in theory, the longer the distance to travel, the more wind assistance would be desirable. The southward track of E5 in 2007 was an indication that, when confronted with unavoidable adverse winds, birds may have a Plan B – in her case, changing course and using following winds to reach New Caledonia. Of course such a plan only really works at a later stage of the journey; further north over the Central Pacific, alternative options are somewhat fewer. There is considerable evidence that these migration strategies may be adaptive; that they evolved to suit predictable climate patterns. Godwits flying from the Yellow Sea to Alaska 'in spring cross one of the most atmospherically dynamic regions on Earth, where intense and frequent storms develop and track east across the North Pacific'.[12] From late August the same phenomenon generates a succession of regular cyclonic systems and associated winds which, for godwits preparing to head south, offer good assistance opportunities every few days.

In the absence of solid data, any account of how a particular migration strategy evolved is necessarily speculative. Bird migration patterns have been a continually evolving process over millions of years. Godwit migration patterns as they exist today may date back no further than the last ice age – some 10–15,000 years ago. Or they could have existed longer than that, but have had to respond to the various glacial–interglacial periods along the way. If the current migration strategies of the *baueri* population *are* strongly dependent on favourable wind patterns, did they evolve in response to palaeo-climatic shifts in storm tracks across the Pacific? Or did they evolve in response to changes in the distribution of available intertidal habitat? If that were the case the use of suitable wind patterns may have then been selected for, as a means to an end. Did there once exist areas of suitable habitat in the Pacific that were then submerged by rising sea levels? Given ocean depths throughout much of the central region, this seems unlikely.

What does seem likely is that ancestors of these birds once migrated down the Asian coastline and then to Australia; and perhaps suitable areas once existed along the way, around the Philippines archipelago, say, or around Papua New Guinea and western Melanesia. Birds in these areas would be only 8000 km from their breeding grounds – a distance well within the range of many shorebirds. If such areas subsequently disappeared, more birds would need to have dispersed elsewhere, such as to Australia and New Zealand. In this scenario, birds may have successively fanned out in a southeasterly arc, with New Zealand as the extreme boundary of their range.[13] Perhaps the nonstop trans-Pacific route evolved through 'progressive corner cutting', involving longer and longer nonstop over-water flights.

> *Steps in the evolution of long distance barrier crossing can be inferred from existing patterns of variation. They would allow gradual development of a long-distance migration system over hostile substrate, without the need for a sudden step-change in either direction or migratory fattening. This makes it easier to understand how such long and difficult migrations might have evolved, but it does not of course prove that they did evolve in this way.*[14]

It has also been suggested that what we see as an immense ocean barrier, godwits see as an avenue of opportunity. Migration is a hazardous business, so any risk minimisation strategy could be selected for; and in flying nonstop across the Pacific a godwit certainly reduces the time spent actually migrating. A further advantage is that there are few predators along the way. The route also reduces exposure to parasites and pathogens, perhaps allowing the bird to divert energy from its immune system.[15]

Bar-tailed godwit.
IAN SOUTHEY

Evidence that birds can live side by side with us, if given appropriate space and habitat: a roadside roost of godwits at Miranda. BRIAN CHUDLEIGH

One outcome of the satellite telemetry project is that it is now possible to do time-and-motion studies of these birds. The migration speed for E7 is the total time she spent on migration; that is, from the time she began initial fuelling for the journey – assumed to be 1 January for the purpose of the study – to the time she arrived back in New Zealand, a total of 249 days, during which she was tracked for 174 days. Of her time away from New Zealand, over 11 percent was spent on major flights; over 47 percent at staging sites; and only 40 percent on the breeding grounds. Of all the birds tracked, 60–80 percent of the total time away from the nonbreeding grounds was spent in migration rather than breeding.[16] According to recent research, this extraordinary annual cycle requiring massive nonstop flights is also tied to a rather rigid schedule of departures.

The stellar performances revealed to us by a few individual godwits such as E7 enthral us; however, the biologists' mantra is: it is the population, not the individual, that is important. As it happens, at the Manawatu Estuary there is a small population of godwits – between 200 and 280 birds – that now also have a prominent position in the history of long-distance migration studies. The advantages of these birds for the purposes of study are: there are not too many of them, though enough to be scientifically useful; they occupy a relatively small site that can be regularly monitored; and, like all godwits, they exhibit strong site fidelity. A further advantage is that 25 percent of the Manawatu godwits are colour-banded, and some also have geolocators. For the three migration periods of 2008–2010, using direct observation and digital photography, Jesse Conklin monitored the exact time and date of departure of individual godwits. The exact day of departure was known for 84 percent of marked birds; and to within a day for the remaining 16 percent. Calculating the mean departure date (MDD) for each bird, he found an astonishing degree of consistency. Most individuals departed within a one-week period each year, confirming that 'the bird making the longest known non-stop flights also has the most rigid migration departure schedules yet reported'.[17]

Generally favourable conditions were experienced over most of the study period, so weather rarely presented an obstacle to departure. In each year the first major peak in departures occurred during 10–15 March, a period when no headwinds or heavy rain occurred during the entire study. Seven birds used the 'departure window' each year, including one bird that departed on 13 March in all three years. In 2008 and 2009, a second departure peak occurred between 21 and 24 March, during which about 40 percent of the population departed. In 2010 however, there were sustained headwinds and rain during this period, and eight consecutive days without departures. Yet immediately prior to this, on 17 March, 37 percent of the migratory population departed. In these departing flocks were 'on-schedule' birds as well as five godwits leaving 4–10 days earlier than their MDD. Not only did these birds avoid the potential delay over the next eight days, they experienced better conditions than any that were available during their expected departure windows. This clearly suggests birds anticipated sustained poor conditions, and avoided those by departing on the last favourable day before a dramatic change in weather. Interestingly, winds on 17 March were also among the most favourable for the whole study, and conditions north of New Zealand 'suggested significant wind assistance along the migratory path for perhaps 2–3 days after departure'. So a bird that is yet to achieve a full fuel load, 'may be "promoted" to readiness by favourable winds, because wind assistance effectively decreases the fuel load required for the flight'.[18] In other words, an unusually easy flight may trump the costs of an early departure.

It would seem, then, that godwits have a fixed 'departure window' that is governed by overall migration speed and the need to arrive in good time on distant breeding grounds. Departure times for individual birds were remarkably consistent from year to year, and yet they were able to tolerate delays of 3–4 days or, in the case of prolonged periods of bad weather, even longer periods. So each individual has an optimal departure schedule that is flexible enough to respond to unpredictable circumstances.

In a further component of his study, Conklin established that the time a bird left New Zealand was exactly correlated to its eventual destination on the breeding grounds, which extend over 1000 km of latitude. Among colour-banded individuals of both sexes, larger birds departed earlier than smaller birds; and birds that left later were travelling further north than those that left earlier. Data from live captures, field photography, museum specimens, and individuals tracked from New Zealand, revealed a north–south cline, or gradient, in body size in Alaska, in which the smallest individuals of each sex occurred at the highest latitudes. There was also a cline in breeding plumage, with the brightest males occurring further north. That birds at higher latitudes had shorter bills is consistent with Allen's rule: that body or surface area is minimised in colder climates. Bird bills can be a big source of heat loss, so longer bills will be a disadvantage at higher latitudes. It is possible that habitat differences at different latitudes are a factor as well. Paler, more patchy body plumage among birds on the YKD is known to be more cryptic for both incubating and non-incubating birds, providing very effective camouflage. However, in northern Alaska the brighter breeding plumage of males – a striking red neck and breast – is very conspicuous: it draws attention to them, and often away from their more cryptic mates. It is suggested there may be a trade-off between being cryptic and quickly attracting a mate. For instance, competition for mates may be more intense in the north; or the brevity of the northern breeding season may require rapid mate acquisition.[19] However if size and plumage and time of departure are correlated with specific regions within the breeding range, the same does not apply in New Zealand, where birds from all over Alaska may be found distributed throughout the country. Godwits up to two years old are known to wander New Zealand and eastern Australia before settling on specific sites. Once they have done so, they then remain extremely faithful to that site as adults.

Through the work of the likes of Gill, Battley and Conklin, along with colleagues around the world, the *baueri* population of godwits has gone, in less than a decade, from one of the least known to the best known, in some respects, of any long-distance migratory shorebirds. Also revealed has been a consistent tendency to underestimate the capabilities of these birds. The trans-Pacific flight represents extreme endurance unknown elsewhere in the animal kingdom; and this suggests godwits may be flying at the edge of their limits. However, concluded Conklin, 'the maintenance of rigorous schedules and high survival rate (over 90 percent individual return rate in this study) do not suggest a bird near the edge of its capabilities'.[20] How many more surprises do these birds hold for us?

LONG-HAUL CHAMPIONS – CHALLENGERS ON THE WING

Compared with many tundra shorebirds, sharp-tailed sandpipers (Calidris acuminata) have a fairly restricted breeding range – if 40 degrees of longitude can be described thus! In the Russian High Arctic they breed from the Lena Delta across to the Chaun Gulf, east of the Kolyma Delta; after which the bulk of the population migrates to Australia, with a few dozen reaching New Zealand. There is something about the juveniles, however, that began raising eyebrows among Alaskan biologists. After breeding, adult birds migrate south along the east coast of Asia, which makes perfect sense if Australia is the destination. However, several thousand juvenile birds were being recorded in Alaska through September, representing a detour of 1500–3400 km from the most direct route taken by adults. It also represents a striking exception to the general rule that adult and juvenile Arctic shorebirds follow the same migration route.[21] Why would juvenile sharp-tailed sandpipers make this long detour? In evolutionary terms there seem to be obvious objections to doing so. It would not only use more time and energy, but could pose navigational challenges for a bird flying on a west–east axis. It is suggested, for instance, that the complex pattern of magnetic fields in the Bering Sea region may reduce the effectiveness of its magnetic compass. In addition, the time shifts associated with rapid longitudinal displacement at such high latitudes complicate the use of its sun compass. It is predicted, therefore, that evolution would select against such a potentially complicated flight route. Moreover, experience from this first journey would be of no use to the sandpipers later in life, 'unlike birds that follow the same route all their lives'.[22]

If, however, fuel deposition rates at the detour site are high enough to outweigh the costs of a longer flight, then it would start to make sense. A study of over 300 juvenile sharp-tails on the YKD in September 2004 and 2005 found they were getting immensely fat. Fuel deposition rates were calculated to be about 6 percent per day, among the highest recorded for a migratory shorebird of that size. By the time birds left the area at the end of September, some were carrying fuel loads close to 100 percent of lean body mass. Further calculations suggest this is sufficient fuel for a nonstop flight of between 7100 and 9800 km, 'presumably including a trans-oceanic flight to the southern hemisphere'.[23]

It is suggested that juvenile sharp-tailed sandpipers 'most likely have the capacity to fly nonstop from Alaska to Australia, but firm evidence for such long flights is still needed'. However a comparison of aspect ratio – the shape and surface area of wings – with bar-tailed godwits, a known long-haul migrant, supports this suggestion. Long narrow wings allow energy-efficient flight; and in this, sharp-tailed sandpipers are in a similar league to godwits.[24] Indeed they may possibly be even more efficient. The costs associated with flapping flight differ among species in a predictable allometric relationship. According to this theory it is more costly for a large shorebird carrying maximum fuel load to undertake migration, compared with a small species. Therefore the maximum flight range of a small species is greater than the larger bird's, because flight is more energetically demanding of a large bird with a big load.[25]

Godwit formation. ATHENA DRUMMOND

Newly arrived sharp-tailed sandpiper, Miranda. IAN SOUTHEY

Flocking during the nonbreeding season – a characteristic of many shorebirds – is particularly pronounced in species such as the red knot. IAN SOUTHEY

CHAPTER FIFTEEN
SPECIALISATION BLUES: THE TROUBLED FUTURE OF KNOTS

Most of the world's surface is useless to a shorebird – too wet, too dry, too forested, too mountainous, too farmed, too urban, too this, too that. Much of the wetland habitat on which many species depend has been lost. So the relatively few places that still suit the birds' needs are important beyond measure.
—Scott Weidensaul[1]

At first glance there is nothing glamorous about it – a dumpy, nondescript grey bird busily probing where the tide meets the mud. When it is seen among its immediate neighbours, this impression strengthens: there is no spectacularly long bill like the godwit's, or dramatically curved one like the whimbrel's. The crisp contrast between black and white plumage in the stilts and oystercatchers is absent, too. Nor is there anything of bright colour – no slash of orange like an oystercatcher bill; and the dark grey legs are far removed from, say, the pink legs of a stilt or the vivid orange of a turnstone. The grey plumage itself is subdued, unlike the scalloped appearance of the sharp-tailed sandpiper foraging a few metres away – its upper plumage a pageant of chestnut and black, each feather edged with cream. Yet this drab creature is not all that it seems. For one thing it makes some of the most spectacular journeys of any migratory bird. There is also its annual metamorphosis, when from this modest chrysalis there emerges one of the most beautiful of all waders.

Metamorphosis: compare the drab plumage of these foraging knots in September (bottom left), with the birds (top and top right) seen in late February when they are well advanced in their pre-breeding moult – one of the essential preparations for imminent migration. IAN SOUTHEY
A flock of knots descending to roost on the Stilt Ponds at Miranda (bottom right). BRIAN CHUDLEIGH

This red knot *Calidris canutus* is part of a clan that is circumpolar in its breeding range and truly global in its migrations. It breeds as far north as it can go – on the very edge of the land, just 800 km from the North Pole; and it winters from New Zealand and South Africa to Tierra del Fuego, 3000 km from the South Pole.[2] There are few other creatures as widely dispersed as these, but they are among the most specialised of all shorebirds. The preferred prey of knots outside the breeding grounds are thin-shelled, shallow-buried bivalves that are swallowed whole, and then crushed in the bird's particularly large and powerful gizzard. The bill tips in many shorebird species contain sensory organs used to detect prey buried in the substrate – a feature that is particularly highly developed in knots. Rapid vertical probing by the bill pushes water remaining in the sediment to form pressure contours that, upon striking a buried shellfish, cause deviations detectable by the bill. Dependence on a particular food source can pose a problem, however, because such food may only be found in the required quantities in a few places. So while they may be flung to the far corners of the earth, over vast tracts of land and sea, at critical intervals during their migrations they are pushed together in huge, dense flocks at only a handful of suitable locations on the entire planet. Their ecology determines this – at the

A tight carpet of roosting knots sprinkled with godwits. In the background are more knots, with a few wrybill and turnstones. IAN SOUTHEY

same time making them dangerously vulnerable.

It is in the nature of knots outside the breeding grounds, then, that wherever they appear they are usually in some numbers. This, together with their dark flesh and fattiness – a feature of long-distant migrants – no doubt explains the long European tradition of knots as table fare. 'They are valued for the table, and as they occur with us in considerable numbers, are sold pretty extensively in the markets.'[3] For Dutch researcher Theunis Piersma – one of the world's leading authorities on shorebirds, and for whom the knot has been a major study species – there is irony in a reference to a practice from the sixteenth century. 'There are even records . . . of knots held in captivity and fattened for the table on a diet of grain – a curious parallel with the migration and energetic studies on captive knots now being made.'[4] It is even suggested that its culinary qualities appealed to the Danish King Canute, from whence come both its common and scientific names. However, other suggestions hold that it is their Canute-like behaviour – standing on the edge of the waves – that gives them their name. For others the name derives from their '*cnut*' calls.[5] Whatever the reason – and no one is entirely sure – in the English-speaking world they are known by what must be one of the most prosaic names for any bird.

Separate knot populations are distributed across the High Arctic, the nominate subspecies nesting on the northern Taymyr Peninsula of central Russia. Further west are *Calidris canutus islandica*, breeding on the islands of the High Canadian Arctic and northern Greenland; *C. c. rufa* further south in the Canadian Arctic; and *C. c. roselaari* in northern Alaska and on Wrangel Island. South of Wrangel on the Chukchi Peninsula is where we find the New Zealand and Australian knots – *C. c. rogersi* and *C. c. piersmai*. Genetic evidence indicates knots diverged from ancestral stock approximately 5–6 million years ago, making their lineage one of the oldest among the sandpipers.[6] But DNA also turned up another surprise about knots: despite their venerable lineage and enormous geographical distribution, they have very little genetic diversity.[7] The lack of genetic variation within each subspecies shows that all these birds are descended from one breeding population, which recently went through a demographic bottleneck. That is, the numbers of birds breeding successfully became so low that much genetic variation in their mitochondrial DNA was lost. 'For red knots this bottleneck occurred around 10,000 years ago and during this time only a few hundred female knots remained.'[8] Conditions during the climatic optimum of the current Holocene caused knots to find themselves in a tight spot. As forests expanded, with the treeline in Siberia advancing 300–400 km north of the boundary today, tundra-breeding habitat decreased.[9] This may have also led to the separation of the *piersmai* and *rogersi* populations – the former breeding on the New Siberian Islands, the latter in Chukotka.

Red knots are the second most common tundra-breeding shorebird in New Zealand: around 30,000 are present here each year, most of which are thought to be from the *rogersi* population. Most *piersmai* birds winter in northern Australia although there is overlap between the two populations, and *piersmai* birds are known to occur in New Zealand as well.[10] Beyond that, remarkably little was known about either the population status or migration strategies of each subspecies until very recently. The last official estimate was a combined population of 220,000 red knots within the East Asian–Australasian Flyway.[11] This figure, based on data up to 30 years old, is now known to be grossly in error. Part of the problem was no one knew where knots were staging during migration. It was assumed that many, if not all, would be using the Yellow Sea; and given the nature of red knot habitat requirements, if they occur at a site they will most likely be there in big numbers. Prior to the late 1990s no large numbers of knots had ever been recorded in the region – until Australian researcher Mark Barter found over 14,000 near Tianjin in the Bohai Sea. Yet once all available data from counts around the Yellow Sea was compiled and assessed, only 66,300, or 30 percent of the supposed population, could be accounted for.

The riddle was partly solved during a survey in 2009 when nearly 40,000, or about 18 percent of the supposed population, were counted at another, previously unknown site in Bohai Bay. Daily counts during the migration season, along with estimates of birds from each population – based on plumage differences and records of banded or flagged birds, together with count and banding data from Australia and New Zealand – allowed researchers to roughly estimate the size of each population. They suggest the world population of *piersmai* is likely to be between 48,000 and 60,000 birds; and that of *rogersi* between 50,000 and 62,000.[12] So the revised estimate of the flyway population is now around 105,000 knots – in which case the 2009 Bohai count represents 38 percent of the population. However, when the estimated number of first-year birds – those not old enough to migrate north and so presumably still in New Zealand and Australia – was taken from the equation, the population estimate stood at just over 87,000 adults, 45 percent of which were staging along a 20-km section of the Chinese coast.[11]

In a study funded by the Global Flyway Network, Australian-based researchers Chris Hassell and Adrian Boyle joined with Chinese colleagues in monitoring the knot migration through the Bohai site. The first migrants were counted in early April, with numbers building up steadily to peak at around 36,000 in early May. Numbers then remained high until late May before declining rapidly, with only 26 birds counted on 2 June. The proportion of birds identified as *piersmai* increased steadily from late April throughout May as the proportion of *rogersi* declined until, by the end of the

Distinctive plumage differences are an indication that these birds are from separate breeding populations – rogersi from Chukotka (left) and piersmai from northern Siberia (right). IAN SOUTHEY

Orange and yellow flags indicate this bird passed through South Australia on its way to New Zealand. Banding data indicate that most juvenile knots migrate to south eastern Australia in their first year, before many come across the Tasman. Once established in New Zealand however, they do not return to southern Australia during subsequent migrations. IAN SOUTHEY

A mixed roost of knots, godwits and wrybill. The degree of breeding plumage in knots may vary among individuals and over time, with some birds more advanced in their moult than others. IAN SOUTHEY

study period, only *piersmai* remained. The *rogersi* birds not only arrived earlier, they stayed longer, averaging a month; *piersmai* averaged three weeks, with some birds staying less than 14 days. The arrival dates for *piersmai* birds corresponded closely with known departure dates from northwestern Australia, suggesting a direct flight to the Bohai Sea; while similar data for *rogersi* showed they arrived much later than observed departure times from New Zealand would suggest, meaning they were likely using an unknown staging area or areas elsewhere, before arrival in Bohai Bay.[13]

This variation may relate to differences in breeding range, with *rogersi* occurring over a more extensive area. Or it could be to do with conditions encountered en route and at the destination. *Piersmai* need to make a long overland flight before reaching the shores of the eastern Siberian Sea, which are still frozen in late May and early June. Perhaps their departure schedule is more rigid, so that they can time their arrival on the breeding grounds as close to the beginning of the thaw as possible. In contrast, the likely route from Bohai Bay to Chukotka is parallel to the northwestern shores of the Sea of Okhotsk, where satellite images suggest there are ice-free areas by late May: if *rogersi* birds encounter adverse wind conditions or heavy snow cover, there are numerous estuaries, tidal flats and coastal lagoons for stopovers if needed.[14]

The annual cycle of knots is a story of living on the edge and being totally dependent on a handful of suitable locations. Their High Arctic breeding grounds are as far north as any other shorebird, on terrain where vegetation cover is seldom more than 25 percent, and where conditions can be harsh – even during summer. Most nests have been found on elevated tundra, often on windswept ridges. Nests in Siberia usually occur 'within 30 km of the Arctic coast in gently sloped, hilly or low mountain landscapes where moss tundra and marshes of sedge grass are present at middle and lower parts of the slopes'.[15] Birds often arrive on the breeding grounds before the snow has cleared, and before insects and other invertebrate prey are available to them. And once again this bivalve-eating specialist has a surprise for us; for, like other species such as turnstones, for a brief time some knots become vegetarians. A study in the Canadian Arctic found newly arrived birds at the beginning of June were taking grass shoots, seeds and other vegetable matter. When the stomach contents of birds were examined later in the season, insects had become part of the diet, along with some seeds and marine invertebrates.[16] A later study also found mostly vegetable matter in stomachs early in the season, with increasing volumes of insects as the season advanced, but never exclusively insect contents.[17] Such a diet initially may not be sufficient in itself for a bird that needs to switch into breeding mode almost immediately after arrival, so the surplus energy stores that birds carry from their last stopover assume critical importance.

Successful migration for knots hinges, then, on those few-and-far-between stopover sites. One such place is Delaware Bay on the east coast of the United States, where the *rufa* population migrating north from Tierra del Fuego stops over en route to the Canadian Arctic. Other knot populations that stop over during migration on the Dutch Wadden Sea and at Bohai Bay appear to be true to form – feasting on great quantities of tiny bivalves – whereas *rufa* are something of an anomaly. Each May during spring tides, hordes of horseshoe crabs, which are singularly intriguing creatures distantly related to spiders, come ashore to spawn. These ancient animals, over 300 million years old, have become an essential factor in the migration of knots along the East Atlantic flyway. As the crabs deposit their eggs – billions of them, laid in dense masses along the beach – knots and other shorebirds are already gathering. Many more are in transit, in the air somewhere between there and Brazil. Unlike bivalves – the normal food for knots away from the breeding grounds – horseshoe crab eggs are easily digested and metabolised into fat and protein. One study estimated that 95,530 knots stopping at Delaware Bay during spring would consume 226.1 tonnes of horseshoe crab eggs and gain 5.2 tonnes of fat; during the stopover, an average individual would consume 1052 g of eggs and would gain 54 g. Mass gains in birds at Delaware Bay are among the highest recorded in knots; they need to make only a 10–14 day stopover, compared with 21–28 days in other parts of the world.[18] What this also means, of course, is there may now be no other place in the flyway suitable for them as a stopover site. It is this place or nowhere. So if there are massive problems at this site, what are the implications for the population?

In the 1990s local fishermen began harvesting horseshoe crabs as bait, and by 1997 up to two million were being taken annually. Inevitably there was a dramatic decrease in spawning crabs, and thus less food for knots – followed by a steep decline in bird numbers. Peak counts of knots between 2002 and 2007 averaged 66 percent less than counts between 1998 and 2002.[19] Weights of birds arriving at Delaware Bay average 90–120 g, and by the time they leave they should be 180 g or more. If a bird cannot reach this weight, it is vulnerable to starvation or freezing once it arrives in the Arctic. An analysis of departure weights of departing birds and subsequent survival rates revealed some disturbing trends. 'From May 2000 to May 2001, 37 percent fewer adults survived than in previous years, and the number of immature birds in wintering flocks declined by 47 percent.' Departure weights were clearly significant: birds seen alive in later years were heavier when they arrived in the bay than birds that were never seen again. From 2000 to 2002, the population size in Tierra del Fuego, the largest and most important wintering site, declined alarmingly from 53,000 to 27,000. Biologists were clear about the reason: 'There can be no doubt that the Delaware Bay food supply has played a critical role in rufa's decline.'[20] 'Based on the low annual survival rate and the poor production of young in the Arctic,' writes researcher Alan Baker, 'we built a demographic model and predicted that if this decline continued apace, the subspecies could approach extinction in as little as 10 years.'[21] By 2008, that outcome seemed ominously closer as the population had tumbled further, to just 14,800 – an overall decline of 78 percent, 'the most precipitous population decline witnessed in the history of avian conservation'.[22]

Biologists came up with a rescue plan that hinged on stringent protection measures for horseshoe crabs. The crab population at Delaware Bay needed to be restored to pre-1997 levels to allow at least 80 percent of knots to reach sufficient departure weights. A total crab-harvesting ban for five years, or at the very least a sharply decreased harvest, was essential to achieve this. 'As well, adult survival among the red knots has to be increased to the normal level of about 85 percent or more, and production of young has to be at least 20 percent, as it was in the past, so that the breeding population can expand.'[23]

If red knots are such specialist bivalve feeders, why are they so dependent at this one site on horseshoe crab eggs – which seem a long way removed from their normal hard-shelled prey? It may be that the present-day concentration of knots at Delaware Bay is a comparatively recent phenomenon; just as the overharvesting of horseshoe crab eggs is recent. It is quite likely that knots have traditionally used horeshoe crab eggs along with a variety of other food as well, such as mussels (which they still take on the coast of Virginia). It is suggested that depletion of other marine resources through overfishing on the eastern coast of the US has, over the last 100 years or so, pushed more and more birds into Delaware Bay seeking sustenance. Subsequent overharvesting of horseshoe crabs merely exacerbated an already growing problem for knots.[24]

A world away, in New Zealand, suitable areas of habitat for knots are also limited. Their preference for swallowing whole bivalves places an upper limit on the size of prey a knot can swallow. There is also a lower limit beyond which prey becomes unprofitable. Even

An essential feature of a knot's annual cycle is to get immensely fat prior to a long migration flight. This bird, seen on the Manukau Harbour in late March, is in full breeding plumage and may have departed within days or even hours of this photograph being taken. IAN SOUTHEY

though most intertidal areas are rich and diverse in the benthic life they support, suitable food for knots does not occur everywhere, though where it does occur, you may find lots of knots. January count data from Chile shows a high proportion of the *rufa* population spends the northern winter concentrated in a single bay, Bahía Lomas, near the eastern end of Strait of Magellan.[25] The pattern in New Zealand is similar, if not so clearcut. Unlike godwits, which can occur on almost any harbour or estuary in the country, knots seldom show up in big numbers anywhere except a few sites, such as the southern Manukau Harbour. Between 1983 and 1994 the average count for red knots in New Zealand was 51,000; by 2003 this had fallen to just under 42,000 – a decline of 14 percent. In 2006 the number had fallen further, to below 30,000.[26]

The bulk of the New Zealand summer population tends to be concentrated around Auckland, Northland and the Nelson bays; but the significance of one site in particular increases dramatically for the wintering population. An average of 78 percent, though as many as 94 percent of winter knots may be found on the Manukau Harbour. Between 1983 and 1994, the Manukau average for wintering birds was only 66 percent – so the importance of the site has increased. 'These wintering birds are hugely important for the overall population because they are mainly pre-breeding birds; they are, should they survive, the next wave of recruits into the breeding population.'[27] Which makes the Manukau Harbour an essential site for red knots in the flyway. However, the decline in knot numbers in New Zealand may be only slightly related to conditions in this part of the world; while it cannot be ruled out entirely, the answer more likely lies a few thousand kilometres further to the north. There, as we shall see in a later chapter, a potential catastrophe for knots is quickly unfolding.

A flock of knots over the Manukau Harbour shows the typical shape of long-distance migratory shorebirds – most notably, the long pointed wings. IAN SOUTHEY

Winter evening, Rakaia. JOHN DOWDING

PART II: TROUBLED FUTURES

Knots and godwits: outside the breeding season many shorebirds are rather sociable, and massed flocks are a common sight on harbours and estuaries around the country. IAN SOUTHEY

CHAPTER SIXTEEN
WINNERS AND LOSERS: HOW ARE OUR SHOREBIRDS DOING?

It is gratifying to be able to record that [the banded dotterel] appears to be one of the more fortunate species that is not much disturbed by settlement; of late it has been observed to breed on farms, in some instances in the immediate neighbourhood of homesteads . . . It is pleasing to be able to place on record that it seems disposed to accept the situation of settlement rather than submit to banishment or extermination. — T.H. Potts[1]

The birds are huddled into the cool sou'wester. Their location determines our position – and the need for our spotting scopes to be beam on to the wind. Tightly massed like this, they are not easy to count, even without the added distraction of a shaking scope. Nevertheless a reasonably accurate count of the flock of mainly godwits is achieved, just before a further problem arrives in the shape of a rain squall; counting large numbers of birds can be difficult enough, without the added complexity of rain on optical lenses. These conditions are not untypical of a June wader census – a regular fixture on the calendar of many dedicated volunteers. Today's count is part of an ongoing project that is essential if we are to monitor the wellbeing of our shorebird populations.

At the core of wildlife biology is the concept of population: an individual bird is interesting, but only knowledge of the population will reveal its relative health or otherwise. How many of these birds are there? How are they distributed throughout their habitat? Which are the sites supporting the biggest concentrations of birds? What are the population

A carpet of knots, densely packed together like these flocks on the southern Manukau Harbour, presents a challenge for the shorebird census taker.
IAN SOUTHEY

trends at each of those sites? What are the overall trends within the entire population – are they increasing or decreasing or is the population stable? Difficult though it may be, the only way to gather some of this information is to count birds. During the breeding season they are dispersed everywhere – over broad riverbeds or farm paddocks, or in wetlands; and on the northern tundra they are scattered over 1000 kilometres of latitude. At low tide on their wintering grounds, they are spread widely and, if it is a large estuary, invisibly. At high tide, however, most are gathered in flocks on the shoreline, and it is then that counting them is 'easier'.

Gathering such data over a period long enough to give useful trend information is even more important. Counts of shorebirds on the Firth of Thames and Manukau Harbour began in 1960; then, recognising the need for data on national populations, OSNZ initiated the National Wader Count scheme in 1983. The aim was to determine numbers and distribution of shorebirds at coastal sites throughout New Zealand, as well as seasonal and annual changes. Winter counts are made nationally in June or early July, while summer counts are made in the North Island in November or early December, and February in the South Island. It is a challenging assignment, going to places, some quite remote, to count birds. The remarkable thing about these annual counts is that not only have they produced one of the longest-term data sets in the world, they have been carried out almost entirely by volunteers. Every weekend during the count periods, people have turned out in all weathers – often at first light, depending on the tides – and stood around for hours counting birds.

Useful though this data set is, however, it does have serious limitations. As one biologist points out, to establish trends in shorebird populations accurately 'we need to distinguish biologically significant declines or increases from short-term fluctuations'.[2] A single count may not provide a representative sample of a whole season, especially when bird numbers at a site may fluctuate over several weeks depending on the date of the count. The accuracy of a single count is also dependent on a number of variables – weather, tide height, species behaviour, and observer experience and behaviour. Where in the country a site is located may also be a factor; the Auckland harbours and the Firth of Thames have been well covered in most years, largely because there is a sufficient pool of volunteers available. In other regions – such as Northland and Southland – sites are no less important, but there are fewer people to do the work. There has also been wide variability in the frequency of counts and coverage of some sites.[3] Multiple repeat counts of at least the most important sites would help solve this problem, and bring a degree of constancy to the data. However, the almost total dependence on volunteers, together with limitations imposed by the tidal cycle – there are only so many spring tides available on which to conduct counts – make this goal largely unreachable as things stand today.

Nevertheless we have learned a lot about our shorebirds. We know for instance that in 2003 there was an average summer total of 121,866 birds counted, of which 101,000 were migrants and 20,864 were residents. Of course the disparity comes from the fact that most natives were away breeding – as is seen in the reversal of the pattern in winter, with an average total of 120,805 natives and 11,128 migrants.[4] Counts such as these, if made over a suitably long period, can reveal population trends. They can tell you what has happened but they cannot tell you why it has happened: for instance, if a population is declining, the cause of that trend may not be clear.[5] Despite such limitations there is enough data – particularly from key sites – to give a reasonable baseline for assessing changes in the distribution and abundance of some species. They can tell us, for instance, whether Potts' prognosis for the fortunes of banded dotterel has come to pass. Or can they?

Of all the New Zealand breeding shorebirds, the banded dotterel is one of the most difficult to monitor. For most species, much of our data comes from the OSNZ counts; but not only do a substantial number of dotterels migrate to Australia each year, many others form feeding flocks inland – away from coastal sites where census data is gathered. In the 1990s the figure widely used for the total banded dotterel population was 50,000 birds, of which 30,000 headed for Australia. This total was based on counts from Australia; data from breeding sites; and the proportions of colour-banded birds seen at nonbreeding sites. Yet of the 20,000 birds estimated to remain in New Zealand each winter, only 11,000 could be accounted for in the 1983–94 census data. Dispersed inland flocks, together with birds that were known to winter in the Mackenzie Basin, were not counted, and this was suggested as an explanation for the discrepancy.[6] However, recent data indicates the figure of 20,000 was grossly inaccurate, and that the true population is considerably lower, with estimates of just 5000–7300 birds. One assessment concluded that, while a number of important wintering sites were not counted, and allowing for the fact some birds remained inland, 'it is difficult to justify a figure of 20,000 from the counts considered here'.[7] Trends at particular sites support this: on the Firth of Thames, for example, annual counts have dropped from as many as 2000 in the 1940s to less than 200 today, and they are no longer breeding in the Firth; the last breeding record was in 1983.[8] The number of birds in Australia was also called into question; it is likely to be considerably less than 30,000. As a result the threat status for banded dotterel has been upgraded from Gradual Decline to Nationally Vulnerable. With other species, of course, the situation is different.

With their dramatic plumage and bill colour, pied oystercatchers are usually highly visible. They are made even more prominent by the numbers in which they can occur, and at some sites, particularly the northern harbours and estuaries from January to June, you may see thousands. In count data over the last 50 years, their trajectory is unmatched by any other New Zealand breeding shorebird. At two sites – Firth of Thames and Manukau Harbour – they went from fewer than 500 in 1941, to 12,000 in 1972, to 38,000 in 1994 – representing an overall increase of 310 percent since 1972.[9] So, like spur-winged plovers, these oystercatchers have been quite successful in recent times. However it was not always so: Buller described variable oystercatchers as 'far more abundant in New Zealand than the pied oystercatcher'.[10]

banded dotterel in August on the Waimakariri River, ready for another breeding season. JOHN DOWDING

Ready to go: a banded dotterel flock in breeding plumage on a beach in the Bay of Plenty in July, shortly before dispersing to their breeding grounds. The scattered dispersal of this species throughout the year, makes it very difficult to accurately assess the population. BRIAN CHUDLEIGH

In the early years of European settlement of Canterbury, pied oystercatchers appear to have been plentiful. 'Years ago,' wrote Potts in 1885, 'before the harbours and estuaries were so much frequented, this shore bird was exceedingly abundant; in June, 1858, on the mudflats at the estuary formed by the Heathcote and Avon rivers, thousands of these birds were to be observed. As late as 1871 there were large flocks on the mudflats and Port Cooper [Lyttelton].'[11] Potts considered the decline in numbers then becoming evident was due to human disturbance. In 1905 Buller confirmed that pied oystercatchers were widely distributed though nowhere abundant. For Dick Sibson they were a notable omission from earlier birding literature. In the mid 1930s Robert Falla was reporting flocks of 2–3000 on the Waimakariri estuary, yet it is 'curious' that neither Stead nor Guthrie-Smith 'devoted a chapter or even a few paragraphs to *finschi*, though both these great naturalists were interested enough in the other birds typical of South Island riverbeds'.[12] One problem for oystercatchers was they were considered a good table bird, and between 1870 and 1940 they came under considerable pressure from hunting. Then two things happened: they received legal protection; and they broadened their breeding horizons.

Original oystercatcher breeding habitat seems to have been the riverbeds of the eastern South Island: on stable banks of sand, gravel or shingle on the braided sections of the rivers, or on short turf areas with exposed gravel bars or banks. Sometime around 1950 they began expanding onto nearby agricultural land – a trend that in more recent years has been documented by Paul Sagar. Growing up in South Canterbury, he got involved with shorebirds early: 'I started doing wetland counts at Washdyke Lagoon when I was 15 and I am still doing them so I have got 40 odd years of records there now.'[13] In 1987 he and his colleague, Ashburton fireman Don Geddes, began a study of oystercatchers nesting on farmland in mid Canterbury. They found breeding success of farmland pairs was considerably higher than for those in the original riverbed habitat. Adult survival rates – which, as these can be long-lived birds, are a key determinant of population size – were consistently high through the study.[14] Birds clearly found the situation to their liking, for their numbers climbed dramatically: in 1973 the estimated national population was 49,000; and by 1994 it was around 112,000 – an increase of 128 percent.[15]

Two specimens collected on the Manukau Harbour in 1880 – now in the Auckland Museum – indicate that pied oystercatchers were known as visitors to the Auckland region. While there are scattered reports after that from the Manukau, no large flocks are mentioned. If numbers in their South Island home range had fallen from the late nineteenth century, this should not be surprising. In March 1936 Charles Fleming reported a flock of 24 near Puketutu; but after the birds gained legal protection, numbers began to rise, with 450 overwintering in 1945, and over 2000 by the 1960s. The number of nonbreeders remaining over summer on the Firth of Thames in 1965 exceeded any winter counts made in the 1940s. There were also likely to be other flocks elsewhere. For instance, while Sibson suspected there were even more birds on the Kaipara Harbour, its 'great size and awkward shape' meant it was difficult to survey.[16]

Today these northern harbours are still hugely valuable for this species. More than 68 percent of all oystercatchers counted during winter census were in the Auckland region. In June 2003 the Kaipara, Manukau and Firth of Thames between them had 63,500, about half the estimated world population.[17] The next biggest concentrations occur in the Nelson region, with nearly 12 percent.[18] Then come the estuaries and lagoons of the eastern South Island, particularly the Avon–Heathcote, although this area is even more important during migration. Christchurch ornithologist and City Council ranger Andrew Crossland suggests that many more oystercatchers pass through than the up to 5000 that may be present at any one time, and that 20–50 percent of the entire population may use this site during migration.[19]

If early records from the Auckland region indicate oystercatchers have long been winter migrants to the area, the question is how many of the population actually did migrate north? The flocks Falla saw on the Waimakariri estuary suggested many birds stayed within close distance of breeding areas. It is thought that ecological pressure from population expansion since 1940 has forced increasing numbers of birds to migrate in search of new feeding areas, and 'as the migratory instinct is best developed in juvenile first year birds . . . they tended to colonise northern New Zealand'.[20] It was also suggested that 'at the current rate of increase, the numbers of this species will probably come under density-dependent control in the next few decades'.[21] Recent evidence suggests this prediction was correct.

The vast food resources of the northern harbours

Nesting wrybill on the Upper Rangitata. JOHN DOWDING

were clearly underutilised by oystercatchers before 1940, and so were able to support the increasing population. But there are always limits to resources. Recent census data seem to indicate the oystercatcher population has reached a plateau, and is now in decline. Over the period 1994–2003 there was a lower rate of increase in the population than during the previous decade. A marked decline in oystercatcher numbers on the Firth of Thames is mirrored by declines in some other species, and may be linked to rapid mangrove expansion over the last two decades. Mechanical harvesting of cockles occurs in Golden and Tasman bays; and while the use of harvesters varies considerably, the net outcome is decreased prey for oystercatchers.[22] Whether the increase has slowed because of winter habitat limitations, or because of recent changes in breeding areas, or a combination of the two, is unclear. There are indications that accelerating conversion to dairy farming in Canterbury has reduced breeding success, as cattle trample a greater proportion of nests than sheep.[23] On the other hand, oystercatchers have begun to colonise North Island sites in the Wairarapa and Hawkes Bay, and this foothold may be the prelude to further expansion of their breeding range.[24] The official threat ranking for the species has been changed from Not Threatened to Declining.[25]

If trends in the pied oystercatcher population seem relatively clear, the same cannot be said for wrybill. What we know of their status at the beginning of the twentieth century comes largely from Buller. In 1895 Mair reported to him a large wrybill flock at the mouth of the Piako River in the Firth of Thames, where 'they are to be seen in thousands, and are so tame you may knock them over with a stick.'[26] Flocks of several hundreds had been recorded on the Manukau in the 1880s and Buller also had a report of 'plentiful' numbers of wrybill on the Kaipara Harbour. So wrybill were present in large numbers in the three key locations where their biggest winter concentrations occur today. During the first half of the twentieth century however, wrybill numbers were thought to have declined.

On a visit to Muriwai Beach in March 1940, Sibson was 'duly satisfied' to see two wrybill for they 'are now believed to be very rare'.[27] In April the following year he encountered over 200. 'Wrybills were thought to be among our rarest birds. No such assemblage had been recorded for half a century. A senior authority remarked that he thought this would be the bulk of the population.'[28] It was to be Sibson himself, along with his comrade in ornithology Ross Mackenzie, who would discover later that year how wrong that assessment was. On one of their first expeditions to the Firth of Thames they discovered not only a flock of black-billed gulls, far to the north of their known range, but over 1000 wrybill, 'the largest gathering of [the species] recorded since the nineteenth century.'[29] Population counts of 1500–2000 were being made by 1950, increasing to over 4000 by 1960. Numbers then appear to have remained relatively stable over the next 20 years at around 5000.[30] Current indications are the population hovers around 5500, with between 85 and 90 percent of all wrybill at just two sites – Manukau Harbour and the Firth of Thames. But just how much these numbers tell us about trends within the overall population remains unclear.

Sibson wrote: 'I am inclined to believe that the figures for the Manukau reflect a steady increase in the population after a serious decline; though even when the numbers were at their lowest, the Wrybill was much more numerous than suspected, because the Firth of Thames was not known.'[31] Early observers were operating from a limited knowledge base. Today we know much more about both the major wintering sites for wrybill, and the way birds use them. For instance, banding has shown fidelity to a wintering site may not be particularly strong for some birds, with numerous records of movements between harbours. The Firth of Thames and the Manukau Harbour have been much studied over recent decades so we now know where to look for the major wrybill flocks.

Given our knowledge of how habitat degradation and loss together with the arrival of mammalian predators has affected our shorebird populations, it seems highly likely that the wrybill population was once higher than it is today. For instance, much riverbed habitat has been lost to wrybill through the spread of exotic weeds. A description of the lower Rakaia in 1936 by Guthrie-Smith gives a good benchmark. Below the rail bridge 20 km from the mouth, the bed was largely bare of vegetation but invasive species were becoming established around the estuary and these have since spread upstream. Stead reported wrybill commonly occurred on the lower reaches of the Canterbury rivers but this is no longer the case today. A survey of 5 km of Rakaia riverbed further upstream in 1977 confirmed this; only five individual wrybill were found where a relatively dense population

Perpetual cacophony: pied stilts are restless, noisy birds, always making their presence known. The dark neck of the bird (top, centre) indicates it is a hybrid.
ATHENA DRUMMOND

Roosting wrybill: though seemingly asleep, most shorebirds maintain a level of alertness.
IAN SOUTHEY

Roost with a view: a warehouse roof in South Auckland, near the flight path to Auckland International Airport, is considered a suitable roost by these wrybill – perhaps more than a third of the world population of the species.
JOHN DOWDING

had occurred just two years earlier.[32]

Hydroelectric development in the Upper Waitaki Basin spelt further loss of ground for wrybill. Not only did large areas of braided river habitat disappear under the hydro lakes, the entire flow regime of the Waitaki system was substantially modified.[33] The effects of this can be seen clearly seen today with most of the lower Waitaki riverbed choked with weeds.

Then there is the question of predators. A three-year study in the 1970s showed most nest losses were due to natural events such as flooding, and recorded no substantial predation on wrybill. However a 1990s study in the Mackenzie Basin during years of high stoat density showed predation had a devastating effect in the Tasman Valley, yet at a similar time there was little problem in the Tekapo Basin. Nevertheless a clear pattern emerged: adult survival of wrybills is higher in areas subject to predator control, and there is a bias against males in survival rates – thought to be because they brood and incubate at night when predators are more active. It could be that predators are responsible for a trend that John Dowding and others have noticed about some of the big rivers.

> Based on what we know about wrybill and the kind of habitat they use, there is just acres and acres of places for them in lots of those upper rivers. Huge areas of the upper Rakaia and large parts of the lower Rangitata look suitable, places that used to have wrybills but don't any more. So I am not in any doubt that there is ample habitat.[34]

And if much of what appears to be suitable breeding habitat is subject to predator pressure, the net result is a reduction in habitat that ensures breeding success.

Historically there were reports of wrybill on the Awatere and Clarence rivers in Marlborough, and the Waiau and Hurunui in North Canterbury, although Guthrie-Smith doubted these records and considered the Waimakariri to be the northern range limit. Up until the 1970s wrybill appeared to be confined between the Ashley and Waimakariri in the north and the confluence of the Waitaki and Hakataramea in the south. In the late 1960s and early 70s came reports of breeding pairs on the Hunter, Makarora and Matukituki; that birds had not been recorded in earlier surveys suggested this was perhaps an extension in range.[35] More recent counts in 2000 found 21 birds in the Matukituki and 18 in the Hunter. Furthermore birds have been found in good numbers in the Dart Valley; four counts of 30–44 birds between 1990 and 2002 represent almost one percent of the world population.[36] In 1977 Hay found wrybills breeding on the south branch of the upper Ashburton in an area previously surveyed two years earlier. To the north wrybill were recently found on the Waiau and Hurunui, and at least one pair was also found on the Wairau in 2010. However whether these reports represent range expansion or the discovery of previously unknown birds through better surveying methods is uncertain.[37] One thing is clear: core wrybill-breeding range remains the three big systems – the Rakaia, the Rangitata and the Upper Waitaki.

A more conventional high-tide roost for these godwits and knots at Miranda. KEITH WOODLEY

The wrybill population may have been much higher than it is now, although we will never know. Best guess however suggests it was probably higher by only a few thousand birds. It seems likely that from the late nineteenth century birds were lost to habitat modification and predation, and that the population may have declined further following hydroelectric developments in the Upper Waitaki. Yet it also seems likely that wrybill have never been particularly plentiful. They exploit limited and very marginal habitat and therefore may have a low level of breeding success. Conditions on the rivers such as flooding may mean they successfully breed only every few years. Under normal circumstances this would not be a problem because they are long-lived birds. Habitat limitations most likely mean the wrybill population itself has always been limited.

Count data that suggest the wrybill population appears to be relatively stable at around 5000–5500 may be cause for celebration, but not complacency. For we are left with the stark ecological facts – they remain a strictly limited population; and they have only the riverbeds, where habitat continues to shrink before the advance of weeds, predators and increasing human pressures, particularly modified flow regimes supporting the farming sector and power generation. And we need to acknowledge another warning flag: because they are long-lived birds, the population could start to decline sharply and it may be some time before that trend is detected. Yet, as one researcher noted: 'Given these pressures, the constancy of the population size seems remarkable, and is perhaps due in part to the management of their breeding habitats in the Mackenzie Country by the Department of Conservation.'[38] As we shall see, that management is not without its problems, and may indeed be having only limited success.

Many beaches and rocky shores around the country feature a pair of variable oystercatchers, although two thirds of the estimated population are in the North Island. Nationally, numbers have increased from 2000 birds in 1970–71 to about 7000 in 2006.[39] Reasons for this increase are not clear, although there is some evidence that management of northern New Zealand dotterel sites may be having a beneficial effect for oystercatchers as well. Both species tend to favour the smaller harbours and estuaries along the northeastern North Island, which is where much of this management has been directed. Since the 1980s predator control and management of human disturbance has occurred at key sites, and 20 percent of breeding pairs of dotterels now occur at protected sites. Variable oystercatchers occupy similar habitats, so 'it is tempting to also attribute the continuing increase

Earthworks on the edge of Thames offer as good a roost as any for these oystercatchers.
BRIAN CHUDLEIGH

Artificial roost: high-tide roosting space is sometimes at a premium, and many shorebirds are not averse to using human constructions – such as this carpark at a boat-launching site, deemed suitable by these oystercatchers. IAN SOUTHEY

in their numbers to this management'.[40] However, it has been pointed out that numbers of birds had begun increasing at some sites before dotterel management began; and also in regions where breeding dotterels do not occur: the number of birds in Tasman Bay and the Avon–Heathcote Estuary in Canterbury has increased considerably since the 1990s. Waimea Inlet now has a substantial population of subadult VOCs and appears to act as a 'regional nursery or crèche'.[41] One further pattern seems clear: these oystercatchers are expanding their range. 'Near the smaller estuaries that were identified as holding large numbers, there now seem to be adjacent sites where large populations have developed in the last 10 years.' Birds from Waipu appear to have expanded to Whangarei Harbour and Ruakaka; and banded birds from the population at Kaikoura have been seen on the Avon–Heathcote and at Tasman Bay.[42] They may even be beginning to move away from the coast: 'In North Canterbury and down in Oamaru there are records of all black birds breeding inland.'[43] This could be leading to the formation of mixed pairs: a bird caught at Nelson in 2011 appeared to be a hybrid; it had the size and structure of a SIPO but the smudgy plumage of a VOC.[44]

Currently there are estimated to be around 20,000 pied stilts, although monitoring this species can be rather difficult. Many stilts live inland and are essentially sedentary, particularly in the northern North Island. Whether or not they visit the coast may depend on conditions, such as rainfall or drought, affecting their inland habitat.[45] What this means, of course, is they cannot be relied on to turn up at census sites. However, several factors still allow reasonable population estimates to be made. Firstly, over 85 percent of the winter population occurs in the North Island, with heavy concentrations in the Auckland region; in 1989 more than half the birds counted were in the Auckland or South Auckland area. So counts on the Firth of Thames – perhaps the major site in the country for this species – and Manukau Harbour can give good indications of population trends. Between 1994 and 2003, numbers at these sites increased by 22 percent overall. The total number of pied stilts appears to have increased by about 20 percent since the previous decade.[46]

So the fortunes of some of our shorebirds show some variation. Both oystercatchers seem to be doing quite well; the wrybill population may be more or less stable, for the moment at least; while banded dotterel appear to be in trouble. We shall look at some of the wider-scale factors behind these trends, such as the predator problem; degradation and loss of habitat; disturbance; and the role of riverflows. First, there are further species to consider, whose status is such that they have their very own recovery plan . . . at least, for the moment they do.

Black stilt at Glentanner, near Mt Cook. IAN SOUTHEY
(right) Black stilt recovery manager Dean Nelson, at the
programme facilities at Twizel. KEITH WOODLEY

CHAPTER SEVENTEEN
HELPING HANDS: RECOVERY GROUPS AND PLANS

The visitor centre is a modest affair, tucked away in a small terraced basin on the Lower Ohau River just outside Twizel. Here two notable features of the contemporary Mackenzie Basin exist side by side. The forest of pylons around the facility advertises the economic status of the place – for it is literally a national powerhouse: the Upper Waitaki hydroelectric power scheme. The other feature is evident immediately adjacent to the visitor centre: two black stilts in a small aviary. The two nonbreeding females have been tasked with public display duties – and this may be the closest many people will ever get to birds of this critically endangered species. The interpretation displays inside the centre, though somewhat tired-looking, nevertheless give the visitor a good overview of the species recovery programme and the conservation issues it is charged with solving. In a way the resource-limited interpretation facilities are a good sign, for they suggest scarce conservation resources may be going where they are most needed, such as to essential activities elsewhere in this building. For this is where the black stilt captive breeding programme is based.

Active management of black stilts began in 1979–1980 and focused primarily on increasing egg production and controlling predators. Fortunately they have shown themselves to be quite cooperative when it comes to churning out extra eggs. Like other riverbed birds adapted to the prospect of natural disasters such as floods, they are able to lay multiple clutches in a season. Pairs have laid up to five clutches a season in captivity, and up to four in the wild, presenting good opportunities for increased production through manipulation. Eggs were taken from early nests and the nest destroyed to encourage the birds to re-lay. The eggs were artificially incubated and then fostered to other pairs, including black with pied, black with hybrid, and hybrid with hybrid. Second clutches were also taken, only this time they were replaced with artificial eggs so the parents would continue to incubate. These eggs were artificially incubated then returned to the parents just before hatching.

Before long there emerged a serious flaw in this plan. First-clutch chicks fostered to hybrid and pied pairs 'acquired at least one behavioural characteristic of their foster species – they migrated out of the Mackenzie Basin during winter', which meant pair bonding that happens in winter and early spring was taking place away from the nucleus of black stilts. Only four of 59 chicks that fledged between 1981 and 1986 were recruited into the Mackenzie Basin breeding population.[1] Black stilt juveniles reared by two black parents were found to have a greater chance of survival than those reared by hybrid or pied foster parents. Moreover, the offspring of black pairs tended to remain in the basin and, although there was still high post-fledging mortality, were recruited into the population.

In addition to egg manipulation, two predator-proof enclosures with electric fences were built around traditional nesting habitats, with traps also laid in other nesting areas. Improved fledging success was the result. Between 1977 and 1980, 70 percent of nests failed – 41 percent of them as a result of predation; and of 31 percent of eggs that hatched, only 2 percent fledged. But once management began, 43 percent of eggs hatched and 14 percent fledged. After predator-proof fences were erected, overall breeding success increased from nil in 1977–79 to 83 percent in 1993.[2]

Meanwhile, in 1979 eggs removed from nests in the Mackenzie Basin were artificially incubated and the chicks reared at the Pukaha Mount Bruce Wildlife Centre. All eight birds – three males and five females – became the nucleus for a captive breeding programme. Unfortunately this was not entirely successful either, as few young birds survived once released. One problem was captive-reared birds tended to be very tame; so modifications were made to the programme to try and make young birds more predator-wary.[3] It was suggested that the breeding programme be moved to the Mackenzie Basin to allow black stilts to be reared within their 'natural' range; and in 1986 the Kaki Recovery Programme centre was established on land owned by what was then Electricorp. Three aviaries were in place by 1991; and the current centre – including an incubator room, food preparation room, laboratory and eight brooder compartments with adjoining aviaries – was opened in 1992. Which is where, in late October 2010, I meet Dean Nelson, manager of the Kaki Recovery Programme.

With a species in such a precarious position, fastidious precautions are required. We put on special shoes to go inside the food preparation area, where a staff member is busy mixing up a combination of minced ox heart and Wombaroo insectivore rearing mix for supplementary feeding. As with most shorebirds, stilt chicks are fully mobile and find their own food soon after hatching, which means they will only take live prey. So chicks in captivity are fed on aquatic invertebrates, harvested from nearby rivers, for at least the first 10 days; after which they are given live mealworms. Eventually they are moved to a diet of the food combinations being prepared in front of us.

Kaki Recovery Programme aviary at Twizel. KEITH WOODLEY

This adult is a part of the black stilt captive breeding programme at Isaac Wildlife Trust near Christchurch. KEITH WOODLEY

Working to save critically endangered species requires discovering just what it is the birds need. Sometimes – and this is particularly true of the programme to save those confounding parrots, kakapo – this comes down to lateral thinking: literally trying to get inside the bird's head. Sometimes it is just trial and error – although we can't afford too much of the latter. Early in the programme it was found that juvenile stilts were not surviving due to an iodine deficiency – a problem that was quickly solved through diet adjustments. A further discovery was that the intestines of captive-reared birds were shorter than those of wild birds, which meant they could not process enough food to maintain their basic metabolism. Clearly their diet was not giving them all the resources they needed, so a six-week soft-release programme was established to get birds better prepared and allow them to develop a longer gut. These birds are fed every day, though the amount of food is gradually decreased.

The next stop is a long corridor lined with eight small box-like cubicles, each with a hatch, fabric netting on the floor and a food bowl. These are connected to larger outside enclosures laid with small pebbles – giving the impression of a Zen-like courtyard. Each contains precious inhabitants: broods of black stilts of various ages, from chicks to the almost fledged. Stringent measures are taken to avoid implanting on humans. Success rates from the programme gradually improved as techniques were honed and refined. In the 1992–93 breeding season, 32 juveniles were reared with minimal human contact and released at nine months. Three months after release, 23 were still alive and feeding in natural and artificial ponds around the aviary site, while some were also frequenting the nearby river for feeding. Six months after release, 16 were still alive.[4] With additional facilities at the Isaac Wildlife Trust near Christchurch, holding capacity for the black stilts project is 100 birds; any birds over that number need to be released when they are a little over three months old. The survival rate of these birds is not high; for birds that are held over the winter and released at nine months of age, it is slightly higher. The project is currently concentrating on two main release areas – the Godley and Cass rivers, and the Tasman.

So where is the black stilt recovery programme today? Despite years of effort, the number of birds remains critically low – although the trend is gradually upwards.

It is fairly clear from previous data that if we walked away from it they would go extinct in a relatively short

period of time. I guess we are still optimistic we can get them to a point where we can get them over the hump, but it's just taken a bit longer than we hoped.[5]

There were 85 adults in the wild as at February 2010. The key figure however, is the number of productive pairs that produce eggs in the wild; and in 2009 that stood at 16. In the February 2011 census the number of productive pairs stood at 17.

We talk about the magic figure of 100 in the wild – it would be nice to get over 100 – but we have not got there yet . . . We have got to the point where we are regularly producing in excess of 100 chicks a year . . . some years they have good survival rates and sometimes they don't. There's no real pattern to it.[6]

Whatever the problems may be, there are limited options available to black stilt. For this species, offshore islands are currently not available for establishing a backstop population, so they will need to continue to be managed in situ. Other river systems have been mooted to be included in the project, such as the Upper Rakaia and Rangitata rivers, although both will need intensive – and very expensive – ongoing predator control. In the short term, however, great efforts are being made to make the existing programme more effective.

Pied oystercatchers have, until recently, done very well over the last 70 years, and variable oystercatcher numbers are steadily increasing in most areas; however, the status of the Chatham Island oystercatcher (CIO) population remains problematic: in 1998 there were only 142 birds. So what was wrong? People and their camp followers, of course. Fourteen bird species are believed to have gone extinct in the 500 years since Moriori arrived on the Chathams; and a further seven since European settlement. Oystercatcher bones in middens and dune deposits indicate hunting by Moriori. By the second half of the nineteenth century, their relative scarcity increased their value to collectors: one specimen in Te Papa came from Pitt Island in 1871; and in 1890 a further 10 specimens were dispatched to the Rothschild collection in the UK. 'This type of collecting . . . may have had a significant impact on the small oystercatcher population.'[7] However, it was change on a wider scale in the Chathams that caused much of the problem.

Agricultural development and associated vegetation changes have severely affected oystercatcher habitat. One example was damage to the natural dune systems in the islands – low mounds and ridges sparsely vegetated with herbs and grasses, which offered good nesting opportunities. Grazing and trampling by stock heavily modified these areas and destabilised the dunes. The subsequent use of exotic marram grass for restabilisation proved most successful; indeed too successful. The heavily vegetated dunes not only limited nesting opportunities, they also changed beach topography, resulting in narrower beaches in front of the dunes. This in turn forced nesting birds nearer the high-tide line, where more nests were lost; between 1994 and 1997, 48 percent of eggs laid were washed away.[8]

But probably the major threat to these oystercatchers

On the edge: Chatham Island oystercatchers at Owenga. IAN SOUTHEY

One-day-old Chatham Island oystercatcher chicks on Pitt Island. JOHN DOWDING

Chatham Island oystercatchers on Pitt Island. Through active management their numbers have increased, but the rarest oystercatcher in the world remains Conservation Dependent. JOHN DOWDING

dates from the early nineteenth century, when more exotic mammals arrived on the islands. Rats, mice, possums, pigs, sheep and cattle all did their bit in tilting the playing field unfavourably for resident birds. Ironically a further intruder that was causing problems was an endemic New Zealand bird originally confined to the mainland. In 1905 weka were introduced to the Chathams as an insurance policy for the Canterbury weka population. They were so successful that they became – and still are – a food source for local people. Remote video cameras were used to film predators at oystercatcher nests: of 17 incidents, cats were responsible for 13, weka three, and sheep-trampling one. Of course there were also more natural causes, such as being washed away by the sea; or predation by red-billed gulls, black-backed gulls and skuas.

In 1998, a six-year programme of intensive management began on a 16-km section of the northern coast of Chatham Island. This involved predator trapping, relocation of nests above storm tides, and the exclusion of farm stock. The results were telling: once again, in a pattern that has been repeated many times on the mainland, where native species are given a good helping hand, most invariably recover very well. From a little over 100 oystercatchers in 1987, the population by 2006 was over 300, with most of this increase occurring during the six-year management period. Increased breeding density also resulted in expansion into suitable habitat elsewhere in the islands. In the period 1999–2001, chicks fledged from 39 percent of managed eggs compared with only 6 percent of unmanaged eggs. Annual productivity in the northern Chatham Island area increased, with an output of 18–35 fledglings per year, which – together with chicks from elsewhere in the islands – meant up to 50 juveniles were entering the population each year.[9]

There is still a way to go, however. The CIO, wrote one researcher, 'is less precarious than it was a few decades ago, although the small population size and restricted range of the species still means it is vulnerable to extinction.'[10] A further problem is the resources required for intensive management are seldom available for the long term. The boosted recruitment into the population benefited mainly birds in the northern part of Chatham Island, so in 2005 management activity was shifted south to Pitt Island, in an effort to boost the population in its southern range. Unfortunately not only were few chicks produced there – for reasons that are not yet understood – productivity in the formerly managed area also fell away. In fact there was high mortality of adults on northern Chatham Island once management ceased; and increased predation by cats is believed to be the primary cause. In a classic 'two steps forward, one back' situation, the population has fallen again to around 250 birds, meaning a great deal of help is still required. For help, read resources: as in so many areas of conservation in New Zealand, success is hampered not by lack of knowledge of what needs to be done, just the lack of resources with which to do it.

For many people, these chunky birds have charisma. Perhaps it is something in the nature of the dotterel clan – the way they run and stop along the beach. Perhaps it is the handsome features; or the large eyes trained on

New Zealand dotterels on the southern Manukau Harbour. IAN SOUTHEY

A close shave: a dotterel nest on the edge of wheel tracks – an indication of just how vulnerable these birds are as they share the beaches with us. BRIAN CHUDLEIGH

Signage produced by local children at northern dotterel nesting sites at Omaha Spit. JOHN DOWDING

An area of Mangawhai Spit fenced off to protect nesting dotterels and fairy terns. KEITH WOODLEY

the observer. Or maybe it is something to do with the places where one finds them, on the very margins of the land – before a backdrop of surf; along a fringe of dunes; or ahead of the tide sliding across the flats. It is these same places, though, that bring us into conflict. For when the New Zealand dotterel seeks to breed, it uses the very places where we like to gather, at the very time we want to be there. Yet from this collision of interests, there has arisen a culture of caring. At many key dotterel sites around the upper North Island, individuals and community groups have emerged to confront problems and protect the birds. For some, this bird has been the pathway to conservation activism.

Attached to the southern dotterel population are several conservation classifications that collectively reveal its parlous circumstances: it is listed as Nationally Critical: Conservation Dependent; and it occurs in just one location. In a glimmer of optimism, however, the population is also described as stable. The northern population, by comparison, is in good shape – except that it is listed as Nationally Vulnerable: Conservation Dependent, meaning that if management ceased, bird numbers would decline.[11]

A management plan for New Zealand dotterels needs to address each of the negative pressures on the population: mammalian and avian predation; disturbance; loss or degradation of breeding habitat;

and flooding. The North Island east coast holds more than 80 percent of the northern subspecies; it is also where dotterel habitat requirements – sandy beaches and estuaries – most often clash with human activities – housing and marina developments, and recreational use of the coastline.[12]

Dotterels tend to be widely and thinly spread, and at most sites there are only a few birds. This presents a perception problem: the negative effects of human activities at a particular site may seem acceptable because only a few birds are likely to be affected. However, given the concentration of the population on the northeast coast, where most human pressure occurs, cumulative effects on numbers and range of the population are likely to be severe.

Then there are the predators. Near Ohope, in 1995, the remains of 11 New Zealand dotterels were recovered from one stoat den. Of eight captive-reared juveniles released at Omaha, a stoat had got six within two days. In 1.5 km of dunes at Tawharanui, 400 hedgehogs were trapped over two years, though enough remained to take all dotterel eggs.[13]

The New Zealand Wildlife Service (NZWS) began management of northern dotterels at some sites in 1983, but did not include control of mammalian predators. Intensive management, which did include predator control, began at Opoutere, Coromandel Peninsula, in 1986. Momentum gradually built up and, by the 1990s, a clear trend was emerging. In some coastal areas of the North Island, members of the public were coming to see dotterels as a highly valued part of the ecological community. Because the dotterels are endemic and in low numbers, and because of their vulnerability to predators and development, people began advocating for their protection. Harnessing this public energy has been a key to subsequent successes. The model that has evolved since the late 1980s includes: appointment of a beach warden; signage and fencing of nesting areas to reduce trampling and disturbance; measures to reduce loss of nests and small chicks to high tides and storm surges; predator control to reduce losses of eggs, chicks, and adults; and advocacy to raise awareness of threats to the species and explain the need for management.[14]

Much of the research on dotterels, as well as promotion of its threatened status, has been undertaken by two NGOs: OSNZ and Forest and Bird. Members of both have participated in national censuses, and are regularly active in monitoring and data collection. Forest and Bird has also promoted and funded some research, management and advocacy initiatives at several sites. While it has kept a coordinating role, in recent years actual management of New Zealand dotterels has increasingly fallen outside the Department of Conservation, to these other organisations, groups and individuals. In the greater Auckland area the former Auckland Regional Council, through management of species within its regional parks, did much to raise public awareness. Since 2000 Miranda Shorebird Centre has annually run a highly effective training course on conservation and management of dotterels. Graduates include DOC and local government staff, as well as many community-based wardens and volunteers. But while there is a moderate level of public awareness of dotterels in some areas of the northern North Island, overall it remains quite low – although it must be said that the birds are doing their bit to raise their profile. As we have seen, construction of the Northern Busway was held up by a few pairs of dotterels.[15]

Although the northern dotterel population is widely dispersed, the bulk of it is on the northeastern coast of the North Island. Within that overall distribution, two clear patterns have emerged: that internationally important numbers occur at key sites; and that two subpopulations appear to have developed – one in Northland and Auckland, and the other including Great Barrier Island, Coromandel and the Bay of Plenty – with little or no interchange between them. Birds have dispersed from the Coromandel to the Bay of Plenty and vice versa, and there are also records linking Great Barrier with Opoutere and also the mouth of the Waihou River in the Firth of Thames; however, no link between Auckland/Northland and Great Barrier has been found. Reasons for this separation are unclear: it could be a relatively recent and temporary development – the product of a low-density population as a legacy of the arrival of mammalian predators. Another factor may be the scarcity of high-quality breeding habitat around the coastline of the Firth of Thames – the boundary between the two populations. Whatever the cause, that there is little or no interchange between the two means they need to be managed as separate units, as 'management in one provides no benefit to the other'.[16]

With over 20 breeding pairs of dotterels, Matakana Island in Tauranga Harbour was identified in the early 1990s as a significant site, but one facing considerable pressure from predators and human disturbance. Large numbers of black-backed gulls were causing heavy losses of dotterel eggs and chicks. Initial warnings about

Most management of northern dotterels occurs at key sites on the east coast of the North Island; on the west coast, where almost no management occurs, birds continue to struggle. Michelle Lewis of DOC with a dotterel on the Waikato coast. JOHN DOWDING

the effect that gulls were having went unheeded, until concerns grew at the complete failure of dotterel chicks to fledge. Remote cameras revealed that gulls – 6000 were estimated to be on the island – were the main culprits. Once controls on the gull population were instigated, the situation began to improve; by 2005 there were no longer any gulls nesting on the island, with huge benefits for dotterels.[17]

Management began in 1992, and by 1999 breeding pairs had increased by 39 percent, while the number of fledglings per season increased by 560 percent. In managed habitat, loss to predation during incubation was 12.5 percent of nests, while at unmanaged sites it was over 52 percent.[18] Indications were the island was approaching, or had reached, its maximum carrying capacity for dotterel pairs, and that birds were dispersing elsewhere in the region. This suggested two things. First, further population increases would depend on fledglings establishing and surviving at other sites, in which case more sites would need to be managed to retain the overall benefits. Second, given the average life expectancy of adult dotterels – about 13 years, although some birds live to at least 30 – there would be no need for predator control every year. This leads to the possibility that some sites could be 'pulse-managed': a given number of sites are successively managed for, say, every three or possibly five years. In this way resources could be focused on particular sites during a season, so there would always be some management going on within the overall range of the population.

If Matakana Island offers a model for individual site management, the adjacent Coromandel Peninsula shows what can be done on a regional scale. At Opoutere, no chicks fledged in the three seasons immediately prior to appointment of a full-time warden in 1986; chicks have fledged in all seasons since. In the late 1990s OSNZ member Bev Woolley began monitoring dotterels on the peninsula during the breeding season, during which time a highly successful partnership developed between DOC, goldmining company Newmont Waihi Gold Ltd, and community dotterel minders. Goldmining? A dotterel pair was found breeding at the mine site and, requiring consent for a new tailings dam, the company agreed to assist the dotterel programme as part-mitigation. Management of dotterels now occurs around most of the peninsula, and the results speak for themselves. From 1996 to 2004 the Coromandel population increased from 176 to 278 birds – an increase of 58 percent. With breeding success remaining poor at unmanaged sites, this was clearly down to management. That the population increase on the Coromandel was much higher than in any other region reflected the higher proportion of birds under management. Elsewhere, in 1998–99, about 20 percent of dotterel pairs were formally managed; but on the Coromandel, over 75 percent of monitored pairs had wardens or minders. In 2004–05, at least 87 percent of the 126 pairs monitored had some predator control. At Matarangi, where numbers had been steadily growing, 158 birds were counted in April 2010, making it the biggest flocking site on the peninsula.[19]

Recent indications are that the dotterel population may have reached the carrying capacity on the peninsula, so expansion into other areas is likely. Productivity on the Coromandel currently exceeds the rate required to keep the entire New Zealand dotterel population stable, and there is capacity for further growth. 'The minder network on Coromandel is now well developed and extensive. The recovery plan aim of having at least 15 percent of the northern dotterel population managed by agencies other than DOC by 2014 has already been well exceeded in this region.'[20] A national dotterel census was scheduled for November 2011, after which decisions would be made on future management options. For instance, it may be possible to reduce management, 'because the Coromandel population could be sustained by considerably lower levels of productivity than are seen at present'.[21] Or the continued production of juveniles on the peninsula could provide birds to other areas, such as around the Firth of Thames, possibly ending the current separation of the two subpopulations.

Counts of birds at other key sites at the end of 2010 provided further proof of the effectiveness of management. Birds follow a regular annual routine: after breeding they move to a post-breeding flocking site nearby for a few months before returning to nesting areas. In the context of the overall dotterel population three such sites loom large: as well as the 158 at Matarangi, 184 birds were recorded at Mangawhai Spit, and 106 at Omaha. 'For the first time on record three New Zealand dotterel flocks in the North Island each contain more than 100 birds.'[22] The count at Mangawhai is the highest count of dotterels at a single location, and represents about 10 percent of the population. Between them, the three sites contain nearly a quarter of the global population, and it is surely no coincidence that all three locations have been subject to intensive management. At Mangawhai, management of fairy terns by DOC, the New Zealand Fairy Tern Trust and OSNZ volunteers has had a spin-off for dotterels; as have the efforts of a community group at nearby Te Arai. The recent formation of the Omaha Shorebird Protection Trust has 'revitalised and formalised management by local volunteers that has been in place, with the support of DOC and local councils, since 1997'. This has been further augmented by high dotterel productivity at two managed sites nearby – Tawharanui Regional Park, now administered by Auckland Council; and Pakiri Beach, where DOC Warkworth and community volunteers have been managing both dotterels and fairy terns.[23] However, while community management has been highly successful in areas like Coromandel, elsewhere – notably the west coast from Northland to Waikato, where there is no management – dotterel numbers continue to decline. Furthermore, in the 2011–12 breeding season, as a result of cuts to an already stretched DOC budget, no predator control occurred on Matakana Island for the first time in nearly 20 years. The results were immediately noticeable with some dotterel nests lasting barely three days before being visited by predators. This is further evidence of just how conservation dependent this species still is.

Nothing in nature – success or otherwise – exists in a vacuum; and on the Coromandel, successful management of dotterels has created an intriguing problem. Throughout the range of northern dotterels, variable oystercatchers favour a similar habitat, and the two species often overlap. Nationally, as we have seen, the VOC population has increased sharply, and where both species are at high density, 'aggressive interactions

Post-breeding flock: outside the breeding season many dotterels flock together, with some sites – such as this one at Omaha Spit – particularly favoured. Pictured here is about 2 percent of the world population. JOHN DOWDING

One outcome of successful management of New Zealand dotterels is an increase in variable oystercatchers that share similar habitat – so successful that, at some sites such as Opoutere on the Coromandel, competition between the two species has become a problem. IAN SOUTHEY

Potent threat to dotterel productivity: black-backed gull colonies on Matakana Island were responsible for heavy losses of dotterel eggs and chicks. BRIAN CHUDLEIGH

between them are not uncommon. At Opoutere and elsewhere, there are now many documented examples of VOCs usurping dotterel nests and killing chicks, and one case of an oystercatcher killing an adult dotterel.'[24] As numbers of both continue to increase around the peninsula, dotterel density and breeding success at some sites may suffer – which may be what has happened at Opoutere. The peak of 15 pairs recorded between 1998 and 2002 may represent the site's carrying capacity; and the recent decline to 10–11 pairs the result of increasing competition for resources with the growing number of VOCs. All of which may present conservation managers with a tricky dilemma. However, there is some anecdotal evidence 'that much of the problem is caused by a few highly aggressive individual oystercatchers. In some cases, consideration may need to be given to identifying and removing such individuals where they persistently reduce dotterel productivity.'[25]

If management of New Zealand dotterels has thus far produced significant conservation gains, it has not yet secured their future. That they remain acutely vulnerable was revealed on 5 October 2011, when the 38,788-tonne container ship *Rena* grounded on the Astrolabe Reef off Tauranga Harbour. Oil gushing from the stricken vessel began coming ashore at Mount Maunganui and along Papamoa Beach. There was a widespread public perception that official responses to this disaster were, in the first few days, sluggish and cumbersome; but at least one sector was up and going within 24 hours. A Wildlife Response Centre was established at Mount Maunganui and was soon receiving oiled birds – primarily blue penguins and some seabirds. However what could be done for birds that were not yet affected, but that lay in the path of projected oil slicks coming ashore? More particularly, what could be done for the New Zealand dotterels along the Bay of Plenty coastline, which by then were well into their breeding season? It was decided to capture and hold up to 60 adults until the danger had passed. With the limited resources available it was not practicable to consider also taking any eggs for artificial incubation: in essence the 2011–12 breeding season in affected parts of the Bay of Plenty would be sacrificed in order to save breeding adults.

Internationally important flock: after breeding, a large percentage of the southern dotterel population cross Foveaux Strait to flock at Awarua Bay, near Invercargill. IAN SOUTHEY

A purpose-built aviary complex was soon home to 60 adult dotterels taken off beaches from Matakana Island to Matata. Because birds at this time of year – particularly males – are highly territorial, each of the captives needed to be held in individual enclosures. An initial diet of mealworms was then replaced by a combination of ox heart and Wombaroo insectivore mix – the same fare used in the black-stilt breeding programme. At least two birds were initially thought to be in danger – one had oil on its tongue and was rapidly losing weight – but after a few days both had recovered. The mean weight for a northern dotterel at this time of year is 144 g; on 30 October weights of the captive birds ranged from 130 g to 155 g, which was heartening for the response team managers.

This was breaking new ground. Nowhere else had pre-emptive capture of birds been attempted ahead of an anticipated oil spill. Capturing and holding dotterels for more than a few days was an enormous gamble, as there was precious little in the way of precedent for such a measure. Apart from a few injured birds brought in for rehabilitation, there is little previous experience of holding dotterels in captivity. A captive rearing programme, using eggs taken from the wild, was started at Auckland Zoo in the 1990s specifically to learn techniques as a contingency for emergency management of southern New Zealand dotterels, should it became necessary.

By mid November, most of the oil had been removed from the *Rena* but the ship remained at risk of breaking up, discharging the estimated 100 tonnes of oil that remained in its bilges if it did so. Furthermore, was it possible to clean beaches completely, down to the last specks of oil that could otherwise enter the food chain? It would still not be safe to release dotterels until checks had been made of their invertebrate prey. There would be no point releasing a dotterel only to have it take sandhoppers that were affected by oil. So it was quite likely birds would have to be held for at least six weeks. There were also many unknowns once birds were released. Would they find sufficient food? Removing territorial birds at this time of year represented a colossal disruption of 'dotterel society': would a captive pair find its territory had been occupied by other birds? Would birds attempt to resume their breeding season?

The release of 17 dotterels on 24 November was, initially, cause for celebration. However, before further birds could be liberated there was a major hitch. On Matakana Island, two days of strong onshore winds had lifted the top few centimetres of sand, uncovering patches of oil. A dotterel nest containing one egg was found surrounded by tar-balls. Despite massive beach clean-up operations by an army of people ranging from New Zealand Defence Force personnel to community volunteers, dotterel habitat was still severely compromised. There were growing fears that, even if no further oil leaked from the *Rena*, it would be months before some beaches were totally clear. Then in early December more oil emerged from the vessel and headed for the beaches.

Meanwhile prolonged captivity was beginning to cause problems for the other 43 birds: some were showing minor ailments and injuries that, because of stress, were slow to heal. Wildlife managers were faced with a growing dilemma: pressure to release birds as soon as possible, into habitat that was still risky for them.

Four birds died in captivity but all others were released. At least three are known to have recommenced breeding operations but for others the immediate outlook was less positive. One female from a long-standing pair returned to her territory to find her mate had taken a new partner, and so found herself evicted.

One positive outcome of the disaster was that Maritime New Zealand agreed to fund monitoring of Bay of Plenty dotterels for at least a year. This will be invaluable for assessing long-term effects on birds affected by the *Rena*. Here also was the opportunity to gain useful information that could inform responses to future pollution incidents. In short, there were lessons that could apply elsewhere in the world.

The aim of the current New Zealand dotterel recovery plan is to achieve a 'population of 400 southern New Zealand dotterels that is self-sustaining or requires minimal management to exist on Stewart Island/Rakiura by 2030'. The major obstacle to achieving that seemingly modest, yet hugely ambitious number is simple: *Felis catus*. In the absence of mustelids, cats on Stewart Island remain the most lethal threat to dotterel survival. Unless they can be eradicated from the island, some form of cat control will be necessary in perpetuity. Not only is the island a large and rugged one, it has a sizeable human community – albeit largely gathered in one area. There was a time, of course, when the idea of removing pests from such a vast area appeared quite impossible; then successful operations on increasingly larger islands – Tiritiri Matangi, Kapiti, Little Barrier and

New Zealand shore plover numbers have increased, thanks to intensive management and the establishment of populations on other islands, such as Mana, north of Wellington. ALEX SCOTT

Grooming on the mainland: a preening shore plover at Plimmerton, opposite Mana Island. BRENDON DORAN

Shore plovers at Plimmerton: the reason for the exodus of birds to the mainland is believed to be a rat that reached Mana sometime in 2011. NEIL FITZGERALD

remote Campbell Island – saw the 'impossible' adjusted to 'difficult but achievable'. As it is, in the absence of eradication, cat control operations are expensive, and new techniques are probably going to be required to allow sustainable predator control over a large area.[26]

The shore plover that turned up at Miranda one Sunday evening in October 2000 was literally a flag-bearer for a recovery programme for its kind. It had arrived in the Firth of Thames, not after an epic ocean crossing from the Chathams, but from an island just a few kilometres to the north.

With the remnant population largely confined to just one island, an insurance policy had been needed, so a captive breeding programme was begun at Mount Bruce, with a view to eventually establishing populations on other islands off the mainland. Two early choices were Mana, just north of Wellington; and Motuora in the inner Hauraki Gulf. Both appeared to have suitable shore plover habitat and no predators – or, more correctly, no introduced predators. However an unforeseen hitch quickly revealed itself on Motuora – in the form of moreporks (which do not occur on the Chathams). Thus when five shore plovers were released on the island in 1994, a native species found itself served up with a highly endangered and naïve snack. Whether because of moreporks or for some other reason, the shore plovers showed little inclination to remain where they were put, and three of the five birds promptly departed.

Between September 1994 and March 2000, 75 birds were released on Motuora, although only one breeding pair remained on the island at the end of the 1999–2000 breeding season.[27] Nevertheless, the programme has continued – and has started to achieve considerable success. In addition to finetuning captive breeding and release methods, a second breeding programme was begun at Isaac Wildlife Trust. Populations of shore plover have now been established at several locations around the North Island; one of which has been extremely successful. Another, on Mana Island, has also met with good success – except for one unfortunate development, which has grown steadily more serious. Once again it is the problem of birds not remaining where they are put.

New Zealand has a growing network of birders among whom sightings of rare or unusual birds arouse considerable interest. Such was the case when shore plover began being reported on the mainland, particularly at Titahi Bay and Plimmerton, opposite Mana Island. Usually the reports involved only one or two birds – although that was sufficient to generate great enthusiasm amongst birders: a species one would normally have to go to Rangatira to see – or not see, because of stringent restrictions on access to that island – could be found on a highly public beach just north of Wellington. Then, in June 2011, OSNZ members returning from the society's annual conference reported a flock of shore plovers at Plimmerton. Eventually 35 birds were counted, all on the mainland and all – even more alarmingly – showing signs of remaining there. Late in 2011 a reason for the exodus was discovered; not only had a rat reached the island, it had killed and cached a number of shore plovers, illustrating the ongoing effort required to secure a future for these birds.

The New Zealand Fairy Tern Recovery Plan 2005–2015 set a clear goal: to 'increase the number of New Zealand fairy terns to 100 by 2021. Then to increase numbers . . . to at least 250 birds and the population to one capable of long-term survival, with minimal levels of protection, maintaining the population at key coastal sites'.[28] However, the critically low numbers of remaining birds pose considerable problems for those charged with implementing the plan. How do you increase the number of birds wanting to breed each year? Adult survival is reasonably high and the average lifespan is thought to be at least six years, although birds can be long-lived; two birds banded as chicks at Mangawhai were still alive 19 years later. However in 2005 only 43 percent of the population attempted to breed, and only 38 percent of eggs hatched. Survival of chicks to fledging was quite high, at 63 percent, yet recruitment into the breeding population was very low: of 55 birds banded between 1991 and 2003, only 32 percent had attempted to breed. Although capable of breeding after two years, birds were not attempting to breed until the fourth or even sixth year, suggesting that habitat may be a limiting factor.

Optimal breeding habitat for fairy terns seems to have an ocean coast on one side and a shallow estuary on the other – a perfect description of a spit, and of all four known breeding sites. A breeding pair also maintains a foraging territory, and such real estate

A rare visitor at Miranda: New Zealand fairy tern. IAN SOUTHEY

may be in short supply. On the other hand, this merely describes sites where fairy terns occur today. Could it be that, as with takahe and shore plover, there is a danger of regarding current habitat as optimal rather than as merely remnants of a formerly wider range? Other areas where fairy terns nested historically, such as Matakana Island, as well as areas adjacent to current breeding sites, like Te Arai near Pakiri, still seem to have suitable habitat available. A further question is, why are New Zealand fairy terns solitary nesters when the Australian fairy terns (*Sternula nereis nereis*) nest in colonies? A further difficulty with the situation today is the low number of eggs hatching – because many eggs are found to be infertile. 'The population could be suffering from inbreeding depression and this may be the cause of the high levels of egg infertility.'[29]

Keeping the New Zealand fairy tern population away from the abyss of extinction is a continuing challenge. One hurdle that dogged the recovery programme until recently was the taxonomic status of the New Zealand birds. If the same species occurs elsewhere and in larger numbers, particularly in Australia, why should scarce conservation dollars go to this programme rather than to other projects involving endemic species? Given the negligent level of funding directed to conservation by the current and past governments, it was a good question. The response of conservation advocates that fairy terns were part of our biodiversity and hence had intrinsic value was valid, but carried little weight with some conservation managers. There were, however, indications of some morphological and behavioural differences among the three populations of fairy tern. The New Zealand birds (*Sternula nereis davisae*), for instance, had longer wings than the other two subspecies. Then in 2006 an analysis of DNA samples from the three populations showed all three were genetically distinct. It also revealed an inherited group of genes that was found only in the New Zealand population. Here was incontrovertible evidence that the 'continuation of the Recovery Plan to conserve and expand this distinct population is warranted'.[30]

This should add weight to the recovery programme; although there are other problems to be tackled as well. One is that the New Zealand fairy tern population is split between Northland and Auckland regional conservancies of DOC. Differences in policy and priorities between

Tire tracks through fairy tern nesting habitat on Mangawhai Spit. JOHN DOWDING

Lonely vigil: a fairy tern warden on duty monitoring birds . . . and people. BRUCE SHANKS

the two have, in the past, created difficulties for those working with the birds. Recent moves to devolve more and more fairy tern management to community groups, while not without merit, also have drawbacks. The passion and drive of well-meaning individuals have produced enormous conservation gains in this country, and continue to do so. The length of the country there are community groups engaged in specific projects – mainland islands, habitat restoration, predator control and monitoring of endangered species. Within such groups there is always the danger of divergent goals. Some community projects continue from strength to strength while others have stalled, or even unravelled, before such hurdles. At Mangawhai, community groups are at loggerheads over management of the spit where half the fairy tern population currently nests. In 2011 an application for consents by the Harbour Restoration Society to clear mangroves and dredge the harbour channel was declined by Northland Regional Council in a decision that rested to a considerable extent on predicted effects on fairy tern habitat. Somewhat inevitably, this was appealed. Considerable work has already been done by the Harbour Restoration Society to stabilise the Mangawhai Spit with a bund and barrier fencing, along with replanting. While this may have achieved the desired effects for protecting the harbour, it has severely affected fairy tern habitat. The group is also seeking to continue replanting work – in September, at the very time the breeding season for both fairy terns and dotterels is getting underway. Members of the community advocating for fairy terns and those supporting the harbour group find themselves in opposing camps; and in the middle of it all is this country's most endangered species.

Community projects can be very effective in cases where it is known what caused a species decline, and a clear prescription exists as to what is needed to improve the situation. But with New Zealand fairy terns, there are too many unknowns. More research is needed – and such research is not the role of a community group. Nor is management of such a vulnerable species, until such time as a clear and effective prescription is developed. Under these circumstances, relying mainly on community effort to preserve our most critically endangered bird is risky at best. It is surely advisable to maintain the recovery programme primarily within a statutory agency.

Line-up of villains: each mammalian predator has affected our shorebirds in different ways, but the net outcome has been catastrophic. Clockwise, from top left: **stoat** ROD MORRIS; **ferret** ROD MORRIS; **cat** JOHN DOWDING; **kiore** ROD MORRIS; **hedgehog** JOHN DOWDING.

CHAPTER EIGHTEEN
WAR WITHOUT END: DEALING WITH PREDATORS

We may infer what havoc the introduction of any new beast of prey must cause in a country, before the instincts of the indigenous inhabitants have become adapted to the stranger's craft or power. — Charles Darwin[1]

In Dusky Sound in 1773 there was a ship – the *Resolution* – and on board there was a 'sly cat'; as Forster records, having 'no sooner perceived so excellent an opportunity of obtaining delicious meals, than she regularly took a walk in the woods every morning and made great havoc among the little birds, that were not aware of such an insidious enemy'.[2] Of course it is quite possible that rats had also left this ship – and the *Endeavour*, several years earlier. These visits were the vanguard of the second echelon of mammals to encounter New Zealand wildlife. Hundreds of years earlier had come the advance scouts: kiore in combination with the Polynesian settlers who brought them; so the mainland snipe were gone. Once the second echelon arrived, shore plover were gone from the mainland and New Zealand dotterel from the South Island. In the late 1880s came the third, and perhaps the deadliest wave of all – the mustelids: a trio of villains of which probably the stoat has had the most devastating effect.

Chatham Island snipe: one of five subspecies that remain on offshore islands, after the *extermination* of mainland birds by cats and rats. JOHN DOWDING

The continued viability of the southern dotterel population depends completely on the control of cats on Stewart Island. JOHN DOWDING

If we ignore for a moment the dreadful effects stoats have had on this country's wildlife and consider their qualities dispassionately, there is much to admire about these animals. Whatever they do they seem to do it very well. They swim and climb, and are highly mobile – travelling great distances relatively quickly. Within 20 years of their release in eastern parts of the South Island, they had reached the wettest areas of southwest Fiordland. Once they reached coastal areas, they then swam to – and colonised – most of the islands within 2–3 km of the coast. They can take prey several times their own body weight; and, taking advantage of periods of high prey densities, can breed rapidly. They are also 'patient and persistent. In short they are extremely efficient predators.'[3] The critical problem about stoats, of course, is that they have thrived in a country where they do not belong.

What these newcomers encountered was a suite of ground-nesting shorebirds that were behaviourally naïve towards mammalian enemies – and thus easy pickings. The birds had evolved in the presence of avian predators that hunted from perches or in flight, and usually by day and by sight.[4] Their cryptically coloured eggs and chicks are difficult to see, especially once chicks crouch and freeze in the presence of danger. On the Chatham Islands, shore plover and snipe nest in holes or under cover. Some species have developed fine arts of dissembling, feigning injury and other distraction displays, to mislead the intruder. None of these techniques, no matter how elaborately performed, offered protection from newcomers hunting by sight, hearing and scent, and often at night. Not only were our birds ill equipped to defend themselves, their breeding biology was such that recovering from repeated loss of eggs and chicks was extremely difficult.

Most New Zealand shorebirds show remarkable longevity compared to similar continental species. A variable oystercatcher at Ruakaka was known to be at least 33 years old when last seen; and there are wrybill and shore plover that are known to be over 20 years old. One corollary of living a long time is that there is less urgency for a bird to breed and replace itself. Many species delay breeding until they are two or three years old (or, in the case of variable oystercatcher, up to six). They lay smaller clutches and so produce fewer offspring each year. Many have extended incubation times, so eggs, chicks and adults are all vulnerable for longer. Fledging times of New Zealand shorebirds are especially protracted. Biologists refer to these as K-selected species.[5] The net result is a sort of circular argument for shorebirds. They live a long time but they do not have to breed as early or as fast or as successfully to replace themselves – because they live a long time. Until, that is, they are confronted with a circuit breaker in the form of new predators. Breeding strategies that evolved over tens or hundreds of thousands of years are impossible to change over a few hundred years. Once adult lifespans are reduced by predation, birds are no longer living long enough to replace themselves on average, and the whole population begins to decline.

The outcome for New Zealand species is disproportionate by world standards. Of the world's 2078 bird species classified as Threatened, 18 percent face threats from introduced species.[6] This figure tends to be higher for island populations – and nowhere is this more the case than here, where introduced species are considered a threat to 25 of the 45 threatened bird species. New Zealand currently has five of the world's rarest shorebird taxa – three species and two subspecies, all with populations of 150 or fewer.[7] Of New Zealand's 11 remaining endemic shorebird species, four are confined to predator-free islands, and a fifth is found only in the Chathams. Populations of three of the six species surviving on the mainland have declined and are threatened. Five of the six species that breed primarily in South Island braided riverbeds are classed as threatened, and a major cause of decline for these species is predation by introduced mammals.[8]

As we have seen, mainland snipe could not cope with kiore and departed early on, whereas other species were less affected. It is instructive to compare the relative fortunes of four plover species subsequently: all are broadly related, all are ground-nesters and three are of similar size, and all showed different susceptibility to predation. Shore plover had gone from the mainland by about 1872, most likely because of cats and rats. The southern New Zealand dotterel had been declining also, and after the 1880s introduction of mustelids, their decline accelerated. Northern New Zealand dotterels continue to survive, though they too have suffered; in one study predation was responsible for 70 percent of nest losses. Wrybill have persisted, but predators have been a problem for them too; while rates of predation seem to vary at different places, there is a clear pattern of higher wrybill productivity in areas of predator control.

Only banded dotterel are still relatively 'common' and widespread, possibly because 'it may be a more recent arrival in New Zealand than the other species and may have retained more effective anti-predator behaviours from its original range'.[9] Nevertheless, they too are vulnerable to predators. A study in the Mackenzie Basin found that 50 percent of banded dotterel eggs were lost to predators; and a further study found considerable improvements as the result of predator control: 49 percent of nests in non-trapped areas were lost, compared with 22 percent where trapping had occurred.[10] For other species the effects of predators are all too clear. Mammalian predators were largely responsible for the black stilt population plummeting from around 1000 to just 23 adults.[11] Black-fronted terns have also struggled against the onslaught: a study on the Ohau River found predators were responsible for over 47 percent of recorded mortalities, and the primary cause of egg loss in the nest.[12]

DEFENDING THE NEST

A variety of tricks and techniques for defending nests, eggs and chicks is displayed by New Zealand shorebirds; but none is effective against mammalian predators hunting by sight and smell, and at night.

Crèche of black-billed gull chicks on the Ashley River. JOHN DOWDING
(left) The cryptic eggs of a wrybill. KEITH WOODLEY

Size doesn't count: a fairy tern harassing a New Zealand dotterel that has strayed too close to its nest. BRUCE SHANKS
(left) Wrybill distraction display. JOHN DOWDING

A major threat to nesting shorebirds, numbers of the native black-backed gull increased unnaturally since European settlement of New Zealand. IAN SOUTHEY

On the South Island riverbeds there now exists a complex ecological relationship between predator and prey species. Various predators occur throughout the systems, in fluctuating densities. On some rivers, such as the Tasman, Godley and Ahuriri, stoats are major predators of wrybill and black-fronted terns; while on the Ohau River, Norway rats were found to be more prevalent than stoats.[13] In a five-year study in the Upper Waitaki Basin, video cameras were used to monitor 172 nests of banded dotterel, black stilt and black-fronted tern. Of 77 'lethal events' recorded, cats were responsible for 43 percent, hedgehogs 20 percent and ferrets 18 percent. Only cats were seen to take adult birds. Ninety percent of visits by predators or potential predators happened between sunset and sunrise.[14] Interestingly, only two nests were lost to aerial predators – one a harrier and the other a magpie. Given the way things used to be hundreds of years ago, only the visit of the harrier could be considered to be a 'natural event'. Or could it? The predator situation facing shorebirds is compounded by the fact that, as a result of human activities, harriers and black-backed gulls now occur in higher densities. Their effects are now likely to be considerably greater than in the past – merely adding further to pressures from mammalian predation and habitat loss.[15]

While the nature of predators varies widely among different habitats and in different regions, there is no doubt that one is a particular problem for shorebirds. As one report noted: 'Among conservation managers the stoat is now widely regarded as the most intractable mammalian pest species in New Zealand.'[16] A study in the Tasman River valley, in which the contents of 219 stoat dens were examined, found most of their diet consisted of rabbits and birds. Bird remains were found in 81 percent of dens, and three of the 10 bird species most commonly identified were threatened endemic shorebirds. Remains of banded dotterel, the most common shorebird in the Tasman, were found in 15 percent of dens. The wrybill population in 1992–94 was estimated to be about 150, but this had fallen to 100–120 by 2002. Remains found in a female stoat den excavated in June 2001 included one adult banded dotterel, one adult black-fronted tern and at least seven adult wrybills. Wrybill remains were found in 8 percent of all dens, indicating stoats may be having a huge effect on this species: 'The 24 adult wrybills found in dens during the study constituted roughly 20–24 percent of the wrybill population in this river; as not all stoat dens would have been found, this is likely to be an underestimate.'[17] The litany continues with black-fronted terns. In April 2001 a male stoat den excavated in the Tasman Valley contained the remains of at least 13 adult black-fronted terns. Researchers concluded: 'the presence of tern remains in 10 stoat dens, with a minimum of 25 adults counted, suggests that where stoats are at the densities we encountered, they must be considered a serious threat to black-fronted terns'.[18]

The situation in the eastern South Island becomes even more complex once *Oryctolagus cuniculus* enters the equation. Introduced in Southland in 1864, rabbits soon began doing what rabbits do so well – and before long they had become an economic disaster. Witnessing this rapid multiplication of pests, pastoral farmers formed the not unreasonable view that this was an unnatural phenomenon caused by the absence of the natural predators that presumably kept rabbit numbers under control in their original northern hemisphere home. So, to restore the 'balance of nature', natural enemies of rabbits were required – ferrets, stoats and weasels. And so, as we all know, a catastrophe was used to try and solve a disaster: 'It is a matter for regret that the zeal of the early acclimatizers was greater than their knowledge, and that mistakes were made by them fraught with evil results of a far-reaching and permanent nature.'[19]

The arrival of mustelids spelt particular problems for black stilts, and as it happens, a case could be made that Adolf Hitler was responsible for their sharp decline in the 1950s. In the 1920s and 30s extensive effort and resources went into trying to control rabbits with some

(top) Terrrible toll: the contents of this stoat den unearthed in the Tasman Valley, include the leg-bands of several wrybill. JOHN DOWDING
Predator traps at Mangawhai. KEITH WOODLEY

and in those areas of the Mackenzie Basin where rabbit populations were sharply reduced, clutch predation rates at banded dotterel nests were higher than those normally found in breeding seasons where rabbit control did not occur – and were similar to the predation rates after a rabbit poisoning programme. It is clear, then, that a shift in predator diet immediately follows a decline in rabbits.[22] As rabbit numbers fell all over the Mackenzie Basin, more predators were found on riverbeds rather than in the adjacent pasture that they normally preferred. For birds there did seem to be some security in numbers, however; areas with the highest density of nests experienced lower clutch predation than areas of low nest density, where only 10 percent of clutches survived.

Yet even where rabbits are present, birds remain vulnerable. This was revealed by examination of the stomach contents of three predator species – 375 cats, 371 ferrets and 86 stoats – trapped over three breeding seasons from 1997 to 2001. Birds were a substantial prey item for all three animals; tellingly, they were found in a much higher proportion of predator diets in the spring and summer of 1997 – after RHD was introduced – than in any other previous diet study.[23] Rabbits are also common around North Island dune areas, where variable oystercatchers, New Zealand dotterels and fairy terns breed. The DOC RHD response plan listed six birds that were particularly vulnerable to prey-switching, including black stilt, northern New Zealand dotterel and wrybill.[24]

success, until interrupted in the 1940s by the war, when rabbit numbers soared once again. In the 1950s control efforts intensified again, with considerable success, and rabbit populations were rapidly reduced. However this meant their predators, which had also been doing very well, were left to find alternative prey. This prey-switching – as Ray Pierce has persuasively argued – was likely behind the fall in stilt numbers.[20]

There is now considerable evidence showing a strong correlation between rabbit control and shorebird nesting success. A study of banded dotterel between 1977 and 1995 found that nest predation rates were a lot higher in areas where rabbit poisoning operations had been carried out.[21] In 1997 the rabbit haemorrhagic disease (RHD) virus was illegally introduced to New Zealand;

Table 1.1 Proportion of prey found in predator guts 1997–2001				
Predator	% of prey found in guts for each predator species			
	rabbit	birds	lizards	invertebrates
Cat	70	47	30	36
Ferret	69	28	–	–
Stoat	50	51	21	23

From surveys of 11 rivers between 1991 and 1994 it was estimated that the Mackenzie Basin contained a minimum of 85 percent of the world population of black stilts; 15 percent of the world population of wrybill (although this is thought to be an underestimate); and 32 percent of the world population of black-fronted terns.[25] Seen in this context, the effects of predators in the region have to be of enormous concern. So what can be done to protect riverbed birds from predators?

Catching and then releasing a stoat seems counter-intuitive, yet stoats attached with a radio-tracking collar like this one, have yielded priceless information on the animal's ecology and home ranges. JOHN DOWDING

We have the interesting situation that a moderately high, stable rabbit population is generally good for shorebirds – and may also determine which predators are present. Around the riverbeds, ferrets and cats tend to specialise in taking rabbits. In areas of high rabbit densities, a predator 'should encounter a rabbit fairly early on in the hunting cycle and that should do them'.[26] But where rabbit densities are too low there may not be so many cats and ferrets around. This opens opportunities for stoats, which can feed on smaller animals such as rodents and lizards, and can actually get by on those smaller animals. The intriguing possibility, therefore, is that maintaining a stable rabbit population may be the answer. Of course, if that were even possible – and there is much to suggest it is not – it would be a difficult idea to sell to high-country farmers. Which leaves active trapping and poisoning of predators.

There is abundant evidence that targeted predator control at particular locations can be effective, at least in the short term: numerous studies show that birds breed more successfully in trapped than in non-trapped areas. Usually the aim is to try and protect at-risk species by reducing predator abundance, so the more pests you remove the better. But this does not guarantee you will increase target populations or halt their decline. This is mainly because of the complexities of predator-prey relationships. Vulnerability to predation is more than just a matter of how many predators there are. For instance, how many of the prey species are there? How many are there of alternative prey species such as rabbits? What is the relative abundance of the different predator species?[27] Then there are further complicating factors. For example, effective predator control in the riverbed environments is also difficult because of high rates of immigration by predators into the trapped areas.[28]

While the vast scale of these riverbed systems makes controlling predators a monumental challenge, there are possible approaches for conservation managers to consider. Models have been developed that allow predictions of 'where on the riverbed predation risk may be the highest, where predation risk is low, and where predator control of introduced mammalian predators should be targeted'.[29] For example, an area showing declining rabbit numbers could be targeted for trapping, and if rabbit numbers continued to decline the trapping could run for more than one shorebird breeding season. Alternatively trapping could be done in areas of low nesting density, or in areas along riverbed margins where predator use is more frequent.[30]

For black-fronted terns, narrowing the control regime to target two key species could prove easier than targeting all predator species combined. For example, cats are clearly a major problem for tern survival at the chick, juvenile and adult life stages; and they are also one of the major predators of eggs. Norway rats are also a threat to terns at all stages; whereas hedgehogs pose a threat only at the egg stage.[31] Another possibility is to select the major tern colonies, and intensively trap around them. On the Ohau River, for instance, predator

Awesome landscape and enormous management challenge: intensive research on predator control in the Tasman Valley has produced some positive results, but has also underlined the difficulties and costs involved. Despite the expense, only continued large-scale predator control in such environments will secure a future for our unique riverbed species. JOHN DOWDING

control on an ongoing basis would most likely increase the population in that area and have a spillover effect into adjacent rivers.

The requirement is all too clear: to stop the decline and possible extinction of birds such as black stilt, black-fronted tern and southern New Zealand dotterel, long-term predator control is essential. Easier said than done, of course. Consider just one target species: stoats. They are flexible and opportunistic in their diet; they can take a wide range of prey in a wide variety of habitats; and their home ranges can be enormous. A study in the Tasman Valley, using radio-tracking collars, found stoat home ranges varied between males and females, and also changed seasonally. One male had a spring range of 809.7 ha, the largest recorded in New Zealand. In comparison, a female was found to occupy a spring range of 21.7 ha and a core range of just 3.2 ha. 'Ranges of this order,' concluded researchers, 'would clearly require a high density of traps or bait stations to ensure that all females have access to a control station.'[32]

The spread of predator species in a valley like the Tasman is also immensely varied. A seven-year predator control programme had some positive results in its early stages, in that ferrets disappeared from the trapped zone, though they were still found in the adjacent areas. Most stoats became confined to the forested sides of the valleys, although it was still not unusual for individuals to be found on the riverbed. Cats were the most difficult species because they are highly mobile, so that peak numbers would occur in buffer areas followed by a peak elsewhere. Early thinking was that intensive trapping for several years would reduce cat numbers but, as has been found elsewhere, that does not seem to happen. 'Create a vacuum and they just keep coming at you. What it has pointed out to us is that there is a phenomenal number of cats in the environment which you just don't realise, until you start doing this sort of thing.'[33] There is also the risk of trap-shy stoats and cats avoiding capture and breeding annually within the control area. So although its continuation is absolutely essential, predator control is only part of the picture. There is also a critical need to maintain what shorebird habitat remains, on a wide enough scale to be ecologically effective. To examine this further, we need to return once again to the braided rivers.

Wrybill nests are usually on clear gravel areas elevated above the level of major channels. Access to channels, particularly minor ones, is a key component of good nesting habitat. KEITH WOODLEY

CHAPTER NINETEEN
NATURAL FLOWS: ESSENTIAL INGREDIENT FOR A SHOREBIRD FUTURE

The tearing nor'-wester with its feverish hot breath comes not alone, in its train comes the heavy down-pouring rain, the melting of the snow in the 'back ranges' to keep the noisy blusterer company and work spells, sudden and fitful, on the swift-flowing rivers . . . —T.H. Potts[1]

Even before the recent goldrush scramble into dairy conversions, the agricultural industry in the central South Island was a thirsty endeavour. The braided river systems of Canterbury and the Mackenzie Basin have long been in the covetous sights of farmers, but proposals to increase water abstraction seldom gave any real weight to wildlife considerations. In the early 1980s Ken Hughey began a research project that aimed to fill a crucial gap in what was known about how the ecology of river species related to river hydrology. Two representative rivers were chosen: the lower reaches of the glacier-fed Rakaia; and the smaller Ashley River, which rises in the foothills east of the Main Divide. He was able to draw on earlier work on wrybills in the Upper Rakaia by Ray Pierce and Rod Hay, as well as on considerable work done by Pierce in the Mackenzie Basin. With a focus on river hydrology he was also entering largely uncharted realms.

Using four river-breeding birds – wrybill, banded dotterel, black-fronted tern and pied stilt – as indicator species, Hughey investigated how the hydrology of unstable, flood-prone rivers affects habitat use and breeding success. Flooding has two major effects on river birds – destruction of nests and fluctuations in food supply. During the 1982 and 1983 breeding seasons, 50 percent of wrybill nests were lost – over 72 percent of them to flooding, and 24 percent to predation. On the

Gathered together by the tide: while these wrybill at Miranda spend most of their year in the north, they are utterly dependent on riverbed habitat over 800 km to the south. JOHN DOWDING

A wrybill pair on the Waimakariri River. JOHN DOWDING

Rakaia, nest losses of other species were also mainly due to flooding; while on the Ashley, predation caused most nest losses.[2]

The 1982 season was nevertheless a good one for wrybill, with no major floods until November, by which time many first clutches had hatched successfully. This offset subsequent losses when floods destroyed most second clutches. The following season, early flooding delayed breeding until late September to October, and subsequent floods destroyed all first-clutch nests and did not allow birds to obtain sufficient energy to successfully renest. So fledging success on the Rakaia fell from 29 percent in 1982 to just 4 percent in 1983. Nesting success for pied stilts and black-fronted terns on the Rakaia was even lower, probably because they both tend to nest later and at lower elevations on the riverbeds. On the smaller, more stable Ashley River, success for all species was generally higher. For example, in 1983 more young birds were recruited into the population from six pairs of wrybill on the Ashley than from 30 pairs on the Rakaia.[3]

Balancing this is the relative effect of predators on breeding success on both rivers. Hughey found that while predation caused over 35 percent of banded dotterel nest failures overall on both rivers, it was responsible for nearly half the losses on the Ashley alone. This suggests the braided pattern on the larger rivers such as the Rakaia – which are also subjected to more frequent and extensive flooding – provides some protection from mustelids, compared with the smaller Ashley. This is supported by Hay, who found predators were an insignificant cause of breeding failure of wrybills on the Upper Rakaia.[4] However, the operative word here is 'some': as we have seen, mustelids – particularly stoats – will cross substantial channels to reach a tern colony.

Bird home ranges and nest locations appeared to be related to riverflow. On rivers such as the Rakaia, minor channels provide better foraging habitat than major channels, and home ranges for dotterels and wrybill tend to be smaller. Stable flows during winter and early spring produce higher densities of invertebrates in all aquatic microhabitats. At such times, wrybill nests and, to a lesser extent, those of banded dotterels were more likely to be near minor braids. However in years when regular flooding resulted in substantially lower food levels, both species moved to seepage zones where medium to low floods and freshes caused less disruption to aquatic invertebrates. This shift was greater for wrybills than for the less specialised banded dotterels and black-fronted terns. Wrybill are more dependent on aquatic microhabitats than either the more generalist dotterel, or the colonial nesting tern that can forage far from breeding areas.[5]

Wrybill generally choose nest sites at higher elevations than banded dotterel or black-fronted tern; so except for bank-to-bank discharges, when all nests may be lost, they are less susceptible to flooding. Pied oystercatchers on the riverbeds also generally nest

Large and small: research on the Lower Rakaia River and the smaller Ashley River (bottom right JOHN DOWDING) revealed much about shorebird ecology in relation to riverflows, and also the relationship between flows and predation risk. KEITH WOODLEY

The Rakaia in flood: a bank-to-bank flood like this sweeps away everything in its path, including shorebird nests. JOHN DOWDING

at higher levels. Banded dotterels may nest at lower levels, though they are just as likely to use less flood-prone areas away from major channels. This leaves the problematic black-fronted terns. Whether it is their preferred habitat, or where habitat loss elsewhere has pushed them, they now breed mainly on the riverbeds – which places them at risk. They tend to nest in loose colonies in areas of varying elevations, much of which are flood-prone. Nesting in loose colonies – rather than tight colonies at higher elevations – means they are spread over a wider area that is at risk from medium-level floods. They also nest later, initiating in late October and November, when there is a higher probability of flooding. So on rivers like the Rakaia, black-fronted terns face considerable challenges. Are they likely to fare better on the smaller, more stable Ashley? Well, yes as far as flood risk is concerned; however, there they face greater dangers from predators and human disturbance.

Floods reduce wrybill foraging options; on the Rakaia, floods are generally shortlived – often less than one day, with water beginning to clear within

Major and minor channels on a river provide different habitats at different times for shorebirds, so both are essential to the overall ecology of the river systems and the species dependent on them. KEITH WOODLEY

(top right) While strong natural flows do not always prevent stoats from reaching island nests, evidence shows the overall risk of predation is reduced. JOHN DOWDING
(middle right) Budding menace: young lupins establishing on the Upper Rakaia. KEITH WOODLEY
(bottom right) Mayfly: a common inhabitant of clear riffles where wrybill like to forage. Populations fluctuate with flooding but quickly build up again when river levels drop. ROD MORRIS
(bottom left) Wrybill foraging in the shallows. KEITH WOODLEY

a few days of the peak – and as water levels drop, the supply of available food increases sharply. Many invertebrates become stranded along the water edge or in disconnected pools and small side eddies, providing a rich feeding habitat. Birds may also find it profitable to forage along riparian margins which are unaffected during small to medium floods; however, during higher or more prolonged floods they are forced to move to more terrestrial margins further beyond the river. On the lower reaches of rivers such as the Rakaia, such terrestrial margins are now heavily vegetated and unsuitable for wrybill, forcing birds to leave the riverbed altogether. This probably explains what happened in

Water abstraction for irrigation is usually beneficial to exotic plant species that are all too ready to colonise the riverbeds. Encroaching vegetation may force birds to nest at lower elevations, where they are more vulnerable to flooding, as well as at increased risk from predators. Riverbed birds such as wrybill prefer open spaces away from vegetation, relying on cryptic colouration as a defence against avian predators. Vegetation may also serve to consolidate otherwise shifting substrate, thus modifying the natural flow regime. Reduced depth and velocity of riverflow reduces islands and makes predator access easier. In addition, increased human usage may mean more predators are led to nesting areas by following human scents across land.
KEITH WOODLEY

1983 when, following frequent and heavy flooding, a notable increase in wrybill was recorded on Lake Ellesmere.[6]

During periods of milky flow, as the river levels began to drop, Hughey noticed an increase in wrybill mating behaviour. He hypothesised that this may be an adaptive advantage on rivers such as the Rakaia – or, to put it another way, a gamble. Floods may occur at any time, so the odds of another flood occurring must increase as flows become clearer and lower (that is, as the time since the last flood lengthens). Wrybill incubation period is about 30 days, so nesting as soon as is metabolically possible after the last flood peak may reduce the chances of losing the nest to the next flood. So while breeding behaviour will still be initiated by photoperiod cues, activities leading to egg-laying 'could be advanced by flood peaks. As the time since the last flood lengthens, invertebrate populations also increase, which is good for newly hatched chicks.[7] Yet while an increase in invertebrate densities with lower riverflow is good news for wrybill, there is a catch. Because for them vegetation and nest sites do not mix, periodic floods are still needed to clear the shingle banks of weeds, to maintain clear nesting habitat and give some protection from predators. Hughey concluded that of the four indicator species, wrybill are the most specialised but also the least directly affected by flooding, so they are the best adapted for unstable environments such as the Rakaia.[8]

If riverflow levels were reduced on a long-term basis for human purposes such as water abstraction, it would affect different birds in different ways. Take the stilts, for example. Ultimately, for black stilts reduced flows would not be good news. At first glance they appear to hold an advantage over pied stilts in that they have more foraging options. They are better adapted for feeding in flowing habitats, and during spring floods and freshes they make more use of bars, major channels and ponds. In addition, during periods of low flow outside the breeding season when pied stilts have migrated out of the area, wetlands adjacent to the river are also available to black stilts.[9] Yet if the number of channels available for feeding were reduced, black stilts would be forced to make more use of static permanent water bodies, thus increasing competition with pied stilts. This, in turn, would facilitate species interaction and may lead to more mixed pair formation and hybridisation. While it is now known that black stilt will choose a black partner if one is available, such is the precarious status of the population that any increase in hybridisation is

River-dependent birds: for both wrybill (left JOHN DOWDING) and black fronted tern (right IAN SOUTHEY), the braided rivers are irreplaceable habitat; but each has different requirements when it comes to river flows.

undesirable. Black stilts also prefer to breed in braided river locations, usually surrounded by water, and reducing such habitat availability may force them to other wetland types, where there is an even higher risk of predation.[10]

A comparison of the habitat needs of wrybill and black-fronted tern further illustrates the complexity of the riverflow equation. Wrybill need both high and low flows to occur. They show a marked preference for feeding in minor channels, which are among the first to disappear as river levels drop. During high flow on the Ashley River, 50 percent of discharge occurred in the main channel; when the river was at its lowest, 95 percent of flow occurred in the main channel. Moreover, as the channel width contracted, so did aquatic habitat – from 10.2 sq m to 2.8 sq m.[11] In such conditions there is no longer any wrybill habitat. The terns, on the other hand, have completely different habitat use. A study on the Ahuriri River showed 70 percent use of main channels in autumn, 55 percent in winter, 60 percent in spring and 30 percent in summer. For wrybills increased flow means a decrease in riffles and runs available for foraging; for terns it means business as usual. Reduced flows would improve wrybills' feeding opportunities, but ultimately degrade both wrybill and tern habitat. Under normal flow conditions there is a balance of major and minor channels that minimises species overlap.[12]

Although wrybill require major floods, there are limits: they can cope with short-term effects of periodic flooding, but not with frequent floods such as occurred on the Rakaia in 1983. The specialist wrybill, concluded Hughey, are a species with a finely balanced, inflexible time budget. They will struggle to cope with any changes to habitat – such as alterations to riverflow – which lead to an increase in time spent foraging. Unlike the more generalist pied stilt for example, which can exploit a variety of habitats, wrybills cannot simply leave the river and breed elsewhere. 'This restriction, the limited flexibility of wrybill time budgets, and the unpredictable nature of the physical habitat, all combine to put [them] at risk from natural and man-induced changes in habitat quality.'[13]

For black-fronted terns, natural riverflows may be the prerequisite for their continued survival. As we have seen, establishing an accurate estimate of the black-fronted tern population has been problematic. However, a recent analysis of 47 years of count data for the species, and a comparison of earlier counts with more recent ones, revealed a population decrease of 14 percent. In recent counts, more than 200 terns were counted on only 12 rivers (14 percent of rivers surveyed); but between them those rivers held 70 percent of all terns counted.[14] While no accurate figure could be gleaned from the data, overall it indicated a black-fronted tern population of just over 8000. It also showed that rivers with flows of greater than 30 cumecs were critically important for this species:

Our data support the hypothesis that the amount of water in a braided river is important for black-

Wrybill chicks. KEITH WOODLEY

Major channel, Rangitata. KEITH WOODLEY

fronted terns. Tern numbers appeared to be highest on rivers with larger than average flows and the largest contemporary counts . . . were all from rivers with relatively high, little-modified flows.[15]

Where downward trends were detected, they were all on rivers with no pest control.

One of the largest declines in tern numbers occurred on the Pukaki River where, because of water diversion for electricity generation, average flows have been reduced by 97 percent. A decline also occurred on the Ashburton where flows were 60 percent lower. Rivers with low or medium flow supported just over 50 percent of terns in old counts, and only 32 percent in recent counts. The only river where the tern population actually increased was the Eglinton, where flow was unmodified but a continuous landscape-scale mammalian predator control project (directed mainly at yellowheads or mohoua) was being carried out over 10 years of the monitoring period. For these terns the situation is gravely serious. According to IUCN criteria, a species is endangered if the probability of extinction in the wild is at least 20 percent within five generations. In 2002, Keedwell predicted a decline of 60–75 percent over 25 years, or just 2.5 generations. The latest study concludes: 'Even if populations on larger rivers were stable, we predict the total population will decline by 50 percent over the next 25 years if trends on smaller rivers continue, and if management focused on recovering populations is not instigated with some urgency.'[16]

Conservation of a representative range of river systems is essential for protection of riverbed species. Rivers need to be managed in a way that maintains all the characteristics of natural flow regimes. This includes allowing natural erosion to occur on riverbed margins, resulting in the provision of stable side channels and other habitats for birds forced off the river by floods.[17] Stopbanks and willow planting obstruct this process, and so the river floods bank to bank. During the breeding season, 'low flow' characteristics are important as they provide food supplies and feeding habitat, while flood flows provide or maintain suitable nesting habitat.[18] These dynamic systems need dynamic management to maintain the range of microhabitats required by different species. It is an enormous task that will require considerable effort and resources. It may even require something of all of us:

Management of entire catchments is probably the only option for conserving these birds. It requires that we not only accept the ongoing monetary costs of conservation, but that New Zealanders reduce their demands on the environment and accept restrictions on some recreational activities.[19]

Beginning of a problem for shorebirds: mangrove seedlings establishing on an area of mudflat used by birds for sub-roosting on the incoming tide. BRIAN CHUDLEIGH

CHAPTER TWENTY
AQUA BLUES: THE PROBLEMS WITH WATER

Jim Archibald is possibly smiling in the photo, although it could also be a grimace, reflecting astonishment or incredulity. The then CEO of Tourism Coromandel is standing on the banks of the Waihou River, the new Kopu Bridge under construction in the background, holding a wine glass full of brown liquid – river water. At this spot the river is always brown, its sediment-laden waters sweeping by in one last broad arc before spilling into the Firth of Thames. However the contents of the glass reflect more than that. A report by the Parliamentary Commissioner for the Environment had just labelled the Waihou the third most polluted waterway in the country. The report identified three main pollutants: sediment from erosion; bacteria from animal and human waste; and excess nutrients, mostly nitrogen, from farm activities. It is estimated that the Waihou River contributes over 1900 tonnes of nitrogen and 138 tonnes of phosphorus to the Firth of Thames each year – and these are *conservative* estimates.[1] The story in the *Hauraki Herald* goes on to quote a senior Environment Waikato manager as saying he was not surprised at this finding, and that if the study had covered the nearby Piako River as well, 'it would have rated even worse'. Around 90 percent of nutrient loads originating from the Waikato are discharged into the Firth of Thames via the two rivers, and 'the condition of both rivers is a risk to the southern Firth of Thames'.[2]

The 3600 sq km catchment of the Firth of Thames, like many other large catchments around the country, bears the marks of total transformation – the legacy of over 600 years of human endeavour. Some burning of forest by Polynesian settlers occurred around Thames, and although this did not devastate the forests it 'did have an adverse cumulative effect over time'.[3] Once Europeans settled the

Damning evidence: a glass of water from the Waihou River, third most polluted river in New Zealand. HAURAKI HERALD

Piako River mouth, Firth of Thames: this was where the famous godwit E7 began and ended her migration in 2007. The broad mangrove zone extends unbroken around the entire southern coast of the Firth of Thames, separated from the Hauraki Plains beyond by the stop banks that have contributed to the mangrove expansion. KEITH WOODLEY

area – and particularly after the 1870s – considerable economic benefits came from logging and mining on the western slopes of the Coromandel Ranges to the east, together with forest clearance, drainage and intensive agriculture over all but a few natural remnants of the Hauraki Plains to the south. These activities also carried massive implications for shorebird habitat in the Firth. How bad is the problem? Over the past 6500 years, the southern coastal margin of the Firth has extended seaward at a rate of around 2 km every 1000 years. The rate of sedimentation and seaward expansion have increased markedly during the last 50 years, largely as a result of human activities in the catchment.[4] Each year the Waihou and the Piako discharge an estimated 230,000 and 35,000 tonnes of sediment respectively. Environment Waikato research revealed rates of sedimentation in the estuaries of the Coromandel Peninsula were now up to 10 mm per year, compared with just 0.1–0.2 mm per year before human settlement. Sediments are now accumulating in many east coast Auckland estuaries at a rate of 2–4 mm per year; but on the intertidal flats of the Firth of Thames the rate is 25 mm per year. Within the mangrove zone, which is expanding on average 20 m per year, the sedimentation rate is 50–100 mm per year. The annual amount of sediment entering the Firth is estimated to be 56 tonnes per square kilometre, which is considered a 'relatively low rate compared to the national average for estuaries'.[5]

The amount of sediment retention in an estuary depends on factors such as topography, tidal flushing patterns and wind. While some material gets carried as suspended solids into the open ocean, most of it settles. Sedimentation together with erection of stopbanks, which prevent the natural grading and settling of sediment by tidal action, produce ideal conditions for mangroves. Beginning in the 1950s mangroves began to expand along the southern Firth of Thames where they did not previously grow, and once they got established, sediment retention rates became even higher. Since then the mangrove zone has expanded by between 900 and 1000 m into the southern Firth of Thames.[6] Currents within the Firth move in a clockwise fashion around the southern part of the bay, which is where the bulk of the 8500 ha of mudflats are, and hence also where the biggest concentrations of foraging shorebirds can be found. It is also where the bulk of the sediments and nutrients settle out, and where the mangrove zone now occurs – with serious consequences for the benthic prey of birds.

Fine silty sediment reduces diversity on the mudflats. The material pouring into the Firth in recent times – fine grain-size, organically rich terrestrial sediments – has covered old sandbars and formerly extensive shell beds.[7] In situations that are not unlike those faced by invertebrates coping with floods on braided rivers, the tidal cycle and strong winds stir up these sediments, causing turbidity and sediment movement, and not a few problems for filter-feeding animals. Limited light penetration and sediment movement reduce the rate of microbenthic algal production that is so essential to the estuarine food chain. Bivalves such as cockles and pipi can feed effectively in an environment of increased suspended sediments for periods of up to one week before detrimental effects occur. In one study, populations of wedge shell *Macomona liliana* – a major shorebird prey species – were adversely affected by higher sediment levels; most had died after 14 days. Sedimentation also adversely affects polychaete fauna, which are major food items for birds such as godwits.[8]

A study of the Waitemata Harbour in the 1990s found marked decreases in benthic fauna abundance and distribution since a previous study in the 1930s, and pointed to land-use changes in the catchment area as the primary cause. Increased sedimentation since forest clearance began in pre-European times, along with extensive subdivision in west Auckland and on the North Shore since the 1930s, meant greatly increased quantities of clay and mud entering the harbour, contributing to the largely muddy substrate. Urbanisation of the catchment in the past 60 years meant greatly increased freshwater, sediment and pollution runoff into the harbour at times of heavy rain. 'This is reflected in heavy metal concentrations in the harbour sediments and possibly in salinities periodically lower than would have been the natural range.'[9] These patterns of sedimentation and runoff apply to most of our harbours and estuaries.

On the other hand, with sediment there may come nutrients as well and, in the right forms and concentrations, these can be beneficial to intertidal invertebrate communities. Too much nutrient, though, leads to problems. From the 1990s to 2011 there was a fivefold increase in the use of nitrogen on Waikato farms. In the southeastern Firth of Thames levels of cadmium, from phosphate fertilisers and a legacy of former mining operations, now exceed acceptable thresholds. The equivalent of 32 truckloads of urea enters the Firth of Thames each week.[10] Nutrient enrichment – particularly from nitrogen and phosphorus – may lead to the growth of algal blooms, which then reduce light penetration and disrupt the production of that vital building block of the food web – phytoplankton.

We have seen how farming practices have been partly beneficial to some shorebirds such as pied oystercatchers and spur-winged plovers; for most species, however, it is a relationship that is far from symbiotic. Nowhere is

Uneasy connections: these pied oystercatchers in dairy pasture at Miranda are well used to such terrain – they may even be the same birds that breed in farm paddocks in the South Island. The mangroves in the background represent a growing threat to shorebird habitat in the Firth of Thames, and intensive dairy farming is implicated in their expansion.
KEITH WOODLEY

this more readily seen than in the central South Island, where the misguided dairy conversion bonanza is in full swing. In late 2010, under the heading: 'More cows than people', the *New Zealand Herald* reported an increase of 144,000 animals in the national dairy herd since the previous year. 'The nation's milking cow population has overtaken the human population – the 4.4 million cows now outnumber the 4.39 million people.' The average herd size has tripled in the last 30 years, and increased by more than 100 animals in the past eight years. And much of this increase occurred in the South Island, which 'now accounts for 39.3 percent of total milk solids produced'. A large part of that expansion has been in Canterbury where, from 1990 to 2003, dairy stock numbers increased 390 percent, while sheep numbers fell 24 percent.[11] The amount of land used by dairying has increased from 63,000 ha in 1995 to 146,000 ha in 2004, while total agricultural land used has remained relatively constant.[12]

The relevance of all this to shorebirds is quite simple: it is all about water. Dairying is a water-intensive industry, and expansions of production on this scale can only occur if sufficient water is available. As we have seen, the hydrology of the alluvial Canterbury Plains is a complex system of rivers, aquifers and associated wetlands. Low average rainfall and high evaporation rates deprive dairy farmers of a water source that is more readily available elsewhere in the country, such as in the Waikato. So the rivers and related aquifers are the

Dairy herd and irrigator, South Canterbury. KEITH WOODLEY

natural place to look for their needs.

Twenty-five kilometres south of Christchurch, State Highway 1 crosses the Selwyn River. Rising in the Big Ben Range in the Canterbury foothills and flowing into Lake Ellesmere, this river represents a notable footnote in the ornithological history of our shorebirds: several wrybill specimens now in the British Museum were collected here. Where it flows into the lake it may once have been one of the best fisheries in New Zealand. According to Martin Clements, North Canterbury chairman of Fish and Game New Zealand, records show that over 65,000 trout used to return to spawn each year; in 2007 there were just 87.[13] Back at the bridge 20 km upstream, it is easy to see why trout are scarce: there is no water. The bed is bone dry and the ridges and islands of gravel are now choked with thick vegetation – mainly broom and willow.

> It is these insidious creeping changes in the rivers [as] they are quietly de-watered and all of a sudden people just accept them as being dry riverbeds. Hundreds of thousands of people drive over the bridge and think it is just an old gravel riverbed but in the past it used to be a vibrant river system.[14]

What has happened to the Selwyn should be a wake-up call for us all. You would think it would be etched in the minds of all farmers, planners and government officials. But this does not seem to be the case. For the expansion of dairying on these plains is only possible with the assistance of rows and rows of centre-pivot irrigators operating 24 hours a day, if necessary. Land under irrigation increased by 74 percent between 2002 and 2008.[15] In the 2011 budget the government allocated a further 35 million dollars for irrigation projects, and during the 2011 general election campaign indicated even more could be allocated from proceeds of state asset sales. With more and more water abstracted from rivers and aquifers, the entire hydrology of the region is put under stress – and this is compounded by the downstream effects of intensive farming. Ninety percent of lowland streams are now classed as 'poor' or 'very poor', compared with less than 30 percent in 1999. In 10 percent of wells monitored by Environment Canterbury, nitrate levels exceed the standard for New Zealand drinking water. Some aquifer-fed streams are now dry in summer, wetlands are disappearing and river biodiversity is declining.[16]

In 2010 a National Institute of Water and Atmospheric Research (NIWA) study of water quality in New Zealand lakes presented a sorry picture, especially for Canterbury. Of 68 lakes with reliable monitoring data between 2005 and 2009, the water quality of 19 had declined, and no less than 15 of those lakes were in Canterbury.

> The most significant finding . . . is that pastoral land use in New Zealand is associated with eutrophication (from excessive nutrients) and ecological deterioration . . . Furthermore the condition of some lakes currently in good condition is declining, most likely as a result of nutrient enrichment and livestock farming.[16]

At Waituna Lagoon in Southland, drainage and dairying are seriously degrading one of this country's six Ramsar wetlands sites (on the Ramsar List of Wetlands of International Importance). Together with the adjoining Awarua Bay, the lagoon is an important shorebird site. Farm drains channel nutrients and sediments directly into these waterways: 'It's almost an unavoidable consequence of farming in Southland. Studies are hinting that we're pumping around twice as much phosphates into Waituna as it ought to absorb.'[17]

Surface waterways get contaminated through runoff from water and effluent irrigation, directly through effluent discharge, or by the stock entering the waterway. Many waterways on farmland do not incorporate riparian buffers and are not fenced off, and large animals eroding riverbanks are a major problem. Sediment in streams causes two main problems: fine sediment stops photosynthesis in turbid waters and subsequently kills plants, starving those dependent on them for food; and in streams with inadequate flow, sediment falls to the bottom, filling up the gaps in the gravel bed to the detriment of fish and invertebrate life.[18]

Many farmers are genuinely motivated to achieving good environmental outcomes from their activities. According to one Federated Farmers executive member, farmers are 'highly conscious of the environment we live in and take a great deal of pride in it'.[19] However, the authors of a Lincoln University study looking at the external costs of dairying in Canterbury found that 'attitudes of dairy farmers to sustainability and the environment have at best a limited role in influencing their propensity to adopt sustainable management practices'.[20] And there is a tendency among farmers to pay lip-service only to environmental protection. 'Environment Canterbury (ECan) figures showed less than 60 percent of the 861 dairy farms monitored in the region last season fully complied with effluent-disposal', and '73 farms were seriously non compliant'.[21] Nationally '40 percent of farmers were not complying with their resource consents governing the treatment and discharge of dairy-shed effluent'.[22]

The consent and regulatory procedures of Environment Canterbury were also under stress, as the council became inundated with water consent applications. Each year since 2000 consent applications increased 11 percent. Each year this was the equivalent of irrigating the total area already consented in Otago; in one three-month period 'the volume of water being sought by consent applications in Canterbury was equivalent to the total volume of water allocated in Taranaki in the last 20 years. By 2006 two thirds of all irrigation consents being applied for in the country were in Canterbury.'[23] The consent process underlined once again a fatal flaw in the Resource Management Act. The complex and interlinked hydrology of the region means even incremental increases in water extraction will have a cumulative effect. 'Yet when ECan tried to take a precautionary approach, declining one high profile groundwater application because its cumulative effects would be detrimental, the Environment Court overturned the decision, insisting it must have scientific proof that the additional water take would damage the aquifer system.'[24] Besieged on all sides – by farmers complaining of slow processes, by local mayors complaining regional growth was being obstructed and by environmental groups and recreational users of the rivers urging restraint in water abstraction – ECan struggled to fulfil its obligations. The issue was one of the factors behind the drastic and ill-considered central government decision in early 2010 to dismiss the regional councillors and appoint a commissioner. As these events unfolded, none of those involved was advocating on behalf of shorebirds.

Human modification of the Upper Waitaki Basin probably began with moa hunters, who were particularly active in the fourteenth and fifteenth centuries. By the sixteenth century moa hunting had diminished, although wide-scale harvesting of birds – most commonly waterfowl, weka and brown quail – continued. It is thought that over the last 3000 years, as the climate became drier, natural fires may have destroyed much of the forest cover of the basin floor. While it is unclear how much forest remained when people arrived, indications are that it succumbed to human activities. Pre-European vegetation would have been a complex mosaic of dryland grasslands and shrub communities that surrounded wetland complexes.[25] What is clear, however, is that after 1850, substantial changes came to the area – for which people were entirely responsible. Around 1850 the Upper Waitaki Basin had 45,500 ha of braided river and 22,900 ha of open water habitat, with 200 km of shoreline habitat. There was also 70,700 ha of wetlands, of which 19,200 ha was swampland, and the remaining areas a variety of wetland habitats – tarns, small lakes, flushes – as well as dryland vegetation communities.[26]

Between 1850 and 1999, development for pastoral farming – which meant burning vegetation and draining wetlands – removed 29,000 ha, or 40 percent, of wetlands in the basin. 'Of the wetlands that remained 30 percent retain low levels of their original character, 50 percent retain moderate levels of naturalness and only 20 percent retain high levels.'[27] Modifications to vegetation patterns and distribution within remaining permanent and seasonal wetlands caused reductions in local groundwater tables through increased evaporation rates and reduced runoff response times. There were also disruptions to natural river flow and changes to channel behaviour, as farmers sought to protect land from flooding as well as abstract water for irrigation and farm supply. Drainage, pasture improvements and stock grazing all directly affected adjoining wetlands and shorebird habitat.

But significant though these farming impacts are, they become relatively minor when compared to the colossal hydroelectric power developments in the region. The formation of four hydro lakes and modification to the levels of two natural lakes inundated approximately 22,250 ha of land – including 16 percent of the open braided river habitat and 20 percent of the total area of swamplands in the area pre-1850. Over half of the lost river habitat was on the Tasman River.

Weed-busting: weed control is a major focus of Project River Recovery. Before and after images of a vegetation transect in the Tasman Valley. CHRIS WOOLMORE

The Tekapo River before and after a discharge of water from the hydroelectric power scheme. JOHN DOWDING

Approximately 4200 ha of braided river floodplain in the Pukaki, Tekapo and Ohau rivers – nine percent of the original braided river floodplain area, has had the main source of flow diverted, reducing natural functioning and dynamics of rivers and making [them] more vulnerable to weed encroachment.[28]

There is also good news, however. Project River Recovery (PRR) was born out of the hydro development scheme, and is funded by Meridian Energy in mitigation for some of its environmental impacts. The objective of PRR is 'to carry out jointly agreed programmes of wetland habitat enhancement with the goal of providing habitat and conditions equivalent to or greater than the net loss of habitat and conditions attributable to the Waitaki Hydro Electric Project.' It is a bold goal, but is it achievable? One study concluded: 'it is unlikely that the area of natural active braided rivers or adjoining wetlands inundated could be recreated or replaced, given the total area involved or the dynamic natural character of the habitat types'.[29] In its core work – focusing on maintaining habitat in the high-quality riverbeds that remain in the Upper Waitaki since the development, and trying to mitigate some of the negative effects it had in the more modified rivers – the project has been 'pretty successful'.[30] Indeed, it is probably one project where that otherwise much misused word 'mitigation' still means something.

The project has made considerable progress in restoring some riverbed habitat. In the Tasman, for instance, Russell lupins – those colourful flowers gracing countless postcards and calendars with Aoraki Mt Cook as a backdrop – are for the most part gone from the valley. On the other hand they remain widespread in the Ahuriri River valley, although other invasive species such as broom, gorse, buddleia, tree lupin and crack willows have been reduced or eradicated. What has become clear during the progress of PRR is just how much variation there is between river systems. To the casual viewer, many of these rivers look very similar; and you might assume that conservation actions in one river would be a model for all, or at least most other rivers. A survey classifying all the plant communities in the braided rivers in the Upper Waitaki revealed great variations – not only in the types of communities in the different systems, but in the relative distribution of plant communities within different systems. Even though they share the same origins in the Southern Alps, each part of the system is subject to variations in altitude, climate, sediment supply and flood regimes. An attempt to do a similar survey classifying invertebrate faunas of the region has revealed similar complexities. Provisional examination of some of the 100,000 specimens collected to date has revealed many endemic species within each river system.[31]

So what needs to be done to maintain these rivers as shorebird habitats? Clearly the challenges of managing habitats over an entire river system are huge.

Conflicting interests on riverbeds: willows planted as a flood control measure completely alter the hydrology of the river and destroy shorebird habitat. JOHN DOWDING

Recognising the unique complexity of each river system would be a start. Since the 1980s there has been a black stilt recovery group and recovery plan, but there has been nothing similar for other braided river species such as wrybill, banded dotterel, black-fronted terns or black-billed gulls. The Department of Conservation has recently moved away from individual species recovery plans, seeking to establish a broader approach, managing habitat types or ecosystems to the benefit of multiple species. The reasoning is that by managing critical areas of habitat you will be able to manage all of those species. As we have seen, shorebird distribution over the various river systems is complex, with some rivers more important for certain species than others. For instance there is a good population of wrybill in the Tasman but fewer black-fronted terns, and even fewer pied oystercatchers. In general, breeding oystercatchers and wrybills tend to be quite dispersed, while terns and gulls may be clumped in large colonies or dispersed in looser ones. Where we see an individual river, birds may see habitat spread over several rivers, using different areas at different times – depending on conditions such as climate and flow regimes. Then there is the complexity of both mammalian and avian predator distribution and abundance.

A recently completed seven-year predator control programme in the Tasman Valley is a case in point. The goal was to manage a 25,000 ha area, of which 45 percent is riverbed or river flats, 'to see if predation rates can be reduced to levels that will allow a range of bird, lizard and invertebrate species to either maintain stable, high populations, or [allow] historically low populations to increase'.[32] A joint project by PRR and DOC, the programme was an extensive – and expensive – operation involving over 1300 traps and a million trap nights. Thousands of predators were caught. But has it been worth the colossal expense and human resources required of it? More to the point, has it worked – and if so, can it be used as a model for other areas? The outcome is still being assessed, but some indications are positive. For instance, where hatching success for shorebirds can, from year to year, range from 30 to 70 percent nationally, some years during the project achieved 90 percent.[33] A progress report at the end of the breeding season in 2007 showed that, of 76 black-fronted tern nests for which the outcomes were known, 58 failed: 39 of those failures were the result or predation, and 11 were due to flooding. Wrybill fared somewhat better, with 84 percent of known nests hatching.[34] However it has been calculated that productivity of 0.75 chicks per pair per year is required for the wrybill population to stabilise and grow; in the Tasman only 0.6 per pair was achieved, which is not enough. It remains to be determined whether the Tasman model is a successful one that can be applied to other river systems. The bottom line is that ongoing predator control in these areas is still an absolute necessity. That alone however, is not sufficient: it needs to be backed up with strategies for managing weeds and maintaining natural flows as much as possible.

All of which makes the recent establishment within DOC of a technical advisory group (TAG) to look at broad-scale management of braided rivers a promising milestone. The bad news, though, is that work by the TAG on developing a conservation plan for the rivers was substantially delayed by restructuring within the department in 2011. With the ever-diminishing resources being allocated to DOC, it remains to be seen whether the group even survives, let alone achieves conservation outcomes for shorebirds.

Applicants for irrigation consents are usually keen to determine 'minimum flows' for a given river, meaning any water above that should be available for abstraction. Unfortunately there is no definitive answer to what constitutes minimum flow. In terms of shorebird habitat, each river system is a complex matrix of variables – the relationship between flow and islands; and the relationship between breeding success and islands and predators. The braided rivers provide more than just bird habitat. They are the vehicle for moving gravels down from the mountains; they manage flood flows; and they are essential for the recharging of aquifers. Only by maintaining their dynamic qualities can we ensure that they keep providing these services. It is, says DOC officer Andy Grant,

> . . . the dynamic of flood and low flow that makes these rivers work. The floods flush the system and provide nutrients, and you have got to have those floods, those freshes and the low flows. It is maintaining that diversity of flow that keeps these habitats. All those little systems are understood to some degree but you just don't know what dewatering is going to do in the long term. Focusing on rivers for development purposes risks losing sight of long term consequences for rivers which are essential for birds, plants, invertebrates and people.[35]

A potentially positive development in June 2011 was publication of a National Policy Statement for Freshwater Management (NPS) that followed a report to government by a board of inquiry. One objective of the statement was 'to improve integrated management of fresh water and the use and development of land in whole catchments, including the interactions between fresh water, land, associated ecosystems and the coastal environment'. The statement set out to give guidelines to regional councils for managing water quality and allocation. For instance, when considering a consent application the consent authority must consider 'the extent to which the change would adversely affect safeguarding the life-supporting capacity of fresh water and of any associated ecosystem'. However these policies are not binding rules: 'decision-makers have to weigh them up alongside other matters when considering resource consent applications'.[36] It is instructive that a key recommendation by the Board of Inquiry that natural and in-stream values of freshwater systems be maintained, or where practicable restored and enhanced, was not adopted by government. A Cabinet paper on the NPS considered 'this gave *precedence to environmental values*' so it was deleted 'to provide a better balance of all values'.[37]

The NPS has also been criticised for not setting clear national objectives for water quality; and for giving regional councils until 2030 for full implementation.

The lack of national standards that apply to all water bodies and the likely long period for implementation, combined with new subsidies for irrigation schemes that are likely to result in further intensification of land use, suggest that despite the NPS the condition of New Zealand's lakes, rivers and wetlands is likely to continue to decline for several more years and possibly longer.[38]

Maintaining natural flows on the braided rivers remains essential for the future of key species such as wrybill and black-fronted tern. It seems highly questionable that in the current political and economic climate the NPS is capable of ensuring that outcome.

Under the Canterbury Water Management Strategy (CWMS) a series of Zone Implementation Programmes (ZIPs) has been established. Each zone committee, comprised of community stakeholders and district and regional council representatives, is charged with drafting a management plan recommending 'actions and approaches for integrated water management solutions to achieve the CWMS principles, targets and goals encompassing economic, social, cultural and environmental outcomes'.[39] The draft plan for the Ashburton ZIP states that 'sufficient and reliable river flows need to be available for fishing, swimming, birds, plants, fish and invertebrates, and to enable mahinga kai gathering and farming'. It also recognises that water quality, natural character and remaining indigenous biodiversity on the two rivers bordering the zone – the Rakaia and the Rangitata – 'need to be protected and maintained'. There are many laudable aims in the plan, with considerable emphasis given to environmental considerations; but how effective it will be remains to be seen. The zone committees are, after all, advisory

Gravel extraction on the Waimakariri River near Christchurch. JOHN DOWDING

bodies only. They cannot 'commit any Council to any path or expenditure', and each ZIP 'has no binding force in its own right. It is a set of recommendations to the Ashburton District Council, Environment Canterbury, and other stakeholders.'[40] Nevertheless, in the right hands and with political will, there is potential for achieving good outcomes for shorebirds.

Ken Hughey suggests a need to think outside the square, and notes that some people, including at least one energy company, are starting to do that. The answers to increasing demands for water in Canterbury lie in being smarter about water storage and circulation and avoiding using main-stem channels for storage. On the Rakaia, for example, Hughey thinks Lake Coleridge could be used in ways that have minimal impact on the river. On the Hurunui, the idea of a large storage dam on a tiny tributary that flows at about 1 cumec – and less for much of the time – but could supply over 100 million cubic metres of water is being investigated. 'The environmental costs', says Hughey, 'are absolutely negligible, the gains potentially enormous. A project such as this alongside weed control and predator control could, with a bit of will, a bit of time, and having good modern farmers [working with us] which is what we have got, achieve net conservation gains.'[41]

There are other issues that need to be addressed. Besides water abstraction for agriculture, rivers are subjected to other development pressures, such as encroachment onto riparian areas. Far from maintaining or replanting riparian margins, in areas such as along the Waitaki there is a lot of farm development creeping right onto the river margins. In one example, a farm development occurred on a wildlife reserve. Gravel extraction is another activity which, if not managed carefully, can cause destruction of ecologically sensitive areas such as the black-billed gull habitat on the Oreti River. It is also a major problem in Canterbury – and this will no doubt intensify during the post-earthquake rebuilding of Christchurch. Recreational use of the riverbeds continues to increase, too. The use of 4WD vehicles in river systems is seen by some as a fundamental right – a view that is continually reinforced by the advertising industry. Clearly people are not aware of the damage they may be causing. One study found that while recreationists generally agree with bird conservation, most did not think their activities would affect nesting birds.[42] Says Andy Grant, 'There's pressures coming from everywhere and I guess it is up to us to try and maintain as much of the integrity of habitat for species as well as allowing development to happen.'[43]

Another recent development that may prove beneficial to the rivers was the formation of BRaid or Braided River Aid. It is an umbrella group of representatives from local riverside communities, central and local government departments (including ECan and DOC), recreational and conservation groups, professional ecologists, universities, and companies with commercial interests in braided rivers. Its stated objectives are to protect, enhance and restore braided river ecosystems, encourage cooperation among stakeholders in facilitating research, and encouraging community involvement in helping protect the rivers. In times of financial restraint it is always tempting to put commercial gains associated with braided rivers ahead of their other values and services, thus downplaying the international significance of Canterbury's braided rivers as essential habitat for many threatened endemic species. Environment Canterbury, as a key participant of BRaid, has stated its commitment to the goal of the CWMS to 'correct the decline' and 'enhance the breeding population of indigenous braided river birds'.[44] It remains to be seen how effective this initiative is, but it is to be hoped that ECan has the potential, in view of its commitments, to implement the NPS extensively and quickly. If, that is – given the current economic and political climate – it is able to do so.

Then there is making the best of what you have got. One of the defining features of the approaches to Christchurch is the Waimakariri River: running across the northern edge of the city, it is something of a playground for the people of Christchurch. It is also a microcosm of the many pressures facing the braided rivers. In a recent initiative, parts of the river near the city have been incorporated in the Waimakariri Regional Park. The park sets aside different parts of the river for different things. The area nearest to the city is popular for all manner of recreation; though it would appear the interests of shorebirds have yet to be fully addressed – there are wrybills and black-fronted terns on the river, as well as a colony of over 1000 black-billed gulls, in the designated recreation area. However city bird ranger Andrew Crossland takes a positive view: the park's very proximity to the city gives a unique opportunity:

> *If you look at the ability to protect the birds long term, say over the next 500 years, it has got to be on a river beside a big city, because that is where you have got the resources, the volunteer base, the councils, regional councils with money and rangers and vehicles, shotguns and traps to look after things.*[45]

Sharing the beach: a flock of godwits in mid-January at Matarangi, Coromandel. KEITH WOODLEY

CHAPTER TWENTY-ONE
COASTAL PRESSURES: COMPETING FOR THE MARGINS

The shellbank roosts along the southern Manukau Harbour seethe with movement: masses of oystercatchers and godwits, knots and wrybills, turnstones and gulls. Pushed off by the tide elsewhere on the harbour, late-arriving birds jostle for landing space on the teeming deck. This avian pageant almost fills the view through the spotting scope – except for the huge airport complex shimmering in the background. It is a few kilometres away across the bay and in the heat haze largely indistinct; yet it too is clearly a busy place.

One of the key requirements for a major airport is plenty of flat land; and, unsurprisingly, many suitable sites happen to be in coastal areas. Thus many of the world's major airports are built on or near the coast; and some, such as Seoul Incheon and Shanghai Pudong, are built over former mudflats. Napier, Nelson and Invercargill airports are all built immediately adjacent to shorebird habitat. So too is the main runway at Auckland International Airport, on the shores of the Manukau – which also happens to be the most important shorebird site in the country. 'As the constructors of the new Auckland airport thrust their huge runway further and further over the tidal flats between Pukaki and Ihumatao,' wrote Dick Sibson in 1963, 'they encroached upon a rich feeding ground for many thousands of waders.' However, he noted, they were also creating 'a most handy and spacious roost' which thousands of shorebirds were not slow to use. Looking ahead he could see potential difficulties for the airport authorities: '2000 oystercatchers alone, rising solidly together, would pose a problem when the airport came into use.'[1]

An airport in close proximity to what can be massive flocks of birds is a recipe for trouble. In May 1996 a Boeing 737 taking off from Wellington struck a flock of nine black-backed gulls. Some birds were sucked into one engine, which had to be shut down; and others struck the leading edge of the wing on either side of the other engine. The aircraft made an emergency landing, with over a million dollars' worth of damage. In July 1985 a Boeing 747 with 373 people on board struck three oystercatchers while taking off from Christchurch. Two engines were damaged, and the plane had to climb with the two remaining engines to dump fuel before making an emergency landing. Only limited reverse thrust was available to assist in slowing the aircraft on the runway, and all wheel brakes were overheated by the time the plane came to a halt. Damage to the aircraft amounted to hundreds of thousands of dollars.[2]

Deadly encounter: carcasses of some of the almost 100 wrybill killed after flying close to a taxiing aircraft at Auckland airport. JOHN DOWDING

In 1994 the estimated spur-winged plover population was over 3600 birds, although given the widely dispersed nature of this species this was almost certainly an underestimate. The steady march north since their Southland beachhead in the 1930s eventually landed them in rather hot water. During the 1990s the Minister of Conservation began receiving requests to review their fully protected status. These came from a very broad spectrum: private individuals, regional councils, conservation organisations, and hunting interests. According to a DOC discussion document, there were concerns for horticultural crops; in some market garden areas they are 'considered a pest, causing damage to green-leafed vegetable crops such as cauliflower, broccoli and lettuce'. They were also believed to be causing problems for other native species – there is video footage of a spur-wing destroying a New Zealand dotterel egg; and there are also limited reports of attacks on other native birds. However 'while they are aggressive and may displace other indigenous species from habitats, their overall effects on other native species are considered insignificant'.[3]

The main points of concern related to 'interactions' with aircraft – and when it comes to hazards to aviation, it is an altogether different ball game. In the period between October 1999 and September 2004, a total of 5111 bird incidents were recorded at New Zealand airports: 2221 bird strikes and 2890 near strikes (or near misses). In March 2001 a Metroliner aircraft approaching Tauranga airport struck a spur-winged plover, causing the failure of the left-hand engine. It turned out to be just one of many such incidents, as spur-wings are the species most commonly involved in aircraft bird strikes and near misses in New Zealand. Of the 1406 reported incidents where the species involved was identified, 37 percent were spur-wings.[4] The proportion of incidents appeared to increase as the spur-wings expanded through the country: 8 percent in 1988, 11 percent in 1989, 14 percent in 1990 and 22 percent in 1991. Nearly half of reported incidents were strikes.[5] This was a major factor behind the removal of protection for the species in 2010.

Casualties involving a steadily growing population are one thing; what if there are air strikes involving more vulnerable species? One such incident occurred in 1998 at Auckland, when a flock of several hundred wrybill flew past the engine exhaust of a taxiing airliner. Between 50 and 100 birds – up to 2 percent of the total population, were killed. There were further casualties in 2006, when a small flock of wrybill on the ground refused to get out of the way of an approaching ATR 72 (turboprop), in spite of Bird Frite shots being fired.[6] Fortunately such losses do not occur regularly, and there have been no similar incidents reported since; although given the limited population, any events of this magnitude are very serious indeed. Auckland is the only airport with a large number of wrybill in the surrounding area. A bird ranger is employed there, but the birds can be difficult to move: the ranger 'reported that one day he used more then 30 charges of bird scare trying to move the flock out of the danger area'.[7]

Shorebirds colliding with an aircraft could lead to a major disaster – perhaps that is why it tends to be one of the more high-profile bird/human interactions. Countless other interactions occur as well – often unnoticed or disregarded by the people concerned. Some, such as a coastal development, may be large in scale but its effects – such as degraded foraging or roosting habitat – may not emerge until further down

Immediately south of this campervan site at Miranda is the Taramaire Stream mouth – once an important high-tide shorebird roost, as well as a nesting site for white-fronted terns, black-billed gulls and New Zealand dotterel. Today, with almost constant people presence, it is little used. IAN SOUTHEY

If undisturbed, godwits are content to roost on the edge of a new suburban development. However such sites are ephemeral, lasting only until the next disturbance or development. BRIAN CHUDLEIGH

the track. Others may seem minor in scale, though with more immediate effects – such as a person or a dog causing a bird to leave its nest. Many of these events may not attract our attention; indeed, some may be so low-profile that even the people causing them remain oblivious. There is, however, one thing common to almost all such contacts with our birds: they are invariably the ones that are disadvantaged.

How do we measure such effects? Is it, indeed, even possible? One way is to monitor the carrying capacity of an estuary or an area of coastal wetland to try and assess its quality as shorebird habitat. If we count the birds that annually use the site over several years and find the number of birds declining, it would perhaps suggest something was wrong with the site. Or perhaps not – for the problem could be elsewhere. Most birds seen on a New Zealand estuary at any given time breed elsewhere, and many of those are dependent on stopover habitat during migration. One measure would be how many migratory birds survive the nonbreeding season in good enough condition to migrate to their breeding grounds and breed successfully. If, under current climatic conditions, feeding conditions at the site are 'sufficient to maintain the survival rate and body condition at the current bird population size, then the quality of that estuary is being maintained'. But if the population using the site declines despite this, 'then the cause of that decline needs to be sought elsewhere'.[8] For instance, if there were a decline in reproductive rate, or increased mortality on the breeding grounds, the size of the larger population would decrease – which could explain why fewer birds were at the nonbreeding site, 'even though its quality had not changed'.[9]

UK researchers developed a model to assess which factors determine carrying capacity at shorebird wintering sites. The results suggested that 'the amount of food required to maintain the current survival rate of the birds may be eight times greater than the amount the birds actually consume during winter'. It all hinges on populations, distribution and densities of the benthic animals that shorebirds feed on. How big do benthic populations have to be to provide birds with the amount of food they need, while leaving sufficient numbers to maintain the health and viability of those populations? How big an area of tidal flat is required to support this overall system? Maintaining the health of the estuary so that food supply does not fall below a certain level should also ensure the ability of the site to support birds at their present level of fitness. Other factors that have an influence on fitness, such as disturbance, predators and parasites, can also be included in the assessment of the site's carrying capacity.[10] Of course, a wide range of such factors threatens the health of shorebird habitats.

One is the population of the birds themselves, and competition that foraging birds may face from either their own kind, or from other species. For example, while red knots and oystercatchers both like bivalves, the much smaller knots can only handle prey that is less than 15 mm in size; any bigger, and the bivalve is safe from the knot – though not from the oystercatcher. If knots consume too much of this small prey, there will be less to grow bigger, as food for other birds: 'Whether predation by knots results in any discernible change to an oystercatcher's food supply a year or more later is unknown.'[11] Conversely, as there are now many more oystercatchers than there used to be, are they taking too many of the larger molluscs and leaving fewer to reproduce – and so leaving less future food for knots, or indeed for themselves? Such considerations are all part of the larger equation determining carrying capacity.

While there is still much to learn about such predator–prey dynamics, we only have to look at many of our harbours and estuaries to find that the pressures birds face are mainly from human activities. Many of us like to live on or near the coast. The problem is that urbanisation is not always good for our coastal environments. An American study clearly identified developed land-cover as the primary stressor on shorebird habitat in Chesapeake Bay. It identified two key pathways for negative effects on waterbird communities: increased nutrients and contaminants such as PCBs and heavy metals; and fragmentation and isolation of adjacent terrestrial habitats.[12] Shorebirds at a site affected by such development may find not only their food supply diminished; their high-tide roosting habitat may also be degraded or even lost entirely. The situation would be even worse for species that breed around the site.

A study of oystercatchers on two Auckland harbours found lead levels 146 percent higher in birds at Mangere Inlet on the Manukau than on the Kaipara. This was perhaps not surprising, given that Mangere was a particularly polluted area, with higher lead concentrations in surface sediment compared even with other areas within the Manukau Harbour. Juvenile oystercatchers had markedly higher levels than adults: this correlated with studies around the Baltic Sea that showed higher lead levels in juvenile dunlin and curlew sandpipers. However, it is not known whether higher levels in the juveniles at Mangere 'represent developmental and physiological differences in the dynamics of lead in this species, or a genuine difference in exposure to lead, resulting from different feeding areas or types of prey ingested'.[13] Overseas studies of waterfowl revealed threshold lead levels above which deleterious effects could result. Over a certain level it may affect the process of synthesising haem, which is incorporated into haemoglobin and used in liver detoxification. The birds at Mangere were mainly under this threshold, though two individuals were above it. Although they are highly site-faithful, adult oystercatchers are not present on the Manukau all year, which means their overall exposure to contaminants is reduced. While the heavy metal concentrations found in the study sample are unlikely to represent a toxicological threat, there are potential warning signs here, particularly regarding resident species. A study at Nakdong Estuary, Korea, found elevated concentrations of PCBs in the muscle tissue of birds. However, levels in migratory birds such as bar-tailed godwits were considerably lower than those in resident species such as gulls.[14]

The Manukau Harbour, around which sprawls much of the city of Auckland, including a large proportion of its industrial zones, currently supports over 20 percent of the total New Zealand shorebird population. It is further estimated that 'more than 60 percent of all shorebirds occurring in New Zealand may use the harbour either temporarily, before or following migration, or seasonally as a feeding habitat'.[15] Maintaining the health of this habitat presents several challenges.

I did not see the skua approach; but the foraging birds, widely scattered across the flats, certainly did. The more northerly birds reacted first, peeling off the mudflats and successively recruiting more and more birds into the air, like a furling plume of wood before the carver's chisel. Soon everything was airborne, wheeling noisily above the flats and the distant tideline. Only a solitary white-faced heron remained, steadfastly working the edge of the inner channel. The flocks were following two primal instincts when confronted with danger: rely on mobility, and find safety in numbers. Within a few minutes the arctic skua had veered out over the bay in pursuit of two white-fronted terns. Piracy against terns is a skua staple; but for many of the birds aloft its presence here was a reminder of their tundra breeding grounds, where it is a major predator of eggs and chicks. For now the

Unnecessary energy expense: vehicle driving through an oystercatcher roost. JANIE VAUGHAN

threat was past and gradually birds began to return to the flats and their foraging. For these shorebirds such disturbances are in the natural scheme of things, and such interactions have occurred for millennia. Today, though, birds are also faced with disturbances that are far from natural; and that cumulatively serve to reduce habitat quality.

In simple terms, a person walking or running on a beach can be classed as a disturbance, particularly if it is an area where birds are nesting. Occasional disturbances matter much less than regular or prolonged ones. From the bird's perspective, a person walking with a dog may be threatening; a dog running free even more so. The dog and its owner may be on the beach briefly, so disturbance is of limited duration. A succession of such incidents, each one brief and therefore perceived by each person as insignificant, presents cumulative difficulties for nesting or roosting birds. And we engage in many activities on our coasts. For example, an increase in the number of campervans parked on the beach immediately north of Miranda has seen use of a once major shorebird roost decrease sharply.

During spring high tides, around 3000 godwits and 2000 knots leave Whangarei Harbour to roost at Ruakaka. Unfortunately for them, the same time and place are now popular with kite surfers. One study recorded 12 disturbances per hour, with kite surfers present from 30 minutes before high tide to four hours after.[16] Some of the Manukau Harbour roosts, among the most important in the country, are increasingly threatened by similar disturbances. During February and March, immediately prior to migration, increasing numbers of birds have abandoned the area for roosts elsewhere on the harbour, or across the isthmus at Whitford, on the Hauraki Gulf. The reason appears to be high-tide use of the area by kite surfers.[17] On a particularly high tide in March, one observer reported 'large flocks of waders in the air continuously for 30 minutes seeking space to rest over the peak of the tide while the kite surfers enjoyed the sheltered water around the largest shellbank and the other shellbanks were already full to bursting with birds'.[18]

These roosts need to be seen in a wider context. Farmland adjacent to feeding and roosting areas may be available as alternative roost sites during high tides that coincide with rough weather. For a bird, a secure roost is one that offers 360 degrees of visibility. If, for example, grass in a farm paddock is too long, it is of no use. Fewer sheep on farms means grass is usually longer; and lifestyle blocks are gradually replacing market gardens, which means fewer ploughed paddocks. It all adds up to more and more birds being confined to the shellbanks. Access to some of the key sites on the southern Manukau is currently over private land and hence restricted to the public, but council planning documents indicate there are intentions to improve access to the harbour, and increase recreational opportunities.[19] If this occurs without appropriate management, shorebird roosts will be further compromised, with potentially serious ramifications elsewhere on the harbour.

The wastewater treatment plant at Mangere, north of the airport, has been substantially upgraded, with the former oxidation ponds opened to the harbour. This area, too, supports large numbers of shorebirds, many of which roosted at the old treatment works. As part of the upgrade, it was recognised that enhancement of existing roosts and provision of new ones would be essential to prevent birds moving elsewhere. This was a critical consideration because the next most suitable roosting area is the airport. Since 2008, over 3.2 ha of roost space has been enhanced or created, and is being used by birds.[20] To ensure this continues to be used, ongoing maintenance, such as vegetation control, is essential. However, this is just one part of the equation: if the major roosts on the southern Manukau are not sufficiently protected as well, it is highly likely many displaced birds will move north. And increased movements of bird flocks past the airport would be of great concern. Finally, if birds need to commute too far between feeding and roosting sites, their energy budgets will go into deficit. This could reduce the quality and hence carrying capacity of the harbour.

The effects of disturbances on birds are often hard to quantify. In response to a perceived threat a flock takes off, circles for a time and then lands again and, apparently, settles. Depending on just where within a bird's annual cycle the disturbance occurs, it potentially threatens its fitness and future wellbeing. As a feeding bird becomes aware of an intruder approaching, its heart rate increases – and so do the metabolic costs. As it becomes more vigilant, its feeding rate slows or stops, which means its energy intake has fallen just as its energy expenditure increases. Birds secrete stress hormones in response to danger and to assist with escape flights, and chronically elevated hormone levels have been shown to have negative effects. The time it takes a bird to recover will vary with the severity of the disturbance; prolonged displacement from its original

A most successful knot: birds need to find sufficient food to make a living and, when the time comes, build up fat reserves prior to migration. This obese bird was photographed on the Manukau Harbour in early April, and most likely departed on migration soon after – if it could get into the air! IAN SOUTHEY

The energy required to burst into flight is evident in these godwits, lifting off from the Avon-Heathcote Estuary, Christchurch. Unnecessary disturbance, particularly for birds preparing for migration, carries heavy costs for them. IAN SOUTHEY

activity will clearly have an effect. The balance between food intake and energy expenditure is a major factor in determining whether a given estuary is suitable habitat. For example, a safe and secure high-tide roost adjacent to feeding areas is ideal; the longer distance a bird needs to fly to a good roost site, the higher its energy expenditure. 'Large areas of good feeding habitat go unused when there are no acceptable roost sites within a reasonable distance of them. The extreme consequence of losing a roost site to disturbance could be the loss of feeding habitat if no acceptable alternative roosts are available.'[21] Disturbance was implicated in long-term declines in shorebird abundance at a staging site in Massachusetts.[22]

Just what is at stake here? If we take godwits and knots as examples, excessive disturbance may set them back in their schedules. From the time they arrive in New Zealand each spring until their departure in March, they have essential tasks to complete. First they need to find the energy to replace their old flight feathers with a set of new ones, which may take up to 17 weeks. Then they must begin preparations for their next migration: perform a full body moult into breeding plumage and begin laying down fat stores for the forthcoming journey. During all these tasks they need to minimise energy expenditure. Unnecessary flight in response to disturbance incurs costs: it diverts energy from finding and digesting food, growing feathers and storing fat. A study of great knots in Australia found that birds spending an extra 30 minutes during each tidal cycle in 'alarm flights' increased their energy use by 13.3 percent.[23] Such expenditure, especially during migration preparations, is not good. Another study in the UK showed that excessive disturbance causes birds to abandon a particular site.[24] Birds prevented from using their preferred estuary have been shown to depart on migration with less than optimal weight, and are less likely to return from migration.[25]

The most obvious situation, where effects may be immediate and visible, is when a bird is nesting. At one extreme, of course, is someone standing on a nest – and as all New Zealand shorebirds nest on the ground there is always that risk. But most disturbances are more indirect – such as death of an embryo from prolonged exposure to sunshine or chilling if the incubating bird is kept continuously from its duties. Or the nest could be exposed to greater predation risk; for example, repeated disturbance may result in more bird tracks leading to and from the nest, which, in turn, could represent neon arrows to a passing harrier or gull. One of the key regions for our shorebirds – both nesting and wintering species – is the northeast North Island. The coastline from the Bay of Plenty to Northland abounds with beaches and harbours offering good habitat for birds. Given our penchant for living by the sea, the same region also holds some of the most desirable 'human habitat', almost always in the very same locations favoured by birds – all further pressure on our shorebirds.

There is also our inability to accept a site as it is; we feel the need to 'improve' it. Thus attempts at Mangawhai to stabilise the sandspit, and dredge the channel to facilitate boat traffic; and similarly, the string of consent applications for building marinas at

SHARING SHORELINES

(top right) Attempts to stabilise dunes at Omaha affect shorebird habitat. JOHN DOWDING
(left top) Sharing shorelines I: a boat launching site at Kaiaua. BRIAN CHUDLEIGH
(left) Sharing shorelines II: vehicles and beaches, a dangerous mix for nesting birds. BRIAN CHUDLEIGH
(bottom right) Sharing shorelines III: A hare causes a kerfuffle at a roost on the Manukau Harbour. IAN SOUTHEY

places like Tairua on the Coromandel, or Sandspit near Warkworth. Each development proposal, seen in isolation, may seem insignificant: certainly the applicant is keen to downplay any environmental effects as 'negligible' or 'minimal'. But seen from the perspective of a shorebird population, each small development, each section of foraging area or roost site reduced or removed, each load of dredge tailings – all chip away at habitat. Given that the pressures for such developments seem to be continuous, the net outcome is that shorebirds continue to lose out.

'At many other breeding sites in Northland, birds fare very badly because of human disturbance. Some beaches and estuaries offering good feeding and ideal physical sites for breeding, are too heavily frequented by people to enable successful breeding.'[26] A study of New Zealand dotterel found disturbance was a factor affecting breeding success. Sites with low human disturbance were, on average, twice as productive as those with higher levels of disturbance. Resulting differences in breeding success between the two were considered large enough to be of biological significance.[27] A further study looked at effects of disturbance on dotterel chicks. When people were present, chicks spent less time than normal in the intertidal zone – their preferred feeding area. The study concluded that if human access to feeding areas was reduced, fledging success could increase.[28] This has proved to be the case at managed sites such as Opoutere and Matarangi. The New Zealand fairy tern is another species where disturbance is of critical importance. In southern Australia, human disturbance caused the disappearance of fairy terns and little terns from many previous nesting areas, with both species surviving only at intensively managed sites. Given its tiny population, the plight of New Zealand fairy terns is even more desperate.[29] So anything that affects tern productivity assumes enormous significance. Which means that any proposed development at or near fairy tern sites requires rigorous scrutiny.

Another development with potential to threaten the wellbeing of shorebirds is the advent of wind turbines. A brilliant technology that uses a constantly renewable resource, this is clearly needed. Certainly when placed against alternative options that use fossil fuels, wind-generated power is a no-brainer. Like most good things, though, it is not without its problems; the biggest of which, of course, is just where to put the turbines. In 2011, provisional consents were granted for a major windfarm on the northern Waikato coast, south of Port Waikato. The problem with this site is that, not only is it immediately south of the Manukau Harbour, it lies in the flightpath of oystercatchers and wrybills migrating to and from the Firth of Thames. When the Kaipara Harbour is also added to the equation, the windfarm site is within the major flyway for substantial numbers of our shorebirds.

As part of the consent application process, considerable monitoring of bird movements through the

Costly scavenging I: black-backed gull with plastic six-pack tie. BRIAN CHUDLEIGH

Costly scavenging II: young red-billed gull with a fish hook caught through its wing. BRIAN CHUDLEIGH

Sleeping wrybill. IAN SOUTHEY

proposed site was carried out, using both observers and radar technology. However the subsequent data proved to be inconclusive, and expert witnesses at the consent hearings were at odds over the numbers of birds likely to be affected by the windfarm. It was calculated that possible mortality could include a small number of SIPO and several wrybills, but precise figures were elusive. In granting provisional consents, the Board of Inquiry stressed that 'robust review measures need to be in place in case fatalities are more significant than anticipated'.[30] Agreed mitigation measures included a programme of intensive predator control in the Upper Rangitata, specifically aimed at increasing productivity of pied oystercatcher and wrybill to offset possible losses to both species. However, given the complexities involved in such measures – and that a model of predator control confirmed to be totally effective on the scale required is yet to be developed – it remains to be seen whether such mitigation will have the desired outcome. A further mitigation measure may, however, be most useful for New Zealand dotterels: annual funding would be provided for a project on Aotea Harbour in the Waikato to control predators and reduce human disturbance. Given the almost total lack of dotterel management anywhere on the west coast, this would be an advance.

As disturbance of shorebirds is so often due to human activities, one avenue for improvement is to raise public awareness. At some sites, such as some of the managed New Zealand dotterel sites on the Coromandel, this has met with considerable success. Elsewhere it is all too often an uphill struggle to get the message across. Restricting public access to sections of beach during the breeding season is often effective. Signage can also be effective, although perhaps not as much as conservation managers would like. A survey of visitors to two Northland sites with high shorebird values showed, unsurprisingly, that occasional or first-time visitors were less aware of such values than regular visitors; 57 percent of people visiting Waipu for the first time failed to see any signs. Regular visitors also showed low levels of awareness. Signage at the main carpark at Waipu and along an access walkway at Ruakaka describes nest protection and behavioural traits shown by shorebirds 'but appears to have had little effect on the level of knowledge of most visitors about shorebird behaviour'. That over 70 percent of those surveyed disliked dogs on beaches could be regarded as a glimmer of optimism, except that most people 'appeared to be more concerned with impacts of dogs on their experience at the beach rather than with problems of shorebird disturbance'.[31]

Red knot. IAN SOUTHEY

CHAPTER TWENTY-TWO
SHRINKING GAS STATIONS: FLYWAY UNDER STRESS

A better world by sustainable development.
—*Promotional slogan at Caofeidian New Area, China*

The plight of New Zealand's shorebirds is very much a mixed bag. A few seem to be doing well; or, at the very least, their populations appear stable. For others the situation is serious. Without management, fairy terns will be extinct within a few years. If management ceases, the northern New Zealand dotterel population will plummet, and the southern population will vanish. If the required management of black-fronted terns is not forthcoming, their prospects are dire. Likewise the current trajectory of the black-billed gull population suggests they are more at risk of extinction than kakapo. If sufficient natural habitat on the braided river systems cannot be maintained, wrybill may also face a bleak future. The problems facing these species are our responsibility, and only we can take the steps required to secure their futures. For the thousands of Arctic migrants that come here each year – the godwits, knots, turnstones and others – only part of their habitat lies directly within our sphere. It is, however, hugely important habitat, where they spend more time than in any other part of their range. Ensuring the health of our intertidal zones and adjacent high-tide roosting habitat is clearly our responsibility. It is suggested 'that the quality of non-breeding sites in New Zealand . . . could have a large influence on the lifetime productivity of birds maturing here as well as affecting the year-to-year survival and productivity of adults'.[1] Young birds may spend their first two or three years here, learning valuable lessons of survival. So our sites may determine how many young birds are eventually recruited into the breeding population.[2] Which makes the Manukau Harbour, for example, an essential part of the equation for red knots in this flyway.

In the official threat rankings for New Zealand native species are categories such as Critically Endangered, Nationally Threatened, Nationally Vulnerable and Not Threatened. There is also the designation: Secure Overseas, meaning that even if a species is declining within New Zealand, there are other populations elsewhere. Just how valid is this, when one considers the accumulating evidence of colossal habitat loss in the flyway posing real and present dangers to birds such as godwits and knots? It could be argued that the problem lies beyond our shores, and therefore there is little we can or should do, especially with our ever-decreasing conservation dollars. There are, of course, pressures on habitats used by these birds within New Zealand as well. Moreover a relatively small number of sites support the bulk of migrant birds in New Zealand. Between them, Parengarenga, Houhora and Rangaunu harbours in the Far North, the Kaipara and Manukau harbours and the Firth of Thames in the Auckland region, and Farewell Spit hold more than two thirds of godwits and turnstones and over 90 percent of knots. Just how secure are these birds?

All three species occur in New Zealand in internationally important numbers. The conservation threat rankings are based on overall population numbers or rates of decline. Recent count data suggests that perhaps 95,000 godwits, about 30,000 knots and 1600 turnstones are here each summer. If these figures, at first glance, suggest little to be concerned about, the trends over time present a different picture. Comparisons with similar counts made between 1983 and 1994 show that godwit numbers appear stable, knots have declined by 13 percent and turnstones by 46 percent. 'Taken as if they were any other species in the Conservation Status list these figures leave godwits as "Not Threatened" but knots would be technically "At Risk" and categorised as "Declining" while turnstones would be officially "Threatened" and classed as "Nationally Vulnerable".'[3] If we then factor in the situation as it stands at Yellow Sea stopover sites, together with what is known to happen to populations once habitat diminishes and breeding success is severely compromised, is there any room for complacency as to the future of any of these species, including godwits?

The sealed road dips and ends; now there is just coarse sand and tyre tracks coiling out on the flats. Low, thick vegetation extends either side, disappearing into the grey haze. The greens and dark mauve of these salt-tolerant colonisers are virtually the only splashes of colour in a landscape otherwise devoid of tone. Along the distant channel edge, among the lines of thin posts marking fish traps – for some people continue to eke out a meagre existence from this place – a few curlew and a pair of greenshanks forage. There then comes a sound that, in an instant, transports me back to previous visits here. Two F-16s roar off the end of the runway behind us and disappear into the murk above, their flight loud

Dying mudflats in South Korea: until completion of the 33 km Saemangeum seawall in 2006 this area was part of a 41,000-ha estuarine system of mudflats and shallows supporting over 400,000 shorebirds during migration. JAN VAN DE KAM

Four years later it is covered in dense vegetation. KEITH WOODLEY and intrusive, where not so long ago substantial flocks of shorebirds shared these skies. But no more: here at Gunsan, South Korea, near the edge of the largest remaining US air base in Asia, the Saemangeum seawall begins.

Further up the estuary lies the great spit at Okgu where, just four years ago, 60,000 great knots swirled in spectacular formation. Now there are few, if any, using this place. For this area too is cloaked in thick vegetation. Seven large fishing dinghies are moored in what remains of the tidal channel, the catch from one being loaded onto a truck. This activity, too, is just a tiny echo of what was once a thriving fishing community for which the Saemangeum development – the complete enclosure of the combined estuaries of the Mungyeong and the Dangjin rivers – represented catastrophe.

A temple high above the south bank of the Mungyeong offers a panorama of Saemangeum. For visitors unaware of the ecological costs, there is ample evidence of just how impressive is the scale of this development. There are still large expanses of water and tidal flats to be seen on these estuaries, for the rivers still flow. But even from this great distance vegetation is visibly establishing in many formerly tidal areas. On the northern side of the Mungyeong, and on both sides of the Dangjin behind us, a few small settlements sit among vast areas of ricefields – an indication that development is no recent phenomenon here. These areas, too, were once tidal flats that succumbed long before Saemangeum began. What's more, habitat destruction here is by no means over. Work is due to begin building the inner dykes along the river channels to complete the land 'reclamation' process.

To the west, at the end of the peninsula that divides the two estuaries, is Simpo. Here on the edges of what remains of the tide, we find an array of birds – egrets and herons; and a few dozen shorebirds – dunlins, Kentish plovers, great knots, several bar-tailed godwits, and a scattering of curlews. But over the hard sandflats on which we stand, the tide no longer flows. Elsewhere within Saemangeum it still flows – only on an artificial cycle, quite unpredictable for estuarine fauna. Tide heights ranging from 0.25 m to 1.3 m, depending on whether sluice gates are open or not, are far below the 7 m spring tides that existed before the seawall closure. If the control gates remain closed, previously subtidal mudflats may remain exposed for periods of four to five days. Other times they may be submerged for periods longer than is natural. Benthic animals cannot long survive such an erratic regime and its associated fluctuation in salinities. At Simpo, apart from a few scattered shell fragments, there is little to indicate benthic life. Vegetation is starting to establish here and there; and, as if to emphasise just how different this area now is, two cyclists slowly make their way towards us over the former mudflats – the going smooth and firm for them.

Long-distance migratory shorebirds depend on a complex network of interlinked sites during an annual cycle that may have them operating near the limits of their capabilities. A bird's preparations for migration – wing moult, body moult, depositing fuel, and changes to its body composition – followed by the demands of a long flight, all depend on the quality of habitat at the nonbreeding site. The quality of stopover sites is no less important; nor is arrival on the breeding grounds on time and in good condition. A bird that fails to store sufficient deposits of fat at a stopover site may arrive on the breeding grounds in poor condition, with a consequent reduction in its prospects for breeding success. Or the problem may have occurred earlier, on the nonbreeding grounds, when a bird was unable to complete its wing moult in time for optimal departure on northward migration. There are time constraints for these migrants: wind assistance is a key component of most migration strategies, and delayed departures may mean missing optimal wind conditions. Arriving too late on the breeding grounds may mean breeding failure. For the bird, what happens at one site has implications for what may happen elsewhere. It may also have fundamental effects at the population level. There are functional links, for example, between staging and breeding sites; it is on the latter that new generations of birds are born to replace those that died on migration or during the previous winter – an equilibrium that determines long-term population size.[4]

The East Asian–Australian Flyway (EAAF) extends south from northern Russia and western Alaska to encompass East and Southeast Asia, Australia and New Zealand – 22 countries in all, and around 45 percent of the world's human population. It constitutes a diverse network of sites, each one essential for all or part of a species population, for part of its annual cycle. Many sites, close to human settlements, are vulnerable to rapid social and economic development pressures. For over 400,000 migratory birds, Saemangeum was one such site; and for great knots – a species that only occurs in this flyway – it was *the* single most important staging site. Losing it caused a decrease in the global population

The rapidly growing port city of Donggang lies along one edge of the Yalu Jiang reserve. ADRIAN RIEGEN

Most important site in the flyway for New Zealand godwits, the 60-km coastline of the Yalu Jiang National Nature Reserve is almost entirely lined with seawalls, behind which is a grid of fishponds and embankments. ADRIAN RIEGEN

Limited roost options: once the tide reaches the seawall at Yalu Jiang there is nowhere for birds to go except to try and find roosts inland. Some use fishpond embankments, where there is always the likelihood of disturbance. ADRIAN RIEGEN

(above) Flagged destination: this male godwit at Kaiaua on the Firth of Thames bears orange and green flags, showing he was caught and banded at Yalu Jiang, China, during one of his northward migrations. Soon after being photographed in early March, he would have departed again – with Yalu Jiang once more his scheduled stopover. IAN SOUTHEY

of at least 22 percent.[5] Recent research involving satellite and geolocator technology, along with records of banded birds and site surveys, means we now have a better picture of the flyway from the perspective of several other species. Best known are the migration patterns of bar-tailed godwits; and while there are still knowledge gaps, we know enough to make educated guesses regarding red knots. Let us look at the most critical areas for these species.

For the *baueri* population of bar-tailed godwits there are two essential staging sites: Yalu Jiang, China, and the Kuskokwim Shoals, Alaska. Yalu Jiang is also a key site for the *menzbieri* population; and the most recent survey, in April 2010, recorded 85,000 godwits including birds of both populations. However, given that *menzbieri* arrive later than *baueri*, this figure is likely to be an underestimate. Six of the nine *baueri* birds and three of the *menzbieri* birds tracked by satellite used Yalu Jiang on northward migration, and four of eight *menzbieri* passed through or staged at Yalu Jiang on southward migration.[6] The Kuskokwim Shoals on the coastline on the southwest YKD are a series of sandy barrier islands

With secure high-tide roosting space in short supply, birds at Yalu Jiang try to use fishpond embankments where they may be subjected to regular disturbance. KEITH WOODLEY

amidst rich, virtually unmodified tidal flats: the islands provide safe roosting habitat, and the tidal flats abundant food. All satellite-tagged godwits used the 80-km stretch of coast centred on the Kuskokwim Shoals as a fuelling site prior to departing southwards. In addition, all 16 birds fitted with geolocators in New Zealand from which data was retrieved, also staged there.

The dependence of so many birds on so few sites has serious conservation implications. They have the capacity to act as population bottlenecks; and degradation of habitat in one region already appears to be affecting godwit populations. A Japanese study of shorebird count data from 1975 to 2008 showed consistent decline for at least four species, including bar-tailed godwit and ruddy turnstone; godwits declined by over 30 percent. Loss and degradation of habitat on the Japanese coast is thought to be one possible reason. However, it is also likely to be linked with habitat loss elsewhere in the Yellow Sea, causing an overall population decrease, which means fewer individuals are migrating through Japan.[7] For godwits, Yalu Jiang as a staging site is clearly what Delaware Bay is to the *rufa* population of knots, and what Saemangeum once represented for great knots. All of which makes the large-scale tidal flat destruction that is occurring on the fringes, and in some cases inside the reserve, deeply worrying.

Enormous mudflats extend either side of the Yalu River where it flows into the northern Yellow Sea. Immediately to the east is North Korea, and to the west the 101,000-ha Yalu Jiang National Nature Reserve (YJNNR). Running almost the entire 60-km length of the reserve is a system of aquaculture ponds, each one generally 500 x 100 m in size, built over the active tidal zone – almost all of which is contained within an artificial rock-lined seawall. South of the seawall are the mudflats, which extend for several kilometres and which help explain the critical importance of this place for godwits and other shorebirds. Yet essential though these tidal flats are, they are only one part of the equation: birds also need good high-tide roosts, and it is this commodity that tends to be in very short supply at Yalu Jiang. In the absence of natural coastline, which elsewhere within their annual cycle is where birds normally find a roost, birds are forced to seek alternative sites, often inland. But there are over 30,000 people living and working within the reserve. When empty, some of the fishponds – or the earth embankments lining them – may provide sanctuary; however such ponds can be flooded at any time, and there are often people working or transiting along the banks. Sometimes there is nowhere for the birds, and they have been observed circling overhead for up to an hour until the receding tide relinquishes some living space. Given the reason the birds are there – to store energy reserves prior to arrival on the breeding grounds – this waste

Diminishing prospects: red knots landing at Bohai Bay. ADRIAN BOYLE

Gaining land but destroying mudflats: mud being pumped into a walled enclosure on the coast of Bohai Bay. ADRIAN BOYLE

of energy may have serious consequences later in their annual cycle.

Birds are also losing foraging habitat – a lot of it, and quickly. Since 2000, approximately 44 sq km of mudflats at or adjacent to Yalu Jiang have been lost to development. Apart from the actual loss of foraging space, such development – whether inside or outside the reserve – changes the hydrology and thus the ecology of the entire intertidal zone. Massive seawalls are currently being constructed in an area immediately adjacent to the site that traditionally holds the greatest concentrations of birds, including over 40,000 godwits. The nearby Yalu River itself is also an important component of the foraging and roosting equation for the region's shorebirds. But it too is subject to change. At its widest point the estuary was once 3.5 km across; coastal development has already reduced this to 2.5 km, reducing the mudflats on the Chinese side of the river by approximately 7 sq km in recent years.[8] Disturbance levels, at both roosting and foraging sites, are also increasing as human population pressures in the area increase. Fishing and shellfish harvesting are substantial facets of the local economy, which means birds are increasingly sharing the flats with people. Ironically, efforts to raise public awareness of these birds among local people have been rather successful, so that hundreds of visitors now come to the seawalls to see them. Unfortunately this has added to the levels of disturbance.

Meanwhile, 550 km to the west in Bohai Bay, another colossal disaster for shorebirds is rapidly unfolding. Between 1994 and 2010, a total of 450 sq km of offshore area, including 218 sq km of intertidal flats – one third of the original tidal area in the bay – was destroyed for two enormous industrial projects.[9] (By comparison, the 340 sq km Manukau Harbour has 145 sq km of tidal flats.) The Tianjin Binhai New Area, located on the western shore of Bohai Bay, was started in 1994; while further east in Tangshan on the northern coast, the Caofeidian New Area, a huge port and industrial development, was started in 2002. In the past decade, these developments have turned large areas of sea into industrial land; and the rate of tidal flat destruction has accelerated, with other development projects on a similar scale already underway elsewhere in Bohai Bay. What's more, there seems to be no legal impediment to further projects being planned. Researchers present a stark picture of just what is at stake: 'Protection of the remaining tidal flats of Bohai Bay is likely to be essential to the continued survival of Red Knots in the East Asian–Australasian Flyway.'[10]

As we have seen, red knots appear to have limited options when it comes to suitable stopover habitat; and where such habitat occurs, knot numbers are highly concentrated. So what happens if those areas begin contracting? On the Dutch Wadden Sea, where mechanical harvesting of cockles decreased both quality and abundance of available food for red knots, it was found that birds lost 55 percent of their suitable foraging area, and the population decreased by 42 percent. Biologists calculated 'the average mean life span of . . . knots wintering in the western Dutch Wadden Sea shortened by 42 percent in the period 1996–2005'.[11] Overharvesting of horseshoe crab eggs at Delaware Bay severely disadvantaged red knots – loss of body condition was followed by dramatically reduced productivity, recruitment and adult survival, and an overall loss of more than 50 percent of the wintering population between 2000 and 2002.[12]

Since the developments started around the Bohai Sea, red knots and curlew sandpipers – the most common migrants in the area during northward migration – have been forced into ever-diminishing areas. A recent study found that in the core study area in Tangshan, the peak counts of red knots increased from 13 percent of the flyway population in 2007 to 62 percent in 2010, while curlew sandpipers increased from 3 percent of the flyway population in 2007 to 23 percent in 2010. If we plot two graphs – one showing the increase in bird numbers and the other showing the rate of habitat loss – they are mirror images. In 2010, with 970 birds per sq km in the core study area, the density of red knot was four times higher than in the years up to 2007 when the density was 211 birds per sq km.[13] One outcome of this for knots and other shorebirds is that increased densities at a site can lead to increased mortality of displaced birds, and an overall loss of birds to the population. As was found at Delaware Bay, more birds are likely to depart on northward migration with less than optimal fuel reserves, and many of those birds will not be seen again in the Yellow Sea. The authors of the study are blunt in their summary: 'With the proposed continuation of land reclamation in Bohai Bay, we predict waterbird densities in the remaining areas to increase to a point of collapse.'[14]

Red knot flight. ADRIAN BOYLE

SHOREBIRD ADVOCATES

Two programmes aimed ultimately at conserving migratory shorebirds are the EAAF Partnership and the Global Flyway Network.

The EAAF Partnership is an informal and voluntary initiative, aimed at protecting migratory species, their habitat and the livelihoods of people dependent upon them. Launched in November 2006, it has currently 38 partners including 14 governments, three intergovernmental agencies and 22 international non-government organisations. Miranda Naturalists' Trust (MNT) was the only New Zealand representative in the partnership until September 2011 when, following considerable lobbying pressure, the New Zealand government was finally persuaded to join.

The partnership provides a framework for international cooperation, including: maintaining a network of sites of international importance to migratory waterbirds; collaborative activities to increase knowledge and raise awareness of migratory waterbirds within the flyway; and building capacity for the sustainable management and conservation of habitat. The partnership evolved from an earlier model – the EAAF Shorebird Site Network – that was launched at Brisbane in 1996. Within this framework the MNT, a community group based on the Firth of Thames, has been actively engaged with research initiatives in China. In 2004 MNT established a sister site partnership with the YJNNR; and it has been actively involved with shorebird surveys, school visits and other public awareness activities ever since.

The Global Flyway Network is a collaboration of researchers seeking to understand and analyse shorebird population trends and the factors determining them. The partnership has three broad aims.

1 To provide an instantaneous sentinel service for the global conservation community: an early warning system of flyway populations under threat; the early identification of populations in decline and in need of recovery action; as well as monitoring the fates of populations known to be in dire straits.
2 To help generate the stories that need to be told to fuel the imagination and the goodwill of people who can make a difference to the fate of the habitats and populations under threat.
3 To further the science, including the understanding of the historical background and the current demographic processes and ecological, genetic and immunological constraints that determine whether populations flourish or flounder.[17]

Globally the situation for shorebirds looks little better. A 2003 survey found that of 207 shorebird populations with known population trajectories, almost half are now known to be in decline, whereas only 16 percent are increasing.[15] While the causes of these declines are likely to vary between species and regions, it seems reasonable to suggest either climate change and/or human pressures on particular habitats lie behind many of them. With three times as many populations declining as growing, shorebirds must be considered as the most globally endangered segment of the world's long-distance migrants. Each shorebird site is important in itself, but its ultimate value lies in functioning as part of a chain, with the quality of each part influencing the quality of others. Understanding the nature of these links is a basic requirement if effective conservation measures are to be developed.

Only then can we make ecologically sensible predictions of the impact of human activities on migratory wader populations, and explore whether developing alternative sites could provide sufficient compensation if harmful activities cannot be stopped. Also, knowing for which sites or combinations of sites a reduction in quality would impact most on population size would greatly help prioritise conservation efforts.[16]

A further cloud on the shorebird horizon is global climate change. For species breeding on the Arctic tundra there is some good news, followed by quite a lot of bad news. Current breeding distributions encompass much of the Arctic tundra regions, and this is reflected in the two main species occurring in New Zealand: red knot and bar-tailed godwit. Breeding range of godwits, for instance, extends over 1000 km of latitude, straddling the Arctic Circle. Primary productivity and bird breeding densities both tend to be much higher on tundra at lower latitudes. 'Shorebird species richness in the Arctic is to a large degree determined by primary production, the length of the snow-free period, the availability of migratory flyways, as well as the extent of tundra habitat during the last glaciation.'[18]

It also seems clear that laying eggs as soon as possible after arrival is the best strategy. Transforming themselves from 'flying machines' to 'breeding machines' depends on the body stores birds arrive with or can quickly acquire. So conditions both inside and outside the Arctic may determine breeding success.[19]

The quality of stopover sites immediately before arrival is critically important. Soil surface temperatures on the breeding grounds must be above freezing to make sufficient food available for egg production. In the lower Arctic, areas of snow-free habitat usually become available relatively quickly, whereas at higher latitudes, as much as 90 percent of the tundra may remain snow-covered during pre-nesting, which is an obvious limitation on breeding densities there. Food needs to be available in the period from hatching to fledging, yet all over the Arctic weather conditions can be extremely variable, making it quite difficult for a bird to predict the time of peak insect emergence from one year to the next. Hence the value in getting breeding under way as quickly as possible. Not only does this maximise the prospects for chicks of finding enough food, it also may offer the possibility of renesting in case of failure.

In large parts of the subarctic and Low Arctic in recent decades, increases in summer temperatures have meant earlier snow melt and plant growth, which in turn means more food available earlier for both breeding adults and growing chicks. But if shorebirds need to time their breeding for the peak insect emergence, warmer temperatures ultimately represent a problem. The timing mismatch between migration and food availability 'can only be rectified in the longer term by changes to genetic control mechanisms'. Day-length cues trigger departure from the nonbreeding area, a strategy that evolved through natural selection to ensure arrival in the breeding area at approximately the right time.

Only by further evolution acting on this endogenous control mechanism is the trigger for departure date likely to be changed. In this situation, the selection pressure to migrate earlier is applied in the breeding area, but action to accomplish earlier arrival occurs weeks earlier in the wintering area hundreds or thousands of km away.[20]

And as we have seen, the bar-tailed godwit from New Zealand is at least one species that appears to be following particularly rigid schedules.

The effects of climate change over a longer timescale are not quite as clear, except they are predicted to be less beneficial for birds, in that breeding habitat will be lost. Expansion of subarctic shrubland and boreal forest is already reducing tundra breeding areas. One study predicts subarctic shrubs may cover half the Arctic by 2100, followed by forest expansion. Changes in southern parts of the Arctic are likely to have a more immediate effect on shorebirds than the advance of trees and shrubs. A lower water table caused by decreasing permafrost will reduce levels of marshes and ponds with subsequent implications for invertebrate fauna. Warmer summers may also result in different predators, parasites and pathogens appearing in shorebird country, all of which will decrease the suitability of their tundra habitats.[21]

We know that migratory shorebirds are, on the whole, rather resilient. They have to be, to make the colossal migrations some of them do, as well as cope with widely varying weather conditions from one year to the next. Will they, however, prove resilient enough to adapt to an accelerating process of climate change? Already the tundra regions appear to be in a bit of a squeeze: the Arctic is presently at the lowest extent it has been in the last 10,000 years. The High Arctic region, sandwiched between the Low Arctic and the Arctic Ocean, is particularly limited, 'exposed to the most dramatic short-term fluctuations in weather', while reduction in sea ice is likely to alter weather patterns even more dramatically.[22]

Outside the Arctic, shorebirds will find habitats and conditions elsewhere in their annual cycles also affected. For instance, godwit departures from Alaska depend on predictable weather patterns, the result of a regular succession of cyclonic systems moving across the Gulf of Alaska each year from late August. If such weather systems were to alter as a result of climate change, moving further north or south for instance, the consequences could be quite serious. At the same time, sea level rises would be wreaking havoc with intertidal feeding habitat throughout the birds' range. Under 'normal' conditions, gradual sea level rise would advance the intertidal zone inland, with the sediment being graded and deposited to establish new areas of mudflats and saltmarsh. However, much of the global coastline is now subject to hard-edged development – seawalls and stopbanks, causeways and bridges – all serving to prevent this process of natural zonation occurring. Instead, rising sea levels will mean a net loss of intertidal flats. Such 'anthropogenic disturbance and destruction of shorebird non-breeding habitat [continues] at a high rate in many parts of the World, possibly superseding and exacerbating the effects of global climate change'.[23]

A further problem for some shorebirds may already exist in their genes. Due to past population bottlenecks at the end of the last ice age, some Arctic-breeding shorebirds have low levels of intraspecific genetic variability, which may make them more vulnerable to climate change. This seems particularly the case with some High Arctic species such as red knot and curlew sandpiper. 'It remains to be seen whether the reduction in genetic diversity has also reduced their ability to adapt to environmental change, and whether it puts these species more at risk now and in the future.'[24] There are also implications for godwits, which show high site fidelity throughout their annual cycle. This 'could limit birds' knowledge of and ability to move to alternative sites if development compromises traditionally used staging sites, or imply a real absence of alternatives'.[25]

Effective global action on climate change – if indeed it is even possible – will only happen gradually. More immediate steps can and should be taken to address ongoing habitat loss caused by human developments. Effective conservation of shorebird populations requires multinational efforts. Especially for sites within the Yellow Sea, pressure is urgently needed at all levels of government to ensure there is adequate protection of the shorebird habitats. An essential starting point would be a freeze on all developments impinging on key shorebird sites, and a moratorium on future projects. It is the only way red knots have any future in the flyway, and the only way to ensure that the epic feats of godwits, the 'greatest avian endurance migration known [can] continue into the future'.[26]

Miranda godwits at dawn. BRIAN CHUDLEIGH

Morning flock: godwits and knots at Miranda.
BRIAN CHUDLEIGH

CONCLUSION

If habitat loss (both climate induced and human caused) were the only change to have affected New Zealand's native birds, there is no evidence to show that any bird species would have become extinct in the last 800 years. —Alan Tennyson[1]

We lost our mainland snipe and most of the southern New Zealand dotterels. We almost lost black stilts and, without the existence of remote Rangatira Island, shore plover too would have gone. Today black-fronted tern and black-billed gulls face uncertain futures. As for wrybill, they appear to be holding on – but for how long? Of course birds are adaptable, otherwise they would not be one of the most successful orders of vertebrates. Many shorebirds seem to exist reasonably well alongside people and their activities. Our transformed landscape is well suited for some: spur-winged plovers have thrived on New Zealand farmland; oystercatchers, dotterels, pied stilts and black-backed gulls also nest in farm paddocks; oystercatchers, stilts and godwits commonly roost there. Others may opt for a roost with a view. When a supermarket was built in Thames it displaced birds from a regular roost, so oystercatchers took to roosting on its roof. A warehouse roof in South Auckland is sometimes adopted as a high-tide roost by as many as 40 per cent of the world population of wrybill. New Zealand dotterels have found nesting opportunities in seemingly unnatural habitat, such as earthworks and building sites, or beside a gold mine. Both black-backed and red-billed gulls have thrived alongside human settlement. But despite these examples of peaceful (and not so peaceful) coexistence, all too often the playing field is tilted in our favour, and birds lose out.

As critical breeding grounds, the braided rivers of the South Island, particularly those of Canterbury and the Mackenzie Basin, remain pivotal to the future of some of our endemic species. It is essential that development proposals for those areas are required to give due weight to the needs of these birds. Standing beside a river the farmer,

Oystercatcher flock on the southern Manukau Harbour. IAN SOUTHEY

the developer and the politician see water flowing out to sea – they see it 'going to waste'. From this comes the concept of 'minimum flow' – an expression used to justify taking water from the river: if we take the 'surplus' and leave a minimum flow that should be okay. It should be 'sustainable'. What they may not give sufficient value to is 'natural flow': and minimum flow and natural flow are not at all the same thing; indeed they can be polar opposites. What they do not see is that only by maintaining natural flows can we maintain viable habitat for shorebirds. Black-fronted terns and wrybills – both utterly dependent on the riverbeds – each have different habitat requirements during their annual cycles; only rivers that are maintained as close to their natural state as possible will suffice for those species. And what does 'sustainable' mean? Will taking all but 'minimum flow' from the river sustain the economic viability of a farming operation? Quite possibly it will. Will taking all but 'minimum flow' sustain the ecological viability of shorebird habitat? It will not. So what do we mean by sustainable: sustainable for whom or for what?

It may be the backbone of the New Zealand economy, but the dairy industry needs to be managed in a way that does not wreck our waterways. The exponential growth of dairying in Canterbury is a loaded gun aimed directly at the region's rivers and aquifers. Intensification of dairying in eastern Southland has placed Waituna Lagoon at grave risk; and proposals for dairy expansion loom threateningly over the Mackenzie Basin. Under current farming regimes this is environmentally unsustainable. The situation is compounded by the fact that existing regulations regarding effluent treatment and discharge appear to be unevenly implemented around the country, and as many as 40 percent of dairy farms are non-compliant. What's more, the costs of environmental degradation are borne by society at large, not by the farming operation. That environmental degradation includes habitat loss for some of our shorebirds. What price should we put on that? One study in Canterbury concluded dairy production 'negatively impacts surface and groundwater, air, biodiversity and human health at an estimated cost of $28.7 to $45 million per annum – [which] can be compared with an estimate of the total economic farm surplus of $260 million'.[2]

Packed in: roosting wrybills at Miranda KEITH WOODLEY

Necessary messages: educating people about how to share our beaches with shorebirds is an ongoing task. Sadly, all too often such messages fail to reach some beach users. JOHN DOWDING

Sometimes the birds themselves are their own signage. BRUCE SHANKS

Birding tourism is a growing industry worldwide, and New Zealand shorebirds are a major attraction for overseas visitors, such as the clients on this bird tour. BRUCE SHANKS

Around our coastlines we continue to chip away at shorebird habitat. Far removed from the natural ebb and flow governed by moon and gravity, another tide has crept over our shorelines in recent decades. From the Bay of Plenty and around the eastern Coromandel, and northwards from Auckland's North Shore and into almost every harbour and estuary, along each beach or bay, this tide of residential developments has flowed almost unchecked. Looking at some of these coastal sites – environmental jewels all of them – it could be seen as a totally reasonable process, for who would not like to live in such places? But it is a process that has proved costly to shorebirds. Not only in direct loss of habitat; there is also the more insidious manifestation of cumulative disturbance, as more and more people are concentrated on coastal margins, engaged in all manner of activities, in increasing numbers and for more prolonged periods. And with them, of course, come those fellow travellers – their dogs and cats. All of which merely adds to an already entrenched problem for shorebirds, one that is remorselessly taking a huge annual toll of eggs, chicks and adult birds: the predators that remain active round the clock, day and night.

The grounding of the *Rena* in the Bay of Plenty should

be a major wake-up call for this country. Before its encounter with Astrolabe Reef, the ship seemed to leave in its wake a string of questionable incidents that highlighted somewhat lax regulatory standards. Policies of successive governments in cutting back regulations on commercial activities have begun to bear bitter fruit; the maritime industry is a case in point.

A theme of this book has been to highlight the critical importance of the northeast North Island coast as one of the heartlands of our shorebird fauna. As the region contains New Zealand's two busiest ports and its oil refinery, it also has the busiest sea lanes. The effects of the *Rena* debacle, serious though they were, may in time come to seem comparatively minor. Clearing oil off predominantly sand beaches is one thing; but what would happen if there was a major maritime disaster in the Hauraki Gulf? The prospect of the Miranda shellbanks, with their teeming flocks of shorebirds, being covered in oil does not bear thinking about. It is imperative that the shipping industry is more closely scrutinised in future. And suitable contingency planning needs to be in place to ensure that this country can respond quickly and effectively in the event of future oil spills, be they from coastal shipping, tankers, offshore oil wells or sunken wrecks.

In some places the flocking of people to live on our coastlines has produced positive outcomes, even offering substantial mitigation of some of their negative effects. For many people a large part of the appeal of living in these lovely places is the very environmental values of which shorebirds are a prominent component. Out of concern for what they see happening at 'their' site, increasing numbers of people have become active in conservation management and advocacy. In some places community groups have emerged to help protect New Zealand dotterels and other species. Others have sprung up all around the country in response to local issues and concerns, each focused on a particular species, site or ecosystem. Groups like Waihora Ellesmere Trust, Manawatu Estuary Trust, Waituna Landcare Group, New Zealand Fairy Tern Trust, and the Omaha

Empty habitat: a solitary black stilt in the Tasman Valley. IAN SOUTHEY

Pied stilt flock. IAN SOUTHEY

Shorebird Protection Trust represent potentially positive outcomes for shorebirds. Sometimes it is one individual or couple who are compelled to do something for shorebirds: people such as John Groom at Matata in the eastern Bay of Plenty who, supported by his wife Bertha, has for years patrolled his beach, monitoring New Zealand dotterels and relentlessly trapping predators. But such people and community groups need support – particularly from councils and state agencies.

Such groups are often the result of individuals spurred into action by what they see happening at 'their' sites. However, the ongoing viability of such groups rests on group cohesion and adherence to common goals. There is also the need for continuity; for an individual or group can only do so much and for so long: if one particularly motivated and active individual or group of individuals moves on, will the group survive or be as effective? Sometimes yes – though such an outcome is by no means assured. There is a real need for oversight and coordination; and when threatened species are involved, it is appropriate that it comes from statutory authorities.

There appears to be a trend emerging in government policy to devolve more biodiversity responsibilities from DOC to local authorities. Some of these, such as the former Auckland Regional Council, have produced excellent conservation outcomes within their jurisdictions. Shorebirds in the Auckland region have benefited enormously from the expertise and dedication of Auckland Council staff working alongside volunteers. Others, such as Western Bay of Plenty District Council, recognise shorebirds in their draft district plans, proposing: 'To protect, maintain and enhance existing identified shorebird and estuarine bird roosting and nesting areas and ensure that any development or disturbance that may adversely affect the roost sites is avoided.'[3] While it has less focus on species management, the Waikato Regional Council (as Environment Waikato) has been instrumental in establishing rigorous environmental monitoring around the Firth of Thames, the outcome of which is a greater understanding of the links between farm practices and the degradation of shorebird habitat. Environment Canterbury has indicated a commitment to correcting the decline and enhancing the breeding population of indigenous braided river birds. As part of the Canterbury Water Management Strategy, the recently launched Immediate Steps programme will focus on restoration

Stable population? Wrybill and chick. JOHN DOWDING

Species in trouble: black-billed gull. IAN SOUTHEY

Birds without borders: though for five to six critical weeks each year, bar-tailed godwits from New Zealand are Chinese birds. KEITH WOODLEY

projects in the Upper Rakaia and Upper Rangitata catchments and at Lake Ellesmere, 'so we should see some benefits to shorebirds, especially wrybill'.[4]

Nevertheless the level of wildlife management and conservation expertise within regional councils around the country has tended to be quite uneven. In which case reducing the role of a national agency such as DOC may be misguided, unless robust systems are in place to ensure consistency of conservation outcomes. This is particularly important when it comes to managing critically endangered species such as New Zealand fairy tern. For some species, such as New Zealand dotterel, a prescription exists for what needs to be done for effective management. With fairy terns there are still many unknowns, so conservation measures need to be research-based until such time as a prescription can be developed for that species. That is clearly a role for DOC. Yet the science and research component within DOC is rapidly dwindling: a round of redundancies in late 2011 claimed an enormous proportion of that section of the department.

In many ways, current policy indications appear to be taking us even further away from what was once a successful model with a proven track record in wildlife management. The New Zealand Wildlife Service officially ceased to exist in 1987 when it was merged with the Department of Lands and Survey and the Ministry of Forestry to form the Department of Conservation. But for many years subsequently it continued to be a very real presence in the form of DOC staff with NZWS backgrounds. Among them were many particularly talented and experienced people who were well grounded in the theory and practice of species management. Very few of those people remain with DOC: inevitably some have retired, others have drifted away – some to redundancy, others in response to declining morale within a grossly underfunded agency charged with management of an expanding conservation estate. Of course, some remain active in private sector wildlife and conservation work so the net skills base is not entirely lost to the country. Yet if biodiversity responsibilities are being decentralised, where will the national overview and coordination of species management come from?

In some regions considerable skills and resources are going to be required in perpetuity for pest control, for no shorebird management project will succeed without controlling predators. The evidence is all too stark: without management which, to a considerable extent means trapping and poisoning, gains for the northern

New Zealand dotterel population will quickly reverse, and fairy terns will disappear entirely; Chatham Island oystercatcher numbers will resume their decline and southern New Zealand dotterels will also disappear. For the major braided rivers, three interrelated tasks are required, two of which will be immeasurably assisted by the third. Ongoing predator control and maintenance of breeding habitat that, to a large extent, means controlling weeds are both essential for river species, although to be fully effective both also need natural flows on the rivers. Operating in tandem all three will improve the prospects of wrybill and black fronted tern, black stilt and black-billed gull; each one alone will not be sufficient.

These are all factors over which, if we have the resources and the will, we have some influence. For the transequatorial migrants – the godwits and knots, turnstones and sandpipers, we can directly influence only part of their habitat – albeit the part where they spend more time than anywhere else. Nevertheless, they remain dependent on breeding grounds thousands of kilometres from New Zealand, and even more critically, on refuelling stopovers in Asia. It is the latter that is causing grave concern for the future of these remarkable migrations. If development at vitally important stopover sites in China continues at current rates, the future for red knots is exceedingly bleak. There will also be problems for godwits. Miranda Naturalists' Trust is actively engaged in promoting awareness of these issues, particularly through its relationship with YJNNR. The Global Flyway Network in association with groups such as the Australasian Wader Studies Group is working to conserve the red knot site in the Bohai Sea.

Such groups need support, however. As, indeed, do our shorebirds. One way people can contribute is by joining a local community group such as the Omaha Shorebird Protection Trust or the Waituna Landcare Group; or become active in the Ornithological Society of New Zealand, Forest and Bird, Miranda Naturalists' Trust or Braided River Aid. The more friends and advocates shorebirds have, the more likely their habitat requirements will receive the recognition they need. And in some cases, such recognition is needed sooner rather than later. Ironically, given their prominence at certain times – such as a massed roost of oystercatchers on an urban fringe – much of the time our shorebirds remain off the radar. The fairy tern hunched invisibly on a nest goes unremarked – which is exactly what evolution intends. But the head-bobbing of an anxious dotterel patrolling a small strip of beach may also go unheeded. We need to pay more attention to the birds sharing the margins with us.

Wader flock, Firth of Thames. BRUCE SHANKS

GLOSSARY

Allee effect: theory in ecology that low population densities make a species more prone to extinction. Apart from simple reproductive reasons, individuals within a species generally require the assistance of others in order to persist, such as common defence against predators. So the more individuals there are the better. The benefits of this are reduced in populations below a certain size or density, at which time the population becomes more vulnerable to random events, such as adverse climatic conditions or habitat loss. It may then slip below the equilibrium where birth rate equals death rate, and so slide to extinction.

benthic: (from benthos) referring to organisms that live at the lowest level below the sea or a lake, including on and beneath the bottom sediment

Chironomidae: midges

cline: in biological terms this describes a gradual change in characteristics and ecotone over time, in which a series of biocommunities display a continuous gradient

decurved: curved downwards

Elmid beetles: aquatic beetles common in gravelly streams

fresh (or freshet): sudden overflow of a river caused by heavy rain or melting snow

hapu: Maori subtribe

Herbst corpuscles: sensitive mechano-receptors that measure pressure

hyperphagia: defined as excessive ingestion of food beyond that needed for basic energy requirements. Ingestion may occupy unusual amounts of time

hypertrophied: abnormal enlargement of a part or organ

introgression: the introduction of genes from the gene pool of one species into that of another during hybridisation

K selection: selection occurring when a population is at or near the carrying capacity of the environment, which is usually stable: tends to favour individuals that successfully compete for resources and produce few, slowly developing young, and results in a stable population of long-lived individuals

keratin: a strong, fibrous, structural protein that occurs in the outer layer of skin as well as in hair, nails, feathers, and hooves

kiore: Pacific rat (*Rattus exulans*)

mayfly: any insect of the order Ephemeroptera, having delicate, membranous wings with the front pair much larger than the rear and having an aquatic larval stage and a terrestrial adult stage usually lasting less than two days

nominate: when a species is split into subspecies, the originally named subspecies is retained as the 'nominate' subspecies. The nominate species repeats the name of the subspecies, e.g. *Vanellus miles miles*

phototactic: movement of an organism toward or away from a source of light

pingao: golden sand sedge *Desmoschoenus spiralis*, endemic species that is one of the major sand-binders, so helping to form and maintain coastal dunes

plumage node: one of 12 divisions used to indicate the various plumage forms occurring within the stilt populations, ranging from a fully pied stilt to a fully black stilt

polychaete: a hugely diverse group of marine annelid worms with paired fleshy appendages, or parapodia, to which bristles are attached, that are used for swimming

refugia: area remaining unaltered within a wider region that is subjected to great change, such as climate change or a flood, that provides a haven for flora and fauna

riffle: minor rapid or ripple in a river or stream where it passes over a shoal

Ramsar Convention: international agreement on the conservation and wise use of wetlands, established at Ramsar, Iran, in 1971. New Zealand currently has six designated Ramsar sites: Firth of Thames, Farewell Spit, Waituna Lagoon, Whangamarino Wetland, Kopuatai Peat Dome, and Manawatu Estuary

tactile organs: touch receptors that are the most widely distributed receptors in birds

water abstraction: removal of water from a river or lake for human purposes such as irrigation

Zugunruhe: anxious behaviour in migratory animals, especially in birds (from the German: Zug 'move, migration' and Unruhe 'anxiety, restlessness')

ABBREVIATIONS

AWSG:	Australasian Wader Studies Group
BRaid:	Braided River Aid
CIO:	Chatham Island oystercatcher
CWMS:	Canterbury Water Management Strategy
DOC:	Department of Conservation
EAAF:	East Asian–Australasian Flyway
ECan:	Environment Canterbury
IUCN:	International Union for Conservation of Nature
MNT:	Miranda Naturalists' Trust
NIWA:	National Institute of Water and Atmospheric Research
NPS:	National Policy Statement for Freshwater Management
NZJS:	New Zealand Journal of Science
NZJZ:	New Zealand Journal of Zoology
NZWS:	New Zealand Wildlife Service
OED:	Oxford English Dictionary
OSNZ:	Ornithological Society of New Zealand
PRR:	Project River Recovery
SIPO:	South Island pied oystercatcher
TAG:	technical advisory group (DOC)
TPNZI:	Transactions and Proceedings of the New Zealand Institute
VOC:	variable oystercatcher
WSG:	International Wader Study Group
YJNNR:	Yalu Jiang National Nature Reserve
YKD:	Yukon-Kuskokwim Delta
ZIP:	Zone Implementation Programme

NOTES

PROLOGUE

1. McGlone, M. 1989. 'The Polynesian settlement of New Zealand in relation to environmental and biotic changes' in M.R. Rudge (ed.) 'Moas, mammals and climate in the ecological history of New Zealand'. *New Zealand Journal of Ecology* 12. (Supplement), pp. 115–129.

INTRODUCTION

1. Thurston, H. 1996. *The Nature of Shorebirds*. Greystone Nature Series, Vancouver, p. 1.
2. De Luca, W.V., C.E. Studds, R.S. King & P.P. Marra. 2008. 'Coastal urbanization and the integrity of estuarine waterbird communities: Threshold responses and the importance of scale'. *Biological Conservation* 141: 2669–78.
3. del Hoyo, J. et al. (eds). 1996. *Handbook of the Birds of the World. Vol 3: Hoatzin to Auks*. Lynx Edicions, Barcelona, Spain, p. 20.
4. Thurston 1996, *The Nature of Shorebirds*, p. 8.
5. Geering, A., L. Agnew & S. Harding. 2007. *Shorebirds of Australia*. CSIRO, Australia.
6. Thurston 1996, *The Nature of Shorebirds*, p. 8.
7. Ibid.
8. Messenger, S. & D. Taylor. 2005. *Waders of Europe, Asia and North America*. Helm, London.
9. Holdaway, R.N. & T.H. Worthy. 2008. 'Late Quaternary Avifauna' in M. Winterbourn et al. *Natural History of Canterbury*. CUP, Christchurch, p. 456.
10. Ibid.
11. Ibid.
12. Worthy, T.H. & R.N. Holdaway. 2002. *The Lost World of the Moa*. Indiana University Press, Bloomington, p. 467.
13. Grey, A.H. 1994. *Aotearoa and New Zealand: A historical geography*, CUP, Christchurch.
14. McGlone, M.S. 2009. 'Postglacial history of New Zealand wetlands and implications for their conservation'. *NZ Journal of Ecology* 33: 1–23.
15. Atkinson, I.A.E. & P.R. Millener. 1990. 'An ornithological glimpse into New Zealand's pre-human past'. *Acta XX Congressus Internationalis Ornithologici*: 127–92.
16. van de Kam, J., B. Ens, T. Piersma & L. Zwarts. 2004. *Shorebirds: An illustrated behavioural ecology*. KNNV, Netherlands.
17. Dyke, G. & M. van Tuinen. 2004. 'The evolutionary radiation of modern birds (Neornithes): Reconciling molecules, morphology and the fossil record'. *Zoological Journal of the Linnean Society* 141(2): 153–77.
18. Baker, A.J., S.L. Pereira & T.A. Paton. 2007. 'Phylogenetic relationships and divergence times of Charadriiformes genera: Multigene evidence from the Cretaceous origin of at least 14 clades of shorebirds'. *Biology Letters* 3: 205–09.
19. Tennyson, A.J.D. 2009. 'The origin and history of New Zealand's terrestrial vertebrates'. *NZ Journal of Ecology* 34(1): 6–27.
20. Bridge, E.S., A.W. Jones & A.J. Baker. 2005. 'A phylogenetic framework for the

terns (*Sternini*) inferred from mtDNA sequences: Implications for taxonomy and plumage evolution'. *Molecular Phylogenetics and Evolution* 35: 459–69.
21 Baker et al. 2007, 'Phylogenetic relationships and divergence times of Charadriiformes genera'.
22 Banks, J.C. & A.M. Paterson. 2007. 'A preliminary study of the genetic differences in New Zealand oystercatcher species'. *NZJZ* 34: 141–44.
23 Holdaway, R.N., T.H. Worthy & A.J.D. Tennyson. 2001. 'A working list of breeding bird species of the New Zealand region at first human contact'. *NZJZ* 28: 119–87.
24 Ibid.

ONE: DIVERGENT FORTUNES
1 Sansom, O. 1951. 'Spur-winged plover in New Zealand'. *Notornis* 4(3): 138–39.
2 Barlow, M. 1983. *The Year of the Spur-winged Plover*. Craig Printing, Invercargill.
3 Gibbs, G. 2006. *Ghosts of Gondwana: The history of life in New Zealand*. Craig Potton, Nelson, p. 57.
4 Worthy & Holdaway 2002, *The Lost World of the Moa*, p. 35.
5 Marchant, S. & P.J. Higgins (eds). 1993. *Handbook of Australian, New Zealand and Antarctic Birds. Vol II: Raptors to lapwings*. OUP, Melbourne, p. 946.
6 Ibid.
7 Ibid.
8 Moffatt, M. 1981. 'Aspects of the biology of the spur-winged plover (*Vanellus miles novaehollandiae* Stephens 1819)'. Unpubl. MSc thesis, Massey University, Palmerston North.
9 Marchant & Higgins (eds) 1993, *Handbook of Australian, New Zealand and Antarctic Birds*.
10 Oliver, W.R.B. 1955. *New Zealand Birds*. Reed, Wellington, p. 270.
11 Barlow, M. 1972. 'The establishment, dispersal and distribution of the spur-winged plover in New Zealand'. *Notornis* 19: 201–11.
12 H.A. Robertson, pers. comm.
13 Robertson, H.A. & B.D. Heather. 1999. 'Effects of water levels on the seasonal use of Lake Wairarapa by waders'. *Notornis* 46: 79–89.
14 Marchant & Higgins (eds) 1993, *Handbook of Australian, New Zealand and Antarctic Birds*, p. 945.
15 Barlow 1972, 'The establishment, dispersal and distribution of the spur-winged plover in New Zealand'.
16 Moffatt 1981, 'Aspects of the biology of the spur-winged plover (*Vanellus miles novaehollandiae* Stephens 1819)'.
17 Barlow 1972, 'The establishment, dispersal and distribution of the spur-winged plover in New Zealand'.
18 Barlow, M., P.M. Muller & R.R. Sutton. 1972. 'Breeding data on the spur-winged plover in Southland, New Zealand'. *Notornis* 19: 212–47.
19 Marchant & Higgins (eds) 1993, *Handbook of Australian, New Zealand and Antarctic Birds*, p. 950.
20 Barlow 1983, *The Year of the Spur-winged Plover*.
21 Barlow et al. 1972, 'Breeding data on the spur-winged plover in Southland, New Zealand'.
22 Ibid.
23 Barlow 1983, *The Year of the Spur-winged Plover*.
24 Potts, T.H. 1885. 'Oology of New Zealand'. *NZJS* Vol II: 1884–1885, p. 508.
25 Hutton, F. & J. Drummond. 1904. *Animals of New Zealand*, Whitcombe and Tombs, Christchurch.
26 Fleming, C.A. 1982. *George Edward Lodge: The Unpublished New Zealand Bird Paintings*. Nova Pacifica & National Museum of NZ, Wellington, p. 242.
27 Sibson, R.B. 1982. *Birds at Risk: Rare or endangered species of New Zealand*. Reed, Wellington.
28 Fleming, C.A. 1939. 'Birds of the Chatham Islands'. *Emu* 39: 1–15.
29 Holdaway, R.N. & T.H. Worthy. 2008. 'Late quaternary avifauna' in M. Winterbourn et al. *Natural History of Canterbury*. CUP, Christchurch.
30 Fleming 1982, *George Edward Lodge*.
31 Davis, A. 1994. 'Status, distribution, population trends of the New Zealand shore plover (*Thinornis novaeseelandiae*)'. *Notornis* (supp.) 41: 179–94.
32 Ibid.
33 Sibson 1982, *Birds at Risk*.
34 Department of Conservation. 2001. 'New Zealand shore plover recovery plan 2001–2011'. DOC, Wellington.
35 Davis, A. 1994b. 'Breeding biology of New Zealand shore plover (*Thinornis novaeseelandiae*)'. *Notornis* (supp.) 41: 195–208.
36 Ibid.
37 Ibid.
38 Davis, A. 1987. 'The behavioural ecology and management of New Zealand shore plover'. Unpubl. MSc thesis, University of Auckland.
39 Davis 1994b, 'Breeding biology of New Zealand shore plover (*Thinornis novaeseelandiae*)'.
40 DOC 2001, 'New Zealand shore plover recovery plan 2001–2011'.
41 Fleming 1939, 'Birds of the Chatham Islands'.
42 Ibid.
43 J. Dowding, pers. comm.
44 Davis 1994a, 'Status, distribution, population trends of the New Zealand shore plover (*Thinornis novaeseelandiae*)'.
45 Davis 1987, 'The behavioural ecology and management of New Zealand shore plover'.

TWO: ONLY GAME IN TOWN
1 Bridge, J.S. 1993. 'The interaction between channel geometry, water flow, sediment transport and deposition in braided rivers', pp. 13–71 in J.L. Best & C.S. Bristow (eds). *Braided Rivers*. The Geological Society, Oxford.
2 Gray, D. & J.S. Harding. 2007. 'Braided river ecology: A literature review of physical habitats and aquatic invertebrate communities'. *Science for Conservation* 279. DOC, Wellington.
3 Ibid.
4 Jobberns, G. 1927. 'The Canterbury Plains. Their origin and structure' in R.M. Laing, R. Speight & A. Wall. *Natural History of Canterbury*. Philosophical Institute of Canterbury, Christchurch.
5 Hay, J.R. 1984. 'The behavioural ecology of the wrybill'. Unpubl. PhD thesis, University of Auckland, Auckland.
6 Gray & Harding 2007, 'Braided river ecology'.
7 Kilroy, C., M.R. Scarsbrook & G. Fenwick. 2004. 'Dimensions in biodiversity of a braided river'. *Water and Atmosphere* 12: 10–11.
8 Hughey, K.F.D. 1985. 'Hydrological factors influencing the ecology of riverbed breeding birds on the plains' reaches of Canterbury's braided rivers'. Unpubl. PhD thesis, University of Canterbury, Christchurch.
9 Gray & Harding 2007, 'Braided river ecology'.
10 Ibid.
11 Biggs, B.J.F. & C. Kilroy. 2004: 'Periphyton' in J.S. Harding et al. (eds). *Freshwaters of New Zealand*. New Zealand Hydrological Society and New Zealand Limnological Society, Christchurch.
12 Gray & Harding 2007, 'Braided river ecology'.
13 Gray, D., M.R. Scarsbrook & J.S.Harding. 2006. 'Spatial biodiversity patterns in a large New Zealand braided river'. *New Zealand Journal of Marine and Freshwater Research* 40: 631–42.
14 Biggs & Kilroy 2004, 'Periphyton'.
15 Sagar, P.M. 1986. 'The effects of floods on the invertebrate fauna of a large, unstable braided river'. *NZ Journal of Marine and Freshwater Research*. 20: 37–46.
16 Gray & Harding 2007, 'Braided river ecology'.
17 Sagar 1986, 'The effects of floods on the invertebrate fauna of a large, unstable braided river'.
18 Ibid.
19 Ibid.
20 Department of Conservation. 2009. 'River life: Explore the ecology of braided rivers in the Mackenzie Basin'. DOC, Christchurch.

THREE: INTERTIDAL FOOD FACTORIES
1 Sibson, R.B. 1975. 'Some thoughts on the diet of the South Island pied oystercatcher'. *Notornis* 22: 66–82.
2 *OED*.
3 Woodley, K. 2009. *Godwits: Long-haul champions*, Raupo, Auckland, p. 63.
4 van de Kam et al. 2004, *Shorebirds: An illustrated behavioural ecology*, p. 17.
5 Angel, H. 1974. *The World of an Estuary*. Faber, London.
6 Jones, M.B. & I.D. Marsden. 2005. *Life in the Estuary: Illustrated guide and ecology*. CUP, Christchurch.
7 Battley, P.F. & B. Brownell. 2007. 'Population biology and foraging ecology of waders in the Firth of Thames: update

2007'. Auckland Regional Council report TP347.
8 Ibid.
9 van de Kam et al. 2004, *Shorebirds: An illustrated behavioural ecology*, p. 84.
10 del Hoyo et al. 1996, *Handbook of the Birds of the World*, see page 166.
11 van de Kam et al. 2004, *Shorebirds: An illustrated behavioural ecology*, p. 448.
12 McLay, C.L. 1976. 'An inventory of the status and origin of New Zealand estuarine systems'. *Proceedings of NZ Ecological Society* 23: 8–25.
13 Sagar, P.M., U. Shankar & S. Brown. 1999. 'Distribution and numbers of waders in New Zealand, 1983–1994'. *Notornis* 46: 1–45.
14 Whelan, M.B., T.M. Hume, P.M. Sagar, U. Shankar & R. Liefting. 2003. 'Relationship between physical characteristics of estuaries and the size and diversity of wader populations in the North Island of New Zealand'. *Notornis* 50: 11–22.
15 Crossland, A. 1996. *NZ Wader Study Group News*. Miranda Naturalists' Trust.

FOUR: LIFE WITH A TWIST
1 Perry, R. 1938. *At the Turn of the Tide: A book of wild birds*. Lindsay Drummond, London, p. 59.
2 Potts, T.H. 1870. *On the Birds of New Zealand*. TPNZI 3: 93–7; and Marchant & Higgins (eds) 1993, *Handbook of Australian, New Zealand and Antarctic Birds*.
3 Sibson, R.B. 1963. 'A population study of the wry-billed plover (*Anarhynchus frontalis*)'. *Notornis* 10: 146–53.
4 Fleming 1982, *George Edward Lodge*, p. 269.
5 Potts 1870, *On the Birds of New Zealand*.
6 Ibid.
7 Hay, J.R. 1984. 'The behavioural ecology of the wrybill'. Unpubl. PhD thesis, University of Auckland, Auckland.
8 Potts 1870, *On the Birds of New Zealand*.
9 Hutton, F. 1873. 'Notes by Captain Hutton on Dr. Buller's "Birds of New Zealand", with the Author's Replies thereto'. *TNZI* 6, art. XXIX
10 Ibid.
11 Stead, E.F. 1932. *The Life Histories of New Zealand Birds*. Search, London, p. 91.
12 Guthrie-Smith, H. 1925. *Bird Life on Island and Shore*. William Blackwood, Edinburgh.
13 Turbott, E.G. 1970. 'The wrybill: A feeding adaptation'. *Notornis* 17: 25–27.
14 Ibid.
15 R.J. Pierce, pers. comm.
16 Pierce, R. 1979. 'Foods and feeding of the wrybill (*Anarhynchus frontalis*) on its riverbed breeding grounds'. *Notornis* 26: 1–21.
17 Pierce, R.J. 1976. 'The feeding ecology of wrybills in Canterbury'. Unpubl. postgraduate diploma in science thesis, University of Otago, Dunedin.
18 Ibid.
19 Battley & Brownell 2007, 'Population biology and foraging ecology of waders in the Firth of Thames'.
20 Hay 1984, 'The behavioural ecology of the wrybill'.
21 Pierce 1979, 'Foods and feeding of the wrybill (*Anarhynchus frontalis*) on its riverbed breeding grounds'.
22 R. Pierce, pers. comm.
23 R. Pierce, pers. comm.
24 Pierce 1979, 'Foods and feeding of the wrybill (*Anarhynchus frontalis*) on its riverbed breeding grounds'.
25 P. Schofield, pers. comm.
26 Pierce 1979, 'Foods and feeding of the wrybill (*Anarhynchus frontalis*) on its riverbed breeding grounds'.
27 Hay 1984, 'The behavioural ecology of the wrybill'.
28 R. Pierce, pers. comm.
29 Hay 1984, 'The behavioural ecology of the wrybill'.
30 Burton, P.J.K. 1972. 'Some anatomical notes on the wrybill'. *Notornis* 19: 26–32.
31 Ibid.
32 Stead 1932, *The Life Histories of New Zealand Birds*, p. 92.
33 Guthrie-Smith, H. 1936. *The Sorrows and Joys of a New Zealand Naturalist*. A.H. & A.W. Reed, Dunedin.
34 Hay 1984, 'The behavioural ecology of the wrybill'.
35 Ibid.
36 Ibid.
37 Stead 1932, *The Life Histories of New Zealand Birds*, p. 95.
38 Hay 1984, 'The behavioural ecology of the wrybill'.
39 Ibid.
40 Stead 1932, *The Life Histories of New Zealand Birds*.
41 R. Pierce, pers. comm.

FIVE: SHRINKING FORTUNES
1 Watola, G. 2008. *The Discovery of New Zealand's Birds*. Stepping Stone Books, Orewa, p. 162.
2 Bridge et al. 2005, 'A phylogenetic framework for the terns (*Sternini*) inferred from mtDNA sequences'.
3 Buller, W.L. 1882. *Manual of the Birds of New Zealand*. Government Printer, Wellington.
4 Stead 1932, *The Life Histories of New Zealand Birds*, p. 25.
5 Potts, T.H. 1882. *Out in the Open: A budget of scraps of natural history, gathered in New Zealand*. Lyttelton Times Company, Christchurch.
6 Stead 1932, *The Life Histories of New Zealand Birds*.
7 Maloney, R. F. et al. 1997. 'Bird density and diversity in braided rivers in the Upper Waitaki, South Island, New Zealand'. *Notornis* 44: 219–32.
8 Keedwell, R.J. 2002. 'Black-fronted terns and banded dotterels: causes of mortality and comparisons of survival'. PhD thesis, Massey University, Palmerston North.
9 Guthrie-Smith 1936, *The Sorrows and Joys of a New Zealand Naturalist*.
10 Soper, M.F. 1972. *New Zealand Birds*. Whitcombe and Tombs, Christchurch, p. 123.
11 Keedwell 2002, 'Black-fronted terns and banded dotterels'.
12 Stead 1932, *The Life Histories of New Zealand Birds*, p. 27.
13 Child, P. 1986. 'Black-fronted tern breeding at high altitude'. *Notornis* 33: 193–94.
14 Stead 1932, *The Life Histories of New Zealand Birds*, p. 27.
15 Keedwell 2002, 'Black-fronted terns and banded dotterels'.
16 Ibid.
17 M. Bell, pers. comm.
18 Keedwell 2002, 'Black-fronted terns and banded dotterels'.
19 Stead 1932, *The Life Histories of New Zealand Birds*, p. 30.
20 Robertson, C.J.R., C.J.F. O'Donnell & F.B. Overmars. 1983. 'Habitat requirements of wetland birds in the Ahuriri River Catchment New Zealand'. New Zealand Wildlife Service, Department of Internal Affairs, occasional report 3.
21 M. Bell, pers. comm.
22 Keedwell 2002, 'Black-fronted terns and banded dotterels'.
23 Ibid.
24 Ibid.
25 Ibid.

SIX: HIGH-STEPPING IN THE SHALLOWS
1 Jobling, J.A. 2010. *Helm Dictionary of Scientific Bird Names*. Christopher Helm, London.
2 Fleming 1982, *George Edward Lodge*, p. 265.
3 Hill, J. 1999. *An Exhilaration of Wings: The literature of birdwatching*. Viking, N.Y., pp. 31 & 105.
4 Soper 1972, *New Zealand Birds*, p. 125.
5 Fleming 1982, *George Edward Lodge*.
6 Ibid.
7 Pierce, R.J. 1984b. 'Plumage, morphology and hybridization of New Zealand stilts *Himantopus* species'. *Notornis* 31: 106–30.
8 Buller 1882, *Manual of the Birds of New Zealand*.
9 Pierce, R.J. 1984a. 'The changed distribution of stilts in New Zealand'. *Notornis* 31: 7–18.
10 Ibid.
11 Pascoe, J. (ed.) 1957. *Mr Explorer Douglas*. A.H & A.W. Reed, Wellington, p. 250.
12 Pierce 1984a, 'The changed distribution of stilts in New Zealand'.
13 Ibid.
14 Ibid.
15 Buller, W.L. 1874. 'On the Genus Himantopus in New Zealand'. *TNZI* 7, Art. XXIX.
16 Oliver, W.R.B. 1930. *New Zealand Birds*. Fine Arts (NZ), Wellington.
17 Stead 1932, *The Life Histories of New Zealand Birds*, p. 97.
18 Holdaway, R.N. 1995. 'A fossil record of the black stilt *Himantopus novaezelandiae* Gould, 1841'. *NZ Natural Sciences* 22: 69–74.
19 Wilson, K-J. 2004. *Flight of the Huia. Ecology and conservation of New Zealand's frogs, reptiles, birds and mammals*. CUP, Christchurch, pp. 296–7.
20 Fleming 1982, *George Edward Lodge*, p. 266.
21 Holdaway 1995, 'A fossil record of the black stilt *Himantopus novaezelandiae* Gould, 1841'.
22 Pierce, R.J. 1996. 'Family Recurvirostridae (stilts and avocets)' in del Hoyo et al. (eds), *Handbook of the Birds of the World*, pp. 332–47.
23 Ibid.
24 Marchant & Higgins (eds) 1993, *Handbook*

25 Based on R.J. Pierce, unpublished data.
26 Dowding, J.E. & S.J. Moore. 2006. 'Habitat networks of indigenous shorebirds in New Zealand'. *Science for Conservation* 261, DOC, Wellington.
27 Pierce, R.J. 1986. 'Differences in susceptibility to predation during nesting between pied and black stilts (*Himantopus* spp.)'. *Auk* 103: 273–80.
28 Ibid.
29 Stead 1932, *The Life Histories of New Zealand Birds*, p. 99.
30 Pierce 1986, 'Differences in susceptibility to predation during nesting between pied and black stilts (*Himantopus* spp.)'.
31 Holdaway 1995, 'A fossil record of the black stilt *Himantopus novaezelandiae* Gould, 1841'.
32 Reed, C.E.M., D.P. Murray & D.J. Butler. 1993. 'Black stilt recovery plan (*Himantopus novaezelandiae*)'. DOC, Wellington.
33 Pierce 1986, 'Differences in susceptibility to predation during nesting between pied and black stilts (*Himantopus* spp.).
34 Greene, B. 1999. 'Genetic variation and hybridisation of black stilts (*Himantopus novaezelandiae*) and pied stilts (*H.h.leucocephalus*), Order Charadriformes.' *NZJZ* 26: 271–7.
35 Ibid.
36 Pierce 1984b, 'Plumage, morphology and hybridization of New Zealand stilts *Himantopus* species'.
37 Ibid.

SEVEN: ON MUSSEL-PICKERS AND SEA-PIES
1 Newton, A. et al. 1896. *A Dictionary of Birds*, A. & C. Black, London.
2 Jobling 2010, *Helm Dictionary of Scientific Bird Names*.
3 Newton 1896, *A Dictionary of Birds*.
4 Baker, A.J. 1972. 'Systematics and affinities of New Zealand oystercatchers'. Unpubl. PhD thesis, University of Canterbury, Christchurch.
5 Hockey, P.A.R. 1996. 'Family Haematopodidae (Oystercatchers)' in del Hoyo et al. (eds), *Handbook of the Birds of the World*, p. 311.
6 Watola 2008, *The Discovery of New Zealand's Birds*.
7 Fleming 1982, *George Edward Lodge*, p. 234.
8 Ibid.
9 Watola 2008, *The Discovery of New Zealand's Birds*, p. 129.
10 Heppleston, P.B. 1973. 'The distribution and taxonomy of oystercatchers'. *Notornis* 20: 102–12.
11 Baker 1975. 'Morphological variation, hybridization and systematics of New Zealand oystercatchers (Charadriiformes: haematopodidae)'. *NZJZ* 175: 357–90.
12 Heppleston 1973, 'The distribution and taxonomy of oystercatchers'.
13 Ibid.
14 Banks & Paterson 2007; see also T. Crocker, S. Petch & P. Sagar. 2010. 'Hybridisation by SI pied oystercatcher (*Haematopus finschi*) and variable oystercatcher (*H. unicolor*) in Canterbury'. *Notornis* 57(1): 27–32.
15 Hockey 1996, 'Family *Haematopodidae* (Oystercatchers)'.
16 Ibid.
17 Ibid.
18 Orbell, M. 2003. *Birds of Aotearoa: A natural and cultural history.* Reed, Auckland, p. 155.
19 Marchant & Higgins (eds) 1993, *Handbook of Australian, New Zealand and Antarctic Birds*, p. 727.
20 Baker, A.J. 1974. 'Prey-specific feeding methods of New Zealand oystercatchers'. *Notornis* 21: 219–33.
21 Ibid.
22 Ibid.
23 Ibid.
24 Ibid.
25 Baker, A.J. 1973. 'Distribution and number of New Zealand oystercatchers'. *Notornis* 20: 128–44.
26 Marchant & Higgins (eds) 1993, *Handbook of Australian, New Zealand and Antarctic Birds*.
27 Ibid.
28 Child, P. 1969. 'Oystercatchers and banded dotterels nesting high in Central Otago'. *Notornis* 16: 186.
29 Soper, M.F. 1959. 'Nesting habitats on the Shotover riverbed'. *Notornis* 8(6): 1.
30 Pierce, R.J. 1983. 'The Charadriiforms of a high-country river valley'. *Notornis* 30: 169–85.
31 Child 1969, 'Oystercatchers and banded dotterels nesting high in Central Otago'.
32 Fleming, P. 1990. 'Variable oystercatchers nesting at Waikanae Estuary 1971–1989'. *Notornis* 37: 73–76.
33 Marchant & Higgins (eds) 1993, *Handbook of Australian, New Zealand and Antarctic Birds*.
34 Baker 1974, 'Prey-specific feeding methods of New Zealand oystercatchers'.

EIGHT: TRANSTASMAN ODDITY
1 Piersma, T. 1996, in del Hoyo et al. (eds), *Handbook of the Birds of the World,* p. 387.
2 Ibid.
3 Dann, P. 1991. 'Feeding behaviour and diet of double-banded plovers (*Charadrius bicinctus*) in Western Port, Victoria'. *Emu* 91: 170–85.
4 del Hoyo et al. (eds) 1996, *Handbook of the Birds of the World*.
5 Jobling 2010, *Helm Dictionary of Scientific Bird Names*.
6 Newton 1896, *A Dictionary of Birds*. See Chapter 13.
7 Ibid.
8 Orbell 2003, *Birds of Aotearoa*, p. 158.
9 Bomford, M. 1986. 'Breeding displays and calls of the banded dotterel (*Charadrius bicintus*)'. *Notornis* 33: 217–32.
10 Cunningham, J.M. 1973. 'The banded dotterel, *Charadrius bicinctus*: pohowera or tuturiwhatu? – call notes and behaviour'. *Notornis* 20: 21–7.
11 Bomford 1986, 'Migratory shorebirds of the East Asian–Australasian Flyway'.
12 Marchant & Higgins (eds) 1993, *Handbook of Australian, New Zealand and Antarctic Birds*, p. 847.
13 Pierce, R.J. 1989. 'Breeding and social patterns of banded dotterels (*Charadrius bicinctus*) at Cass River'. *Notornis* 36: 13–14.
14 Fleming 1982, *George Edward Lodge*, p. 241.
15 Marchant & Higgins (eds) 1993, *Handbook of Australian, New Zealand and Antarctic Birds*.
16 Child 1969, 'Oystercatchers and banded dotterels nesting high in Central Otago'.
17 Drummond, J. 1909. *In Touch with Nature*, 16 September 1909, Canterbury Museum Archives.
18 Soper 1959, 'Nesting habitats on the Shotover riverbed'.
19 del Hoyo et al. (eds) 1996, *Handbook of the Birds of the World*.
20 Heather, B.D. 1977. 'Foot trembling by the black-fronted dotterel'. *Notornis* 24: 1.
21 Phillips, R.E. 1980. 'Behaviour and systematics of New Zealand plovers'. *Emu* 80: 177–98.

NINE: A GAME OF TWO HALVES
1 Marchant & Higgins (eds) 1993, *Handbook of Australian, New Zealand and Antarctic Birds*, p. 818.
2 Sibson 1982, *Birds at Risk*.
3 A. Polkanov, pers. comm.
4 Watola 2008, *The Discovery of New Zealand's Birds*; and Andrews, J.R.H. 1986. *The Southern Ark: Zoological discovery in New Zealand 1769–1900*. Century Hutchinson, Auckland.
5 Buller 1882, *Manual of the Birds of New Zealand*.
6 Pascoe 1957, *Mr Explorer Douglas*, p. 250.
7 Potts 1885, 'Oology of New Zealand'.
8 Barlow, M. 1993. 'New Zealand dotterel: South Island historical notes and Southland coastal records'. *Notornis* 40: 15–25.
9 Dowding, J.E. 1994. 'Morphometrics and ecology of the New Zealand dotterel (*Charadrius obscurus*), with a description of a new subspecies'. *Notornis* 41: 221–3.
10 J. Dowding, pers. comm.
11 Ibid.
12 Dowding, J.E. & E.C. Murphy. 1993. 'The decline of the Stewart Island population of the New Zealand dotterel'. *Notornis* 40: 1–13.
13 Edgar, A.T. 1969. 'Estimated population of the red-breasted dotterel'. *Notornis*. 16(2): 85–100.
14 Ibid.
15 Ibid.
16 Karl, B.J. & H.A. Best. 1982. 'Feral cats on Stewart Island: Their foods, and their effects on kakapo (*Strigops habroptilus*)'. *NZJZ* 9: 287–94.
17 Dowding & Murphy 1993, 'The decline of the Stewart Island population of the New Zealand dotterel'.
18 J. Dowding, pers. comm.
19 Dowding & Murphy 1993, 'The decline of the Stewart Island population of the New Zealand dotterel'.
20 Dowding 1994. 'Morphometrics and ecology of the New Zealand dotterel (*Charadrius obscurus*), with a description of a new subspecies'.
21 Ibid.
22 Ibid.
23 J. Dowding, pers. comm.
24 Ibid.
25 Marchant & Higgins (eds) 1993, *Handbook*

of Australian, New Zealand and Antarctic Birds.
26. Hammond, P. 2011. 'A very old New Zealand dotterel', *Miranda News* 81, May 2011.
27. Dowding, J.E. & S.P. Chamberlin. 1991. 'Annual movement patterns and breeding site fidelity of the New Zealand dotterel (*Charadrius obscurus*)'. *Notornis* 38: 89–102.
28. Pye, D. & J. Dowding. 2002. 'Nesting period of northern New Zealand dotterel (*Charadrius obscurus aquilonius*)'. *Notornis* 49: 259–60.
29. Ibid.

TEN: PIRACY AND PREJUDICE
1. Gill, B.J. et al. (eds). 2010. *Checklist of the Birds of New Zealand*. 4th edn. Te Papa Press/OSNZ, Wellington.
2. Jobling 2010, *Helm Dictionary of Scientific Bird Names*.
3. Ibid.
4. Oliver 1955, *New Zealand Birds*, p. 310.
5. Stead 1932, *The Life Histories of New Zealand Birds*, p. 45.
6. Potts 1882, *Out in the Open*, p. 217.
7. Orbell 2003, *Birds of Aotearoa*.
8. Ibid.
9. Burger, J. & M. Gochfeld. 1996. 'Family Laridae (gulls)' in del Hoyo et al. (eds), *Handbook of the Birds of the World*, p. 572.
10. Caughley, G. 1966. 'The breeding of black-backed gulls in the South island mountains'. *Notornis* 13: 3: 166–7.
11. Oliver 1955, *New Zealand Birds*.
12. Oliver, W.R.B. 1953. 'Black-backed gull breeding at high altitudes'. *Notornis* 5(3): 82.
13. Stead 1932, *The Life Histories of New Zealand Birds*.
14. Oliver 1953, 'Black-backed gull breeding at high altitudes'.
15. Turbott, E.G. 1969. 'Roof-nesting black-backed gulls'. *Notornis* 16(3): 187–89.
16. Fordham, R.A. 1964. 'Breeding biology of the southern black-backed gull II: incubation to chick stage'. *Notornis* 11(2): 110–26.
17. Stead 1932, *The Life Histories of New Zealand Birds*, p. 47.
18. Worthy & Holdaway 2002, *The Lost World of the Moa*, p. 415.
19. del Hoyo et al. (eds) 1996, *Handbook of the Birds of the World*.
20. Biswell, S.F. 2005. 'Black-backed gulls'. *NZ Geographic* 73: 46–61.
21. McClellan, R. 2009. 'The ecology and management of Southland's black-billed gulls'. Unpubl. PhD thesis, University of Otago, Dunedin.
22. Stead 1932, *The Life Histories of New Zealand Birds*.
23. Fleming 1939, 'Birds of the Chatham Islands', pp. 1–15.
24. Soper 1972, *New Zealand Birds*, p. 146.
25. Fleming, C.A. 1946. 'Breeding of red-billed gull: A preliminary census of Mokohinau colony'. *NZ Bird Notes* 2: 2; 26 (my italics).
26. Oliver 1955, *New Zealand Birds*.
27. Blackburn, A. 1962. 'Feeding behaviour of red-billed gulls, Awapuni Lagoon Gisborne'. *Notornis* 10(1): 42.
28. Brown, B. 1982. 'Unusual feeding of red-billed gull'. *Notornis* 29(1): 77.
29. Buller, W.L. 1888. *A History of the Birds of New Zealand*. London.
30. Buller, W.L. 1894. 'Notes on the ornithology of New Zealand, with an exhibition of rare specimens'. *TNZI* 27: 116–17.
31. Oliver 1955, *New Zealand Birds*.
32. Gurr, L. & F.C. Kinsky. 1965. 'Distribution of breeding colonies and status of red-billed gull (*L. novaehollandiae scopulinus*) in New Zealand and outlying islands'. *Notornis* 12(4): 223–40.
33. Higgins, P.J. & S.J.J.F. Davies (eds). 1993. *Handbook of Australian, New Zealand and Antarctic Birds. Vol III. Snipe to Pigeons.* OUP, Melbourne, p. 517.
34. Oliver 1955, *New Zealand Birds*.
35. Soper 1972, *New Zealand Birds*.
36. Mills, J.A., J.W. Yarrall et al. 2008. 'Impact of climatic variations on food availability and reproductive performance of planktivorous red-billed gull (*Larus novaehollandiae scopulinus*)'. *Journal of Animal Ecology* 77: 1129–42.
37. Ibid.
38. Mills, J.R. 1969. 'The distribution of breeding red-billed gull colonies in New Zealand in relation to areas of plankton enrichment'. *Notornis* 16(3): 180–6.
39. Ibid.
40. Ibid.
41. Ibid.
42. Mills et al. 2008, 'Impact of climatic variations on food availability and reproductive performance of planktivorous red-billed gull (*Larus novaehollandiae scopulinus*)'.
43. Ibid.
44. Ibid.
45. Ibid.
46. McClellan 2009, 'The ecology and management of Southland's black-billed gulls'.
47. Ibid.
48. Buller 1888, *A History of the Birds of New Zealand*.
49. Boud, R. & B.T. Cunningham. 1959. 'Feeding habits of the black-billed gull'. *Notornis* 8: 4: 119–20.
50. McClellan 2009, 'The ecology and management of Southland's black-billed gulls'.
51. Allen, G.G. 1984. 'Black-billed gull food preferences'. *Notornis* 31(3): 224.
52. McClellan 2009, 'The ecology and management of Southland's black-billed gulls'.
53. Williams, P.A. & S. Wiser. 2004. 'Determinants of regional and local patterns in the floras of braided riverbeds in New Zealand'. *Journal of Biogeography* 31: 1355–72.
54. McClellan 2009, 'The ecology and management of Southland's black-billed gulls'.
55. Ibid.
56. Burger, J. & M. Gochfeld. 1996. 'Use of space by nesting black-billed gulls *Larus bulleri*: Behavioural changes during the reproductive cycle'. *Emu* 96: 73-81.
57. McClellan 2009, 'The ecology and management of Southland's black-billed gulls'.
58. Stead 1932, *Life Histories of New Zealand Birds*, p. 219.
59. McClellan 2009, 'The ecology and management of Southland's black-billed gulls'.
60. Ibid.
61. Ibid.
62. Science dictionary.com; see also Courchamp, F., L. Berec & J. Gascoigne. 2008. *Allee Effects in Ecology and Conservation*. OUP, New York..
63. McClellan 2009, 'The ecology and management of Southland's black-billed gulls'.
64. Schmechel, F. 2008. 'Ashburton River 2007/2008 black-billed gull colony.' Environment Canterbury Report RO8/89.
65. Ibid.
66. McClellan 2009, 'The ecology and management of Southland's black-billed gulls'.
67. Ibid.

ELEVEN: ELEGANCE ALOFT
1. Guthrie-Smith 1925, *Bird Life on Island and Shore*.
2. Perry 1938, *At the Turn of the Tide*, p. 95.
3. Higgins & Davies (eds) 1993, *Handbook of Australian, New Zealand and Antarctic Birds, Vol III*, p. 632.
4. Buller 1888, *A History of the Birds of New Zealand*.
5. Medway, D. 1976. 'Extant types of New Zealand birds from Cook's voyages – Part I: Historical and the type paintings'. *Notornis* 23: 45–61.
6. Andrews 1986, *The Southern Ark*.
7. Jobling 2010, *Helm Dictionary of Scientific Bird Names*.
8. Stead 1932, *The Life Histories of New Zealand Birds*, p. 40.
9. Ibid.
10. Higgins & Davies (eds) 1993, *Handbook of Australian, New Zealand and Antarctic Birds*.
11. Cramp, S. and K. Simmons (eds). 1985. *Handbook of the Birds of Europe, the Middle East and North Africa: Birds of the Western Palearctic. Vol IV: Terns to Woodpeckers.* OUP, Oxford, p. 626.
12. Higgins & Davies (eds) 1993, *Handbook of Australian, New Zealand and Antarctic Birds*.
13. Cramp & Simmons (eds). 1985, *Handbook of the Birds of Europe, the Middle East and North Africa, Vol IV*.
14. Barlow, M.L. & J.E. Dowding. 2002. 'Breeding biology of Caspian terns (*Sterna caspia*) at a colony near Invercargill'. *Notornis* 49: 76–91.
15. Sibson, R. 1992. 'Some thoughts on Caspian terns in New Zealand'. *Notornis* 39: 87–93.
16. Ibid.
17. Ibid.
18. Ibid.
19. Worthy & Holdaway 2002, *The Lost World of the Moa*, p. 415.
20. Buller 1888, *A History of the Birds of New Zealand*.
21. Sibson 1992, 'Some thoughts on Caspian terns in New Zealand'.
22. Barlow & Dowding 2002, 'Breeding biology of Caspian terns (*Sterna caspia*) at a colony near Invercargill'.
23. Buddle, G.A. 1951. *Bird Secrets*. A.H. & A.W. Reed, Wellington, p. 54.
24. Barlow & Dowding 2002, 'Breeding biology of Caspian terns (*Sterna caspia*) at a colony near Invercargill'.
25. Ibid.

26. Buller 1888, *A History of the Birds of New Zealand*.
27. Ibid.
28. McKenzie, H.R. & R.B. Sibson. 1957. 'Does the little tern (*Sterna albifrons*) reach New Zealand?' *Notornis* 7: 174–82.
29. Higgins & Davies (eds) 1993, *Handbook of Australian, New Zealand and Antarctic Birds*.
30. Buller 1888, *A History of the Birds of New Zealand*.
31. Higgins & Davies (eds) 1993, *Handbook of Australian, New Zealand and Antarctic Birds*.
32. Hansen, K. 2005. 'New Zealand fairy tern (*Sterna nereis davisae*) recovery plan, 2005–15'. DOC Threatened Species recovery plan 57.
33. G. Pulham, pers. comm.
34. Miskelly, C.M. et al. 2008. 'Conservation status of New Zealand birds 2008'. *Notornis* 55: 117–35.
35. Higgins & Davies (eds) 1993, *Handbook of Australian, New Zealand and Antarctic Birds*.
36. G. Pulham, pers. comm.
37. Threadgold, S. 2000. 'Behavioural ecology of the endangered New Zealand fairy tern (tara-iti) *Sterna nereis davisae*; implications for management'. Unpubl. MSc thesis, Massey University, Palmerston North.

TWELVE: ANCIENT ENIGMAS
1. Barker, D. et al. 2005. 'Discovery of a previously unknown *Coenocorypha* snipe in the Campbell Island group, New Zealand subantarctic'. *Notornis* 52: 143–9.
2. Ibid.
3. Miskelly, C. 2006. 'Bird in the hand: Snipe-hunting on subantarctic Campbell Island'. *NZ Geographic* 80: 104–12.
4. Miskelly, C.M. & B. Norton. 2008. 'A further 1952 record of a *Coenocorypha* snipe on Campbell Island, New Zealand subantarctic'. *Notornis* 55: 162–5.
5. Hayes, S. 2006. 'Seeing snipe'. *NZ Geographic* 81: 7.
6. Barker et al. 2005, 'Discovery of a previously unknown *Coenocorypha* snipe in the Campbell Island group'.
7. McClelland, P. 2002. 'Eratication: The clearance of Campbell Island', *NZ Geographic* 58.
8. Ibid.
9. Miskelly, C.M. & J.R. Fraser. 2006. 'Campbell Island snipe (*Coenocorypha* undescribed sp.) recolonise subantarctic Campbell Island following rat eradication'. *Notornis* 53: 353–60.
10. Barker et al. 2005, 'Discovery of a previously unknown *Coenocorypha* snipe in the Campbell Island group'.
11. Fleming 1982, *George Edward Lodge*, p. 250.
12. Tennyson, A.J.D. & P. Martinson. 2006. *Extinct Birds of New Zealand*. Te Papa, Wellington, p. 90.
13. Roberts, A. & C. Miskelly. 2003. 'Recovery plan for the snipe species of New Zealand and the Chatham Islands (*Coenocorypha* spp.) tutukiwi 2003–2015'. DOC, Wellington.
14. Worthy & Holdaway 2002, *The Lost World of the Moa*, p. 487.
15. Ibid.
16. Jobling 2010, *Helm Dictionary of Scientific Bird Names*.
17. Miskelly, C.M., K.J. Walker & G.P. Elliott. 2006. 'Breeding ecology of three subantarctic snipes (genus *Coenocorypha*)'. *Notornis* 53: 361–74.
18. Higgins & Davies (eds) 1993, *Handbook of Australian, New Zealand and Antarctic Birds*.
19. Tennyson & Martinson 2006, *Extinct Birds of New Zealand*.
20. Medway, D.G. 2007. 'A possible live South Island snipe (*Coenocorypha iredali*) at Dusky Sound 1773'. *Notornis* 54: 237–8.
21. Guthrie-Smith 1936, *The Sorrows and Joys of a New Zealand Naturalist*.
22. Tennyson & Martinson 2006, *Extinct Birds of New Zealand*.
23. Worthy & Holdaway 2002, *The Lost World of the Moa*.
24. Tennyson & Martinson 2006, *Extinct Birds of New Zealand*.
25. Baker, A.J., C.M. Miskelly & O. Haddrath. 2010. 'Species limits and population differentiation in New Zealand snipes (Scolopacidae: *Coenocorypha*)'. *Conservation Genetics* 11: 1363–74.
26. Tennyson & Martinson 2006, *Extinct Birds of New Zealand*.
27. Morris, R. & H. Smith. 1988. *Wild South: Saving New Zealand's endangered birds*. TVNZ & Hutchinson, Auckland, p. 117.
28. Gill et al. 2010, *Checklist of the Birds of New Zealand*.
29. Miskelly, C.M. 1990b. 'Breeding systems of New Zealand snipe *Coenocorypha aucklandica* and Chatham Island snipe *C. pusilla*: Are they food limited?' *Ibis* 132: 366–79.
30. Roberts & Miskelly 2003, 'Recovery plan for the snipe species of New Zealand and the Chatham Islands (*Coenocorypha* spp.) tutukiwi 2003–2015'.
31. Miskelly, C.M. 1990. 'Aerial displaying and flying ability of Chatham Island snipe *Coenocorypha pusilla* and New Zealand snipe *C. aucklandica*'. *Emu* 90: 207–21.
32. Miskelly et al. 2006, 'Breeding ecology of three subantarctic snipes (genus *Coenocorypha*)'.
33. Fleming 1982, *George Edward Lodge*, p. 250.
34. Miskelly, C.M. & A.J. Baker. 2009. 'Description of a new subspecies of *Coenocorypha* snipe from subantarctic Campbell Island, New Zealand'. *Notornis* 56: 113–23.
35. Miskelly 1990, 'Aerial displaying and flying ability of Chatham Island snipe *Coenocorypha pusilla* and New Zealand snipe *C. aucklandica*'.
36. Ibid.
37. Ibid.
38. Miskelly, C.M. 1987. 'The identity of the hakawai'. *Notornis* 34: 95–116.
39. Miskelly, C.M. E.A. Bell; G.P. Elliott & K.J. Walker. 2006. '"Hakawai" aerial breeding display by three populations of subantarctic snipe (genus *Coenocorypha*)'. *Notornis* 53: 375–79.
40. Miskelly, C.M. 2005. 'Evidence for "hakawai" aerial displaying by Snares Island snipe (*Coenocorypha aucklandica huegeli*)'. *Notornis* 52: 163–65.
41. C. Miskelly, pers. com.
42. Miskelly, C.M., M.R. Charteris & J.R. Fraser. 2011. 'Successful translocation of Snares Island snipe *Coenocorypha huegeli* to replace the extinct South Island snipe *C. iredalei*'. Submitted manuscript.
43. One reason suggested for why the display had not been heard on the Snares was that people weren't listening at the right time of year. Furthermore, at certain times it may be just too dangerous for a snipe to be airborne, when, earlier in the season, the skies are thickly filled with masses of returning sooty shearwaters. The number of shearwaters flying overhead at dusk is greatly diminished by April. How many sooties? 'To say muttonbirds are common here fails to convey their overwhelming abundance on the islands. During summer months the sky at dusk is flecked with uncountable numbers of titi returning to their nests from sea.' Warne, K. 2003. 'A wing and a snare: Part II Island of Birds'. *NZ Geographic* 62. 'As we left the shore the air was literally dark with mutton-birds flying in every direction, the owners no doubt of the innumerable nests on the shore. I verily believe they might be numbered by millions as they followed their bewildering courses through the air. I am told that towards night they descend upon the land in such numbers as to overwhelm the fires and threaten the stability of the tent of any one encamped there.' Chapman, F.R. 1890. 'The outlying islands of New Zealand'. *TNZI* 23: 492–522.
44. Baker et al. 2010, 'Species limits and population differentiation in New Zealand snipes (Scolopacidae: *Coenocorypha*)'.
45. Roberts & Miskelly 2003, 'Recovery plan for the snipe species of New Zealand and the Chatham Islands (*Coenocorypha* spp.) tutukiwi 2003–2015'.
46. Miskelly & Fraser 2006, 'Campbell Island snipe (*Coenocorypha* undescribed sp.) recolonise subantarctic Campbell Island following rat eradication'.
47. Miskelly & Baker 2009, 'Description of a new subspecies of *Coenocorypha* snipe from subantarctic Campbell Island, New Zealand'.

THIRTEEN: THE GREAT OE
1. Lopez, B. 1986. *Arctic Dreams*. Vintage, New York, p. 162.
2. Southey, I. 2009. 'Numbers of waders in New Zealand 1995–2003'. DOC Research & Development Series 308. DOC, Wellington.
3. Higgins, P.J. & S.J.J.F. Davies (eds). 1993. *Handbook of Australian, New Zealand and Antarctic Birds. Vol III: Snipe to Pigeons*. OUP, Melbourne.
4. Battley, P. & D. Rogers 2007, in Geering et al., p. 37.
5. Ibid.
6. Newton, I. 2010. *Bird Migration*. Collins, London, p. 314.
7. Ibid.
8. Lindstrom, A. 2003. 'Fuel deposition rates in migrating birds: Causes, constraints and consequences' in Berthold, P., E. Gwinner & E. Sonnenschein (eds). 2003. *Avian Migration*. Springer, Heidelberg.
9. Higgins & Davies (eds) 1993, *Handbook of*

10 Johnson, O.W. & P.G. Connors. 1996. 'Pacific golden plover *Pluvialis fulva*'. *Birds of North America* No. 202.
11 Morris, F.O. 1851. *History of British Birds Vol V*. London.
12 Jobling 2010, *Helm Dictionary of Scientific Bird Names*.
13 Higgins & Davies (eds) 1993, *Handbook of Australian, New Zealand and Antarctic Birds*.
14 Witherby, H.F. et al. 1947. *The Handbook of British Birds Vol IV*. pp. 223–7.
15 Nettleship, D.N. 2000. 'Ruddy turnstone *Arenaria interpres*'. *Birds of North America* No. 537.
16 Higgins & Davies (eds) 1993, *Handbook of Australian, New Zealand and Antarctic Birds*.
17 Jenkins, J. 1971. 'A hitchhiking turnstone'. *Notornis* 18(2): 130–1.
18 Schipper, C.J., M.A. Weston & J.M. Peter. 1996. 'Scavenging behaviour of ruddy turnstone *Arenaria interpres*'. *Stilt* 29: 39–40.
19 Mercer, A.J. 1966. 'Turnstones feeding on a human corpse'. *British Birds* 59: 307.
20 Nettleship 2000, 'Ruddy turnstone *Arenaria interpres*'.
21 Ibid.
22 Hale, W.G. 1980. *Waders*. New Naturalist Series. Collins, London.
23 Nettleship 2000, 'Ruddy turnstone *Arenaria interpres*'.
24 Johnson & Connors 1996, 'Pacific golden plover *Pluvialis fulva*'.
25 Jobling 2010, *Helm Dictionary of Scientific Bird Names*.
26 Johnson, O.W. 1993. 'The Pacific golden plover *Pluvialis fulva*: Discovery of the species and other historical notes'. *Auk* 110: 136–41.
27 Johnston, D.W. & R.W. McFarlane. 1967. 'Migration and bioenergetics of flight in the Pacific golden plover'. *Condor* 69: 156–68.
28 Kinsky, F.C. & J.C. Yaldwyn. 1981. 'The bird fauna of Niue Island, South-west Pacific, with special notes on the white-tailed tropic bird and golden plover'. National Museum of New Zealand, Miscellaneous Series No. 2, April 1981.
29 Thompson, M.C. 1973. 'Migratory patterns of ruddy turnstones in the Central Pacific region'. *Living Bird* 12: 5–23.
30 Ibid.
31 Minton, C.D.T. et al. 2010. 'Initial results from light level geolocator trials on Ruddy Turnstone *Arenaria interpres* reveal unexpected migration route'. *WSG Bulletin* 117(1): 9–14; see also Ruddy hell: turnstone flies 27,000 km – twice!!' in *AWSG Tattler* 21: 6.
32 *NZ Wader Study Group News* 6, Nov. 95, Miranda Naturalists' Trust.
33 Birkhead, T. 2008. *The Wisdom of Birds: An illustrated history of ornithology*. Bloomsbury, London.
34 Newton 2010, *Bird Migration*.

FOURTEEN: TIGHT SCHEDULES, OR EASY AS?
1 Woodley 2009, *Godwits*, p. 36.
2 Oliver 1955, *New Zealand Birds*.
3 Woodley 2009, *Godwits*.
4 P. Battley, pers. comm.
5 Gill, R. E. Jr., et al. 2005. 'Crossing the ultimate ecological barrier: evidence for an 11,000 km-long nonstop flight from Alaska to New Zealand and Eastern Australia by bar-tailed godwits'. *Condor* 107: 1–20.
6 Battley, P.F., et al. 2011. 'Trans-hemispheric migration timing, flight paths and staging in two bar-tailed godwit subspecies'. *Journal of Avian Biology*. Submitted.
7 Ibid.
8 Colwell, M.A. 2010. *Shorebird Ecology: Conservation and management*. University of California, Berkeley, p. 109.
9 Battley et al, 2011, 'Trans-hemispheric migration timing, flight paths and staging in two bar-tailed godwit subspecies'.
10 Ibid.
11 Ibid.
12 Ibid.
13 Woodley 2009, *Godwits*.
14 Newton 2010, *Bird Migration*.
15 Piersma, T. 1997. 'Do global patterns of habitat use and migration strategies co-evolve with relative investments in immunocompetence due to spatial variation in parasite pressure?' *Oikos* 80, 623–31.
16 Battley, et al. 2011, 'Trans-hemispheric migration timing, flight paths and staging in two bar-tailed godwit subspecies'.
17 Conklin, J.R. & P.F. Battley. 2011. 'Impacts of wind upon rigid individual migration schedules of New Zealand bar-tailed godwits'. *Behavioural Ecology* 22(4): 854–61.
18 Ibid.
19 Conklin, J.R., P.F. Battley, M.A. Potter & D.R. Ruthrauff. 2011. 'Geographic variation in morphology of Alaska-breeding bar-tailed godwits (*Limosa lapponica*) is not maintained on their non breeding grounds in New Zealand'. *Auk* 128(2): 363−73.
20 Conklin & Battley 2011, 'Geographic variation in morphology of Alaska-breeding bar-tailed godwits (*Limosa lapponica*) is not maintained on their non breeding grounds in New Zealand'.
21 Lindström, et al. 2011. 'A puzzling migratory detour: Are fuelling conditions in Alaska driving the movement of juvenile sharp-tailed sandpipers?' *Condor* 113(1): 129–39.
22 Ibid.
23 Ibid.
24 Ibid.
25 Newton 2010, *Bird Migration*.

FIFTEEN: SPECIALISATION BLUES
1 Weidensaul, S. 1999. *Living on the Wind: Across the hemisphere with migratory birds*. North Point Press, New York.
2 Piersma, T. & N. Davidson (eds). 1992. 'The migration of knots'. *Wader Study Group Bulletin* 64.
3 Morris 1851, *History of British Birds Vol V*.
4 Piersma & Davidson 1992, 'The migration of knots'.
5 Ibid.
6 Harrington, B.A. 2002. 'Red knot *Calidris canutus*'. *Birds of North America*. No. 563.
7 Buehler, D.M., A.J. Baker & T. Piersma. 2006. 'Reconstructing palaeoflyways of the late Pleistocene and early Holocene red knot *Calidris canutus*'. *Ardea* 94(3): 485–98.
8 van de Kam et al. 2004, *Shorebirds: An illustrated behavioural ecology*, p. 143.
9 Buehler et al. 2006, 'Reconstructing palaeoflyways of the late Pleistocene and early Holocene red knot *Calidris canutus*'.
10 Rogers, D.I. et al. 2010. 'Red knots (*Calidris canutus piersmai* and *C.c. rogersi*) depend on a small threatened staging area in Bohai Bay, China'. *Emu* 110: 307–15.
11 Bomford, M. et al. (2008). 'Migratory shorebirds of the East Asian–Australasian Flyway: Population estimates and internationally important sites'. *Wetlands International – Oceania*. Canberra, Australia.
12 Rogers et al. 2010, 'Red knots (*Calidris canutus piersmai* and *C.c. rogersi*) depend on a small threatened staging area in Bohai Bay, China'.
13 Ibid.
14 Ibid.
15 Harrington 2002, 'Red knot *Calidris canutus*'.
16 Ibid.
17 Ibid.
18 Ibid.
19 Niles, L.J., J. Bart, H. Sitters, et al. 2009. 'Effects of horseshoe crab harvest in Delaware Bay on red knots: are harvest restrictions working?' *Bioscience* 59: 153–64.
20 Ibid.
21 Baker, A.J. 2009. 'Plight of the red knot'. *Royal Ontario Museum Magazine*. Archives Spring 2009.
22 Colwell 2010, *Shorebird Ecology*, p. 7.
23 Baker 2009, 'Plight of the red knot'.
24 T. Piersma, pers. comm.
25 Harrington 2002, 'Red knot *Calidris canutus*'.
26 Southey 2009, 'The conservation status of migrant waders in New Zealand'.
27 Ibid.

SIXTEEN: WINNERS AND LOSERS
1 Potts 1885, 'Oology of New Zealand'.
2 Battley & Brownell 2007, 'Population biology and foraging ecology of waders in the Firth of Thames'.
3 Ibid.
4 Southey 2009, 'The conservation status of migrant waders in New Zealand'.
5 Battley & Brownell 2007, 'Population biology and foraging ecology of waders in the Firth of Thames'.
6 Sagar et al. 1999, 'Distribution and numbers of waders in New Zealand, 1983–1994'.
7 Southey 2009, 'The conservation status of migrant waders in New Zealand'.
8 Battley & Brownell 2007, 'Population biology and foraging ecology of waders in the Firth of Thames'.
9 Sagar et al. 1999, 'Distribution and numbers of waders in New Zealand, 1983–1994'.
10 Buller 1882, *Manual of the Birds of New Zealand*.

11. Potts 1885, 'Oology of New Zealand'.
12. Sibson, R.B. 1966. 'Increasing numbers of South Island pied oystercatchers visiting northern New Zealand'. *Notornis* 13: 94–97.
13. P. Sagar, pers. comm.
14. Sagar, P.M., R.J. Barker & D. Geddes. 2002. 'Survival of Finsch's oystercatchers (*Haematopus finschi*) on farmland in Canterbury, New Zealand'. *Notornis* 49: 233–40.
15. Sagar, P.M. & D. Geddes. 1999. 'Dispersal of SIPO from an inland breeding area of New Zealand'. *Notornis* 46: 89–99.
16. Sibson 1966, 'Increasing numbers of South Island pied oystercatchers visiting northern New Zealand'.
17. Dowding & Moore 2006, 'Habitat networks of indigenous shorebirds in New Zealand'.
18. Schuckard, R. 2002. 'Wader distribution at Farewell Spit, Golden Bay and Tasman Bay'. DOC, Nelson/Marborough Conservancy.
19. Crossland, A. 2002. 'Birds of the Estuary' in S.J. Owen (ed.) *The Estuary: Where our rivers meet the sea, Christchurch's Avon–Heathcote Estuary and Brooklands Lagoon*. Parks Unit, Christchurch City Council, Christchurch.
20. Baker 1972, 'Systematics and affinities of New Zealand oystercatchers'.
21. Baker 1973, 'Distribution and number of New Zealand oystercatchers'.
22. Sagar et al. 2002, 'Survival of Finsch's oystercatchers (*Haematopus finschi*) on farmland in Canterbury, New Zealand'.
23. P. Sagar, pers. comm.
24. Southey 2009, 'The conservation status of migrant waders in New Zealand'.
25. Miskelly et al. 2008, 'Conservation status of New Zealand birds 2008'.
26. Buller, W.L. 1905. *Birds of New Zealand Supplement*. W.L. Buller, London.
27. Sibson, R.B. 1990. *From Penguins to Parakeets*. Waiatarua Publishing, Auckland.
28. Ibid.
29. Ibid.
30. Davies, S. 1997. 'Population structure, morphometrics, moult, migration, and wintering of wrybill'. *Notornis* 44: 1–14.
31. Sibson 1963, 'A population study of the wry-billed plover (*Anarhynchus frontalis*)'.
32. Hay 1984, 'The behavioural ecology of the wrybill'.
33. See Chapter 19.
34. J. Dowding, pers. comm.
35. Child, P. 1973. 'Wrybills in Central Otago: Further records'. *Notornis* 20: 77–8.
36. Dowding & Moore 2006, 'Habitat networks of indigenous shorebirds in New Zealand'.
37. K. Hughey, pers. comm.
38. Southey 2009, 'The conservation status of migrant waders in New Zealand'.
39. Bell 2011, 'A census of variable oystercatcher (*Haematopus unicolor*) in the Marlborough Sounds'.
40. Southey 2009, 'The conservation status of migrant waders in New Zealand'.
41. D. Melville, pers. comm.
42. Southey 2009, 'The conservation status of migrant waders in New Zealand'.
43. P. Sagar, pers. comm.
44. D. Melville, pers. comm.
45. Dowding & Moore 2006, 'Habitat networks of indigenous shorebirds in New Zealand'.
46. Southey 2009, 'The conservation status of migrant waders in New Zealand'.

SEVENTEEN: HELPING HANDS

1. Reed et al. 1993. 'Black stilt recovery plan (*Himantopus novaezelandiae*)'.
2. Ibid.
3. Ibid.
4. Reed, C.E.M. 1994. 'Handrearing and breeding the endangered black stilt *Himantopus novaezelandiae* at Twizel'. *International Zoology Yearbook* 33: 125–28.
5. D. Nelson, pers. comm.
6. Ibid.
7. Moore, P.J. 2008. 'The recovering population of the Chatham Island oystercatcher (*Haematopus chathamensis*)'. *Notornis* 55: 20–32.
8. Ibid.
9. Ibid.
10. Ibid.
11. Miskelly et al. 2008, 'Conservation status of New Zealand birds 2008'.
12. Dowding, J.E. & A. Davis. 2004. 'New Zealand dotterel (*Charadrius obscurus*) recovery plan, 2004–14'. DOC Threatened Species Recovery Plan 58.
13. Walsby, J. 1997. 'Shorebirds under threat'. *NZ Geographic* 36: 96–113.
14. Dowding & Davis 2004. 'New Zealand dotterel (*Charadrius obscurus*) recovery plan, 2004–14'.
15. Needless to say opinion was much divided among Auckland commuters – but the fact a native species was delaying construction was satisfying to some.
16. Dowding, J.E. 2006. 'Management of northern New Zealand dotterels on Coromandel Peninsula'. DOC Research & Development series 252.
17. Biswell 2005. 'Black-backed gulls'.
18. Wills, D.E., J. Murray & R.G. Powlesland. 2003. 'Impact of management on the breeding success of the northern New Zealand dotterel (*Charadrius obscurus aquilonius*) on Matakana Island, Bay of Plenty'. *Notornis* 50: 1–11.
19. Dowding 2006. 'Management of northern New Zealand dotterels on Coromandel Peninsula'.
20. Dowding & Davis 2004. 'New Zealand dotterel (*Charadrius obscurus*) recovery plan, 2004–14'.
21. Ibid.
22. Dowding, J.E. 2010. 'Northern NZ dotterels: East coast good, west coast bad'. *Southern Bird* 42: June 2010, OSNZ.
23. Ibid.
24. Ibid.
25. Ibid.
26. Dowding & Davis 2004. 'New Zealand dotterel (*Charadrius obscurus*) recovery plan, 2004–14'.
27. DOC 2001, 'New Zealand shore plover recovery plan 2001–2011'.
28. Hansen 2005, 'New Zealand fairy tern (*Sterna nereis davisae*) recovery plan, 2005–15'.
29. Ibid.
30. Baling, M. & D.H. Brunton. 2006. 'New Zealand fairy tern: Endangered or common? A study using mitochondrial DNA'. NZES/ESA Conference, Wellington, New Zealand.

EIGHTEEN: WAR WITHOUT END

1. Darwin, C. 1845. *The Voyage of the Beagle*. John Murray, London.
2. King, C. 1984. 'Immigrant Killers: Introduced predators and the conservation of birds in New Zealand'. OUP, Auckland.
3. Worthy & Holdaway 2002, *The Lost World of the Moa*.
4. Ibid.
5. Dowding, J.E. & E.C. Murphy. 2001. 'The impact of predation by introduced mammals on endemic shorebirds in New Zealand: A conservation perspective'. *Biological Conservation* 99: 57–64.
6. Walters, M. (in association with Birdlife International, Australia). 2011. *Endangered Birds: Survey of planet Earth's changing ecosystems*. New Holland, Chatswood.
7. Dowding & Murphy 2001, 'The impact of predation by introduced mammals on endemic shorebirds in New Zealand'.
8. Murphy, E. C., R.J. Keedwell, K.P. Brown & I. Westbrooke. 2004. 'Diet of mammalian predators in braided river beds in the central South Island, New Zealand'. *Wildlife Research*. 31(6): 631–8.
9. Dowding & Murphy 2001, 'The impact of predation by introduced mammals on endemic shorebirds in New Zealand'.
10. Ibid.
11. Pierce 1986, 'Differences in susceptibility to predation during nesting between pied and black stilts (*Himantopus* spp.)'.
12. Keedwell 2002, 'Black-fronted terns and banded dotterels'.
13. Ibid.
14. Sanders, M.D. & R.F. Maloney. 2002. 'Causes of mortality in ground nesting birds in the Upper Waitaki basin, South Island, New Zealand: A 5-year video study'. *Biological Conservation* 106: 225–36.
15. Dowding & Murphy 2001, 'The impact of predation by introduced mammals on endemic shorebirds in New Zealand.
16. Dowding, J.E. & M.J. Elliott. 2003. 'Ecology of stoats in a South Island braided river valley'. Unpublished report on Investigation 3405 to Science & Research Unit, DOC, Wellington.
17. Ibid.
18. Ibid.
19. Bathgate, A. 1898. 'Notes on acclimatisation in New Zealand'. *TPNZI* 30: 266–78.
20. Pierce 1986, 'Differences in susceptibility to predation during nesting between pied and black stilts (*Himantopus* spp.).
21. Rebergen, A., R. Keedwell, J. Moller & R. Maloney. 1998. 'Breeding success and predation at nests of banded dotterel (*Charadrius bicinctus*) on braided riverbeds in the central South Island, New Zealand'. *NZ Journal of Ecology*. 22: 33–41.
22. Norbury, G. & R. Heyward. 2007. 'Predictors of clutch predation of a globally significant avifauna in

Zealand's braided river ecosystems'. *Animal Conservation* 11: 17–25.
23 Murphy et al. 2004, 'Diet of mammalian predators in braided river beds in the central South Island, New Zealand'.
24 Dowding & Murphy 2001, 'The impact of predation by introduced mammals on endemic shorebirds in New Zealand'.
25 Maloney et al. 1997, 'Bird density and diversity in braided rivers in the Upper Waitaki'.
26 R. Pierce, pers. comm.
27 Norbury & Heyward 2007, 'Predictors of clutch predation of a globally significant avifauna in New Zealand's braided river ecosystems'.
28 Keedwell, R.J. & K.P. Brown. 2001. 'Relative abundance of mammalian predators in the Upper Waitaki Basin, South Island, New Zealand'. *NZJZ* 28: 31–8.
29 Kliskey, A.D., A.E. Byrom & G.L. Norbury. 2000. 'Spatial prediction of predation in the landscape: A GIS based approach to predator–prey interactions for conservation management.' 4th International Conference on Integrating GIS and Environmental Modeling (GIS/EM4): Problems, prospects and research needs. Banff, Alberta, Canada, September 2–8, 2000.
30 Norbury & Heyward 2007, 'Predictors of clutch predation of a globally significant avifauna in New Zealand's braided river ecosystems'.
31 Keedwell 2002, 'Black-fronted terns and banded dotterels'.
32 Dowding & Elliott 2003, 'Ecology of stoats in a South Island braided river valley'.
33 D. Nelson, pers. comm.

NINETEEN: NATURAL FLOWS
1 Potts 1882, *Out in the Open*.
2 Hughey 1985, 'The relationship between riverbed flooding and non-breeding wrybills on northern feeding grounds in summer'.
3 Ibid.
4 Hay 1984, 'The behavioural ecology of the wrybill'.
5 Hughey 1985, 'The relationship between riverbed flooding and non-breeding wrybills on northern feeding grounds in summer'.
6 Ibid.
7 Ibid.
8 Ibid.
9 Pierce, R.J. 1983. 'The Charadriiforms of a high-country river valley'. *Notornis* 30: 169–85.
10 Robertson et al. 1983, 'Habitat requirements of wetland birds in the Ahuriri River Catchment New Zealand'.
11 Ibid.
12 Ibid.
13 Hughey 1985, 'The relationship between riverbed flooding and non-breeding wrybills on northern feeding grounds in summer'.
14 O'Donnell, C.F.J. & J.M. Hoare. 2011. 'Meta-analysis of status and trends in breeding populations of black-fronted terns (*Chlidonias albostriatus*) 1962–2008'. *NZ Journal of Ecology* 35(1): 30–43. Rivers were the Ahuriri, Aparima, Hurunui, Mararoa, Oreti, Rakaia, Rangitata, Tekapo, Waiau (Canterbury), Waimakariri, Wairau and Waitaki.
15 Ibid.
16 Ibid.
17 R. Maloney, pers. comm.
18 Hughey, K. 1998. 'Nesting home range sizes of wrybill (*Anarhynchus frontalis*) and banded dotterel (*Charadrius bicinctus*) in relation to braided riverbed characteristics'. *Notornis* 45: 103–11.
19 Wilson 2004, *Flight of the Huia*, p. 299.

TWENTY: AQUA BLUES
1 Anon. 2011. 'State of Our Gulf: Tikapa Moana – Hauraki Gulf State of the Environment Report'. Hauraki Gulf Forum.
2 *Hauraki Herald*, 9 July 2010.
3 Anon. 2011, 'State of Our Gulf'.
4 Ibid.
5 Battley & Brownell 2007, 'Population biology and foraging ecology of waders in the Firth of Thames'.
6 Anon. 2011, 'State of Our Gulf'.
7 Battley & Brownell 2007, 'Population biology and foraging ecology of waders in the Firth of Thames'.
8 Ibid.
9 Hayward, B.W. et al. 1997. 'Faunal changes in Waitemata Harbour sediments 1930s–1980s'. *Journal of the Royal Society of New Zealand* 27: 1–20.
10 M. Bellingham, pers. comm.; and Environment Waikato data.
11 *New Zealand Herald*, 7 December 2010.
12 Tait, P. & R. Cullen. 2010. 'Some external costs of dairy farming in Canterbury'. Lincoln University. 50th AAES Conference, Manly, NSW.
13 MacFie, R. 2010. 'Taking the waters'. *NZ Listener*, 17 April 2010.
14 A. Grant, DOC, pers. comm.
15 MacFie 2010, 'Taking the waters'.
16 Williams, D. 2010. 'Canterbury lake pollution a concern'. *The Press*, 11 November 2010.
17 Hansford, D. 2010. 'Wetlands'. *NZ Geographic* 101: 48–73.
18 Tait & Cullen 2010, 'Some external costs of dairy farming in Canterbury'.
19 *The Press*, 11 November 2010.
20 Tait & Cullen 2010, 'Some external costs of dairy farming in Canterbury'.
21 *The Press*, 11 November 2010.
22 MacFie, R. 2010. 'The price of milk'. *NZ Listener* 14 August 2010.
23 MacFie 2010, 'Taking the waters'.
24 Ibid.
25 Wilson, G.H. 2000. 'Historical changes and the present status of the rivers and adjoining wetlands in the Upper Waitaki Basin'. Unpubl. MSc thesis, University of Waikato.
26 Ibid.
27 Ibid.
28 Ibid.
29 Ibid.
30 C. Woolmore, DOC and Project River Recovery, pers. comm.
31 Ibid.
32 Nelson, D. 2008. 'State of New Zealand's birds 2008: Conservation of birds on the mainland'. OSNZ.
33 R. Maloney, DOC, pers. comm.
34 Cleland, S., E. Wahlberg, S. Stevenson & R. Maloney. 2007. 'Predator control project report for Kaki Recovery Programme. A: Tasman Valley B: Ahuriri Valley March 2006–February 2007'. Kaki Project Internal Report No 07/04, DOC, Twizel.
35 A. Grant, pers. comm.
36 National Policy Statement for Freshwater Management, 2011. Ministry for the Environment.
37 Sinner, J. 2011. 'Implications of the National Policy Statement on Freshwater Management'. Report prepared for Fish and Game New Zealand by the Cawthron Institute.
38 Ibid.
39 Canterbuty Water. 2011. Draft Ashburton Zone Implementation Programme. Environment Canterbury.
40 Ibid.
41 K. Hughey, pers. comm.
42 Smith, D., K. Hughey & K. Booth. 1997. 'Impacts of recreational users on the wildlife of braided rivers – a preliminary study on the Tekapo River'. Unpubl. Department of Resource Management report, Lincoln University, Canterbury.
43 A. Grant, pers. comm.
44 F. Schmechel, pers. comm.
45 A. Crossland, pers. comm.

TWENTY-ONE: COASTAL PRESSURES
1 Sibson 1966, 'Increasing numbers of South Island pied oystercatchers visiting northern New Zealand'.
2 Department of Conservation. 2006. 'Review of level of protection for some New Zealand wildlife: Public discussion document'. Strategy and Policy Group, DOC, Wellington.
3 Ibid.
4 Ibid.
5 Marchant & Higgins (eds) 1993, *Handbook of Australian, New Zealand and Antarctic Birds*.
6 J. Dowding, pers. comm.
7 Ibid.
8 West, A.D., et al. 2005. 'Maintaining estuary quality for shorebirds: Towards simple guidelines'. *Biological Conservation* 123: 211–24.
9 Ibid.
10 Ibid.
11 Battley & Brownell 2007, 'Population biology and foraging ecology of waders in the Firth of Thames'.
12 DeLuca, W.V. et al. 2008. 'Coastal urbanization and the integrity of estuarine waterbird communities: Threshold responses and the importance of scale'. *Biological Conservation* 141: 2669–78.
13 Thompson, D.R. & J.E. Dowding. 1999. 'Site-specific heavy metal concentrations in blood of South Island pied oystercatchers *Haematopus ostralegus finschi* from the Auckland region, New Zealand'. *Marine Pollution Bulletin* 38: 202–6.
14 Choi, J-W., M. Matsuda et al. 1999.

'Contamination of PCBs in Nakdong River estuary, Korea'. *Toxicological and Environmental Chemistry* 72: 233–43.
15. Anon. 2008. 'Project Manukau: Mangere Wastewater Treatment Plant bird roost management plan'. Watercare Services, Auckland.
16. A. Beauchamp, DOC, pers. comm.
17. Southey, I. 2011. 'Shorebirds and disturbance'. *Miranda News* 81, May 2011, Miranda Naturalists' Trust.
18. I. Southey, pers. comm.
19. Southey 2011, 'Shorebirds and disturbance'.
20. Anon. 2008, 'Project Manukau'.
21. Ibid.
22. Pfister, C., B.A. Harrington & M. Lavine. 1992. 'The impact of human disturbance on shorebirds at a migration staging area'. *Biological Conservation* 60: 115–26.
23. Rogers, D.I., P.F. Battley, T. Piersma, J.A. van Gils & K.G. Rogers. 2006. 'High-tide habitat choice: Insights from modelling roost selection by shorebirds around a tropical bay'. *Animal Behaviour* 72: 563–75.
24. Burton, N.H.K., P.R. Evans & M.A. Robinson. 1996. 'Effects on shorebird numbers of disturbance and the loss of a roost site and its replacement by an artificial island at Hartlepool, Cleveland'. *Biological Conservation* 73: 193–201.
25. Burton, N.H.K. et al. 2006. 'Impacts of sudden winter habitat loss on the body condition and survival of redshank *Tringa totanus*'. *Journal of Applied Ecology* 43: 464–73.
26. Pierce, R.J. 2000. 'Implications of subdivision proposal near an important shorebird breeding site'. *Conservation Advisory Science Notes* 274. DOC, Wellington.
27. Cumming, A.B. 1991. 'The New Zealand dotterel (tuturiwhatu) problems and management'. Unpubl. MSc thesis, University of Auckland.
28. Lord, A., J.R. Waas & J. Innes. 1997. 'Effects of human activity on the behaviour of northern New Zealand dotterel *Charadrius obscurus aquilonius* chicks'. *Biological Conservation* 82: 15–20.
29. Pierce 2000, 'Implications of subdivision proposal near an important shorebird breeding site'.
30. Anon. 2011. 'Draft report and decision of the Board of Inquiry into the Hauauru ma Raki Wind Farm and infrastructure connection to grid'. Draft report under s. 148 of the Resource Management Act 1991 as amended in 2005.
31. Bridson, L. 2000. 'Minimising visitor impacts on threatened shorebirds and their habitats'. *Conservation Advisory Science Notes* 32. DOC, Wellington.

TWENTY-TWO: SHRINKING GAS STATIONS

1. Southey, I. 2009. 'The conservation status of migrant waders in New Zealand'. *Miranda News* 74, August 2009.
2. Ibid.
3. Ibid.
4. Schekkerman, H., I. Tulp & B. Ens. 2003. 'Conservation of long-distance migratory wader populations: Reproductive consequences of events occurring in distant staging sites'. *WSG Bulletin* 100: 151–6.
5. McGowan, C.P. et al. 2011. 'Demographic consequences of migratory stopover: Linking red knot survival to horseshoe crab spawning abundance'. *Ecosphere* 2, art 69. [doi: 10.1890/ES11-00106.1].
6. Battley et al. 2011, 'Trans-hemispheric migration timing, flight paths and staging in two bar-tailed godwit subspecies'.
7. Amano, T. et al. 2010. 'A framework for monitoring the status of populations: An example from wader populations in the East Asian–Australasian flyway'. *Biology Conservation* 143: 2238–47.
8. Riegen, A., G. Vaughan & K. Rogers. 2011. 'Yalu Jiang shorebird survey report 1999–2010. A joint project between Yalu Jiang National Nature Reserve – China and Miranda Naturalists' Trust – New Zealand'. Miranda Naturalists' Trust.
9. Yang, H-Y. et al. 2011. 'Impacts of tidal land reclamation in Bohai Bay, China: Ongoing losses of critical Yellow Sea waterbird staging and wintering sites'. *Bird Conservation International* 1–19. BirdLife International.
10. Rogers et al. 2010. 'Red knots (*Calidris canutus piersmai* and *c.c. rogersi*) depend on a small threatened staging area in Bohai Bay, China'.
11. Kraan, C., et al. 2009. 'Landscape-scale experiment demonstrates that Wadden Sea intertidal flats are used to capacity by molluscivore migrant shorebirds'. *Journal of Animal Ecology* 78: 1259–68.
12. Baker, A.J et al. 2004. 'Rapid population decline in red knots: fitness consequences of decreased fuelling rates and late arrival in Delaware Bay'. *Proceedings of the Royal Society of London B* 271: 875–82.
13. Yang et al. 2011, 'Impacts of tidal land reclamation in Bohai Bay'.
14. Ibid.
15. Amano et al. 2010, 'A framework for monitoring the status of populations'.
16. Schekkerman et al. 2003, 'Conservation of long-distance migratory wader populations'.
17. Piersma, T. 2007. 'Global Flyway Network: progress report for 2007'.
18. Meltofte, H. et al. 2007. 'Effects of climate variation on the breeding ecology of Arctic shorebirds'. *Bioscience* 59.
19. Ibid.
20. Newton 2010, *Bird Migration*.
21. Meltofte et al. 2007, 'Effects of climate variation on the breeding ecology of Arctic shorebirds'.
22. Ibid.
23. Piersma, T. & A. Lindström. 2004. 'Migrating shorebirds as integrative sentinels of global environmental change'. *Ibis* 146: 61–9.
24. Meltofte et al. 2007, 'Effects of climate variation on the breeding ecology of Arctic shorebirds'.
25. Battley et al. 2011, 'Trans-hemispheric migration timing, flight paths and staging in two bar-tailed godwit subspecies'.
26. Ibid.

CONCLUSION

1. Tennyson & Martinson 2006, *Extinct Birds of New Zealand*.
2. Tait & Cullen 2010, 'Some external costs of dairy farming in Canterbury'.
3. Wickham, J. 2009. 'District Plan Review planners report natural environment section – to add shorebird and estuarine bird nesting and roosting sites to the District Plan'. Western Bay of Plenty District Council.
4. F. Schmechel, Environment Canterbury, pers. comm.

BIBLIOGRAPHY AND FURTHER READING

BOOKS

Andrews, J.R.H. 1986. *The Southern Ark: Zoological discovery in New Zealand 1769–1900*. Century Hutchinson, Auckland.

Angel, H. 1974. *The World of an Estuary*. Faber, London.

Barlow, M. 1983. *The Year of the Spur-winged Plover*. Craig Printing, Invercargill.

Berthold, P., E. Gwinner & E. Sonnenschein (eds) 2003. *Avian Migration*. Springer, Heidelberg.

Best, J.L. & C.S. Bristow (eds). *Braided Rivers*. The Geological Society, Oxford.

Birkhead, T. 2008. *The Wisdom of Birds: An illustrated history of ornithology*. Bloomsbury, London.

Buddle G.A. 1951. *Bird Secrets*. A.H & A.W. Reed, Wellington.

Buller, W.L. 1888. *A History of the Birds of New Zealand*. John Van Voorst, London.

——. 1882. *Manual of the Birds of New Zealand*. Government Printer, Wellington.

——. 1905. *Supplement to the Birds of New Zealand*. London.

Colwell, M.A. 2010. *Shorebird Ecology: conservation and management*. University of California.

Cramp, S. and K. Simmons (eds). 1985. *Handbook of the Birds of Europe, the Middle East and North Africa: Birds of the Western Palearctic. Vol IV: Terns to Woodpeckers*. OUP, Oxford.

Cromarty, P. & D.A. Scott (eds) 1995. *A directory of wetlands in New Zealand*. DOC, Wellington.

Crossland, A. 2002. 'Birds of the estuary' in S.J. Owen (ed.) *The Estuary: where our rivers meet the sea, Christchurch's Avon-Heathcote Estuary and Brooklands Lagoon*. Parks Unit, Christchurch City Council.

Darwin, C. 1845. *The Voyage of the Beagle*. John Murray, London.

Del Hoyo, J., A. Elliott, J. Sargatal (eds). 1996. *Handbook of the Birds of the World. Vol 3: Hoatzin to Auks*. Lynx Edicions, Spain.

Fleming, C.A. 1982. *George Edward Lodge: The unpublished New Zealand bird paintings*. Nova Pacifica & National Museum of NZ, Wellington.

Geering, A., L. Agnew & S. Harding. 2007. *Shorebirds of Australia*. CSIRO, Australia.

Gibbs, G. 2006. *Ghosts of Gondwana: The history of life in New Zealand*. Craig Potton, Nelson.

Gill, B.J. et al (eds) 2010. *Checklist of the Birds of New Zealand*. 4th edn. Te Papa Press/OSNZ, Wellington.

Gill, B.J. & B.D. Heather (eds) 1990. *A Flying Start: commemorating fifty years of the Ornithological Society of New Zealand*. OSNZ.

Gillespie, O.A. 1958. *South Canterbury: a record of settlement*. South Canterbury Historical Committee & Timaru Herald.

Grey, A. H. 1994. *Aotearoa and New Zealand: A historical geography*. CUP, Christchurch.

Guthrie-Smith, H. 1925. *Bird Life on Island and Shore*. William Blackwood & Sons, Edinburgh.

——. 1936. *The Sorrows and Joys of a New Zealand Naturalist*. A.H. & A.W. Reed, Dunedin.

Hale, W.G. 1980. *Waders*. New Naturalist Series. Collins, London.

Harding, J.S, P.M Mosley, C. Pearson, B. Sorrell (eds). 2004. *Freshwaters of New Zealand*. New Zealand Hydrological Society & New Zealand Limnological Society, Wellington.

Higgins, P.J. & S.J.J.F. Davies (eds). 1993. *Handbook of Australian, New Zealand and Antarctic Birds. Vol III: Snipe to Pigeons*. OUP, Melbourne.

Hill, J. 1999. *An Exhilaration of Wings: The literature of birdwatching*. Viking, New York.

Hutton F.W. & J. Drummond. 1904. *The Animals of New Zealand: An account of the colony's airbreathing vertebrates*. Whitcombe and Tombs, Christchurch.

Jobling, J.A. 2010. *Helm Dictionary of Scientific Bird Names*. Christopher Helm, London.

Jones, M.B. & I.D. Marsden. 2005. *Life in the Estuary: Illustrated guide and ecology*. CUP, Christchurch.

King, C. 1984. *Immigrant Killers: Introduced predators and the conservation of birds in New Zealand*. OUP, Auckland.

Laing, R.M., R. Speight, & A. Wall. 1927. *Natural History of Canterbury*. Philosophical Institute of Canterbury, Christchurch.

Lopez, B. 1986. *Arctic Dreams*. Vintage, New York.

McDowall, R.M. 1994. *Gamekeepers for the Nation: The story of New Zealand's acclimatisation societies 1861–1990*. CUP, Christchurch.

Marchant, S. & P.J. Higgins (eds). 1993. *Handbook of Australian, New Zealand and Antarctic Birds. Vol II: Raptors to Lapwings*. OUP, Melbourne.

Messenger, S. & D. Taylor. 2005. *Waders of Europe, Asia and North America*. Helm, London.

Moon, G.H. 1967. *Refocus on New Zealand Birds*. Reed, Wellington.

Morris, F.O. 1851. *History of British Birds. Vol V*. Groombridge & Sons, London.

Morris, R. & H. Smith. 1988. *Wild South: Saving New Zealand's endangered birds*. TVNZ & Hutchinson, Auckland.

Newton, A., H. Gadow, R. Lydekker, C.S. Roy & R.W. Shufeldt. 1896. *A Dictionary of Birds*. A. & C. Black, London.

Newton, I. 2010. *Bird Migration*. Collins, London.

Oliver, W.R.B. 1930. *New Zealand Birds*. Fine Arts (NZ), Wellington.

——. 1955. *New Zealand Birds*. A.H. & A.W. Reed, Wellington.

Orbell, M. 2003. *Birds of Aotearoa: A natural and cultural history*. Reed, Auckland.

Pascoe, J. (ed.) 1957. *Mr Explorer Douglas*. A.H & A.W. Reed, Wellington.

Peat, N. & B. Patrick. 2001: *Wild Rivers: Discovering the natural history of the central South Island*. University of Otago Press, Dunedin.

Perry, R. 1938. *At the Turn of the Tide: A book of wild birds*. Crown Helm, London.

Potts, T.H. 1882. *Out in the Open: A budget of scraps of natural history, gathered in New Zealand*. Lyttelton Times Company, Christchurch.

Relph, D. 2010. *The Mackenzie Country: A fine plain behind the snowy range*. David Ling, Auckland.

Sibson, R.B. 1982. *Birds at Risk: Rare or endangered species of New Zealand*. Reed, Wellington.

——. 1990. *From Penguins to Parakeets*. Waiatarua Publishing, Auckland.

Soper, M.F. 1972. *New Zealand Birds*. Whitcombe and Tombs, Christchurch.

Stead, E.F. 1932. *The Life Histories of New Zealand Birds*. Search, London.

Sutton, D.G. 1994. *Origins of the First New Zealanders*. AUP, Auckland.

Tennyson, A.J.D & P. Martinson. 2006. *Extinct Birds of New Zealand*. Te Papa, Wellington.

Thurston, H. 1996. *The Nature of Shorebirds: Nomads of the wetlands*. Greystone Nature Series. Douglas & McIntyre, Vancouver.

van de Kam, J., B. Ens, T. Piersma & L. Zwarts. 2004. *Shorebirds: An illustrated behavioural ecology*. KNNV, Netherlands.

Walters, M. (in association with Birdlife International, Australia). 2011. *Endangered Birds: A survey of planet Earth's changing ecosystems*. New Holland, Chatswood.

Watola, G. 2008. *The Discovery of New Zealand's Birds: The first record of every bird species in New Zealand since 1769*. Stepping Stone Books, Orewa.

Weidensaul, S. 1999. *Living on the Wind: Across the hemisphere with migratory birds*. North Point Press, New York.

Wilson, K-J. 2004. *Flight of the Huia. Ecology and conservation of New Zealand's frogs, reptiles, birds and mammals*. CUP, Christchurch.

Winterbourn, M., G. Knox, C. Burrows & I. Marsden. 2008. *Natural History of Canterbury*. CUP, Christchurch.

Witherby, H.F., F.C.R. Jourdain, N.F. Ticehurst & B.W. Tucker. 1947. *The Handbook of British Birds Vol IV: Cormorants to cranes*. H.F. & G. Witherby, London.

Woodley, K. 2009. *Godwits: Long-haul champions*. Raupo, Auckland.

Worthy, T.H. & R.N. Holdaway. 2002. *The Lost World of the Moa: Prehistoric life of New Zealand*. Indiana University Press, Bloomington.

Yate, W. 1835. *An Account of New Zealand; and of the formation and progress of the Church Missionary Society's mission in Northern Island*. Seeley & Burnside, London.

PAPERS & JOURNALS

Allen, G.G. 1984. 'Black-billed gull food preferences'. *Notornis* 31(3):224.

Amano, T., T. Székely, K. Koyama, H. Amano, & W.J. Sutherland. 2010. 'A framework for monitoring the status of populations: An example from wader populations in the East Asian–Australasian flyway'. *Biological Conservation* 143:2238–47.

Anon. 2011. 'Ruddy hell: Turnstone flies 27,000 km – twice!!' *AWSG Tattler* 21:6.

Atkinson, I.A.E. & P.R. Millener. 1990. 'An ornithological glimpse into New Zealand's pre-human past'. *Acta XX Congressus Internationalis Ornithologici*: 127–92.

Atkinson, P.W. 2003. 'Can we restore intertidal habitats for shorebirds?' *WSG Bulletin* 100:67–72.

Baker, A.J. 1973. 'Distribution and number of New Zealand oystercatchers'. *Notornis* 20:128–44.

———. 1974. 'Ecological and behavioural evidence for the systematic status of the NZ oystercatchers (*Charadriiformes*; *Haematopodidae*)'. *Royal Ontario Museum Life Sciences Contributions* 96:1–34.

———. 1974. 'Prey-specific feeding methods of New Zealand Oystercatchers'. *Notornis* 21:219–33.

———. 1975. 'Morphological variation, hybridization and systematics of New Zealand oystercatchers (*Charadriiformes: haematopodidae*)'. *New Zealand Journal of Zoology* 175:357–90.

———. 2009. 'Plight of the Red Knot'. *Royal Ontario Museum Magazine.* Archives, Spring.

Baker, A.J, P.M González, T. Piersma, L.J. Nile, I.S. do Nascimento, P.W. Atkinson, N.A. Clark, C.T.D. Minton, M.K. Peck & G. Aarts. 2004. 'Rapid population decline in red knots: Fitness consequences of decreased fuelling rates and late arrival in Delaware Bay'. *Proceedings of the Royal Society of London* B 271:875–82.

Baker, A.J., C.M. Miskelly, O. Haddrath. 2009. 'Species limits and population differentiation in New Zealand snipes (*Scolopacidae: Coenocorypha*). *Conservation Genetics* DOI 10.1007/s10592-009-9965-2.

Baker, A.J., S.L. Pereira & T.A. Paton. 2007. 'Phylogenetic relationships and divergence times of Charadriiformes genera: Multigene evidence for the Cretaceous origin of at least 14 clades of shorebirds'. *Biology Letters* 3:205–09.

Baling, M. & D.H. Brunton. 2006. 'New Zealand fairy tern: endangered or common? A study using mitochondrial DNA'. NZES/ESA Conference, Wellington.

Banks, J.C, & A.M. Paterson. 2007. 'A preliminary study of the genetic differences in New Zealand oystercatcher species'. *NZJZ* 34:141–4.

Barbosa, A. 1996. 'Relationship between bill morphology and preening behaviour in waders'. *Ethology, Ecology and Evolution* 8:291–6.

Barker, D., J.W.A. Carroll, H.K. Edmonds, J.R. Fraser & C.M. Miskelly. 2005. 'Discovery of a previously unknown *Coenocorypha* snipe in the Campbell Island group, New Zealand subantarctic'. *Notornis* 52:143–49.

Barlow, M. 1972. 'The establishment, dispersal and distribution of the spur-winged plover in New Zealand'. *Notornis* 19:201–11.

———. 1978. 'Spur winged plover longevity record'. *Notornis* 25:2:160

———. 1988. 'Spur winged plover longevity record'. *Notornis* 35:195–6.

———. 1993. 'New Zealand Dotterel: South Island historical notes and Southland coastal records'. *Notornis* 40:15–25.

Barlow, M. & J.E. Dowding. 2002. 'Breeding biology of Caspian terns (*Sterna caspia*) at a colony near Invercargill'. *Notornis* 49:76–91.

Barlow, M., P.M. Muller & R.R. Sutton. 1972. 'Breeding data on the spur-winged plover in Southland, New Zealand'. *Notornis* 19:212–47.

Bathgate, A. 1898. 'Notes on acclimatisation in New Zealand'. *TPNZI* 30:266–78.

Battley, P.F. & T. Piersma. 1997. 'Body composition of Lesser Knots (*Calidris canutus rogersi*) preparing to take off on migration from northern New Zealand'. *Notornis* 44:137–50.

Battley, P.F., N. Warnock, T.L. Tibbitts, R.E. Gill, Jr., T. Piersma, C.J. Hassell, D.C. Douglas, D.M. Mulcahy, B.D. Gartrell, R. Schuckard, D.S. Melville & A.C. Riegen. 2011. 'Trans-hemispheric migration timing, flight paths and staging in two bar-tailed godwit subspecies'. *Journal of Avian Biology.* Submitted.

Beauchamp, A.J. & G.R. Parrish. 1999. 'Bird use of the settlement ponds and roost areas at Port Whangarei'. *Notornis* 46:470–83.

Bell, D. & M. Bell. 2000. 'Discovery of a second natural wild population of the New Zealand shore plover (*Thinornis novaeseelandiae*)'. *Notornis* 47:166–7.

Bell, M. 2011. 'A census of variable oystercatcher (*Haematopus unicolor*) in the Marlborough Sounds'. *Notornis* 57:169–72.

Biswell, S.F. 2005. 'Black-backed gulls'. *New Zealand Geographic* 73:46–61.

Blackburn, A. 1962. 'Feeding behaviour of red-billed gulls'. *Notornis* 10:1–42

Bomford, M. 1986. 'Breeding displays and calls of the banded dotterel (*Charadrius bicinctus*)'. *Notornis* 33:217–32.

———. 1988. 'Breeding of the banded dotterel (*Charadrius bicinctus*), on the Cass River Delta, Canterbury'. *Notornis* 35:9–14.

Boud, R. & B.T. Cunningham. 1959. 'Feeding habits of the black-billed gull'. *Notornis* 8(4):119–20.

Brathwaite, D.H. & G.F. van Tets. 1975. 'The taxonomy and nomenclature of the New Zealand spur-winged plovers'. *Notornis* 22(2):180–1.

Bridge E.S., A.W. Jones & A.J. Baker. 2005. 'A phylogenetic framework for the terns (Sternini) inferred from mtDNA sequences: implications for taxonomy and plumage evolution'. *Molecular Phylogenetics and Evolution* 35:459–69.

Bridson, L. 2000. 'Minimising visitor impacts on threatened shorebirds and their habitats'. Conservation Advisory Science Notes 301. DOC. Wellington.

Brown, B. 1982. 'Unusual feeding of red-billed gull'. *Notornis* 29(1):77.

Buddle, G.A. 1947. 'Breeding of red-billed gull'. *NZ Bird Notes* 2(4):71.

Buehler, D.M., A.J. Baker & T. Piersma. 2006. 'Reconstructing palaeoflyways of the late Pleistocene & early Holocene red knot *Calidris canutus*'. *Ardea* 94(3):485–98.

Buller W.L. 1874. 'On the genus *Himantopus* in New Zealand'. *TPNZI* 7 Art. XXIX.

———. 1894. 'Notes on the ornithology of New Zealand, with an Exhibition of Rare Specimens'. *TPNZI* 27:116–17.

Burger, J. & M. Gochfeld. 1996. 'Use of space by nesting black-billed gulls *Larus bulleri*: Behavioural changes during the reproductive cycle'. *Emu* 96:73–81.

Burton, N.H.K., M.M. Rehfisch, N.A. Clark & S.G. Dodd. 2006. 'Impacts of sudden winter habitat loss on the body condition and survival of redshank *Tringa totanus*'. *Journal of Applied Ecology* 43:464–75.

Burton, N.H.K., P.R. Evans & M.A. Robinson. 1996. 'Effects on shorebird numbers of disturbance and the loss of a roost site and its replacement by an artificial island at Hartlepool, Cleveland'. *Biological Conservation* 73:193–201.

Burton, P.J.K. 1972. 'Some anatomical notes on the wrybill'. *Notornis* 19:26–32.

Caruso, B.S. 2006. 'Effectiveness of braided gravel-bed river restoration in the Upper Waitaki Basin, New Zealand'. *Regulated Rivers: Research & Management* Vol 22(8):905–22.

Caughley, G. 1966. 'The breeding of black-backed gulls in the South Island mountains'. *Notornis* 13(3):166–7.

Chapman, F.R. 1890. 'The outlying islands of New Zealand'. *TPNZI* 23:492–522.

Child, P. 1969. 'Oystercatchers and banded dotterels nesting high in Central Otago'. *Notornis* 16:186.

———. 1973. 'Wrybills in Central Otago: further records'. *Notornis* 20:77–8.

———. 1986. 'Black-fronted tern breeding at high altitude'. *Notornis* 33:193–4.

Choi, J-W., M. Matsuda et al. 1999. 'Contamination of PCBs in Nakdong River estuary, Korea'. *Toxicological and Environmental Chemistry* 72:233–43.

Conklin, J. R. & P.F. Battley. 2011. 'Impacts of wind upon rigid individual migration schedules of New Zealand bar-tailed godwits'. *Behavioural Ecology* 22(4):854–61.

Conklin, J.R., P.F. Battley, M.A. Potter & D.R. Ruthrauff. 2011. 'Geographic variation in morphology of Alaska-breeding bar-tailed godwits (*Limosa Lapponica*) is not maintained on their non breeding grounds in New Zealand'. *Auk* 128(2):363–73.

Conklin, J.R., P.F. Battley, M.A. Potter & J.W. Fox. 2010. 'Breeding latitude drives individual schedules in a trans-hemispheric migrant bird'. *Nature Communications* 1, article 67. [Online, doi: 10.1038/ncomms1072.]

Crocker, T., S. Petch & P. Sagar. 2010. 'Hybridisation by South Island pied oystercatcher (*Haematopus finschi*) and variable oystercatcher (*H. unicolor*) in Canterbury'. *Notornis* 57:1:27–32.

Cunningham, J.M. 1973. 'The banded dotterel, *Charadrius bicinctus*: Pohowhera or tuturiwhatu? – call notes and behaviour'. *Notornis* 20:21–7.

Dann, P. 1991. 'Feeding behaviour and diet of double-banded plovers (*Charadrius bicinctus*) in Western Port, Victoria'. *Emu* 91:170–85.

Davies, S. 1997. 'Population structure, morphometrics, moult, migration, and wintering of wrybill'. *Notornis* 44:1–14.

Davies, S.J. 1991. 'Longevity, breeding success, and faithfulness to wintering sites of wrybill – as suggested by banding data'. *Stilt* 19:26–7.

Davis, A. 1994. 'Status, distribution, population trends of the New Zealand shore plover (*Thinornis novaeseelandiae*)'. *Notornis* (supp.) 41:179–94.

———. 1994b. 'Breeding biology of New Zealand shore plover (*Thinornis novaeseelandiae*)'. *Notornis* (supp.) 41:195–208.

DeLuca, W.V., C.E. Studds, R.S. King & P.P. Marra. 2008. 'Coastal urbanization and the integrity of estuarine waterbird communities: threshold responses and the importance of scale'. *Biological Conservation* 141:2669–78.

Deng, Y., M. Horrocks, J. Ogden & S. Anderson. 2006. 'Modern pollen–vegetation relationships along transects on the Whangapoua Estuary, Great Barrier Island'. *NZ Journal of Biogeography* 33:592–608.

Dowding, J.E. 1994. 'Morphometrics and ecology of the New Zealand dotterel (*Charadrius obscurus*), with a description of a new subspecies'. *Notornis* 41:221–3.

——. 2010. 'Northern NZ dotterels: East coast good, west coast bad'. *Southern Bird* 42: June 2010. OSNZ.

——. 1999. 'Past distribution and decline of the New Zealand dotterel (*Charadrius obscurus*) in the South Island of New Zealand'. *Notornis* 46:167–80.

Dowding, J.E. & S.P. Chamberlin. 1991. 'Annual movement patterns and breeding site fidelity of the New Zealand dotterel (*Charadrius obscurus*)'. *Notornis* 38:89–102.

Dowding, J.E. & E.S. Kennedy. 1993. 'Size, age structure and morphometrics of the shore plover population on South East Island'. *Notornis* 40:213–22.

Dowding, J.E. & E.C. Murphy. 1993. 'The decline of the Stewart Island population of the New Zealand dotterel'. *Notornis* 40:1–13.

——. 1993b. 'Distribution and breeding of the spur-winged plover on Stewart Island'. *Notornis* 40:227–9.

——. 1996. 'Predation of Northern New Zealand dotterels (*Charadrius obscurus aquilonius*) by stoats'. *Notornis* 43:144–6.

——. 2001. 'The impact of predation by introduced mammals on endemic shorebirds in New Zealand: A conservation perspective'. *Biological Conservation* 99:57–64.

Drummond, J. 1909. 'In touch with nature'. 16 September 1909, Canterbury Museum Archives.

Dyke, G. & M. van Tuinen. 2004. 'The evolutionary radiation of modern birds (Neornithes): Reconciling molecules, morphology and the fossil record'. *Zoological Journal of the Linnean Society* 141(2):153–77.

Edgar, A.T. 1969. 'Estimated population of the red-breasted dotterel'. *Notornis* 16:85–100.

Ferns, P.N. 2003. 'Plumage colour and pattern in waders'. *WSG Bulletin* 100:122–9.

Finney, S.K, J.W. Pearce-Higgins & D.W. Yalden. 2005. 'The effect of recreational disturbance on an upland breeding bird, the golden plover *Pluvialis apricaria*'. *Biological Conservation* 121:53–63.

Fleming, C.A. 1939. 'Birds of the Chatham Islands'. *Emu* 39:1–15.

——. 1946. 'Breeding of red-billed gull: A preliminary census of Mokohinau colony'. *NZ Bird Notes* 2(2):26.

Fleming, P. 1990. 'Variable oystercatchers nesting at Waikanae Estuary 1971–1989'. *Notornis* 37:73–6.

Fordham, R.A. 1964. 'Breeding biology of the southern black-backed gull I: Pre-egg and egg stage'. *Notornis* 11(1):3–35.

——. 1964b. 'Breeding biology of the southern black-backed gull II: Incubation to chick stage'. *Notornis* 11(2):110–26.

Gill, R.E. Jr, T. Piersma, G. Hufford, R. Servranckx & A. Riegen. 2005. 'Crossing the ultimate ecological barrier: Evidence for an 11,000 km-long nonstop flight from Alaska to New Zealand and Eastern Australia by bar-tailed godwits'. *Condor* 107:1–20.

Goss-Custard, C.J. & P. Battley. 2003. 'Burning the engine: a time-marching computation of fat and protein consumption in a 5420-km non-stop flight by great knots *Calidris tenuirostris*'. *Oikos* 103:323–32.

Gray, D., M.R. Scarsbrook & J.S. Harding. 2006. 'Spatial biodiversity patterns in a large New Zealand braided river.' *New Zealand Journal of Marine and Freshwater Research* 40:631–42.

Greene, B. 1999. 'Genetic variation and hybridisation of black stilts (*Himantopus novaezelandiae*) and pied stilts (*H. h. leucocephalus*), Order Charadriformes'. *NZJZ* 26:271–7.

Gurr, L. & F.C. Kinsky. 1965. 'Distribution of breeding colonies and status of red-billed gull (*L. novaehollandiae scopulinus*) in New Zealand and outlying islands'. *Notornis* 12(4):223–40.

Handly, J.W. 1895. 'Notes on some species of New Zealand birds'. *TPNZI* 28:360–7.

Harrington, B.A. 2002. 'Red knot *Calidris canutus*'. *Birds of North America* No. 563.

Hay, R. 1985. 'An oystercatcher in Vanuatu'. *Notornis* 32:79–80.

Hayward, B.W., A.B. Stephenson, M. Morley, J.L. Riley & H.R. Grenfell. 1997. 'Faunal changes in Waitemata Harbour sediments 1930s–1980s'. *Journal of the Royal Society of New Zealand* 27:1–20.

Heather, B.D. 1977. 'Foot trembling by the black-fronted dotterel'. *Notornis* 24:1.

Heppleston, P.B. 1973. 'The distribution and taxonomy of oystercatchers'. *Notornis* 20:102–12.

Hinzman, L., N. Bettez et al. 2005. 'Evidence and implications of recent climate change in Northern Alaska and other Arctic regions'. *Climate Change* 72:251–98.

Holdaway, R.N. 1995. 'A fossil record of the black stilt *Himantopus novaezelandiae* Gould, 1841'. *NZ Natural Sciences* 22:69–74.

Holdaway, R.N., T.H. Worthy & A.J.D. Tennyson. 2001. 'A working list of breeding bird species of the New Zealand region at first human contact'. *NZJZ* 28:119–87.

Houston, P. & M. Barter. 1990. 'Morphometrics of ruddy turnstone *Arenaria interpres* in Australia'. *Stilt* 17:17–23.

Hughey, K. 1977. 'The diet of the wrybill (*Anarhynchus frontalis*) and the banded dotterel (*Charadrius bicinctus*) on two braided rivers in Canterbury, New Zealand'. *Notornis* 44:185–93.

——. 1998. 'Nesting home range sizes of Wrybill (*Anarhynchus frontalis*) and Banded Dotterel (*Charadrius bicinctus*) in relation to braided riverbed characteristics'. *Notornis* 45:103–11.

——. 1985. 'The relationship between riverbed flooding and non-breeding wrybills on northern feeding grounds in summer'. *Notornis* 32:42–50.

Hutton, F. 1873. 'Notes by Captain Hutton on Dr. Buller's "Birds of New Zealand", with the author's replies thereto'. *TNZI* 6, art. XXIX.

Jenkins, J. 1971. 'A hitchhiking turnstone'. *Notornis* 18(2):130–1.

Johnson, O.W. 1993. 'The Pacific golden plover *Pluvialis fulva*: Discovery of the species and other historical notes'. *Auk* 110:136–41.

——. 2003. 'Pacific and American golden plovers: Reflections on conservation needs'. *WSG Bulletin* 100:10–13.

Johnson, O.W. & P.G. Connors. 1996. 'Pacific golden plover *Pluvialis fulva*'. *Birds of North America* No. 202.

Johnston, D.W. & R.W. McFarlane. 1967. 'Migration and bioenergetics of flight in the Pacific golden plover'. *Condor* 69:156–68.

Karl, B.J. & H.A. Best. 1982. 'Feral cats on Stewart Island; their foods, and their effects on kakapo (*Strigops habroptilus*)'. *NZJZ* 9:287–94.

Keedwell, R.J. 2005. 'Breeding biology of black-fronted terns (*Sterna albostriata*) and the effects of predation'. *Emu* 105:39–49.

——. 2003. 'Does fledging equal success? Post-fledging mortality in black-fronted terns'. *Journal of Field Ornithology* 74:217–22.

Keedwell, R.J. & K.P Brown. 2001. 'Relative abundance of mammalian predators in the Upper Waitaki Basin, South Island, New Zealand'. *NZJZ* 28:31–38.

Keedwell, R.J. & M.D. Sanders. 2002. 'Nest monitoring and predator visitation at nests of banded dotterels'. *Condor* 104:199–202.

Kilroy, C., M.R. Scarsbrook & G. Fenwick. 2004. 'Dimensions in biodiversity of a braided river'. *Water and Atmosphere* 12:10–11.

Kinsky, F.C. & J.C. Yaldwyn. 1981. 'The bird fauna of Niue Island, South-west Pacific, with special notes on the white-tailed tropic bird and golden plover'. *National Museum of New Zealand*, Miscellaneous Series No. 2, April 1981.

Kirk, T. 1895. 'The displacement of species in New Zealand'. *TNZI* 28:1–27

Kliskey, A.D., A.E. Byrom & G.L. Norbury. 2000. 'Spatial prediction of predation in the landscape: A GIS based approach to predator-prey interactions for conservation management'. *4th International Conference on Integrating GIS and Environmental Modeling (GIS/EM4): Problems, Prospects and Research Needs*. Banff, Canada, September 2–8, 2000.

Kraan, C., J.A. van Gils, B. Spaans, A. Dekinga, A.I. Bijleveld, M. van Roomen, R. Kleefstra & T. Piersma. 2009. 'Landscape-scale experiment demonstrates that Wadden Sea intertidal flats are used to capacity by molluscivore migrant shorebirds'. *Journal of Animal Ecology* 78:1259–68.

Lindström, Å., R.E. Gill Jr, S.E. Jamieson, B.J. McCaffery, L. Wennerberg, M. Wikelski & M. Klaassen. 2011. 'A puzzling migratory detour: Are fuelling conditions in Alaska driving the movement of juvenile sharp-tailed sandpipers?' *Condor* 113(1):129–39.

Lord, A., J.R. Waas & J. Innes. 1997. 'Effects of human activity on the behaviour of northern New Zealand dotterel *Charadrius obscurus aquilonius* chicks'. *Biological Conservation* 82:15–20.

McCaffery, B.J., R.E. Gill, Jr, D. Melville, A. Riegen, P. Tomkovich, M. Dementyev, M. Sexson, R. Schuckard & S. Lovibond. 2010. 'Variation in timing, behavior, and plumage of spring migrant bar-tailed godwits on the Yukon–Kuskokwim Delta, Alaska'. *WSG Bulletin* 117:179–85.

McClelland, P. 2002. 'Eratication: The clearance of Campbell Island', *NZ Geographic* 58.

McLay, C.L. 1976. 'An inventory of the status and origin of New Zealand estuarine systems'. *Proceedings of NZ Ecological Society* 23:8–25.

McGlone, M. 1989. 'The Polynesian settlement of New Zealand in relation to environmental & biotic changes', pp. 115–29 in M.R. Rudge (ed.) 'Moas, mammals and climate in the ecological history of New Zealand'. *NZ*

Journal of Ecology 12 (Supplement).

——. 2009. 'Postglacial history of New Zealand wetlands and implications for their conservation'. *NZ Journal of Ecology* 33:1–23.

McGowan, C.P., J.E. Hines, J.D. Nichols, J.E. Lyons, D.R. Smith, K.S. Kalasz, L.J. Niles, A.D. Dey, N.A. Clark, P.W. Atkinson, C.D.T. Minton & W. Kendall. 2011. 'Demographic consequences of migratory stopover: Linking red knot survival to horseshoe crab spawning abundance'. *Ecosphere* 2: art 69. [Online doi:10.1890/ES11-00106.1]

McKenzie, H.R. 1955. 'Black-backed gulls dispose of enemies by drowning'. *Notornis* 6:4:130–1.

McKenzie, H.R. & R.B. Sibson. 1957. 'Does the little tern (*Sterna albifrons*) reach New Zealand?' *Notornis* 7: 174–82.

Mackenzie, N.B. 1962. 'A new breeding bird for NZ: Black-fronted dotterels in Hawkes Bay'. *Notornis* 9:8.

McKinlay, B. & A. Smale. 2001. 'The effect of jet boat wake on braided river birds on the Dart River'. *Notornis* 48(2):72–5.

Maloney, R.F. 1999. 'Bird populations in nine braided rivers of the Upper Waitaki Basin, South Island, New Zealand: Changes after 30 years'. *Notornis* 46:243–56.

Maloney, R.F., R. Keedwell, N.J. Wells, A.L. Rebergen & R.J. Nilsson. 1999. 'Effect of willow removal on habitat use by five birds of braided rivers, Mackenzie Basin, New Zealand'. *NZ Journal of Ecology* 23:53–60.

Maloney, R.F., A.L. Rebergen, R.J. Nilsson & N.J. Wells. 1997. 'Bird density and diversity in braided rivers in the Upper Waitaki, South Island, New Zealand'. *Notornis* 44:219–32.

Medway, D.G. 2007. 'A possible live South Island snipe (*Coenocorypha iredalei*) at Dusky Sound 1773'. *Notornis* 54:237–38.

Medway, D. 1976 'Extant types of New Zealand birds from Cook's voyages: Part I: Historical & the type paintings'. *Notornis* 23:45–61.

Meltofte, H., T. Piersma, H. Boyd, B. J. McCaffery, B. Ganter, V.V. Golovnyuk, K. Graham, C.L. Gratto-Trevor, R.I.G. Morrison, E. Nol, H-U. Rösner, D. Schamel, H. Schekkerman, M.Y. Soloviev, P.S. Tomkovich, D.M. Tracy, I. Tulp & L. Wennerberg. 2007. 'Effects of climate variation on the breeding ecology of Arctic shorebirds'. *Bioscience* 59:2007.

Mercer, A.J. 1966. 'Turnstones feeding on a human corpse'. *British Birds* 59:307.

Millar, C.D., C.E.M. Reed, J.L. Halverson & D.M. Lambert. 1997. 'Captive management and molecular sexing of endangered avian species: An application to the black stilt *Himantopus novaezelandiae* and hybrids'. *Biological Conservation* 82:81–6.

Mills, J.A, J.W. Yarrall, J.M. Bradford-Grieve, M.J. Uddstrom, J.A. Renwick & J. Merila. 2008. 'Impact of climatic variations on food availability and reproductive performance of planktivorous red-billed gull (*Larus novaehollandiae scopulinus*)'. *Journal of Animal Ecology* 77:1129–42.

Mills, J.R. 1969. 'The distribution of breeding red-billed gull colonies in New Zealand in relation to areas of plankton enrichment'. *Notornis* 16:3:180–6.

Minton, C.D.T., K. Gosbell, P. Johns, M. Christie, J.W. Fox & V. Afanasyev. 2010. 'Initial results from light level geolocator trials on Ruddy Turnstone *Arenaria interpres* reveal unexpected migration route'. *WSG Bulletin* 117(1):9–14.

Miskelly, C.M. 1987. 'The identity of the hakawai'. *Notornis* 34:95–116.

——. 1990. 'Aerial displaying and flying ability of Chatham Island snipe *Coenocorypha pusilla* & New Zealand snipe *C. aucklandica*'. *Emu* 90:207–21.

——. 1990b. 'Breeding systems of New Zealand snipe *Coenocorypha aucklandica* and Chatham Island snipe *C. pusilla*; are they food limited?' *Ibis* 132:366–79.

——. 2005. 'Evidence for "hakawai" aerial displaying by Snares Island snipe (*Coenocorypha aucklandica huegeli*)'. *Notornis* 52:163–65.

Miskelly, C.M. & A.J. Baker. 2009. 'Description of a new subspecies of Coenocorypha snipe from subantarctic Campbell Island, New Zealand'. *Notornis* 56:113–23.

Miskelly, C.M., E.A. Bell, G.P. Elliott & K.J. Walker. 2006. '"Hakawai" aerial breeding display by three populations of subantarctic snipe (genus Coenocorypha)'. *Notornis* 53:375–9.

Miskelly, C.M., M.R. Charteris & J.R. Fraser. 2011. 'Successful translocation of Snares Island snipe *Coenocorypha huegeli* to replace the extinct South Island snipe *C. iredalei*'. Submitted ms.

Miskelly, C.M. & P.J. de Lange. 2006. 'Notes on the breeding biology of the extinct Stewart Island snipe (*Coenocorypha aucklandica iredali*)'. *Notornis* 53:339–52.

Miskelly, C.M., J.E. Dowding, G.P. Elliott, R.A. Hitchmough, R.G. Powlesland, H.A. Robertson, P.M. Sagar, R.P. Scofield & G.A. Tatlor. 2008. 'Conservation status of New Zealand birds 2008'. *Notornis* 55:117–35.

Miskelly, C.M. & J.R. Fraser. 2006. 'Campbell Island snipe (Coenocorypha undescribed sp.) recolonise subantarctic Campbell Island following rat eradication'. *Notornis* 53:353–60.

Miskelly, C.M. & B. Norton. 2008. 'A further 1952 record of a Coenocorypha snipe on Campbell Island, New Zealand subantarctic'. *Notornis* 55:162–5.

Miskelly, C.M., K.J. Walker & G.P. Elliott. 2006. 'Breeding ecology of three subantarctic snipes (genus Coenocorypha)'. *Notornis* 53:361–74.

Moore, P.J. 2008. 'The recovering population of the Chatham Island oystercatcher (*Haematopus chathamensis*)'. *Notornis* 55:20–32.

Moore, P. 2005. 'Predator control to increase breeding success of Chatham Island oystercatcher *Haematopus chathamensis*, Chatham Island, New Zealand'. *Conservation Evidence* 2:80–2.

Murphy, E.C., R.J. Keedwell, K.P. Brown & I. Westbrooke. 2004. 'Diet of mammalian predators in braided river beds in the central South Island, New Zealand'. *Wildlife Research*. 31(6):631–38.

Nettleship, D.N. 2000. 'Ruddy Turnstone *Arenaria interpres*'. *Birds of North America* No. 537.

Niles, L.J., J. Bart, H. Sitters, A.D. Dey, K.E. Clark, P.W. Atkinson, A.J. Baker, K.A. Bennett, K.S. Kalasz, N.A. Clark, J. Clark, S. Gillings, A.S. Gates, P.M. González, D.E. Hernandez, C.D.T. Minton, R.I.G. Morrison, R.R. Porter, R.K. Ross, & C.R. Veitch. 2009. 'Effects of horseshoe crab harvest in Delaware Bay on red knots: Are harvest restrictions working?' *Bioscience* 59:153–64.

Norbury, G. & R. Heyward. 2007. 'Predictors of clutch predation of a globally significant avifauna in New Zealand's braided river ecosystems'. *Animal Conservation* 11:17–25.

O'Donnell, C.F.J. & J.M. Hoare. 2011. 'Meta-analysis of status and trends in breeding populations of black-fronted terns (*Chlidonias albostriatus*) 1962–2008'. *NZ Journal of Ecology* 35(1):30–43.

Oliver, W.R.B. 1937. 'The wry-billed plover'. *Emu* 37:1–4.

——. 1953. 'Black-backed gull breeding at high altitudes'. *Notornis* 5:3:82.

Parrish, G.R. & G.A. Pulham. 1995. 'Population size, productivity and post breeding movements of the New Zealand fairy tern'. *Tane* 35:175–81.

Pfister, C., B.A. Harrington & M. Lavine. 1992. 'The impact of human disturbance on shorebirds at a migration staging area'. *Biological Conservation* 60:115–26.

Phillips, R.E. 1977. 'Notes on the behaviour of the New Zealand shore plover'. *Emu* 77:23–8.

——. 1980. 'Behaviour and systematics of New Zealand plovers'. *Emu* 80:177–98.

Pierce, R.J. 1979. 'Foods and feeding of the wrybill (*Anarhynchus frontalis*) on its riverbed breeding grounds'. *Notornis* 26:1–21.

——. 1983. 'The Charadriiforms of a high-country river valley'. *Notornis* 30:169–85.

——. 1984a. 'The changed distribution of stilts in New Zealand'. *Notornis* 31:7–18.

——. 1984b. 'Plumage, morphology and hybridization of New Zealand stilts *Himantopus* species'. *Notornis* 31:106–30.

——. 1989. 'Breeding and social patterns of banded dotterels (*Charadrius bicinctus*) at Cass River'. *Notornis* 36:13–23.

——. 1999. 'Regional patterns of migration in the banded dotterel *Charadrius bicinctus*'. *Notornis* 46:101–22.

Piersma, T. 1997. 'Do global patterns of habitat use and migration strategies co-evolve with relative investments in immunocompetence due to spatial variation in parasite pressure?' *Oikos* 80:623–31.

——. 2007. 'Global Flyway Network: progress report for 2007'. www.globalflywaynetwork.com.au/reports/2007

Piersma T. & N. Davidson (eds). 1992. 'The migration of knots'. *WSG Bulletin* 64.

Piersma, T. & A. Lindström. 2004. 'Migrating shorebirds as integrative sentinels of global environmental change'. *Ibis* 146:61–9.

Potts T.H. 1885. 'Oology of New Zealand'. *New Zealand Journal of Science* Vol II: 508.

——. 1870. 'On the birds of New Zealand'. *TNZI* 3:93–7.

Pye, D. & J. Dowding. 2002. 'Nesting period of northern New Zealand dotterel (*Charadrius obscurus aquilonius*)'. *Notornis* 49:259–60.

Rebergen, A., R. Keedwell, H. Moller & R. Maloney. 1998. 'Breeding success and predation at nests of banded dotterel (*Charadrius bicinctus*) on braided riverbeds in the central South Island, New Zealand'. *NZ Journal of Ecology*. 22:33–41.

Reed, C.E.M. 1994. 'Handrearing and breeding the endangered black stilt *Himantopus novaezelandiae* at Twizel'. *International Zoology Yearbook* 33:125–8.

Reinfelds, I. & G. Nanson. 1993. 'Formation of braided river floodplains, Waimakariri River, New Zealand'. *Sedimentology* 40:1113–27.

Riegen, A. & J.E. Dowding. 2003. 'The wrybill (*Anarhynchus frontalis*): a brief review of threats & work in progress'. *WSG Bulletin* 100:20–4.

Robertson, H.A. & B.D. Heather. 1999. 'Effects of water levels on the seasonal use of Lake Wairarapa by waders'. *Notornis* 46:79–89.

Rogers, D., H-Y. Yang, C.J. Hassell, A.N. Boyle, K.G. Rogers, B. Chen, Z-W. Zhang & T. Piersma. 2010. 'Red knots (*Calidris canutus piersmai* and *c.c. rogersi*) depend on a small threatened staging area in Bohai Bay, China'. *Emu* 110:307–31.

Rogers, D.I. 2003. 'High tide roost choice by coastal waders'. *WSG Bulletin* 100:73–9.

Rogers, D.I., P.F. Battley, T. Piersma, J.A. van Gils & K.G. Rogers. 2006. 'High-tide habitat choice: Insights from modelling roost selection by shorebirds around a tropical bay'. *Animal Behaviour* 72:563–75.

Roper, D.S., S.F. Thrush & D.G. Smith. 1988. 'The influence of runoff on intertidal mudflat benthic communities'. *Marine Environmental Research* 26:1–18.

Rowe, L. 2008. 'Breeding of variable oystercatchers (*Haematopus unicolor*) at Kaikoura Peninsula, South Island, New Zealand'. *Notornis* 55:146–55.

Sagar, P.M. 1986. 'The effects of floods on the invertebrate fauna of a large, unstable braided river'. *NZ Journal of Marine Freshwater Research* 20:37–46.

Sagar, P.M., R.J. Barker & D. Geddes. 2002. 'Survival of Finsch's oystercatchers (*Haematopus finschi*) on farmland in Canterbury, New Zealand'. *Notornis* 49:233–40.

Sagar, P.M. & D. Geddes. 1999. 'Dispersal of SIPO from an inland breeding area of New Zealand'. *Notornis* 46:89–99.

Sagar, P.M., D. Geddes, J. Banks & P. Howden. 2000. 'Breeding of South Island pied oystercatchers (*Haematopus ostralegus finschi*) on farmland in mid-Canterbury, New Zealand'. *Notornis* 47:71–81.

Sagar, P.M., U. Shankar & S. Brown. 1999. 'Distribution and numbers of waders in New Zealand, 1983–1994'. *Notornis* 46:1–45.

Sanders, M.D. 1999. 'Effect of changes in water level on numbers of black stilts *Himantopus novaezelandiae* using deltas of Lake Benmore'. *NZJZ* 26:155–63.

Sanders, M.D. & R.F. Maloney. 2002. 'Causes of mortality in ground nesting birds in the Upper Waitaki basin, South Island, New Zealand: A 5-year video study'. *Biological Conservation* 106:225–36.

Sansom, O. 1951. 'Spur-winged plover in New Zealand'. *Notornis* 4(3):138–9.

Schekkerman, H., I. Tulp & B. Ens. 2003. 'Conservation of long-distance migratory wader populations: Reproductive consequences of events occurring in distant staging sites'. *WSG Bulletin* 100:151–6.

Schipper, C.J., M.A. Weston & J.M. Peter. 1996. 'Scavenging behavior of ruddy turnstone *Arenaria interpres*'. *Stilt* 29:39–40.

Sibson, R.B. 1963. 'A population study of the wry-billed plover (*Anarhynchus frontalis*)'. *Notornis* 10:146–53

——. 1966. 'Increasing numbers of South Island pied oystercatchers visiting northern New Zealand'. *Notornis* 13:94–7.

——. 1975. 'Some thoughts on the diet of the South Island pied oystercatcher'. *Notornis* 22:66–82.

——. 1992. 'Some thoughts on Caspian terns in New Zealand'. *Notornis* 39:87–93.

Soper, M.F. 1959. 'Nesting habitats on the Shotover riverbed'. *Notornis* 8(6):1.

——. 1967. 'Some observations of black stilts'. *Notornis* 14(1):8–10.

Stead, E.F. 1921. 'Notes on the migratory plovers of New Zealand, with records of some additional species. Read before the Philosophical Institute of Canterbury, 7th September, 1921'. *TNZI* 53.

Stevens, G.R. 1990. 'Geological evolution and biotic links in the Mesozoic and Cenozoic of the southwest Pacific'. *Acta XX Congressus Internationalis Ornithologici*, 361–82.

Tait, P. & R. Cullen. 2010. 'Some external costs of dairy farming in Canterbury'. Lincoln University. 50th AAES Conference, Manly, NSW.

Tennyson, A.J.D. 2009. 'The origin and history of New Zealand's terrestrial vertebrates'. *NZ Journal of Ecology* 34(1):6–27.

Thompson, D.R & J.E. Dowding. 1999. 'Site-specific heavy metal concentrations in blood of South Island pied oystercatchers *Haematopus ostralegus finschi* from the Auckland region, New Zealand'. *Marine Pollution Bulletin* 38:202–06.

Thompson, M.C. 1973. 'Migratory patterns of ruddy turnstones in the Central Pacific region'. *Living Bird* 12:5–23.

Turbott, E.G. 1969. 'Roof-nesting black-backed gulls'. *Notornis* 16(3):187–89.

——. 1970. 'The wrybill: A feeding adaptation'. *Notornis* 17:25–7.

Veitch, C.R. 1978. 'Waders of the Manukau Harbour and Firth of Thames'. *Notornis* 25:1–24.

Veitch, C.R. & A.M. Habraken. 1999. 'Waders of the Manukau Harbour and Firth of Thames'. *Notornis* 46:45–70.

Walsby, J. 1997. 'Shorebirds under threat'. *NZ Geographic* 36:96–113.

Warne, K. 2003. 'A wing and a snare: Part II Island of birds'. *NZ Geographic* 62.

Weber, J.M. 2009. 'The physiology of long-distance migration: Extending the limits of endurance metabolism'. *Journal of Experimental Biology* 212:593–97.

Wenink, P.W., A.J. Baker & M.G.J. Tilanus. 1994. 'Mitochondrial control region sequences in two shorebird species, the turnstone and the dunlin, and their utility in population genetic studies'. *Molecular Biology Evolution*. 11:22–31.

West. A.D., J.D. Goss-Custard, S.A. le V. dit Durell & R.A. Stillman. 2005. 'Maintaining estuary quality for shorebirds: Towards simple guidelines'. *Biological Conservation* 123:211–24.

Whelan, M.B., T.M. Hume, P.M. Sagar, U. Shankar & R. Liefting. 2003. 'Relationship between physical characteristics of estuaries and the size and diversity of wader populations in the North Island of New Zealand'. *Notornis* 50:11–22.

Williams, P.A. & S. Wiser. 2004. 'Determinants of regional and local patterns in the floras of braided riverbeds in New Zealand'. *Journal of Biogeography* 31:1355–72.

Wills, D.E, J. Murray & R.G. Powlesland. 2003. 'Impact of management on the breeding success of the northern New Zealand dotterel (*Charadrius obscurus aquilonius*) on Matakana Island, Bay of Plenty'. *Notornis* 50:1–11.

Worthy, T.H. 1999. 'What was on the menu? – Avian extinctions in NZ'. *NZ Journal of Archaeology* 19:125–60.

Worthy, T.H., C.M. Miskelly & R.A. Ching. 2002. 'Taxonomy of North and South Island snipe (Aves: Scolopacidae: Coenocorypha), with analysis of a remarkable collection of snipe bones from Greymouth, New Zealand'. *NZJZ* 29:231–44.

Worthy, T.H., A.J.D. Tennyson, C. Jones, J.A. McNamara & B.J. Douglas. 2007. 'Miocene waterfowl and other birds from Central Otago, New Zealand'. *Journal of Systematic Palaeontology* 5(1):1–39.

Yang, H-Y., B. Chen, M. Barter, T. Piersma: C-F. Zhou, F-S. Li & Z-W. Zhang. 2011. 'Impacts of tidal land reclamation in Bohai Bay, China: Ongoing losses of critical Yellow Sea waterbird staging and wintering sites'. *Bird Conservation International* 1–19. BirdLife International.

UNPUBLISHED THESES

Baker, A.J. 1972. 'Systematics and affinities of New Zealand oystercatchers'. Unpubl. PhD thesis, University of Canterbury, Christchurch.

Bomford, M. 1978. 'The behaviour of the banded dotterel *Charadrius bicinctus*'. Unpubl. MSc thesis, University of Otago, Dunedin.

Cumming, A.B. 1991. 'The New Zealand dotterel (tuturiwhatu) problems and management'. Unpublished MSc thesis, University of Auckland, Auckland.

Davis, A. 1987. 'The behavioural ecology and management of New Zealand shore plover'. Unpubl MSc thesis. University of Auckland, Auckland.

Hay, J.R. 1984. 'The behavioural ecology of the wrybill'. Unpublished PhD thesis, University of Auckland.

Hughey, K.F.D. 1985. 'Hydrological factors influencing the ecology of riverbed breeding birds on the plains' reaches of Canterbury's braided rivers'. Unpublished PhD thesis, University of Canterbury, Christchurch.

Keedwell, R.J. 2002. 'Black-fronted terns and banded dotterels: Causes of mortality and comparisons of survival'. Unpubl. PhD thesis, Massey University, Palmerston North.

Lalas, C. 1977. 'Food and feeding behaviour of the black-fronted tern (*Sterna albostriata*)'. Unpubl. MSc thesis, University of Otago, Dunedin.

McClellan, R. 2009. 'The ecology and management of Southland's black-billed gulls'. Unpubl. PhD thesis, University of Otago, Dunedin.

Millener, P.R. 1981. 'The quaternary avifauna of the North Island New Zealand'. Unpubl. PhD thesis, University of Auckland, Auckland.

Moffatt, M. 1981. 'Aspects of the biology of the spur-winged plover (*Vanellus miles novaehollandiae* Stephens 1819)'. Unpubl MSc thesis, Massey University, Palmerston North.

Pierce, R.J. 1976. 'The feeding ecology of wrybills in Canterbury. Unpubl. postgraduate diploma in science thesis, University of Otago, Dunedin.

Threadgold, S. 2000. 'Behavioural ecology of the endangered New Zealand fairy tern (tara-iti) *Sterna nereis davisae*; implications for management'. Unpubl. MSc thesis Massey University, Palmerston North.

Wilson, G.H. 2000. 'Historical changes and the present status of the rivers and adjoining wetlands in the Upper Waitaki Basin'. Unpubl. MSc thesis, University of Waikato, Hamilton.

REPORTS

Anon. 2008. 'Project Manukau: Mangere Wastewater Treatment Plant bird roost management plan'. Watercare Services, Auckland.

Anon. 2011. 'Draft report and decision of the Board of Inquiry into the Hauauru ma Raki wind farm and infrastructure connection to grid'. Draft report under Section 148 of the Resource Management Act 1991 as amended in 2005.

Bamford, M., D. Watkins, W. Bancroft, G. Tischler & J. Wahl. 2008. 'Migratory shorebirds of the East Asian–Australasian Flyway, population estimates and internationally important sites'. Wetlands International – Oceania. Canberra, Australia.

Battley, P.F. & B. Brownell. 2007. 'Population biology and foraging ecology of waders in the Firth of Thames: Update 2007'. Auckland Regional Council report: TP347.

Cleland, S., E. Wahlberg, S. Stevenson & R. Maloney. 2007. 'Predator control project report for Kaki recovery programme. A: Tasman Valley B: Ahuriri Valley March 2006–February 2007'. Kaki Project Internal Report No 07/04, DOC, Twizel.

Department of Conservation. 2001. 'New Zealand shore plover recovery plan 2001–2011'. DOC, Wellington.

——. 2006. 'Review of level of protection for some New Zealand wildlife: Public discussion document'. Strategy and Policy Group, DOC, Wellington.

——. 2009. 'River life: Explore the ecology of braided rivers in the Mackenzie Basin'. DOC, Christchurch.

Dowding, J.E. 2006. 'Management of northern New Zealand dotterels on Coromandel Peninsula'. DOC Research & Development series 252.

——. 2006. 'Potential impacts on shorebirds of a proposed subdivision at Te Arai, North Auckland'. A report prepared for the Auckland Conservancy, DOC. DM Consultants contract report number 49.

Dowding, J.E. & S.J. Moore. 2006. 'Habitat networks of indigenous shorebirds in New Zealand'. *Science for Conservation* 261. DOC.

Dowding, J.E. & M.J. Elliott. 2003. 'Ecology of stoats in a South Island braided river valley'. Unpublished report on Investigation 3405 to Science & Research Unit, DOC, Wellington.

Dowding, J.E. & A. Davis. 2004. 'New Zealand dotterel (*Charadrius obscurus*) recovery plan, 2004–14'. DOC Threatened Species Recovery Plan 58.

Gray, D. & J.S. Harding. 2007: 'Braided river ecology: A literature review of physical habitats and aquatic invertebrate communities'. *Science for Conservation* 279. DOC, Wellington.

Hansen, K. 2005. 'New Zealand fairy tern (*Sterna nereis davisae*) recovery plan, 2005–15'. DOC Threatened Species Recovery Plan 57.

——. 2005. 'Protection of shorebirds at three Northland breeding sites – Mangawhai, Waipu and Ruakaka'. DOC Research & Development Series 204. DOC, Wellington.

Pierce, R.J. 2000. 'Implications of a subdivision proposal near an important shorebird breeding site'. Conservation Advisory Science Notes 274.

Reed C.E.M., D.P. Murray & D.J. Butler. 1993. 'Black stilt recovery plan (*Himantopus novaezelandiae*)'. DOC, Wellington.

Roberts, A. & C. Miskelly. 2003. 'Recovery plan for the snipe species of New Zealand and the Chatham Islands (*Coenocorypha* spp) tutukiwi 2003–2015'. DOC, Wellington.

Robertson, C.J.R., C.J.F. O'Donnell, & F.B. Overmars. 1983. 'Habitat requirements of wetland birds in the Ahuriri River Catchment New Zealand'. New Zealand Wildlife Service, Department of Internal Affairs, occasional report 3.

Schuckard, R. 2002. 'Wader distribution at Farewell Spit, Golden Bay and Tasman Bay'. DOC, Nelson/Marborough Conservancy.

Schmechel, F. 2008. 'Ashburton River 2007/2008 black-billed gull colony'. Environment Canterbury Report R08/89.

Sinner, J. 2011. 'Implications of the National Policy Statement on Freshwater Management'. Report prepared for Fish and Game New Zealand by the Cawthron Institute.

Smith, D., K. Hughey & K. Booth. 1997. 'Impacts of recreational users on the wildlife of braided rivers – a preliminary study on the Tekapo River'. Unpublished Department of Resource Management report, Lincoln University, Lincoln.

Southey, I. 2009. 'Numbers of waders in New Zealand 1995–2003'. DOC Research & Development Series 308. DOC, Wellington.

Wickham, J. 2009. 'District Plan Review planners report natural environment section – to add shorebird and estuarine bird nesting and roosting sites to the District Plan'. Western Bay of Plenty District Council.

Woolmore, C., S. Anderson, D. Kimber. 2008. 'Project River Recovery Annual Report 1 July 2007–30 June 2008. DOC, Twizel.

PAPERS AND PERIODICALS

Hauraki Herald 9 July 2010.
NZ Geographic 36:96–113.
NZ Geographic 58.
NZ Geographic lapwings 62.
NZ Geographic 73:46–61.
NZ Geographic 80:104–12.
NZ Geographic 81:7.
NZ Geographic 101:86–91.
Miranda News 74: 2009.
Miranda News 81: 2011. Miranda Naturalists' Trust.
New Zealand Herald 7 December 2010.
New Zealand Listener 17 April 2010.
New Zealand Listener 2 August 2010.
New Zealand Wader Study Group News. 1996. Miranda Naturalists' Trust.
The Press 11 November 2010.
Southern Bird 42: 2010 Ornithological Society of New Zealand.

INDEX

Abbott, Charles 75
Ahuriri River 39, 70, 204, 214;
airport bird incidents 227–8
Alaska 143, 147, 149, 154, 156, 158, 161, 162, 245
Allee effect 120–1
Allen's rule 92, 161
Anarhynchus frontalis (wrybill) 7, 55–65
Anderson, William 124
Antarctic Circumpolar Current (ACC) 28
Antipodes Island snipe 135, 139, 141
Arenaria interpres see ruddy turnstone
Ashburton River 121
Ashley River 21, 56, 99, 118, 181, 203, 209–11, 214
Astrolabe voyage 56, 105
asymmetry 62
Auckland airport 104, 227–8, 231
Auckland Council 251
Auckland Island snipe 134, 135, 136, 139–41
Auckland Islands 138; dotterel 98
Auckland Regional Council 191
Australasian harrier *see* predators
Australasian Wader Studies Group 253
Australia 28, 29; migration to 145; *see also individual species*
Avon-Heathcote Estuary 21, 86, 178, 183, 232; oystercatchers 90, 178
Awarua Bay 106–7, 108, 144, 146, 154, 194, 220;

Baker, Alan: oystercatchers 88
banded dotterel 31, 64, 95–101; breeding range & habitat 98–100; brooding & chicks 100–1; conservation status 177; displays 98, 100; foraging 95–7; migration 145; migratory vs sedentary 98–9; nesting 70–3; nomenclature & historical record 97–8; plumage 95, 97, 98, 177; population counts 42, 43, 177; *see also* plovers
banding: godwit 154–5, 160–1, 168; New Zealand dotterel 103, 107, 108; oystercatcher 86; tern 69, 125; turnstone 149; wrybill 63, 64, 180
Banks, Joseph 87
bar-tailed godwit 15, 20, 48, 49, 51; Campbell Is. specimens 134; flight & geolocator 15; migration 17, 145, 149, 153–63, 240–5
Barlow, Maida 29, 30; NZ dotterel 105
bat, greater short-tailed (extinct) 136
benthic fauna 48–49
Big South Cape Island/Taukihepa 137–8, 139, 141
bill shape & function 51, 52, 88–92, 95, 136, 138, 147–8, 161, 166; *see also individual species* Herbst corpuscles 52, 90, 97, 138
biodiversity *see* braided rivers; intertidal areas
black stilt: bill shape & function 60, 61, 80; conservation status 76–7, 82, 83; interbreeding, hybridisation 74, 82–3; nesting 81; origins, evolution & adaptation 79–80; plumage & colouration 61, 79, 81; population decline 76–9, 81–3; predator vulnerability 81, 204–05; range & habitat 76–80, 81, 83, 250; recovery programme 185–8; *see also* stilts
black-backed gull: benefits from human development 114; parenting, chicks & food begging 113; as predator 62, 111–12, 126, 191–3; survey count 43; *see also* predators
black-billed gull 117–21; breeding range & habitat 118–19; breeding synchrony, predation, colony size & Allee effect 120;

conservation status 117; diet pre-human settlement 118; population decline 118–19;
black-fronted dotterel *100*, 101
black-fronted tern 67–73; banding 69; breeding & foraging range 68, 73; cf banded dotterel 71–3; conservation status 68, 69, 73, 215; cryptic colouration 72; egg hatching asynchrony 71; nesting (colonial) 69, 70, 71–3; nomenclature 67–8; population decline 214–15; predators & defence strategies 69–72, 206–7
surveys: Lake Pukaki 43; Ohau River 68–73; Wairau River 70
Bohai Sea 168–9, 242–3
Bomford, Mary: banded dotterels 98
Borchgrevink, Carsten Egeberg 134
Boyle, Adrian 168
braided rivers 7, 21, 37–43, 61, 209–15, 221–5; *see also individual rivers*; water biodiversity 40–2
exotic vegetation 42, 119, 212, 215, 220, 222, 223
floodplains 38–42, 61, 63, 64, 70, 119–20, 181, 182, 186, 209–15, 222–4
gravel extraction 225
flow regime 39, 41, 209–15, 248; controlled flow 70, 215; effects on home range & nest locations 210–15
food chain 40–2
formation in Southern Alps 37–9, 42, 222
predators 204–7
riverbed restoration 222–5; *see also* water restoration
Braided River Aid (BRaid) 225
Brodrick, T.N. 105
Buffon, G-L.L., Comte de 144
Buller, Walter 32, 34, 68, 87, 154, 177, 178, 179; dotterels 105, 106; gulls 113, 115; oystercatchers 177–8; stilts 76, 77, 79; terns 124, 127, 128, 129; wrybill 57

Calidris acuminata see sharp-tailed sandpiper
Calidris canutus see red knot
    C. c. islandica 167
    C. c. piersmai 167–9
    C. c. rogersi 167–9
    C. c. roselaari 167
    C. c rufa 167, 169–71, 241
Calidris ferruginea see curlew sandpiper
Calidris tenuirostris see knots: great knot
Campbell Island 133–5, 139, 141, 147; pest eradication 134–5, 197
Campbell Island snipe 133–41; breeding 134; origins 138–9
Campbell Island teal 133, 134
Canada goose 42
Canterbury
    Canterbury Water Management Strategy (CWMS) 224–5, 251–2
    Environment Canterbury (ECan) water restoration 220–1, 225, 251–2
Caspian tern 126–28; nomenclature 126–7; breeding & nesting habitat 127–8; population 128; predators 128
Cass River 59; banded dotterel 98
cats *see* predators
Charadriiformes 18, 52, 112
Charadrius bicinctus 98; *see* banded dotterel
    C. b. exilis (Auckland Islands) 98
Charadrius morinellus 97
Charadrius obscurus aquilonius see New Zealand dotterel: northern
Charadrius obscurus obscurus see New Zealand dotterel: southern

Chatham Island oystercatcher *51*, 87, 88, 188–89; brooding & chicks 93, *189*; conservation status 89, 188–9; habitat & morphology 89, 188; predators 189
Chatham Island snipe 20, 135, 137
Chatham Islands 21, 31–3; snipes 135, 137, 138
Chlidonias albostriatus 68–73; *see also* black-fronted tern
Chubbia see snipe
Chukotka 143, 158, 168
Coenocorypha 136; *see* snipe
Coenocorypha aucklandica see Auckland Island snipe
Coenocorypha aucklandica perseverance 141
Coenocorypha barrierensis see snipe: North Is.
Coenocorypha iredali see snipe: South Is.
Coenocorypha pusilla see snipe: Chatham Is.
Conklin, Jesse: godwit migration 160–1
conservation 43, 136, 155–6, 185–99, 238, 252; *see also* water restoration
community groups 250–1
endangered species 202–3
recovery programmes 141, 185–8, 197–9
Cook, Captain James 32, 137, 148
Crossland, Andrew 178, 225
curlew *see* eastern curlew
curlew sandpiper 16, 18, 22, 151, 230, 243, 245; migration 151; *see also* eastern curlew

dairy farming *see* farming
Delaware Bay *see Calidris canutus rufa*
Dent Island 134
Department of Conservation (DOC) 42, 182, 191; habitat recovery 223, 252
Discovery (Cook's voyage) 32, 124, 137
dotterels *see* banded dotterel; black-fronted dotterel; New Zealand dotterel; plover
inland dotterel (Aus.) 18
Dowding, John: dotterel 106–07; wrybill 63, 64, 181
Dusky Sound 32, 87, 104, 108, 112, 115, 137, 201

Earl, Percy 67
East Asian–Australasian Flyway (EAAF) 21, 45–53, 154, 168–71, 239–43
eastern curlew 144, *145*
Edgar, A.T. 107
endangered species *see* conservation; *see also individual species*
El Niño conditions 131
Ellis, William 124
Ellman, J.B. 126–7
Elseyornis melanops see black-fronted dotterel
endangered species *see* conservation
Enderby Island 136
Erebus & Terror expedition 134
estuaries 17, 20–1, 45–53, 60, 85–6, 130, 178, 218–19, 229, 230; sedimentation 218; *see also* Avon–Heathcote; Awarua Bay; Firth of Thames; Omaha; Saemangeum
exotic vegetation *see* braided rivers
extinction 21, 22, 33; *see also individual species*

fairy tern 128–31; breeding sites 129–30; conservation status 128, 129; colouration, camouflage 130; conservation 197–9; & human disturbance 130, 234; predation 130–1
Fairy Tern Recovery Plan 2005–15 (NZ) 197–9
New Zealand Fairy Tern Trust 193
Falla, Robert: oystercatchers 87–8
Farewell Spit 53, 86, 98, 108, 109, 144, 147, 238
farming, farmland 30, 33, 121, 134, 219–21, 248; farmland as habitat 30, 33, 93; habitat reduction 33, 121; nutrients & pollution in waterways 217–19;

dairy farming, conversions 30, 121, 179, 209, 219–21, 248
water abstraction & irrigation 209, 213, 219–21, 223–25
Finsch, Otto 87
Firth of Thames 31, 50–1, 85, 177, 178, 179, 180; sediment 217–19; *see also* Miranda
Fleming, Charles 32, 34, 76, 79, 114, 138, 178
flooding 61, 70, 80, 81, 101, 210–15, 241; *see also* braided rivers
flyways 237–45; *see also* East Asian–Australasian Flyway
foraging techniques: foot trembling 103; visual 96–7; tactile 90–2, 97; turning objects over 104; *see also individual species*
Forbes' harrier (extinct) 62
Forest and Bird 191
Forster, Georg 104
Forster, Johann 32, 67, 87, 201; dotterel 104, 105; snipe 137
fossils 21, 61, 134–5; black stilt 79; black-backed gull 113; Chatham Island snipe 137; Waikari Valley 32
Foxton Beach 15, 16
Fraser, James *135*

Gaimard 56, 105
geolocator: bar-tailed godwit 15; turnstone 149–50
Gill, Robert (Bob): godwit migration 156, 161
Gmelin 104, 124
Global Flyway Network 168, 243, 253
godwits 7, 15, 18, 19, 44, 50, 51, 169, *174*, 182
bill shape & function 52, 135; conservation status 238; flight 232; & human disturbance 231, 232; migration 153–63, 240–5; & pollution 230; roosting near development 229; *see also* bar-tailed godwit
E5 157, 159
E7 157, 160, 218
Gould, John: fairy tern 129
Grant, Andy 224, 225
Gray, G.R. 56, 67
gulls 111–21; cf seabirds 112, 113; diverse habitat 112–13; scavenging 114; *see also* black-backed gull; black-billed gull; red-billed gull
Guthrie-Smith, H. 123, 180–1; black stilt 77; black-fronted tern 69; snipe on Big South Cape Is. 137; wrybill 58, 62

habitat 16, 17, 20–1, 35; degradation 21, 22, 180; pressures 229–35; *see also specific habitats*
habitat loss *see* farming; human development
Haematopus finschi 88
Haematopus longirostris 88
Haematopus reischeki 88; *see also H. unicolor*
Haematopus unicolor (variable oystercatcher) 87, 88
Hakataramea River 79, 181
Hakawai 139; *see also* snipe: South Is.
Hasselborough, Capt. Frederick 141
Hassell, Chris 168;
Hay, Rod: wrybill 60, 61, 62, 63, 181, 210
Herbst corpuscles *see* bills
Himantopus himantopus 75–6; *see also* stilt
Himantopus leucocephalus see pied stilt
Himantopus novaezelandiae see black stilt
Hokio Beach 29, 100
horseshoe crab *see* red knot
Hughey, Ken: river species & hydrology 209–15 *passim*; 225

human development 21, 35, 104, 148, 160, 219, 225, 227–35, 237–45; *see also* farming; flyway; hydroelectric; water
human disturbance 16, 21, 91, *190*, *199*, *225*, 227–35, 249
Hutton, Frederick: godwit 154; snipe 138, 139; wrybill 57–58
hydroelectric development 39, 70, 181–2, 185, 215, 222; *see also* braided rivers: flow regime

International Union for Conservation of Nature (IUCN) 117, 215
intertidal areas 20, 45–53; *see also* estuaries; tidal flats
  sediment as food factory 45–9
Invercargill 27, 29, 127, 128, 154
invertebrates 40–2, 136; *see also individual species*
Isaac Wildlife Trust 187

Jackson Bay 92
Jacquemart Island snipe 133–5; recovery plan 141

Kaiaua *23*, 50–1, 233, 240
Kaikoura 92; red-billed gull 116–17
kakapo 140, 187
kaki *see* black stilt
Kaki Recovery Programme 185–8; chick fostering 186
Kamchatka 144, 149
karoro 112; *see* black-backed gull
Kawhia Harbour 53, 81, 85, 86
Keedwell, Rachel: black-fronted tern 68–73
kiore *see* predators
kite surfers 231
knots 165–71; bill function 166; breeding range 166–9; ecology & food 166–7; lack of genetic diversity 167; plumage 168; *see also* red knot
  great knot (*Calidris tenuirostris*) 239, 241
krill (euphausiids) 115–16
kuaka *see* godwits
Kuskokwim *see* Yukon-Kuskokwim Delta

La Niña: adverse weather 131; food abundance 116
Laishley, Richard 127
Lake Ellesmere *see* Te Waihora
Lake Horowhenua 29
Lake Pukaki 42–3
Lake Wainono 21, 53
Lalas, Chris: black-fronted tern 68
lapwing *see* spur-winged plover
Larus bulleri see black-billed gull
Larus dominicanus dominicanus see black-backed gull
Larus novaehollandiae scopulinus see red-billed gull; *L. n. forsteri* (Pacific) 115; *L. n. novaehollandiae* (Aus.) 115
Lepekhin, Ivan 127
Lewis, Michelle 192
Lichtenstein, Martin 111
Limosa lapponica anadyrensis 154
Limosa lapponica baueri 154, 156, 158, 159, 161, 240
Limosa lapponica menzbieri 154, 158, 240
limpets 90, 91–2
Linnaeus 97, 144, 147, 148
longevity *see* populations
Mackenzie, Ross 180
Mackenzie Basin 39, 61, 81, 99, 185–6, 209; banded dotterel 100, 177; black stilt 83; wrybill 181, 182, 203, 205; *see also* Pierce, Ray
Madagascar 144
Mair, Gilbert 68
Mana Island 196–7

Manawatu Estuary 15, 17, 160
Manawatu Estuary Trust 250
Mangawhai: terns 127–8, 129, 190, 193
  Harbour Restoration Society 199
Mangere Island (Chathams) 32, 35, 137; Little Mangere 137
mangrove expansion 179, 199, *216*, 218–19
Manukau Harbour 17, 85, 104, 118, 171, 178, 180, 183, 227, 230–32, 238, 242; knots 171; oystercatchers 178; Pacific golden plover 146; wrybill 60, 180
Maori bird names, myths & traditions: hakawai (snipe) 139; kaki (black stilt) 20; karoro (black-backed gull) 112; kuaka (godwit) 154; powhera (banded dotterel) 97; tara (white-fronted tern) 123; tarapiroe (black-fronted tern) 68; tarapunga (red-billed gull) 114, 115
  middens (& N.I. snipe) 136
Marlborough Sounds 32
Mason Bay 106–7
Matakana Island 91, 105, 191, 192, 193, 198
Matarangi 105, 192, 193, *226*, 234
mayfly 40, 41, 59, 60, *212*
McClellan, Rachel: gull colonies 119–20
McCormick, Robert 134
Meridian Energy *see* Project River Recovery
migration 15–17, 143–51, 153–63; first/juvenile migrations 151, 162; food & fuel 19, 145, 156, 158, 161, 162, 232, 243, 253; hyperphagia 146; navigation 146; physiology & chemistry 155; satellite tracking 156, 157, 160, 240; strategies & schedules 145–6, 158, 159, 161; transequatorial 144–6; weather & wind 157, 159, 161; *Zugunruhe* (circannual cues) 146, 151; *see also* East Asian–Australasian Flyway; *individual species*
Mills, Jim: gull colonies 116
mining 192, 218, 219
Miranda 7, 44, 46, 49, 50, 56, 76, 79, 86, 115, 118, 126, 158, 182, 210, 219; black-billed gull 118; Caspian tern 126; fairy tern 198; godwits 49, 50, 154–6, 159, 166–7, *182*, *245*; hybrid stilt 79; knots 166; pied oystercatcher 86, 126, 219; pied stilt 76; shore plover 197; short-tailed sandpiper 163; wrybill 56, 210
Miranda Naturalists' Trust (MNT) 56, 243, 253
Miranda Shorebird Centre 7, 9, 191
Miskelly, Colin *135*, 136
Mokohinau Islands 114, 117
molluscs, as prey 89–92, 170
Morris, Rev. 147
Motuora Island 34, 197
Mount Maunganui Wildlife Response Centre 194–5
Mt Cook *see* Aoraki Mt Cook
Murphy, Elaine: dotterel 106, 107
Muttonbird Islands, muttonbirders 137–8, 139, 140

National Policy Statement for Freshwater Management (NPS) 224
Nelson, Dean: Kaki Recovery Programme 185
New Zealand crow (extinct) 113
New Zealand dotterel 31, 103–9, 190–7; banded 'BOW' 103; breeding range & habitat 104–9; conservation 190–6; eggs 109; foraging & foot trembling 103, 104; historical record & nomenclature 104–5; juvenile migration 108; nesting in developed areas 104; plumage 108; predators 191, 193
  northern population 190, 193; breeding range & site fidelity 108–9; longevity 109; *Rena* disaster 195
  southern (Stewart Island) conservation

status 190; population 105–8; breeding & flocking sites 106–7, 108–9; plumage *107*, 108; predation & mortality 107–8
New Zealand Fairy Tern Trust 193
New Zealand falcon 62
New Zealand Wildlife Service 191, 252
Newmont Waihi Gold Ltd 192
Numenius madagascariensis see eastern curlew
Nyctiphanes australis see krill

Ohau River black-fronted tern study 68–73
Ohiwa Harbour 53, 85
Ohope Beach 99, 105
Old Chevak 144
Oliver, W.R.B.: black stilt 79; black-backed gull 112, 113
Omaha: NZ dotterel 109, 190, 191, 193, 233
Omaha Shorebird Protection Trust 250–1, 253
Opoutere 191, 192, 194, 233
Orbell, Margaret 112
Oreti River 119
Ornithological Society of New Zealand (OSNZ): Checklist 88; National Wader Count scheme 176, 177; research & surveys 118, 155, 191, 192
oystercatchers 22, 60, 85–93; bill shape & function 86, 89–92; black vs pied 87–9, 92–3; brooding & chicks 93; foraging & detecting prey 90–2; migratory vs sedentary 88; nomenclature, historical record & evolution 85–8, 90; population expansion & decline 178–9; range 85–7; self-introduced from Aus. 88–9 *see also* Chatham Island oystercatcher 89; pied oystercatcher; variable oystercatcher

Pacific golden plover *146*, 147–9; migration 148–9
Pakiri Beach & estuary 193; dotterels 103, 109; fairy tern 128, 129
Pallas, Simon 127
Perseverance 134, 141
pest eradication 134–5, 141, 195; *see also* predators
phalarope 18
phytoplankton 49, 219
Piako River 217, 218
pied oystercatcher 16, *17*; brooding & chicks 92, 93; cf VOC 88–9, 92–3; habitat 92, 93; mate fidelity 93; populations 43, 177–8
pied stilt *75*–83, *180*; bill shape 61, 80; interbreeding, hybridisation 82–3; nesting 81, 82; population trends 76, 183; range & habitat 80–1; *see also* stilts
Pierce, Ray: wrybill 58–61; black stilt 77, 81, 82, 83; dotterel 99; prey-switching 205; river hydrology 209
Piersma, Theunis 167
Pitt Island 32, 137, 189
plover 27–35, 62; foraging techniques & bill shape 95–7, 147–8; & human development 148; migration 146–9; *see also* Pacific golden plover; shore plover; spur-winged plover; wrybill
plumage 95, 161; breeding, camouflage 18–19, 62, 79; display 98; insulation 61; migration 165; *see also individual species*
Plunket, Lord 134
Pluvialis 148
Pluvialis fulva see Pacific golden plover
polychaete worms 49, 114
Polydora ciliata (marine boring worm) 91
populations 175–83; bird counts 176–7; longevity & breeding 202–3; *see also individual species*

Potts, Thomas 32; gulls 112; NZ dotterel 105; oystercatchers 178; wrybill 56–7
powhera *see* banded dotterel
predators 22, 32–33, 70–1, 107–8, 134–5, 201–07; & black-fronted tern 69–72; & dotterels 107–8; & shore plover 32, 33; & stilts 81; & wrybill 181
    avian 33, 34, 62–3, 81–2; *see also* black-backed gull; skua
    cats 107–8, 134, 195, 201, 207
    control & eradication 134–5, 141, 186, 195, 223, 235
    evolution in absence of 33
    hedgehogs 70
    kiore (Pacific rats) 32, 135, 137, 201, 203
    rats, Norway 70, 81, 107, 130, 134, 137–8, 139, 141, 189, 201, 204, 206
    mammalian & mustelids 32, 70–1, 78, 81, 107–8, 200–7; & birds' behavioural naïvety 202–3; & SI riverbeds 204–5
    prey-switching & rabbit numbers 81, 204–5
    stoats 70, 78, 181, 191, 202, 204–7, 210, 212
Project River Recovery (PRR) 222–3
Pukaha Mount Bruce Wildlife Centre 33; & black stilts 186; & shore plover 33
Pukaki River 215, 222; *see also* Lake Pukaki

rabbits 81, 137, 204–6
Rakaia River 17, 38, 39, 41, 59, 125, *172–3*, 180–1, 209–14, 225; predators 70; restoration projects 251–2; *see also* braided rivers; wrybill
Rakiura *see* Stewart Island
Ramsar List *see* wetlands
Rangatira/South East Island 31, 33–4, 137
Rangitata River 13, 38, 60, 63, 65, 179, 188, *215*; biodiversity restoration 224, 251–2; predator control 235
rats *see* predators
Recurvirostridae 18, 75
red knot 48, 167, 169–71, 241; breeding range 166–7; & horseshoe crab eggs, Delaware Bay 170–1; migration 169–71; specialist bivalve feeders 170; *see also* knots
red-billed gull 34; Australian population 115; coastal roosting colonies 115, 116; conservation watch 117; foraging, hawking & scavenging 114–15; & human activities 115; Kaikoura colonies study 116–17; plankton supply & breeding success 116–17
red-necked stint 144
redpoll 42
Reed, Sylvia 106
Rena disaster response 194–5, 250
Resolution 201
rhyncokinesis 62
riverbed habitat *see* braided rivers
rivers 217–25; *see also* braided rivers; *individual rivers*; water
rocky shore/platform 34
ruddy turnstone 20, *32*, 146–8; bill shape & feeding 147–8; migration 149–50; plumage 146

Saemangeum seawall 238–9
sand plover *see* shore plover
sandpipers 96–7; short-tailed *163*; *see also* curlew sandpiper; sharp-tailed sandpiper
Sandspit 233
Schofield, Paul 61
Scolopacidae 135
sediment & nutrients 21, 41, 45–9, 60, 61, 219; sedimentation 217–20; *see also* water
Selwyn River 220
sharp-tailed sandpiper: foraging 96–7; migration 162, 163; plumage 95, 165
Shoal Bay 109
shore plover 21, 27, 31–5; effects of habitat on breeding, nesting & brooding 33–5; Mana Island 196–97; population decline 32; & predators 34; Pukaha Mt Bruce population 33; Rangatira population 31–5
Sibson, Dick 104, 126, 127, 179–80
SIPO *see* pied oystercatcher
skua 20, *33*; origins 22; as predator 33, 34, 128, 139, 189, 230
    brown skua 34
Snares Island 135, 138–41, 147
snipe (New Zealand) 133–41; aerial displays 139–40; bill shape & function 136, 138; courtship feeding 138; distinctive features 135, 136; fossil record 135–7; genetic impoverishment 140; habitat & range 135; origins 138–9; parental care 138; predation by kiore 135; recovery plan 141; *see also* Auckland Island snipe; Campbell Island snipe; Jacquemart Island
    Antipodes Island snipe 135, 139, 141
    Chatham Island snipe 137, 140
    Chubbia (South America) 138, 139
    Latham's/Japanese snipe 137
    North Island snipe (extinct) 21, 136; fossil record 136
    Snares Island snipe 139, 140
    South Island snipe (extinct) 137, 139–40
Soper, Michael: black stilt 76
South East Island *see* Rangatira
South Island pied oystercatcher (SIPO) *see* pied oystercatcher
Southland 29–30, 80, 81, 89, 99, 118–19, 146, 147
    dairy farming 121, 220, 248
spur-winged plover 27–31; airport incidents 228, breeding 30; chicks 30; habitat 28–30; population expansion 28–30, 228; removal of protected status 29, 31, 35, 228; self-introduction from Australia 28–9
Star Keys Island 137
Stead, Edgar: Big South Cape Is. 137, 138; gulls 112, 113, 114, 120; black-fronted tern 69; stilts 77, 79, 81; terns 69, 125, 126; wrybill 58, 62, 64, 180–1
Sterna albifrons (little tern) 128
Sterna striata see white-fronted tern
Sternula nereis see fairy tern
Stewart Island 106; predators & species loss 107–8, 195; South Island snipe 137; southern NZ dotterel 105–08
stilts 75–83; adaptations 79–80; fossils 79; historical record/confusion 75–80; hybridisation 74, 82–3, *180*, 213–14; predator response 81; *see also* black stilt; pied stilt
stoats *see* predators
subantarctic islands *see individual islands*

Tamaki Estuary: wrybill 60
Tapper, Jules: banded dotterel 100
tara *see* white-fronted tern
taranui, tara kakao *see* Caspian tern
tarapiroe *see* black-fronted tern
tarapunga *see* red-billed gull
Tasman River valley 43, 181, 204, 207, 222–3, 250
Taukihepa *see* Big South Cape Island
Tawharanui Regional Park 193
Te Waihora/Lake Ellesmere 21, 53, 127, 144, 147, 213, 252
terek sandpiper 60
terns 123–31; *see also* black-fronted tern; Caspian tern; fairy tern; white-fronted tern
    little tern (*Sterna albifrons*) 128
Thinornis novaeseelandiae 31–5
Tianjin Binhai New Area 242
tidal flats 21, 45–9; *see also* estuaries
tides 47; marine tides & gull colonies 116
tundra 18–19, 20, 22, 42, 48, 142–7, 162, 168–9, 244–5; *see also* bar-tailed godwit; migration
Turbott, Graham 58
Turituriwhatu 97
turnstone *see* ruddy turnstone
tutukiwi *see* snipe: South Is.

Upper Waitaki Basin 78–9, 83, 181, 185, 204, 221–3

Vanellus miles 27–31; *V. m. miles* 28; *V. m. novaehollandiae* 27
variable oystercatcher (VOC) 16; cf SIPO 88–9, 92–3; chicks 93; plumage 92; predation on dotterels 193–4; range & habitat 88, 92, 93, 182–3
Vernon Lagoons 53
VOC *see* variable oystercatcher

Waihora Ellesmere Trust 250
Waihou River, pollution 217, 218
Waikato Regional Council/Environment Waikato 217–18, 251
Waimakariri River 36, 38, 40, 177, 178, 191, 210, 225; *see also* braided rivers
Waipu 93, 106, 129, 183, 235
Waitaki River 39; *see also* Upper Waitaki Basin
Waituna Lagoon 53, 146, 220, 248
Waituna Landcare Group 250, 253
water 209–15; 217–25
    abstraction for irrigation 209, 213, 219–25
    flooding 61, 70, 80, 81, 101, 210–15, 241
    pollution 217–20, 230
    restoration 222–5
    sedimentation 217–20
Western Reef (Chatham Is) 34
wetlands
    coastal 21, 45–53, 146, 147; *see also* estuaries
    inland 28, 80, 219–22
    Ramsar List of Wetlands of International Importance 220
White, Gilbert 75
white-faced heron *18*, 22
white-fronted tern 33–4, 123–6; breeding 125–6; courtship display 125–6; nesting 126; nomenclature & historical record 124–5
windfarms 324–35
Wilson, Robert 137
Woolley, Bev: dotterels 192
wrybill 7, 12–13, 17, 55–65; bill shape & function 56–63; breeding range 181–2; chicks 62, 64; distraction display 63; feeding actions 59–60; feeding grounds 59, 60; nesting 42, 62–3, 209–10; nomenclature & historical record 56–8; plumage & cryptic colouration 62, 63, 64; population constraints 65, 179–82, 214; predation 62–3, 181
    surveys: Lake Pukaki 42–3; Rangitata 63–5

Yalu Jiang 240–2
Yellow Sea 156, 158, 159, 168, 238, 241, 243
Yukon-Kuskokwim Delta (YKD) 156, 158, 161, 162, 240–1